Teenage TALES

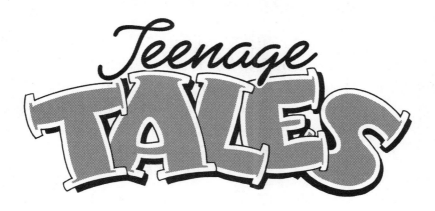

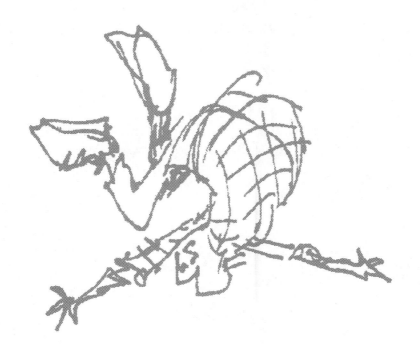

Also by Jerry Scott and Jim Borgman

Zits: Sketchbook 1
Growth Spurt: Zits Sketchbook 2
Don't Roll Your Eyes at Me, Young Man!: Zits Sketchbook 3
Are We an "Us"?: Zits Sketchbook 4
Zits Unzipped: Zits Sketchbook 5
Busted!: Zits Sketchbook 6
Road Trip: Zits Sketchbook 7

Treasuries
Humongous Zits
Big Honkin' Zits
Zits: Supersized

Teenage TALES

Zits® Sketchbook No. 8

by JERRY SCOTT and JIM BORGMAN™

**Andrews McMeel
Publishing**

Kansas City

ATTENTION: SCHOOLS AND BUSINESSES

Andrews McMeel books are available at quantity discounts with bulk purchase for educational, business, or sales promotional use. For information, please write to: Special Sales Department, Andrews McMeel Publishing, 4520 Main Street, Kansas City, Missouri 64111.

Per Isabella, con amore.

—J.S

To Katie Carl. Thanks for making it fun.

—J.B.

Zits
by JERRY SCOTT and JIM BORGMAN

THERE ARE NO WORDS TO EXPRESS THE LIMITLESS DEPTH OF PITY I FEEL FOR THE IGNORANCE BEFORE ME, ASTONISHING IN ITS STARK FRANKNESS, PREDICTABLE AS THE SUNRISE, EVER-EXPANDING AS THE UNIVERSE ITSELF, AND FORTUNATELY – OH! SO FORTUNATELY! – NEITHER GENETIC NOR CONTAGIOUS
ALL I DID WAS EXPLAIN WHICH PEDAL WAS THE GAS AND WHICH WAS THE BRAKE, JEREMY! DON'T GIVE ME THAT LOOK!
WHAT LOOK?

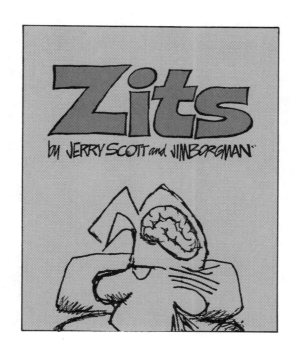

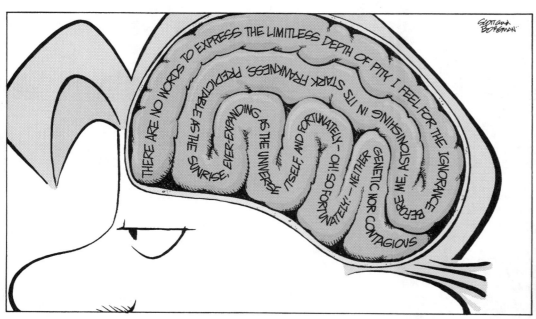

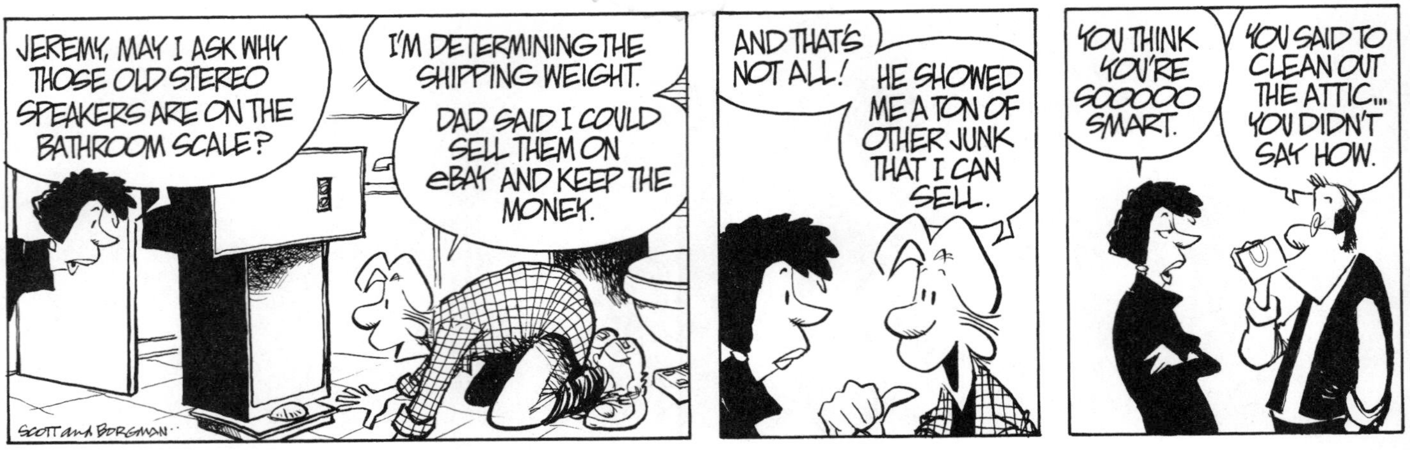
JEREMY, MAY I ASK WHY THOSE OLD STEREO SPEAKERS ARE ON THE BATHROOM SCALE?
I'M DETERMINING THE SHIPPING WEIGHT.
DAD SAID I COULD SELL THEM ON eBAY AND KEEP THE MONEY.
SCOTT AND BORGMAN
AND THAT'S NOT ALL!
HE SHOWED ME A TON OF OTHER JUNK THAT I CAN SELL.
YOU THINK YOU'RE SOOOOO SMART.
YOU SAID TO CLEAN OUT THE ATTIC... YOU DIDN'T SAY HOW.

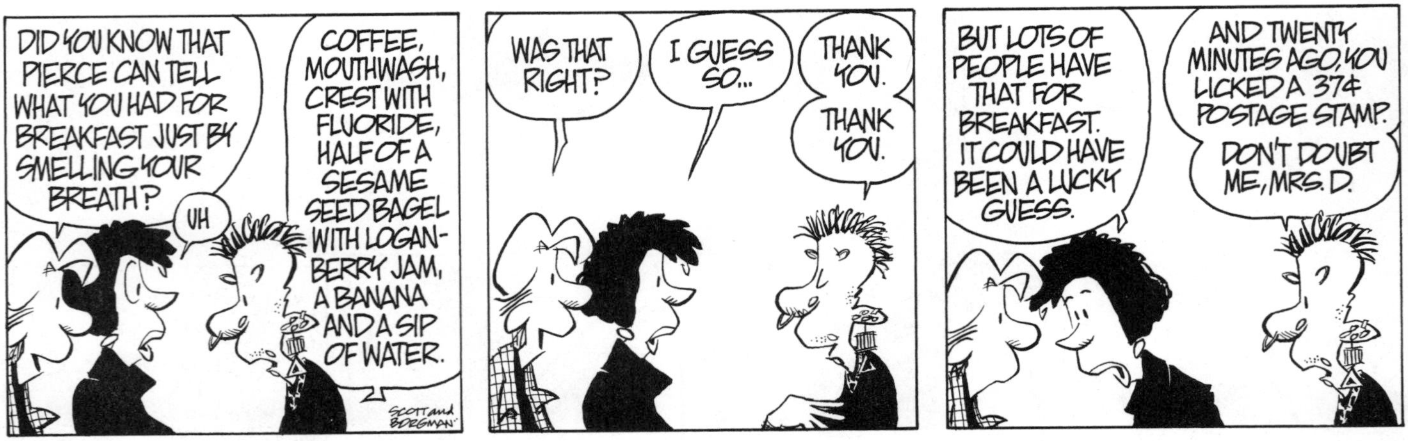
DID YOU KNOW THAT PIERCE CAN TELL WHAT YOU HAD FOR BREAKFAST JUST BY SMELLING YOUR BREATH?
UH
COFFEE, MOUTHWASH, CREST WITH FLUORIDE, HALF OF A SESAME SEED BAGEL WITH LOGANBERRY JAM, A BANANA AND A SIP OF WATER.
SCOTT AND BORGMAN
WAS THAT RIGHT?
I GUESS SO...
THANK YOU.
THANK YOU.
BUT LOTS OF PEOPLE HAVE THAT FOR BREAKFAST. IT COULD HAVE BEEN A LUCKY GUESS.
AND TWENTY MINUTES AGO, YOU LICKED A 37¢ POSTAGE STAMP.
DON'T DOUBT ME, MRS. D.

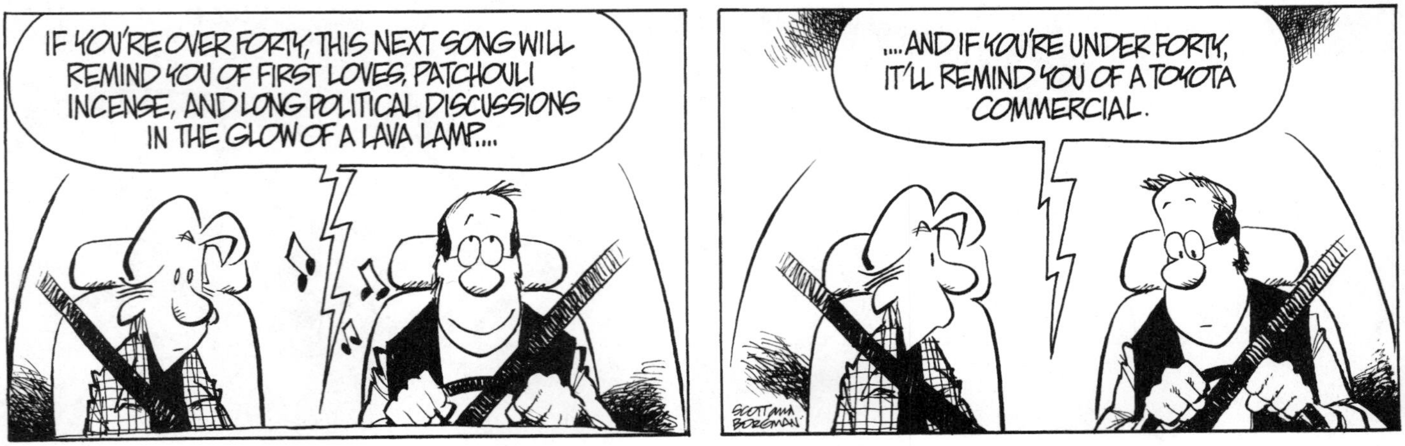
IF YOU'RE OVER FORTY, THIS NEXT SONG WILL REMIND YOU OF FIRST LOVES, PATCHOULI INCENSE, AND LONG POLITICAL DISCUSSIONS IN THE GLOW OF A LAVA LAMP....
....AND IF YOU'RE UNDER FORTY, IT'LL REMIND YOU OF A TOYOTA COMMERCIAL.
SCOTT AND BORGMAN

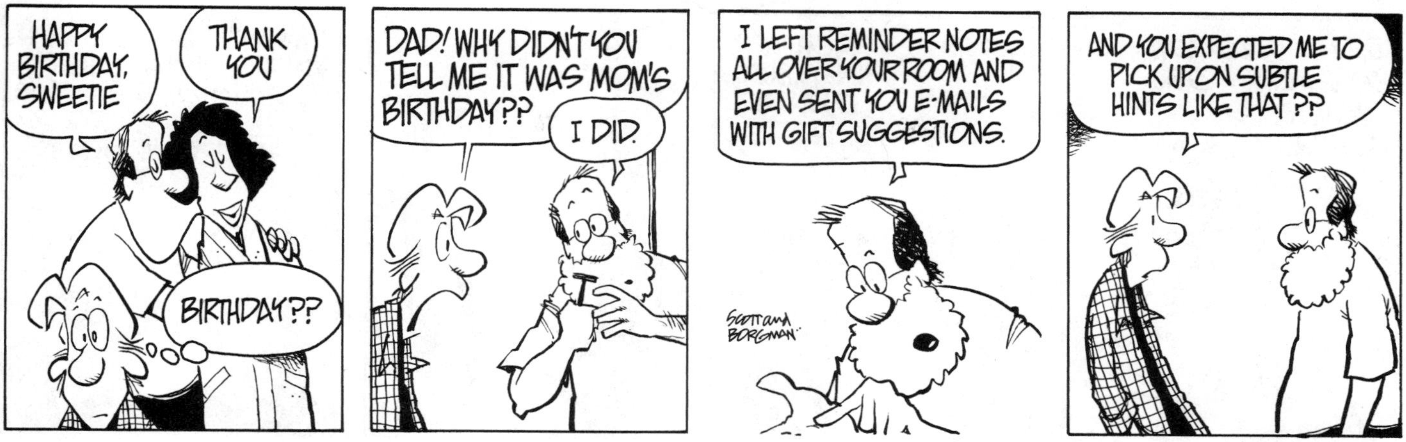
HAPPY BIRTHDAY, SWEETIE
THANK YOU
BIRTHDAY??
DAD! WHY DIDN'T YOU TELL ME IT WAS MOM'S BIRTHDAY??
I DID.
I LEFT REMINDER NOTES ALL OVER YOUR ROOM AND EVEN SENT YOU E-MAILS WITH GIFT SUGGESTIONS.
SCOTT and BORGMAN
AND YOU EXPECTED ME TO PICK UP ON SUBTLE HINTS LIKE THAT??

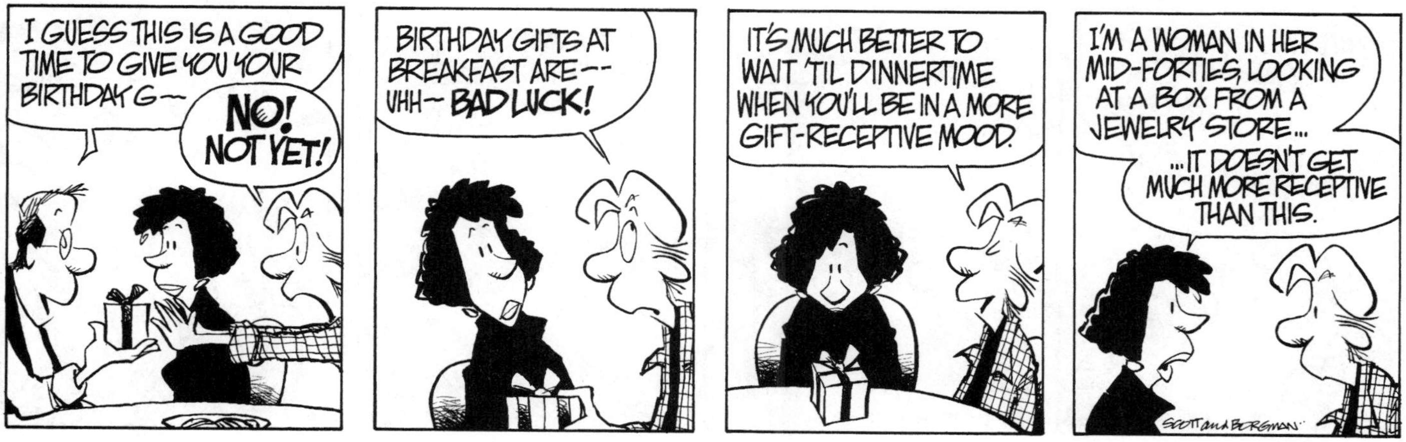
I GUESS THIS IS A GOOD TIME TO GIVE YOU YOUR BIRTHDAY G—
NO! NOT YET!
BIRTHDAY GIFTS AT BREAKFAST ARE-- UHH-- BAD LUCK!
IT'S MUCH BETTER TO WAIT 'TIL DINNERTIME WHEN YOU'LL BE IN A MORE GIFT-RECEPTIVE MOOD.
I'M A WOMAN IN HER MID-FORTIES, LOOKING AT A BOX FROM A JEWELRY STORE...
...IT DOESN'T GET MUCH MORE RECEPTIVE THAN THIS.
SCOTT and BORGMAN

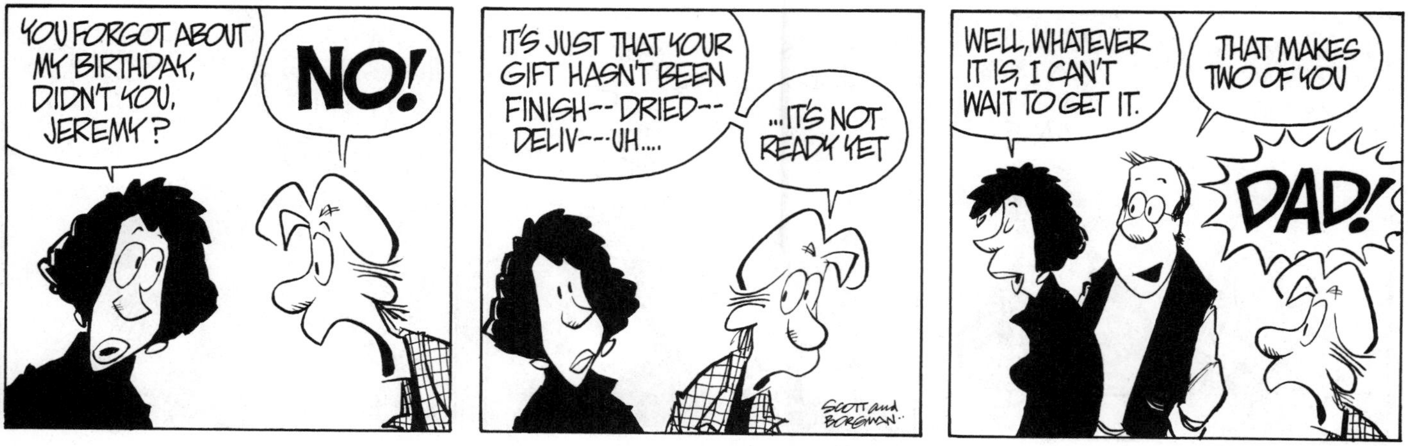
YOU FORGOT ABOUT MY BIRTHDAY, DIDN'T YOU, JEREMY?
NO!
IT'S JUST THAT YOUR GIFT HASN'T BEEN FINISH-- DRIED-- DELIV---UH....
...IT'S NOT READY YET
SCOTT and BORGMAN
WELL, WHATEVER IT IS, I CAN'T WAIT TO GET IT.
THAT MAKES TWO OF YOU
DAD!

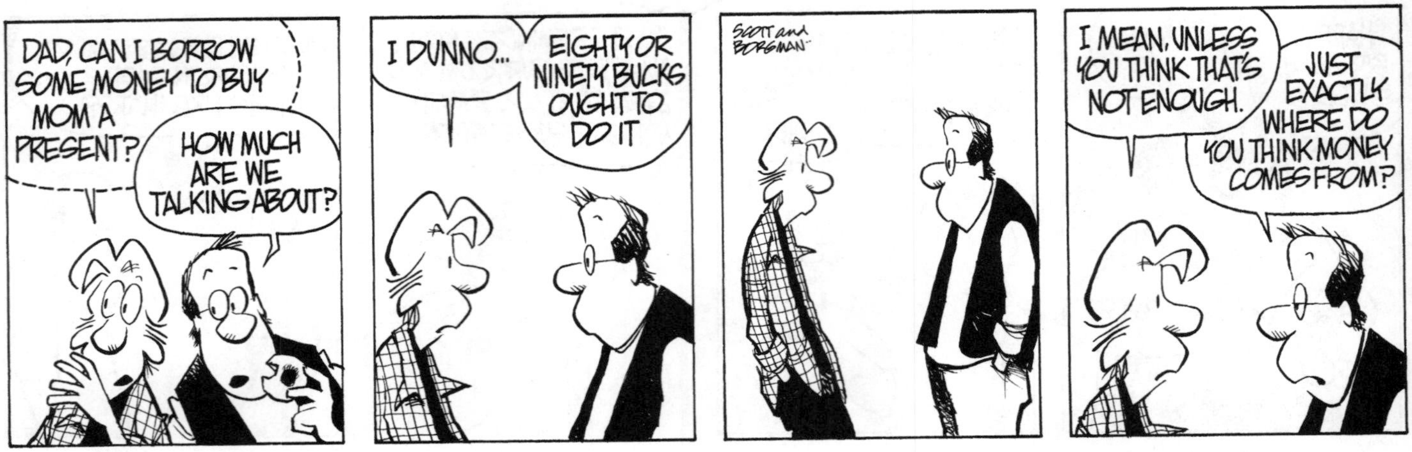
DAD, CAN I BORROW SOME MONEY TO BUY MOM A PRESENT?
HOW MUCH ARE WE TALKING ABOUT?
I DUNNO...
EIGHTY OR NINETY BUCKS OUGHT TO DO IT
SCOTT and BORGMAN
I MEAN, UNLESS YOU THINK THAT'S NOT ENOUGH.
JUST EXACTLY WHERE DO YOU THINK MONEY COMES FROM?

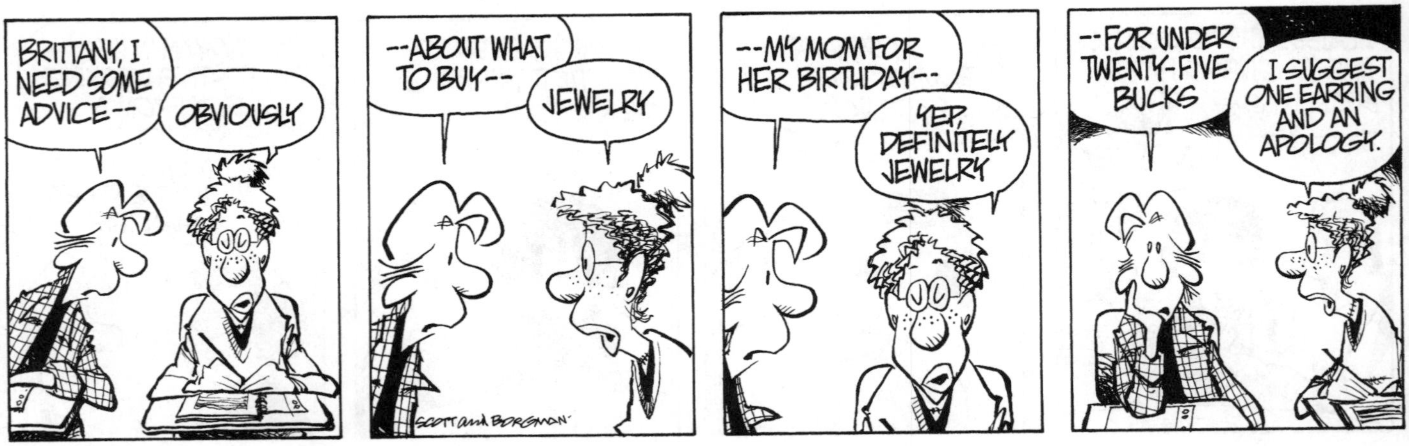
BRITTANY, I NEED SOME ADVICE--
OBVIOUSLY
--ABOUT WHAT TO BUY--
JEWELRY
SCOTT and BORGMAN
--MY MOM FOR HER BIRTHDAY--
YEP, DEFINITELY JEWELRY
--FOR UNDER TWENTY-FIVE BUCKS
I SUGGEST ONE EARRING AND AN APOLOGY.

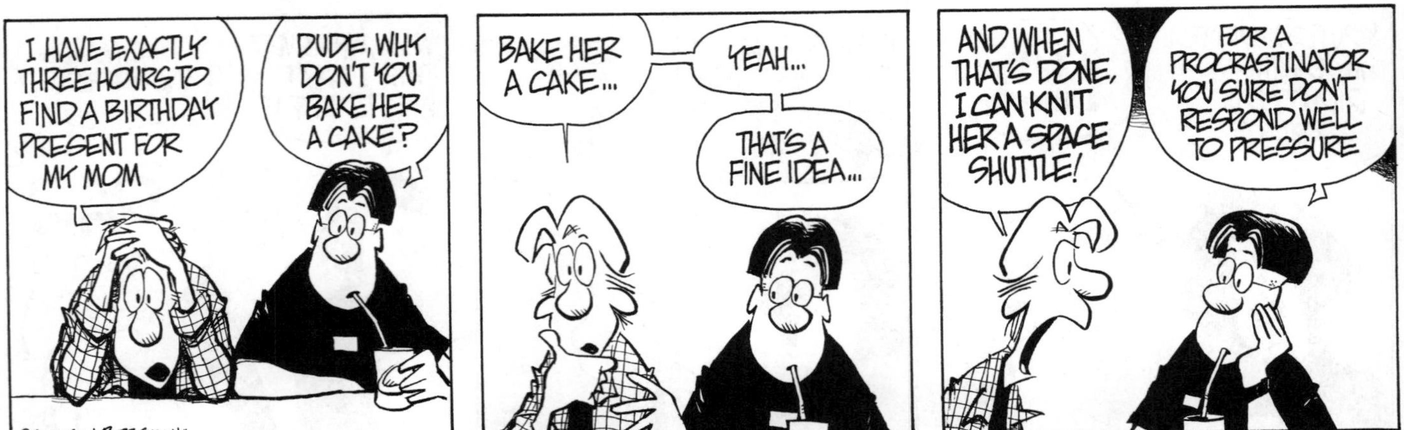
I HAVE EXACTLY THREE HOURS TO FIND A BIRTHDAY PRESENT FOR MY MOM
DUDE, WHY DON'T YOU BAKE HER A CAKE?
SCOTT and BORGMAN
BAKE HER A CAKE...
YEAH...
THAT'S A FINE IDEA...
AND WHEN THAT'S DONE, I CAN KNIT HER A SPACE SHUTTLE!
FOR A PROCRASTINATOR YOU SURE DON'T RESPOND WELL TO PRESSURE

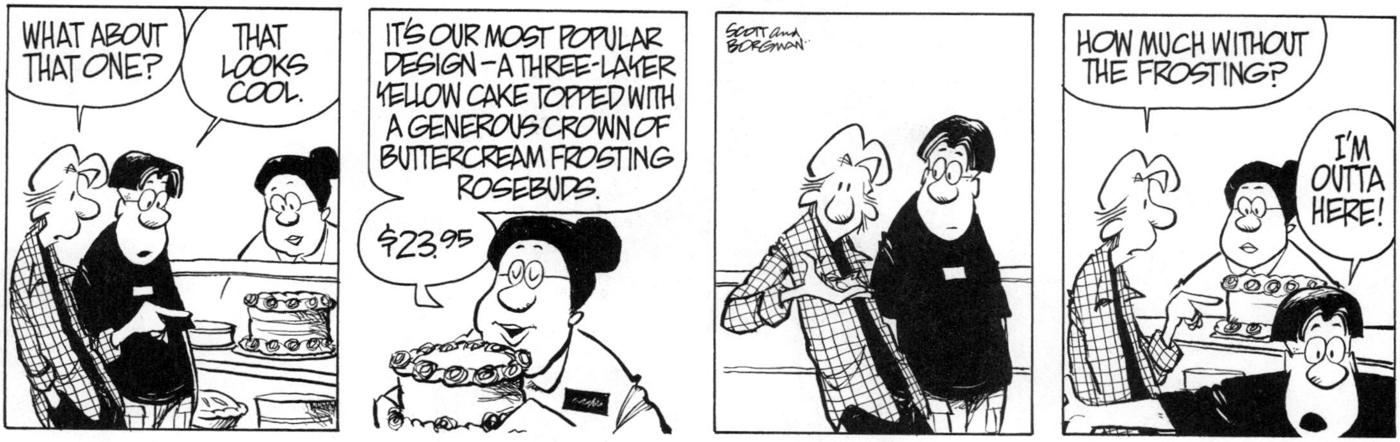
WHAT ABOUT THAT ONE?
THAT LOOKS COOL.
IT'S OUR MOST POPULAR DESIGN—A THREE-LAYER YELLOW CAKE TOPPED WITH A GENEROUS CROWN OF BUTTERCREAM FROSTING ROSEBUDS.
$23.95
SCOTT and BORGMAN
HOW MUCH WITHOUT THE FROSTING?
I'M OUTTA HERE!

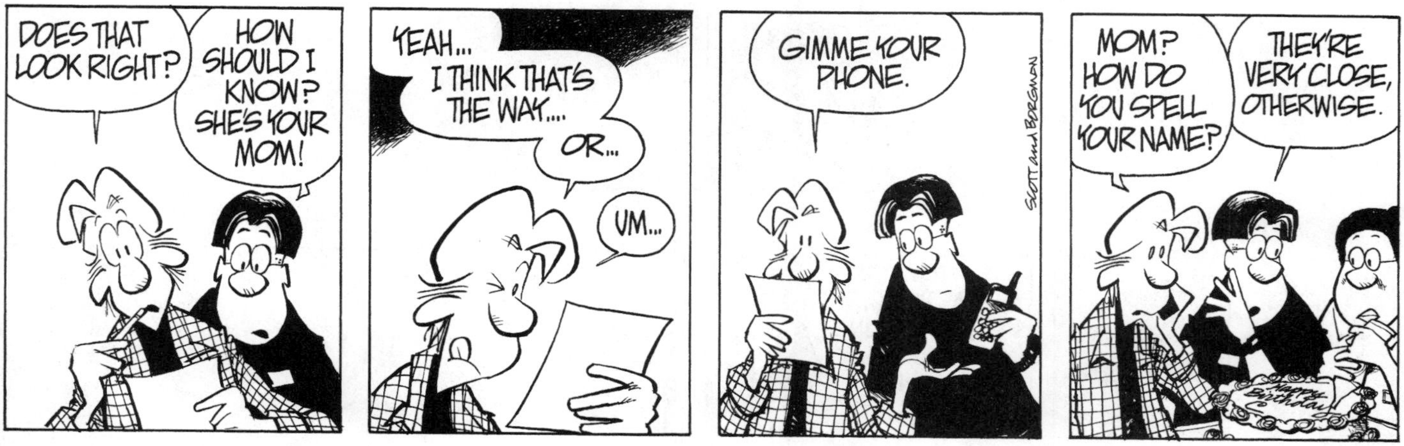
DOES THAT LOOK RIGHT?
HOW SHOULD I KNOW? SHE'S YOUR MOM!
YEAH... I THINK THAT'S THE WAY....
OR...
UM...
GIMME YOUR PHONE.
SCOTT and BORGMAN
MOM? HOW DO YOU SPELL YOUR NAME?
THEY'RE VERY CLOSE, OTHERWISE.

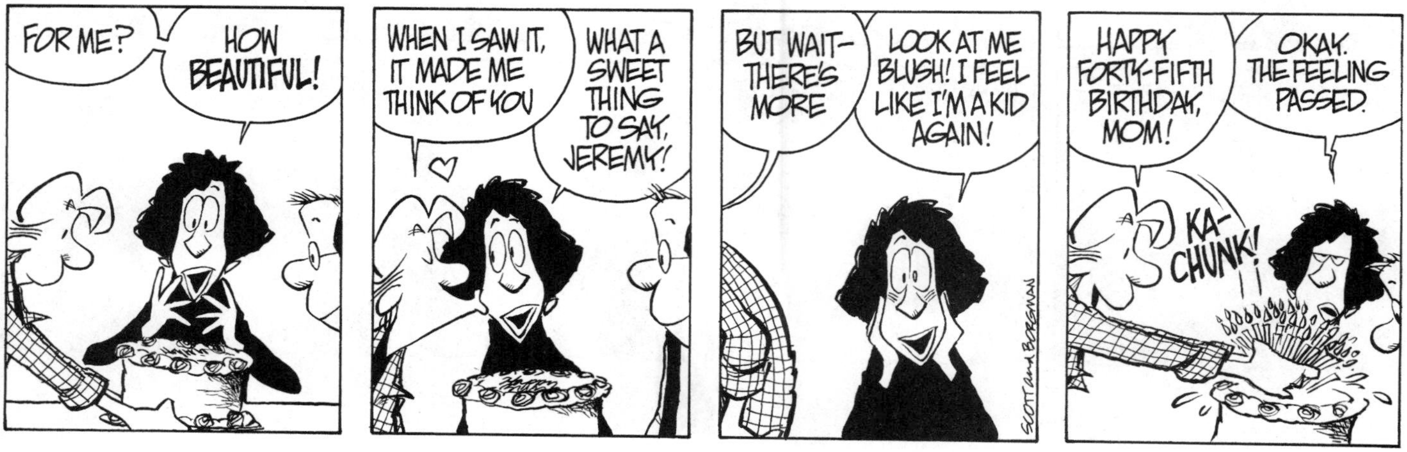
FOR ME?
HOW BEAUTIFUL!
WHEN I SAW IT, IT MADE ME THINK OF YOU
WHAT A SWEET THING TO SAY, JEREMY!
BUT WAIT-THERE'S MORE
LOOK AT ME BLUSH! I FEEL LIKE I'M A KID AGAIN!
SCOTT and BORGMAN
HAPPY FORTY-FIFTH BIRTHDAY, MOM!
OKAY. THE FEELING PASSED.
KA-CHUNK!

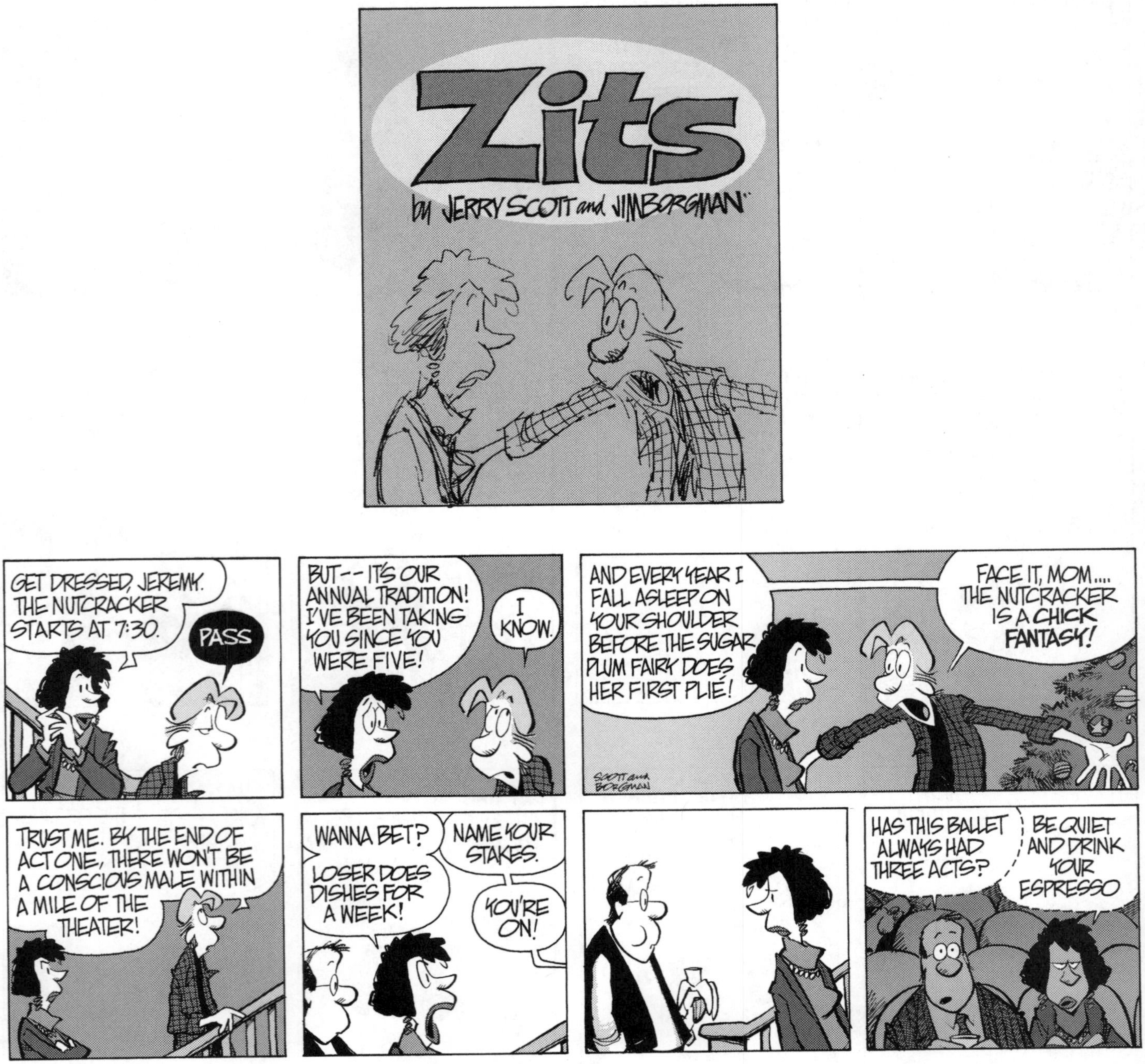
Zits
by JERRY SCOTT and JIM BORGMAN
GET DRESSED, JEREMY. THE NUTCRACKER STARTS AT 7:30.
PASS
BUT-- IT'S OUR ANNUAL TRADITION! I'VE BEEN TAKING YOU SINCE YOU WERE FIVE!
I KNOW.
AND EVERY YEAR I FALL ASLEEP ON YOUR SHOULDER BEFORE THE SUGAR PLUM FAIRY DOES HER FIRST PLIÉ!
FACE IT, MOM.... THE NUTCRACKER IS A CHICK FANTASY!
SCOTT and BORGMAN
TRUST ME. BY THE END OF ACT ONE, THERE WON'T BE A CONSCIOUS MALE WITHIN A MILE OF THE THEATER!
WANNA BET?
NAME YOUR STAKES.
LOSER DOES DISHES FOR A WEEK!
YOU'RE ON!
HAS THIS BALLET ALWAYS HAD THREE ACTS?
BE QUIET AND DRINK YOUR ESPRESSO

Zits
by JERRY SCOTT and JIM BORGMAN

DING! DONG!
OH, HEY. COME ON IN, PIERCE.
MERRY CHRISTMAS, MRS. D.
HI, MR. D.
SCOTT and BORGMAN
JINGLE! JINGLE! JINGLE! JINGLE!
IT'S BEGINNING TO LOOK A LOT LIKE CHRISTMAS.
CURRIER AND IVES THIS AIN'T.

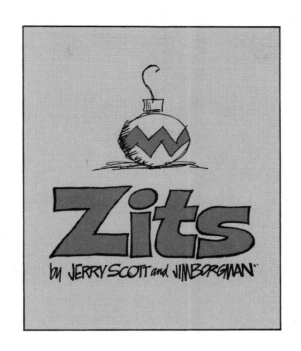

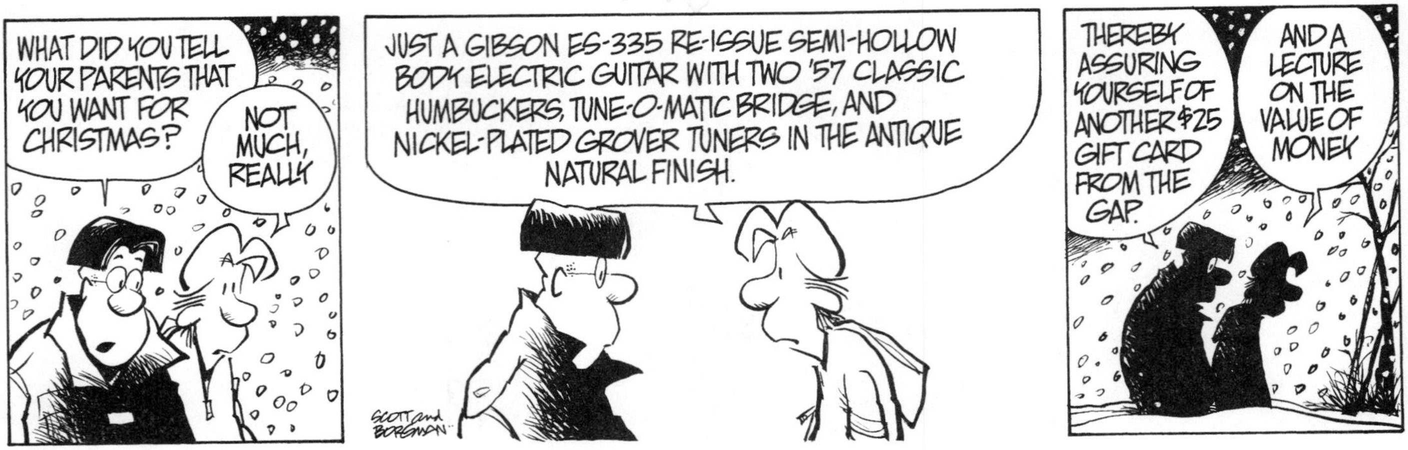
WHAT DID YOU TELL YOUR PARENTS THAT YOU WANT FOR CHRISTMAS?
NOT MUCH, REALLY
JUST A GIBSON ES-335 RE-ISSUE SEMI-HOLLOW BODY ELECTRIC GUITAR WITH TWO '57 CLASSIC HUMBUCKERS, TUNE-O-MATIC BRIDGE, AND NICKEL-PLATED GROVER TUNERS IN THE ANTIQUE NATURAL FINISH.
THEREBY ASSURING YOURSELF OF ANOTHER $25 GIFT CARD FROM THE GAP.
AND A LECTURE ON THE VALUE OF MONEY
SCOTT and BORGMAN

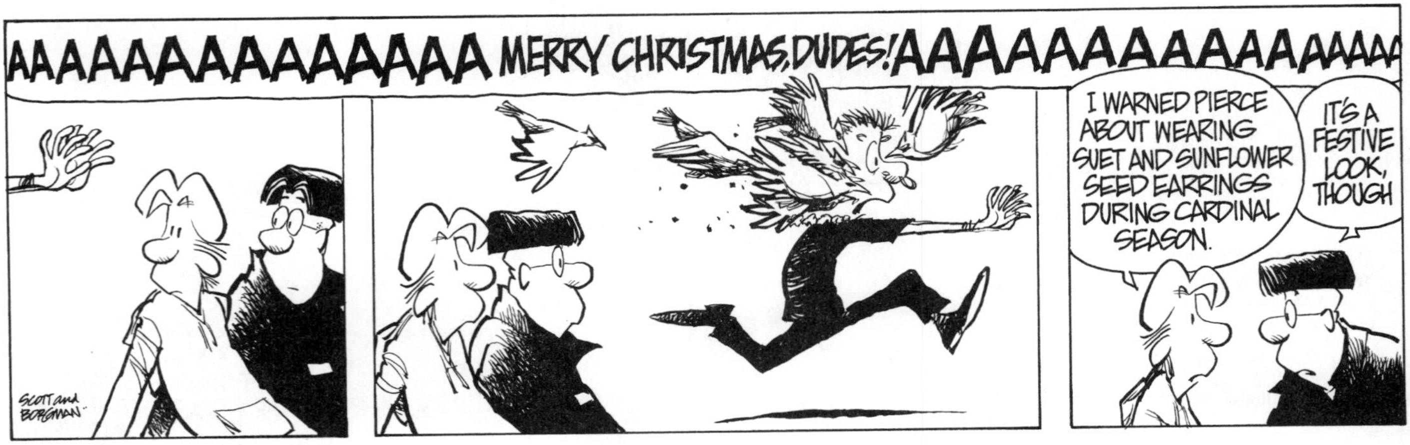
AAAAAAAAAAAAAA MERRY CHRISTMAS, DUDES! AAAAAAAAAAAAAAAA
SCOTT and BORGMAN
I WARNED PIERCE ABOUT WEARING SUET AND SUNFLOWER SEED EARRINGS DURING CARDINAL SEASON.
IT'S A FESTIVE LOOK, THOUGH

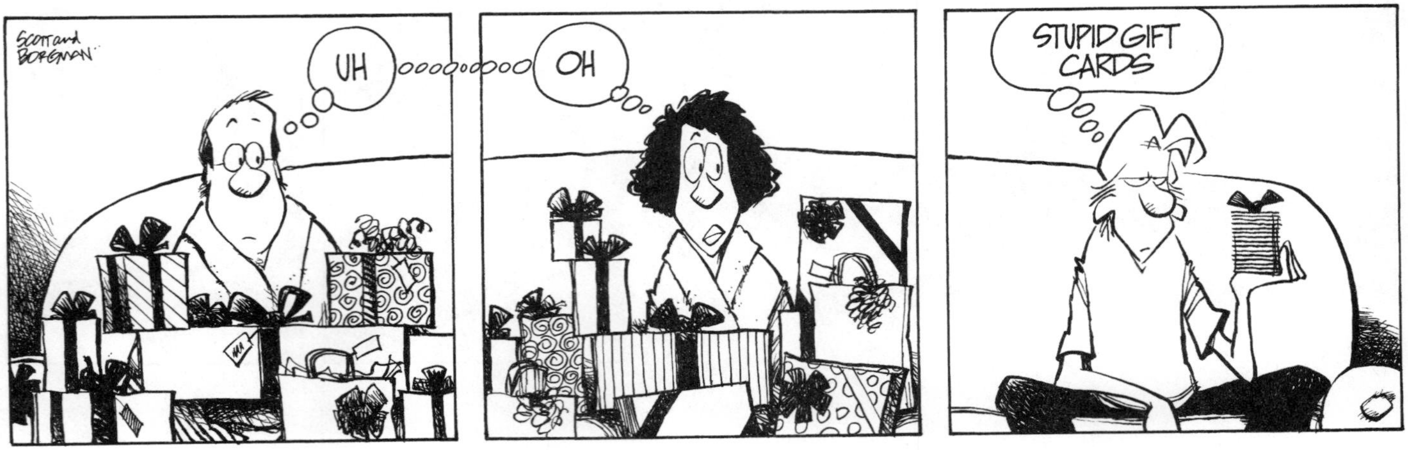
SCOTT and BORGMAN
UH
OOOOOOOOOO
OH
STUPID GIFT CARDS

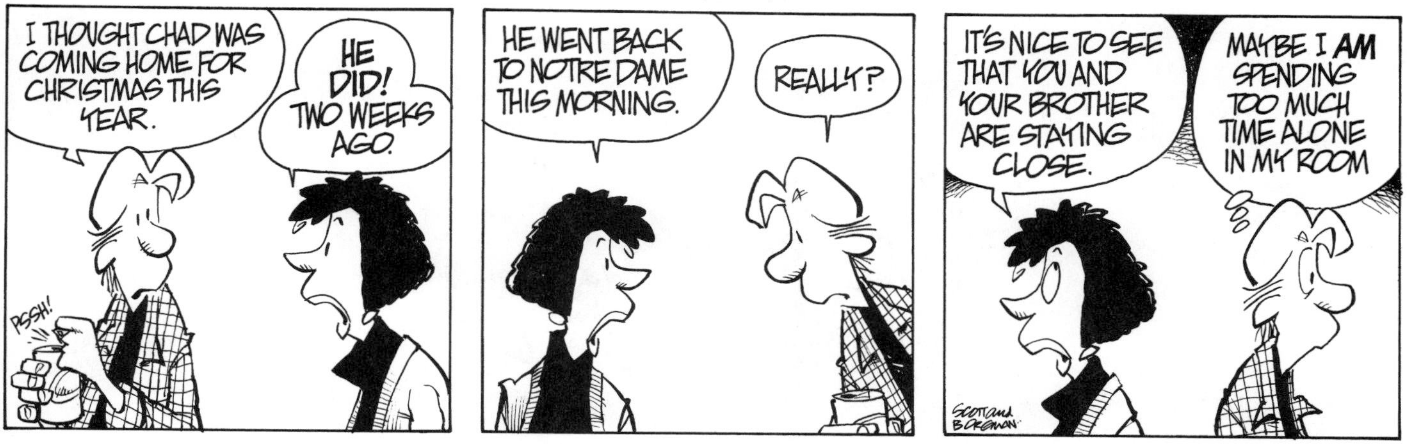
I THOUGHT CHAD WAS COMING HOME FOR CHRISTMAS THIS YEAR.
HE DID! TWO WEEKS AGO.
PSSH!
HE WENT BACK TO NOTRE DAME THIS MORNING.
REALLY?
IT'S NICE TO SEE THAT YOU AND YOUR BROTHER ARE STAYING CLOSE.
MAYBE I **AM** SPENDING TOO MUCH TIME ALONE IN MY ROOM

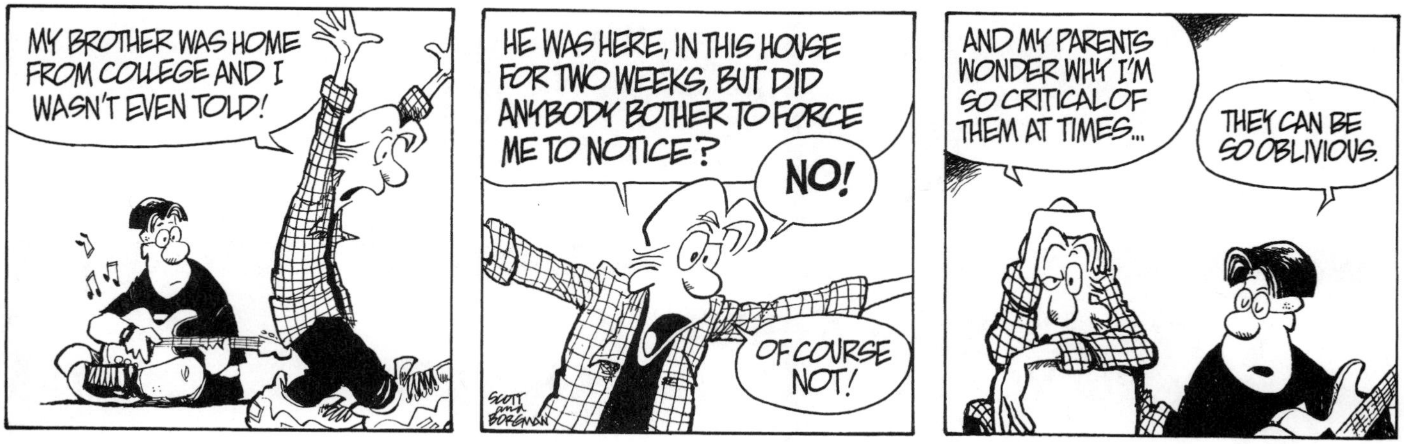
MY BROTHER WAS HOME FROM COLLEGE AND I WASN'T EVEN TOLD!
HE WAS HERE, IN THIS HOUSE FOR TWO WEEKS, BUT DID ANYBODY BOTHER TO FORCE ME TO NOTICE?
NO!
OF COURSE NOT!
AND MY PARENTS WONDER WHY I'M SO CRITICAL OF THEM AT TIMES...
THEY CAN BE SO OBLIVIOUS.

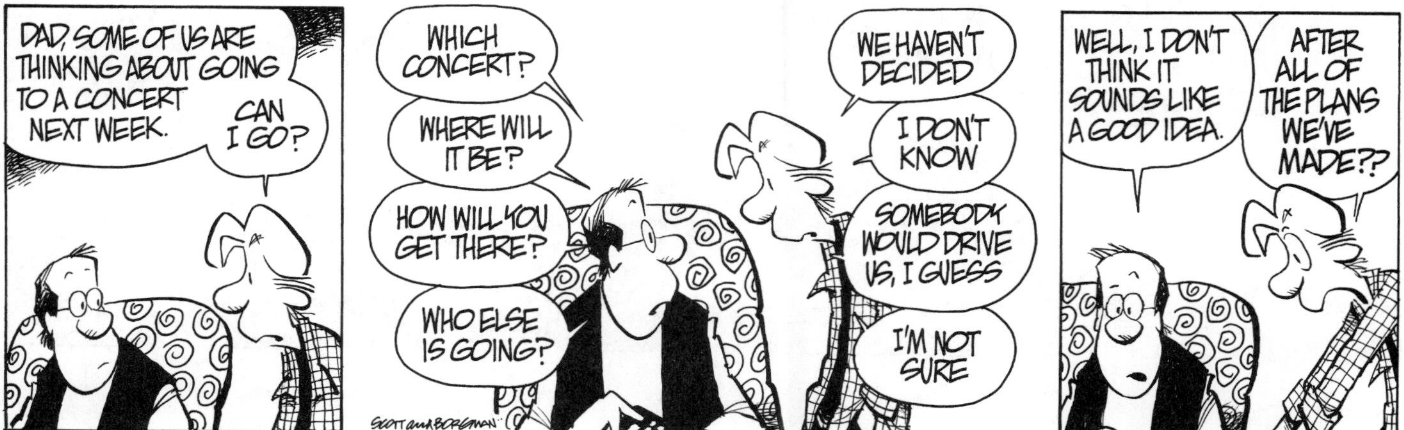
DAD, SOME OF US ARE THINKING ABOUT GOING TO A CONCERT NEXT WEEK.
CAN I GO?
WHICH CONCERT?
WE HAVEN'T DECIDED
WHERE WILL IT BE?
I DON'T KNOW
HOW WILL YOU GET THERE?
SOMEBODY WOULD DRIVE US, I GUESS
WHO ELSE IS GOING?
I'M NOT SURE
WELL, I DON'T THINK IT SOUNDS LIKE A GOOD IDEA.
AFTER ALL OF THE PLANS WE'VE MADE??

Zits
by
JERRY SCOTT
and
JIM BORGMAN

GIVE A TEEN A SNACK AND YOU FEED HIM FOR A DAY,
TEACH HIM TO FIX HIS OWN SNACK AND YOUR KITCHEN WILL BE A WRECK FOREVER.
Chips
Cookies
SCOTT and BORGMAN

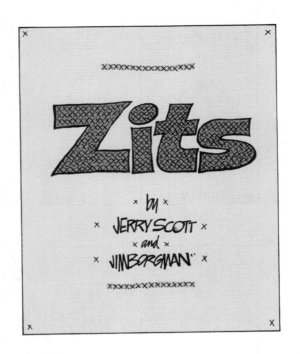

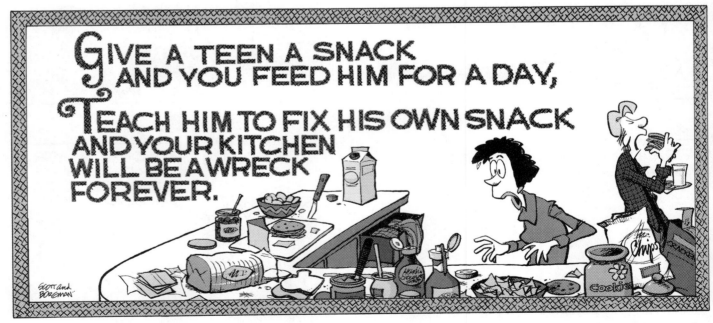

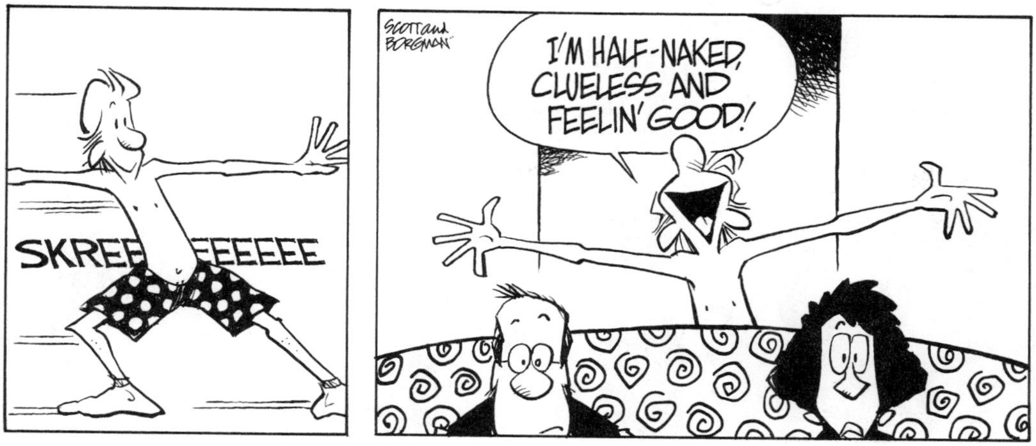
SKREEEEEEEE
SCOTT and BORGMAN
I'M HALF-NAKED, CLUELESS AND FEELIN' GOOD!
TEN BUCKS SAYS THAT THE REST OF THE CHRISTMAS FUDGE IS GONE
HOW MUCH SUGAR HAVE YOU EATEN?

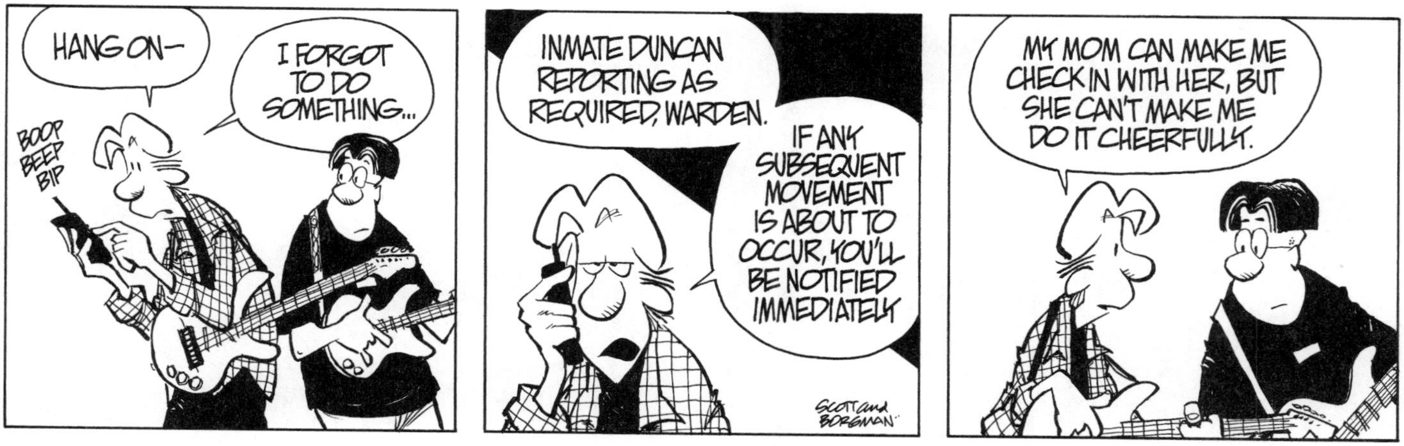
HANG ON-
BOOP BEEP BIP
I FORGOT TO DO SOMETHING...
INMATE DUNCAN REPORTING AS REQUIRED, WARDEN.
IF ANY SUBSEQUENT MOVEMENT IS ABOUT TO OCCUR, YOU'LL BE NOTIFIED IMMEDIATELY
SCOTT and BORGMAN
MY MOM CAN MAKE ME CHECK IN WITH HER, BUT SHE CAN'T MAKE ME DO IT CHEERFULLY.

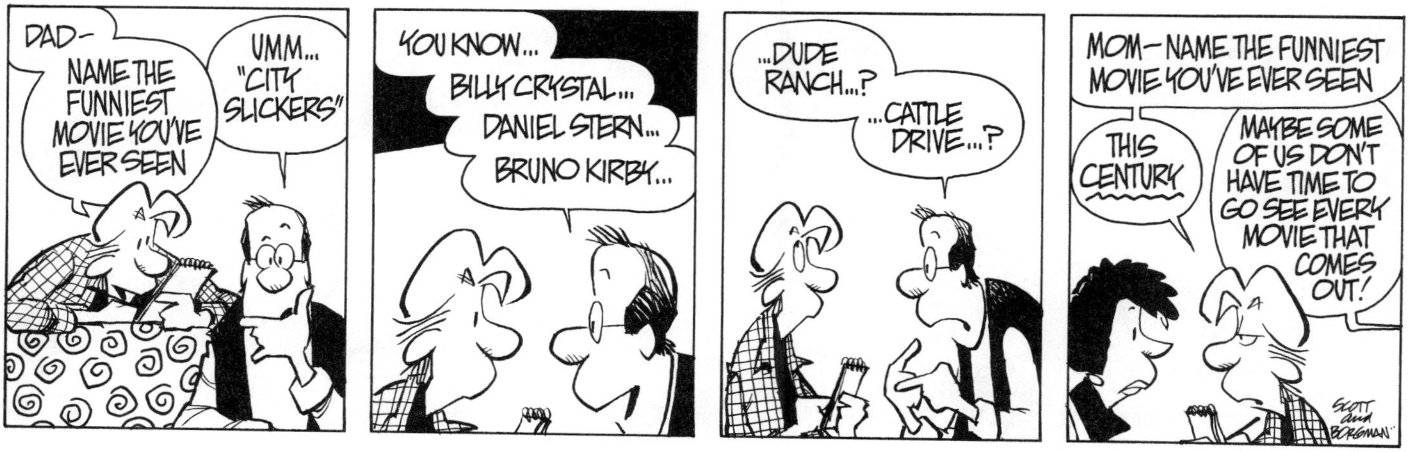
DAD- NAME THE FUNNIEST MOVIE YOU'VE EVER SEEN
UMM... "CITY SLICKERS"
YOU KNOW...
BILLY CRYSTAL...
DANIEL STERN...
BRUNO KIRBY...
...DUDE RANCH...?
...CATTLE DRIVE...?
MOM- NAME THE FUNNIEST MOVIE YOU'VE EVER SEEN
THIS CENTURY
MAYBE SOME OF US DON'T HAVE TIME TO GO SEE EVERY MOVIE THAT COMES OUT!
SCOTT and BORGMAN

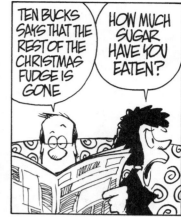

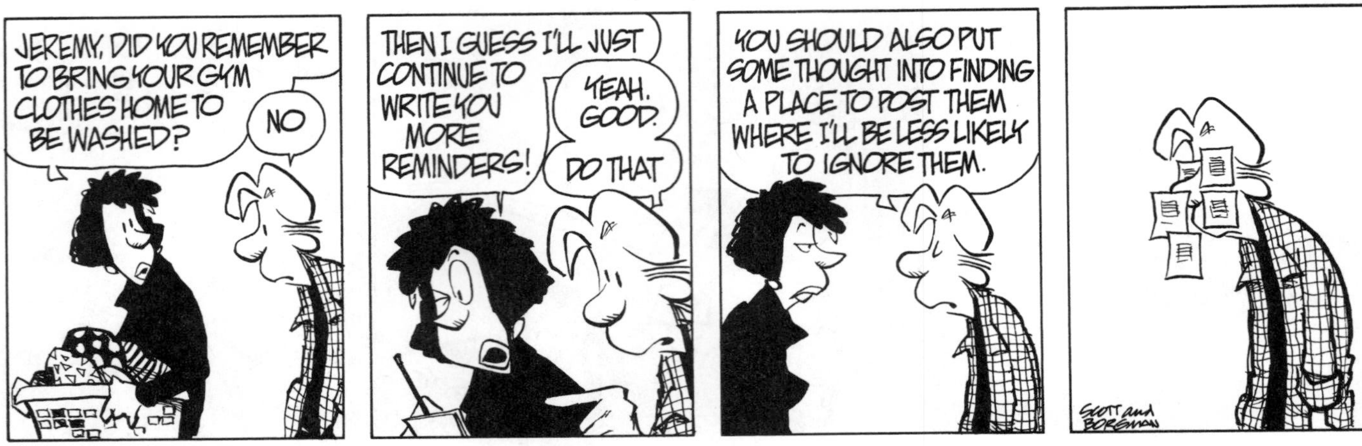
JEREMY, DID YOU REMEMBER TO BRING YOUR GYM CLOTHES HOME TO BE WASHED?
NO
THEN I GUESS I'LL JUST CONTINUE TO WRITE YOU MORE REMINDERS!
YEAH. GOOD.
DO THAT
YOU SHOULD ALSO PUT SOME THOUGHT INTO FINDING A PLACE TO POST THEM WHERE I'LL BE LESS LIKELY TO IGNORE THEM.
SCOTT and BORGMAN

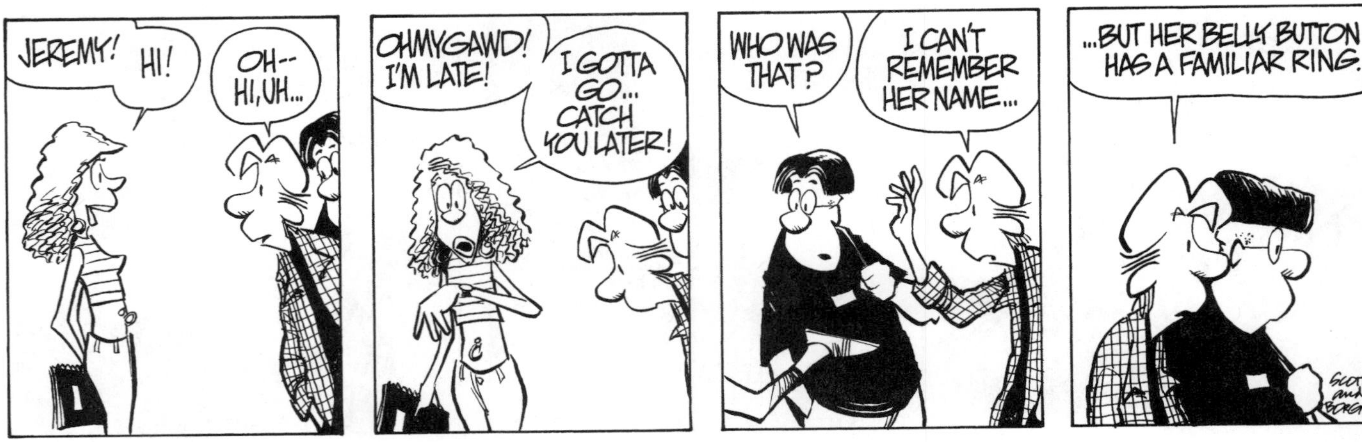
JEREMY!
HI!
OH-- HI, UH...
OHMYGAWD! I'M LATE!
I GOTTA GO... CATCH YOU LATER!
WHO WAS THAT?
I CAN'T REMEMBER HER NAME...
...BUT HER BELLY BUTTON HAS A FAMILIAR RING.
SCOTT and BORGMAN

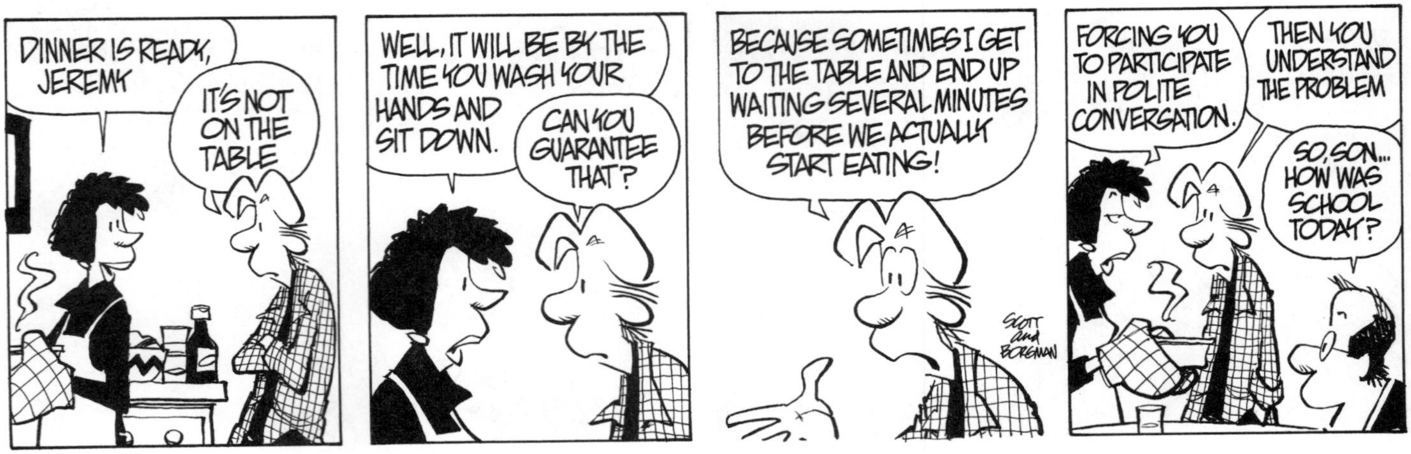
DINNER IS READY, JEREMY
IT'S NOT ON THE TABLE
WELL, IT WILL BE BY THE TIME YOU WASH YOUR HANDS AND SIT DOWN.
CAN YOU GUARANTEE THAT?
BECAUSE SOMETIMES I GET TO THE TABLE AND END UP WAITING SEVERAL MINUTES BEFORE WE ACTUALLY START EATING!
SCOTT and BORGMAN
FORCING YOU TO PARTICIPATE IN POLITE CONVERSATION.
THEN YOU UNDERSTAND THE PROBLEM
SO, SON... HOW WAS SCHOOL TODAY?

Zits
by JERRY SCOTT and JIM BORGMAN"

JEREMY, WHAT ARE YOU DOING?

EATING A BAGEL

SEE, THIS HALF HAS CREAM CHEESE ON IT.

AND THIS HALF HAS PEANUT BUTTER.

NOW, MOST PEOPLE WOULD JUST PUT THE CREAM CHEESE AND THE PEANUT BUTTER ON TOP OF EACH OTHER.

RIGHT?

BUT I'VE DISCOVERED THAT YOU GET A FAR MORE SATISFYING TASTE EXPERIENCE IF YOU KEEP YOUR FLAVORS ISOLATED UNTIL YOU MIX THEM IN YOUR MOUTH.

MMMMMMMMM

YOU SHOULD TRY IT.

YEAH. I'LL DO THAT, "EMERIL."

COULD YOU PASS THE CHOCOLATE AND THE MILK?

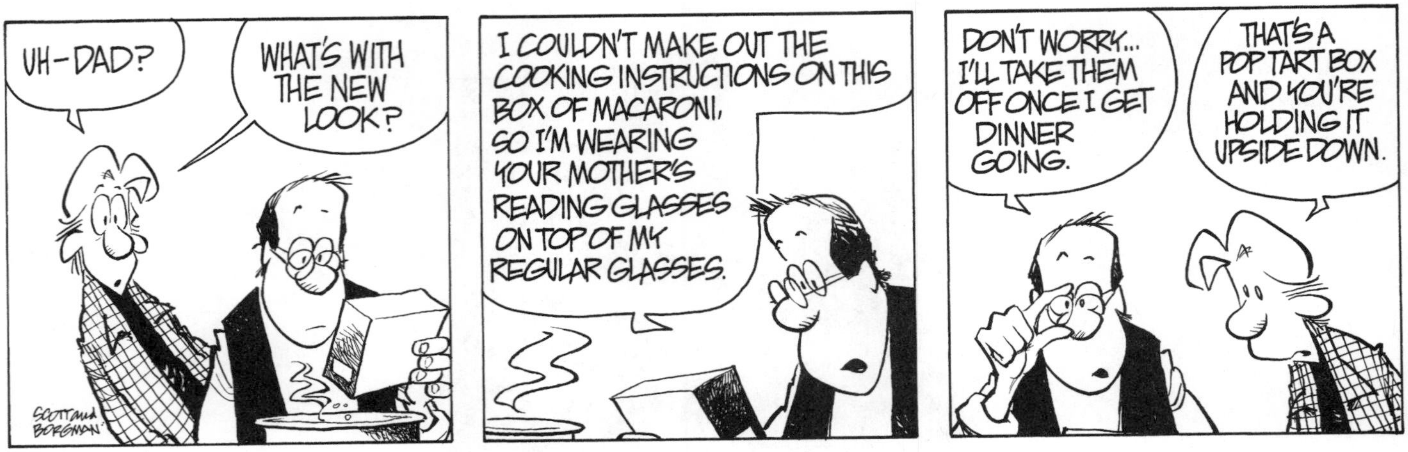
UH-DAD?
WHAT'S WITH THE NEW LOOK?
I COULDN'T MAKE OUT THE COOKING INSTRUCTIONS ON THIS BOX OF MACARONI, SO I'M WEARING YOUR MOTHER'S READING GLASSES ON TOP OF MY REGULAR GLASSES.
DON'T WORRY... I'LL TAKE THEM OFF ONCE I GET DINNER GOING.
THAT'S A POP TART BOX AND YOU'RE HOLDING IT UPSIDE DOWN.
SCOTT AND BORGMAN

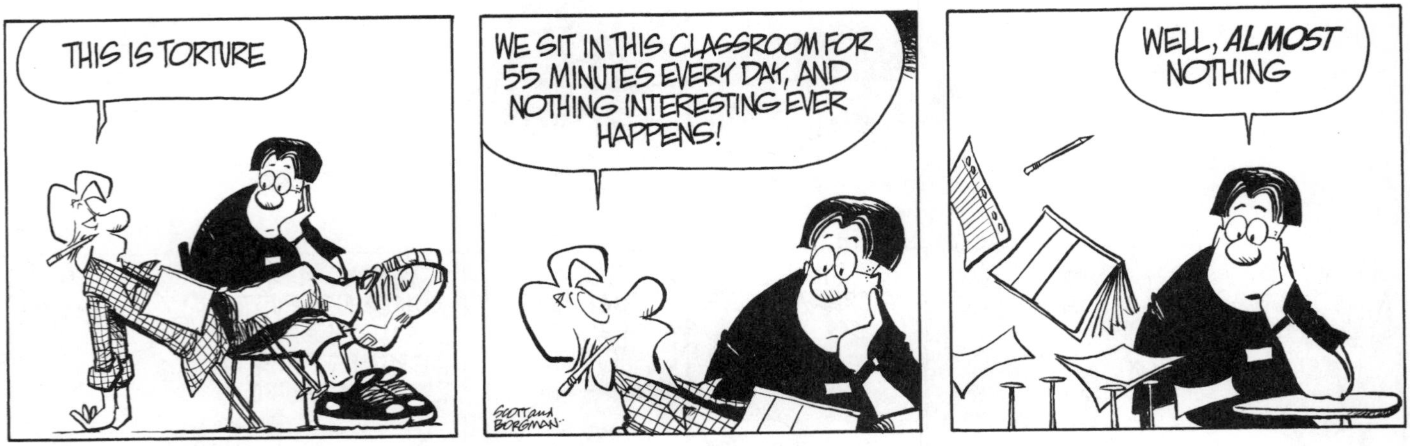
THIS IS TORTURE
WE SIT IN THIS CLASSROOM FOR 55 MINUTES EVERY DAY, AND NOTHING INTERESTING EVER HAPPENS!
WELL, ***ALMOST*** NOTHING
SCOTT AND BORGMAN

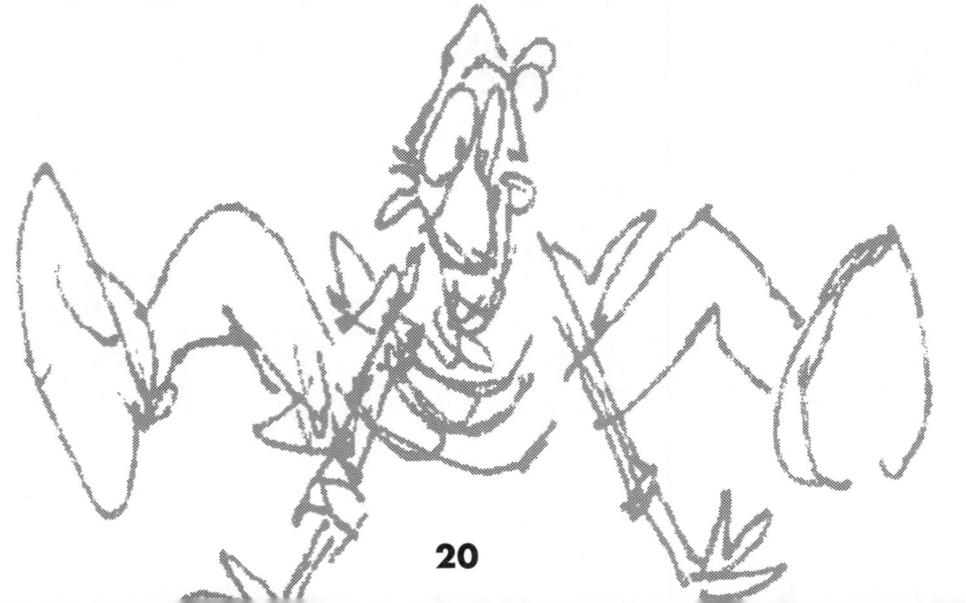

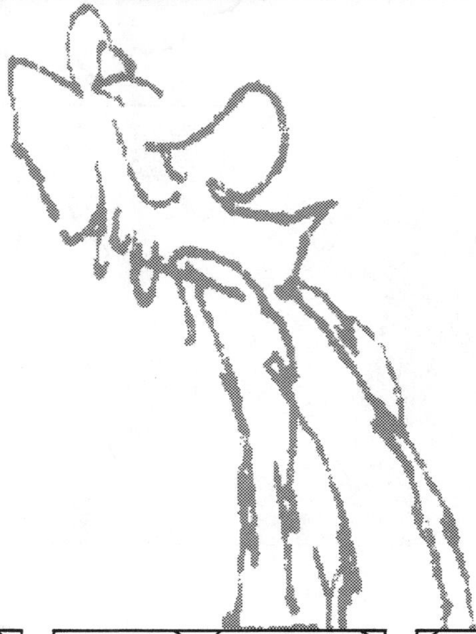

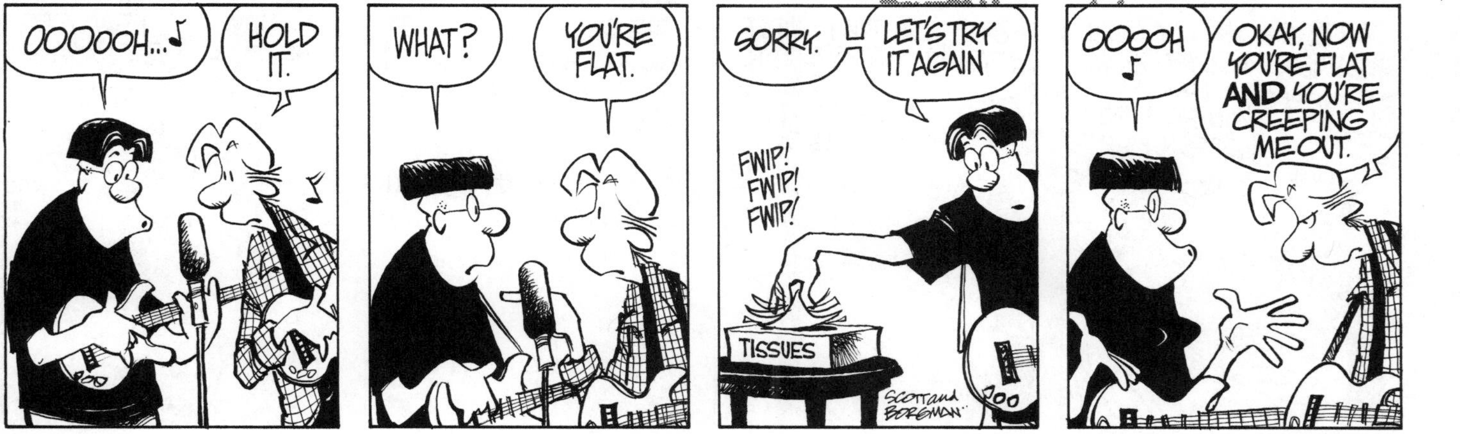
OOOOOH...♪
HOLD IT.
WHAT?
YOU'RE FLAT.
SORRY.
LET'S TRY IT AGAIN
FWIP! FWIP! FWIP!
TISSUES
OOOOH ♪
OKAY, NOW YOU'RE FLAT **AND** YOU'RE CREEPING ME OUT.

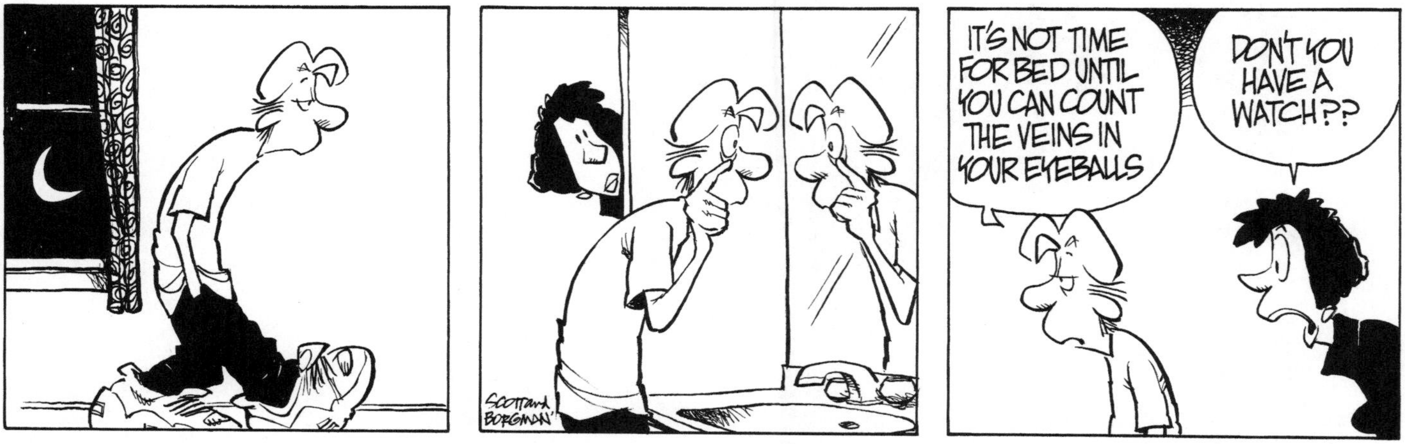
IT'S NOT TIME FOR BED UNTIL YOU CAN COUNT THE VEINS IN YOUR EYEBALLS
DON'T YOU HAVE A WATCH??

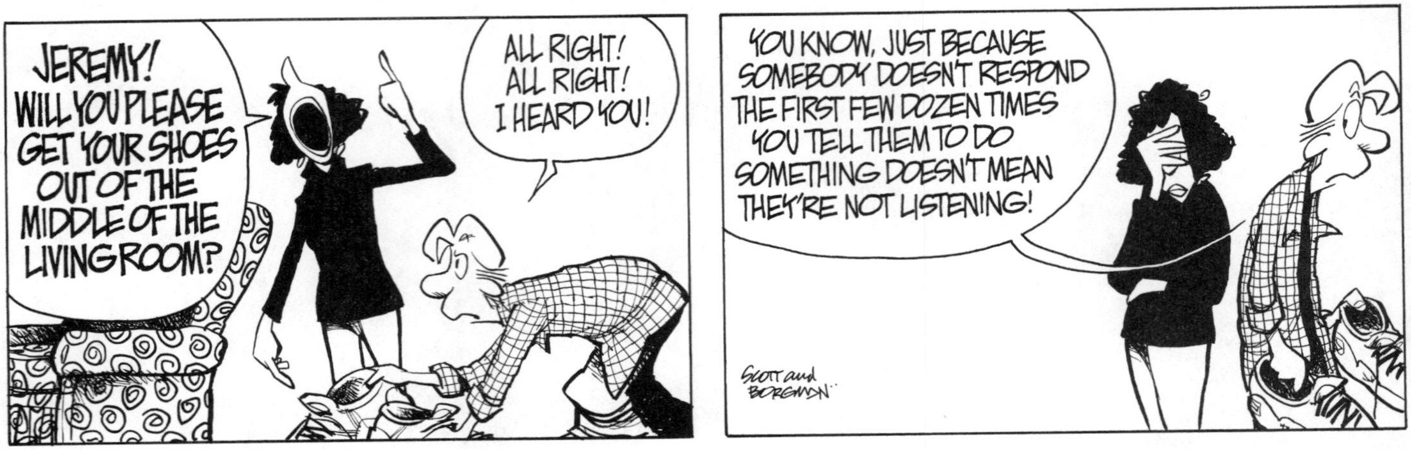
JEREMY! WILL YOU PLEASE GET YOUR SHOES OUT OF THE MIDDLE OF THE LIVING ROOM?
ALL RIGHT! ALL RIGHT! I HEARD YOU!
YOU KNOW, JUST BECAUSE SOMEBODY DOESN'T RESPOND THE FIRST FEW DOZEN TIMES YOU TELL THEM TO DO SOMETHING DOESN'T MEAN THEY'RE NOT LISTENING!
SCOTT and BORGMAN

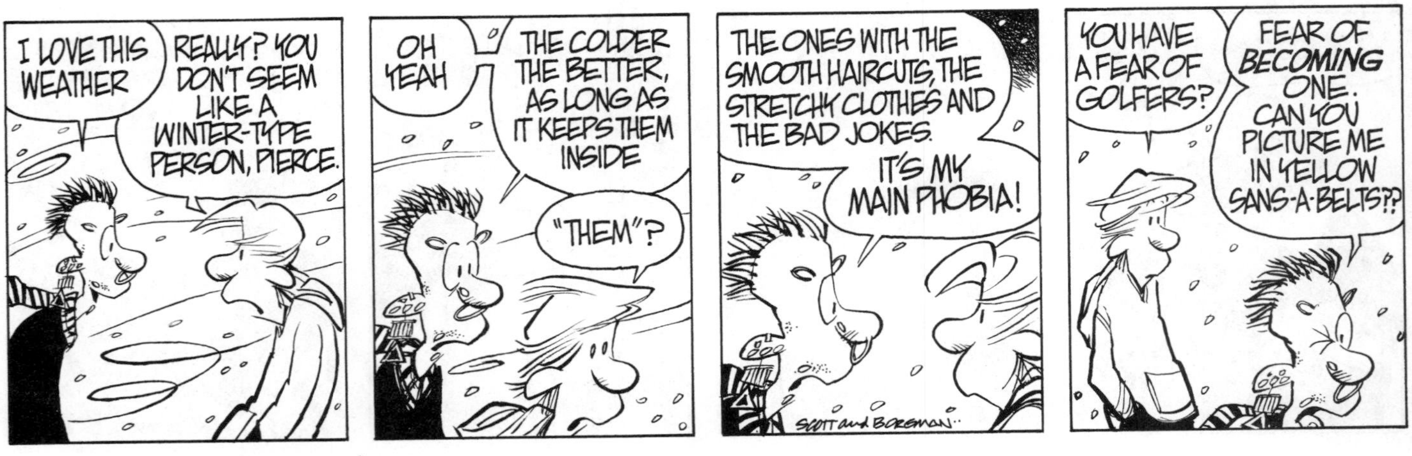
I LOVE THIS WEATHER
REALLY? YOU DON'T SEEM LIKE A WINTER-TYPE PERSON, PIERCE.
OH YEAH
THE COLDER THE BETTER, AS LONG AS IT KEEPS THEM INSIDE
"THEM"?
THE ONES WITH THE SMOOTH HAIRCUTS, THE STRETCHY CLOTHES AND THE BAD JOKES.
IT'S MY MAIN PHOBIA!
SCOTT and BORGMAN
YOU HAVE A FEAR OF GOLFERS?
FEAR OF *BECOMING* ONE. CAN YOU PICTURE ME IN YELLOW SANS-A-BELTS??

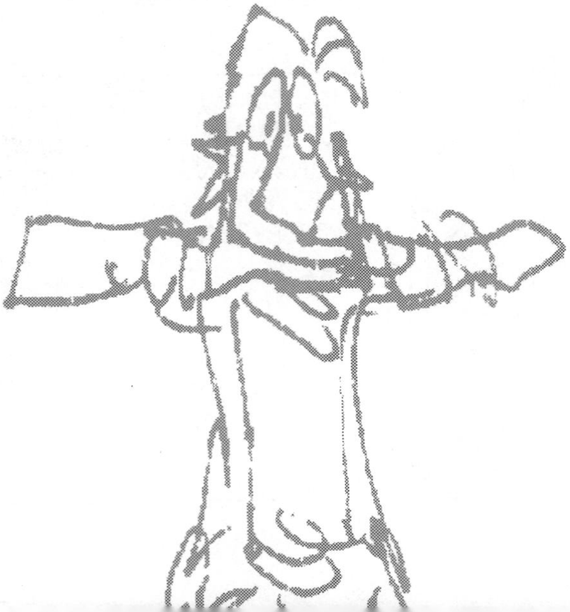

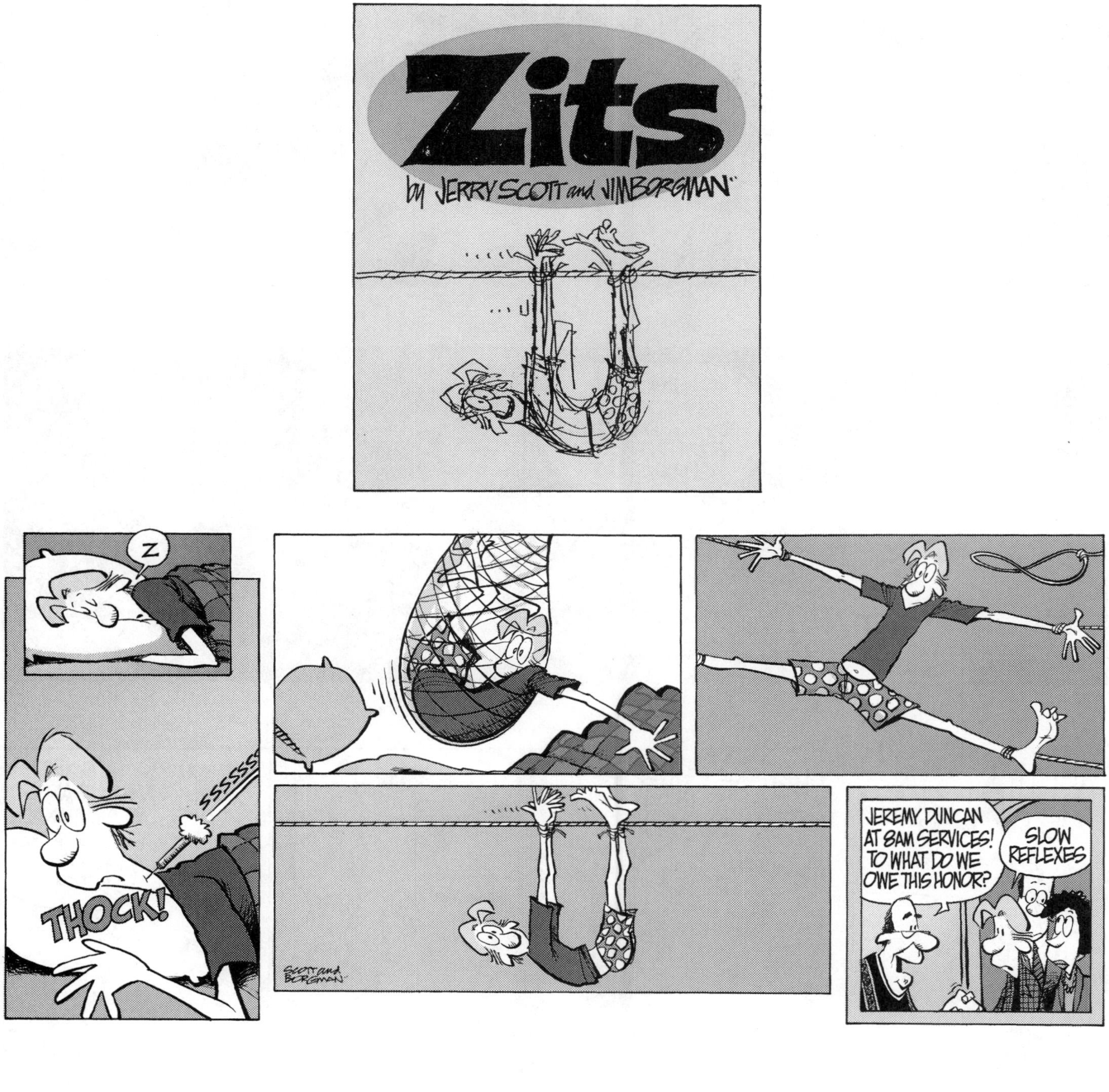
Zits
by JERRY SCOTT and JIM BORGMAN
Z
SSSSSS
THOCK!
JEREMY DUNCAN AT 8AM SERVICES! TO WHAT DO WE OWE THIS HONOR?
SLOW REFLEXES
SCOTT and BORGMAN

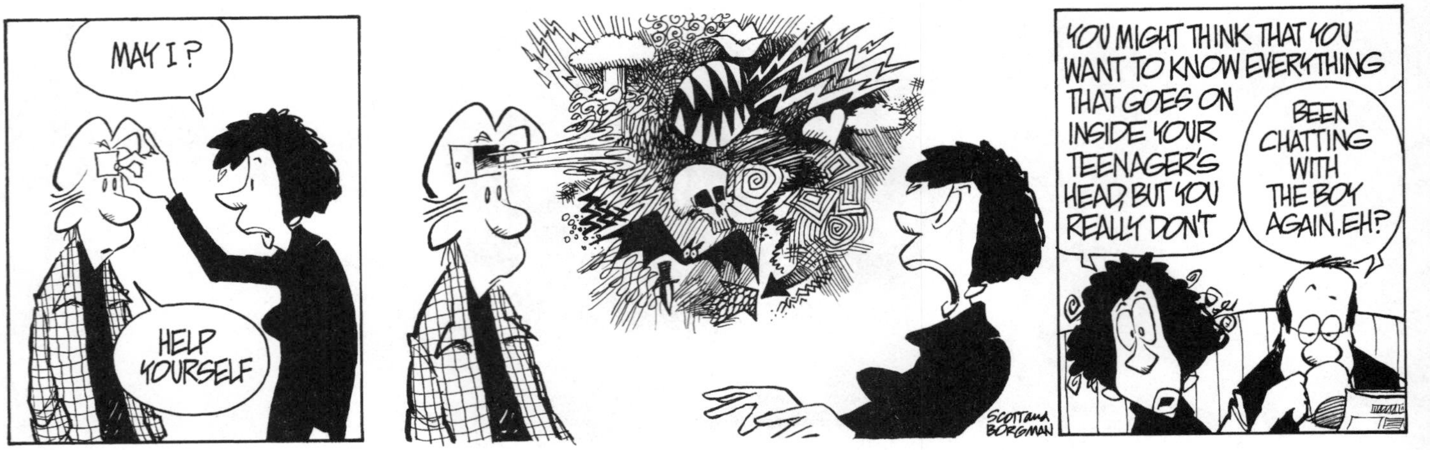
MAY I?
HELP YOURSELF
SCOTT and BORGMAN
YOU MIGHT THINK THAT YOU WANT TO KNOW EVERYTHING THAT GOES ON INSIDE YOUR TEENAGER'S HEAD, BUT YOU REALLY DON'T
BEEN CHATTING WITH THE BOY AGAIN, EH?

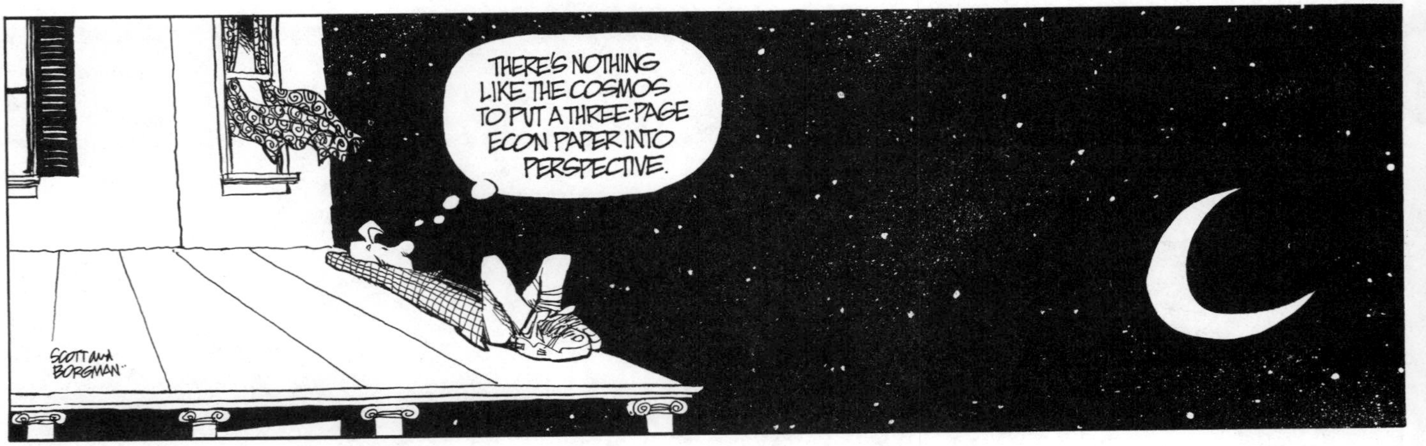
THERE'S NOTHING LIKE THE COSMOS TO PUT A THREE-PAGE ECON PAPER INTO PERSPECTIVE.
SCOTT and BORGMAN

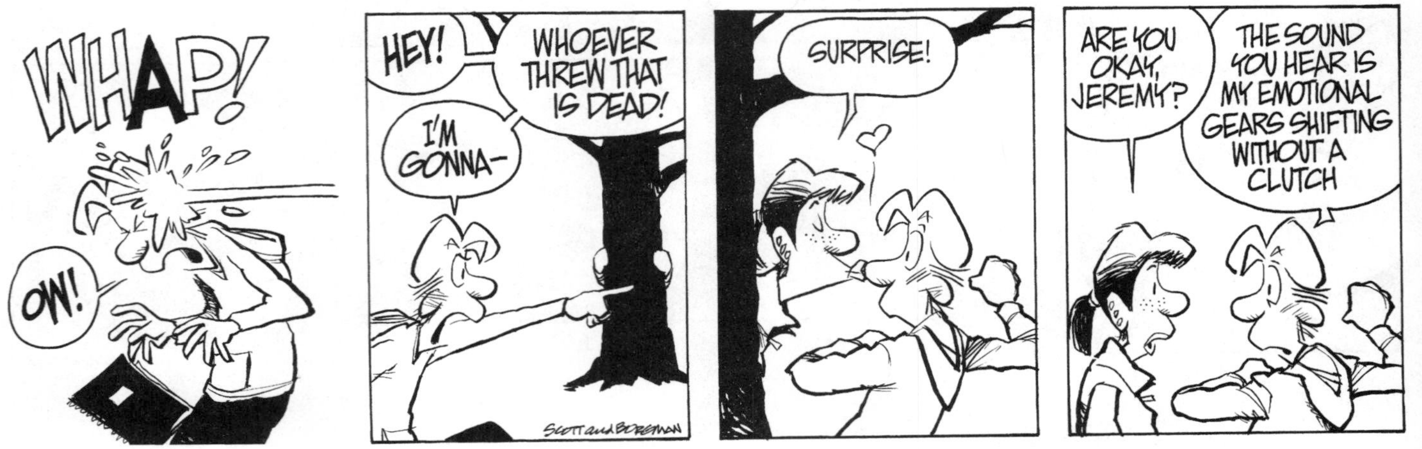
WHAP!
OW!
HEY!
WHOEVER THREW THAT IS DEAD!
I'M GONNA-
SCOTT and BORGMAN
SURPRISE!
ARE YOU OKAY, JEREMY?
THE SOUND YOU HEAR IS MY EMOTIONAL GEARS SHIFTING WITHOUT A CLUTCH

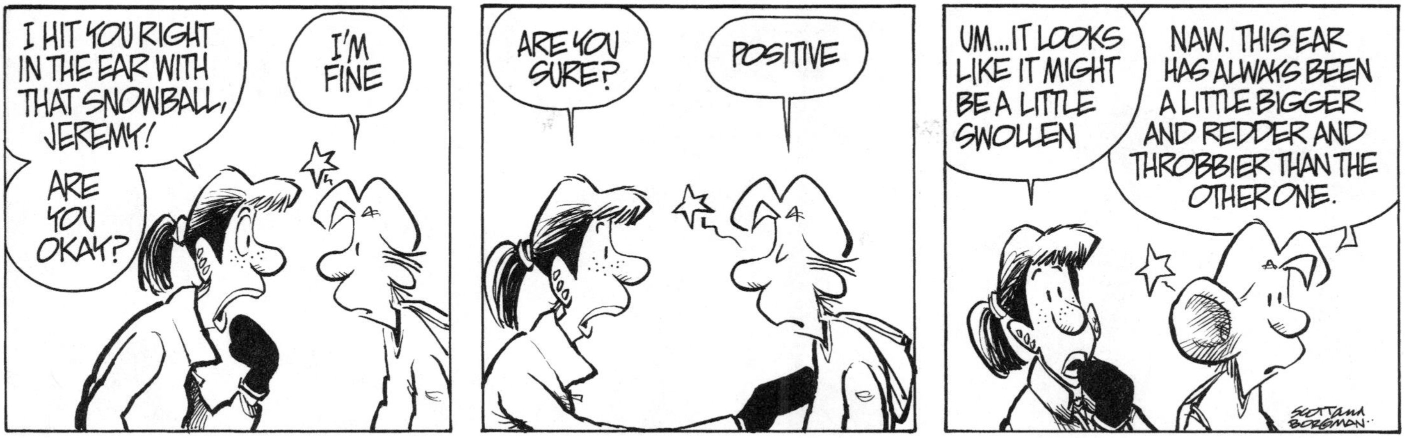
I HIT YOU RIGHT IN THE EAR WITH THAT SNOWBALL, JEREMY!
ARE YOU OKAY?
I'M FINE
ARE YOU SURE?
POSITIVE
UM... IT LOOKS LIKE IT MIGHT BE A LITTLE SWOLLEN
NAW. THIS EAR HAS ALWAYS BEEN A LITTLE BIGGER AND REDDER AND THROBBIER THAN THE OTHER ONE.

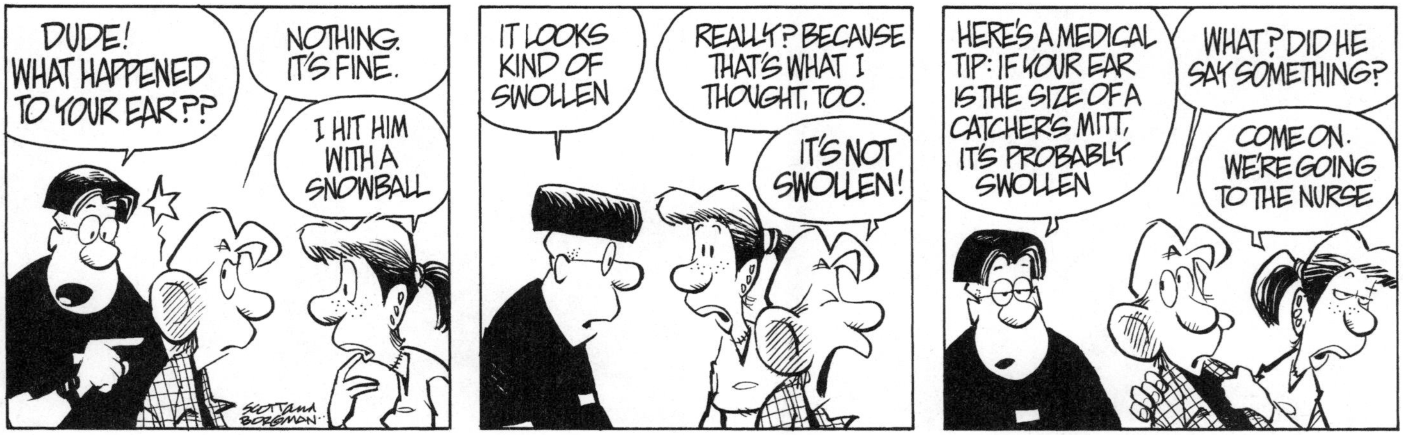
DUDE! WHAT HAPPENED TO YOUR EAR??
NOTHING. IT'S FINE.
I HIT HIM WITH A SNOWBALL
IT LOOKS KIND OF SWOLLEN
REALLY? BECAUSE THAT'S WHAT I THOUGHT, TOO.
IT'S NOT SWOLLEN!
HERE'S A MEDICAL TIP: IF YOUR EAR IS THE SIZE OF A CATCHER'S MITT, IT'S PROBABLY SWOLLEN
WHAT? DID HE SAY SOMETHING?
COME ON. WE'RE GOING TO THE NURSE

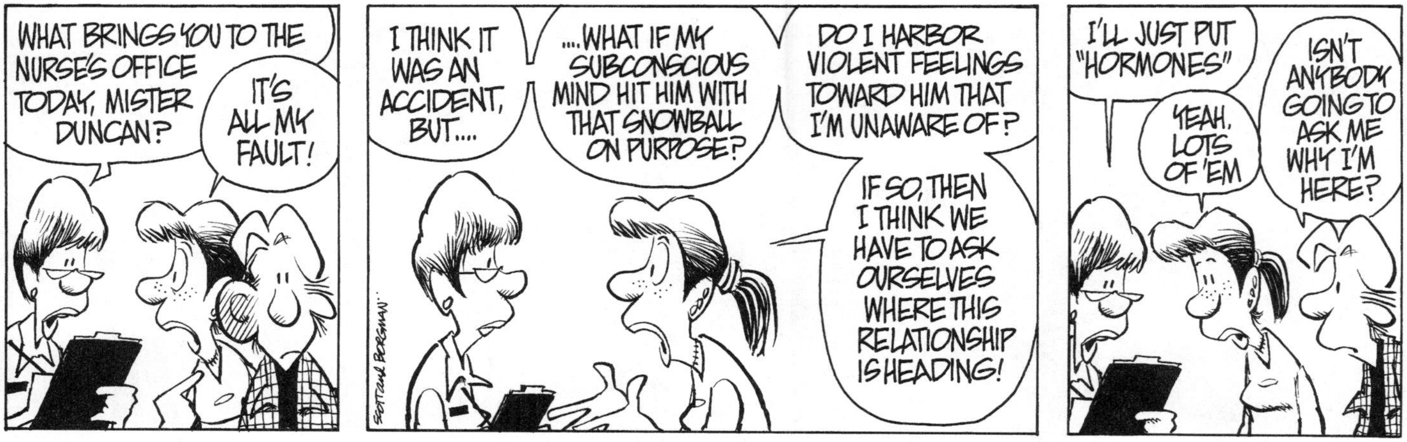
WHAT BRINGS YOU TO THE NURSE'S OFFICE TODAY, MISTER DUNCAN?
IT'S ALL MY FAULT!
I THINK IT WAS AN ACCIDENT, BUT....
....WHAT IF MY SUBCONSCIOUS MIND HIT HIM WITH THAT SNOWBALL ON PURPOSE?
DO I HARBOR VIOLENT FEELINGS TOWARD HIM THAT I'M UNAWARE OF?
IF SO, THEN I THINK WE HAVE TO ASK OURSELVES WHERE THIS RELATIONSHIP IS HEADING!
I'LL JUST PUT "HORMONES"
YEAH, LOTS OF 'EM
ISN'T ANYBODY GOING TO ASK ME WHY I'M HERE?

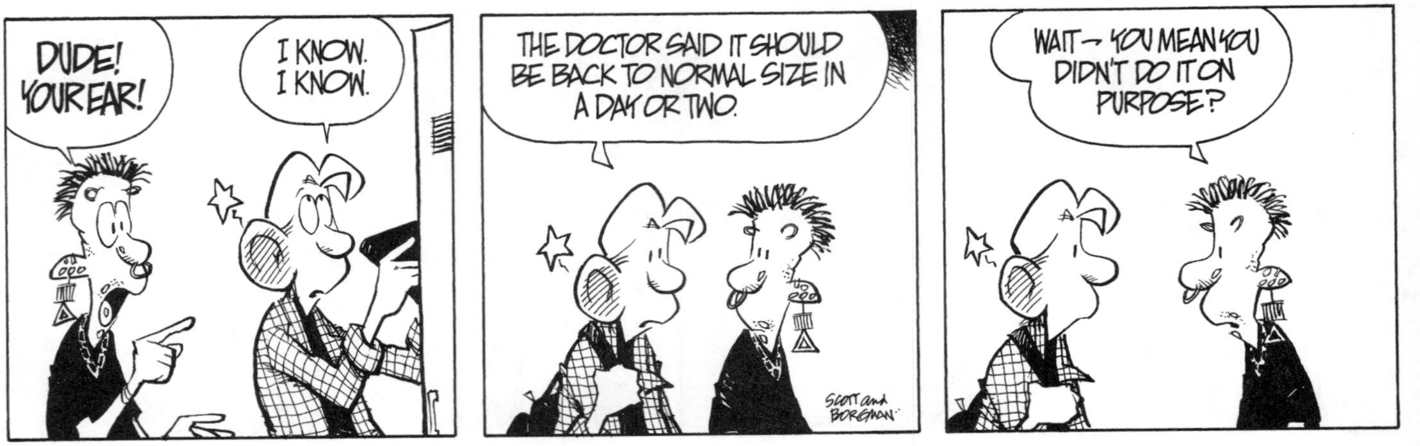
DUDE! YOUR EAR!
I KNOW. I KNOW.
THE DOCTOR SAID IT SHOULD BE BACK TO NORMAL SIZE IN A DAY OR TWO.
WAIT— YOU MEAN YOU DIDN'T DO IT ON PURPOSE?
SCOTT and BORGMAN

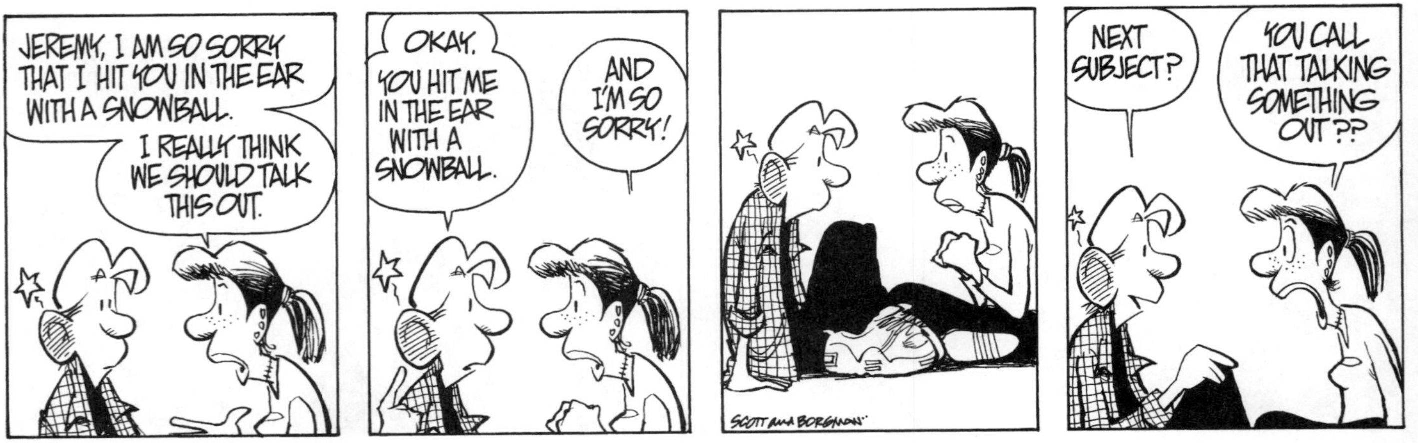
JEREMY, I AM SO SORRY THAT I HIT YOU IN THE EAR WITH A SNOWBALL.
I REALLY THINK WE SHOULD TALK THIS OUT.
OKAY.
YOU HIT ME IN THE EAR WITH A SNOWBALL.
AND I'M SO SORRY!
SCOTT and BORGMAN
NEXT SUBJECT?
YOU CALL THAT TALKING SOMETHING OUT??

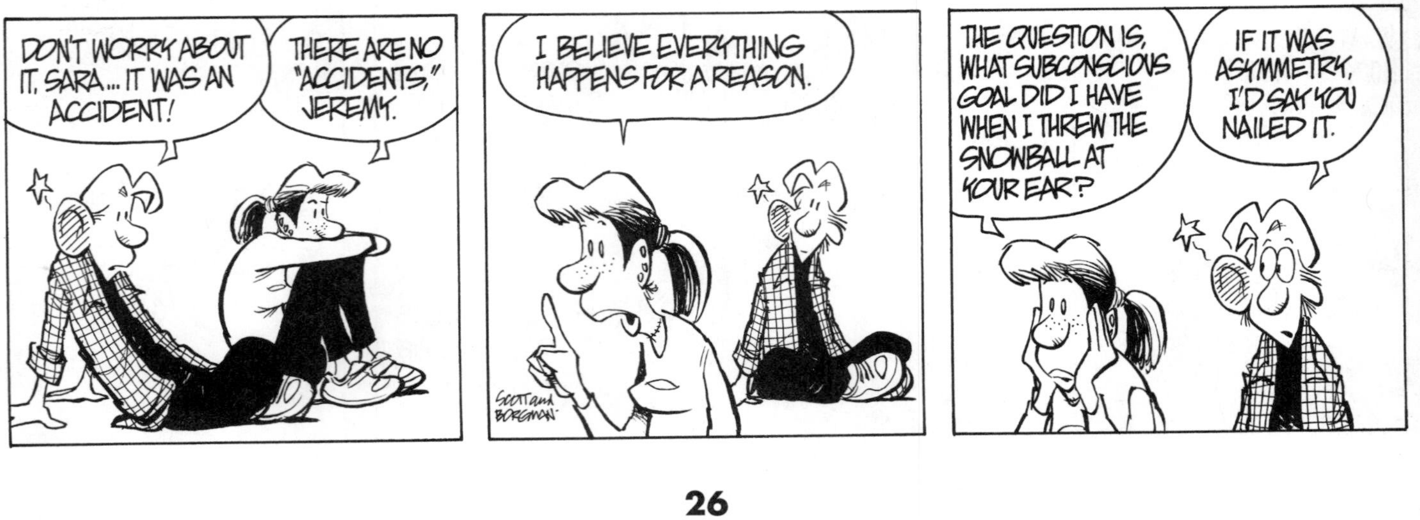
DON'T WORRY ABOUT IT, SARA... IT WAS AN ACCIDENT!
THERE ARE NO "ACCIDENTS," JEREMY.
I BELIEVE EVERYTHING HAPPENS FOR A REASON.
SCOTT and BORGMAN
THE QUESTION IS, WHAT SUBCONSCIOUS GOAL DID I HAVE WHEN I THREW THE SNOWBALL AT YOUR EAR?
IF IT WAS ASYMMETRY, I'D SAY YOU NAILED IT.

Zits
by
JERRY SCOTT and
JIM BORGMAN

SCOTT and BORGMAN
OOPS! GOTTA GO!
WE JUST PASSED YOU THREE MINUTES AGO, PIERCE! HOW CAN YOU BE FINISHED WITH LUNCH ALREADY?
SIMPLE
I CONSUME FROM 12:47 TO 12:50 AND I CHEW FROM 12:50 TO 1:30.
SO THAT'S THE NOISE I HEAR DURING ALGEBRA!

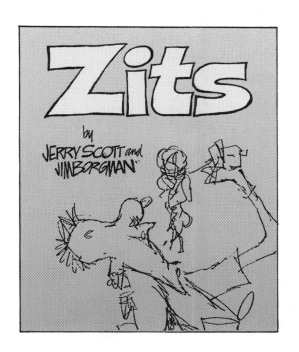

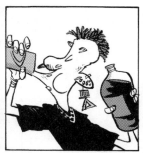

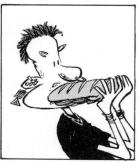

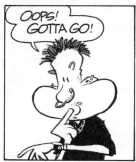

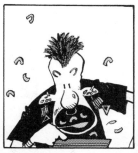

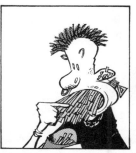

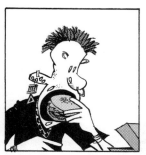

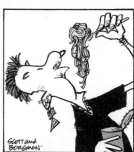

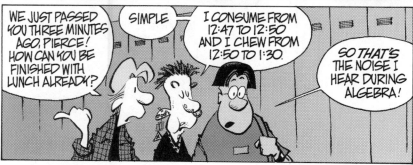

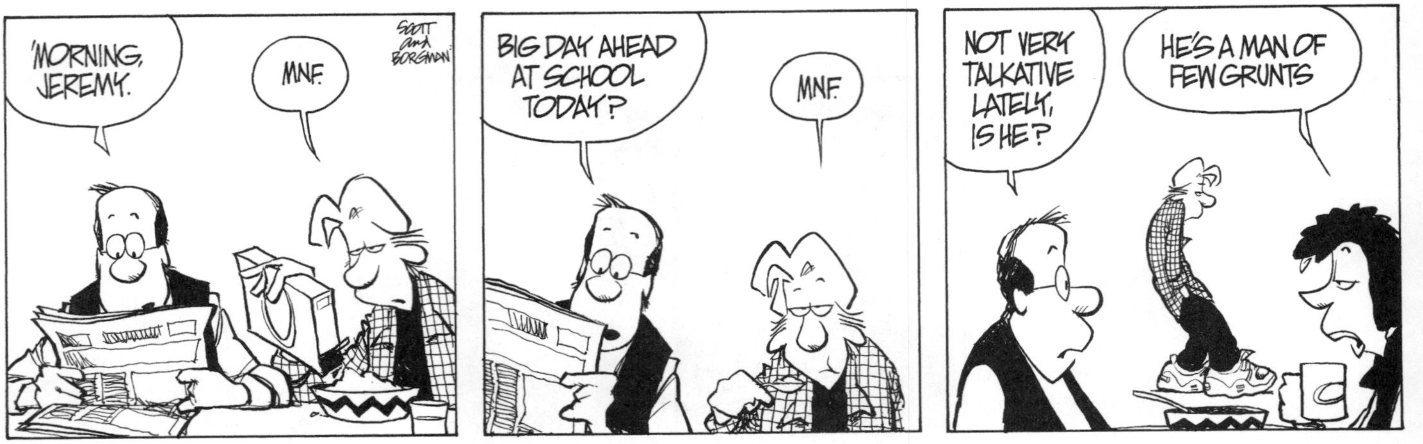
'MORNING, JEREMY.
MNF.
BIG DAY AHEAD AT SCHOOL TODAY?
MNF.
NOT VERY TALKATIVE LATELY, IS HE?
HE'S A MAN OF FEW GRUNTS

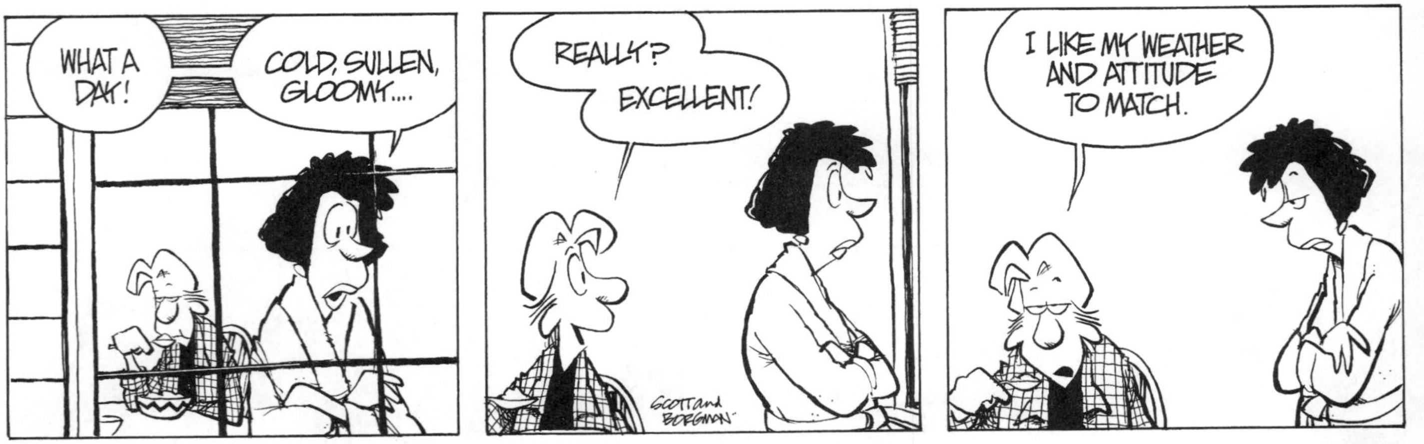
WHAT A DAY!
COLD, SULLEN, GLOOMY....
REALLY? EXCELLENT!
I LIKE MY WEATHER AND ATTITUDE TO MATCH.

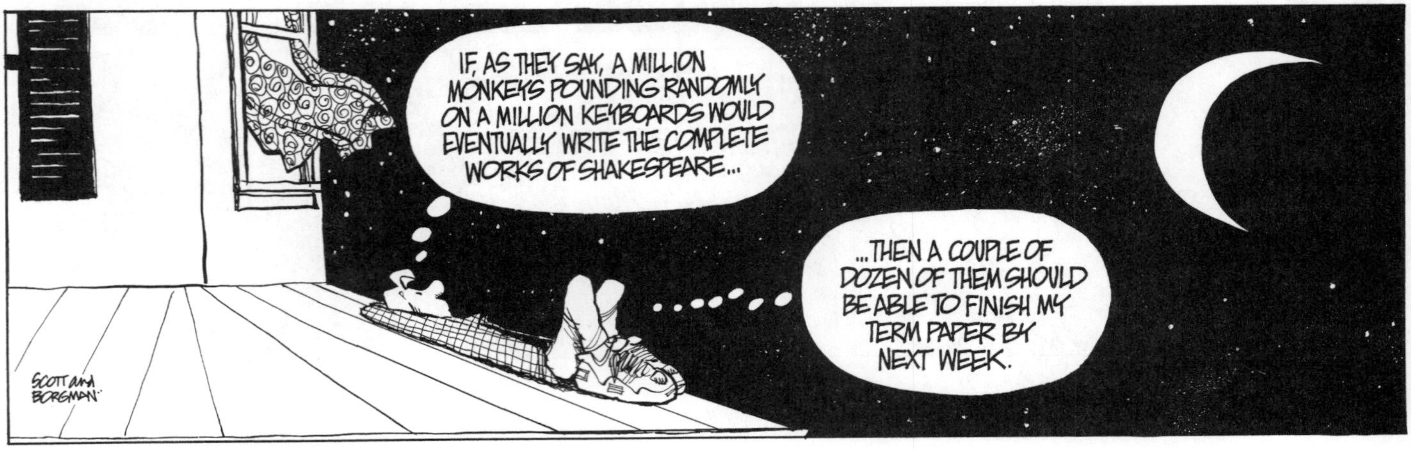
IF, AS THEY SAY, A MILLION MONKEYS POUNDING RANDOMLY ON A MILLION KEYBOARDS WOULD EVENTUALLY WRITE THE COMPLETE WORKS OF SHAKESPEARE...
...THEN A COUPLE OF DOZEN OF THEM SHOULD BE ABLE TO FINISH MY TERM PAPER BY NEXT WEEK.

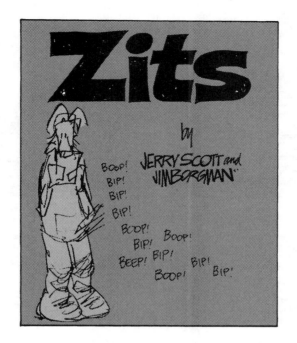

Zits
by
JERRY SCOTT and
JIM BORGMAN
BOOP!
BIP!
BIP!
BIP!
BOOP!
BIP!
BOOP!
BEEP!
BIP!
BIP!
BOOP!
BIP!

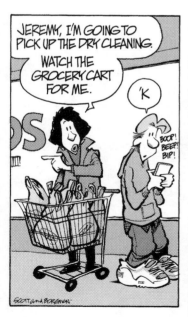

JEREMY, I'M GOING TO PICK UP THE DRY CLEANING.
WATCH THE GROCERY CART FOR ME.
'K
BOOP! BEEP! BIP!
BECAUSE IT'S ON AN INCLINE....
RIGHT.
BOOP! BIP! BEEP!
...NEAR A LOT OF PARKED CARS...
UH-HUH.
BOOP! BOOP! BIP! BIP!
...WHICH IT WILL CRASH INTO IF YOU DON'T---
BOOP! BIP! BOOP! BIP!
ON SECOND THOUGHT, YOU GO PICK UP THE DRY CLEANING.
ARE YOU SURE? BECAUSE I DON'T MIND WATCHING THE CART.

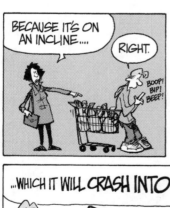

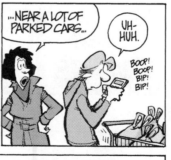

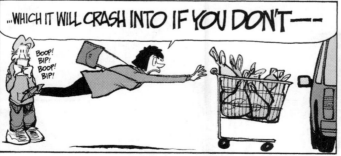

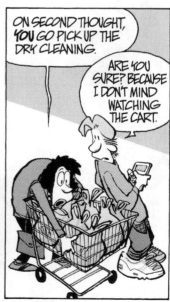

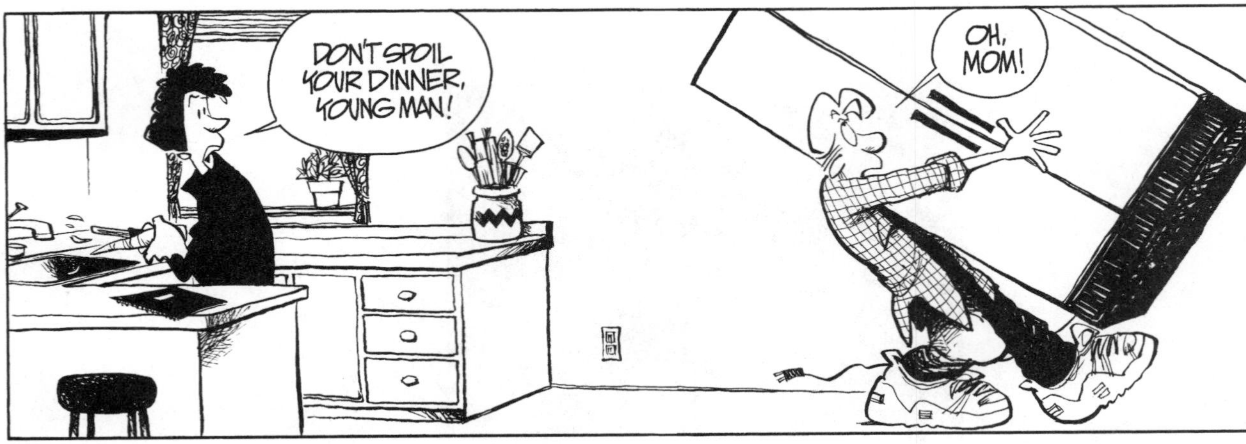
DON'T SPOIL YOUR DINNER, YOUNG MAN!
OH, MOM!
SCOTT and BORGMAN

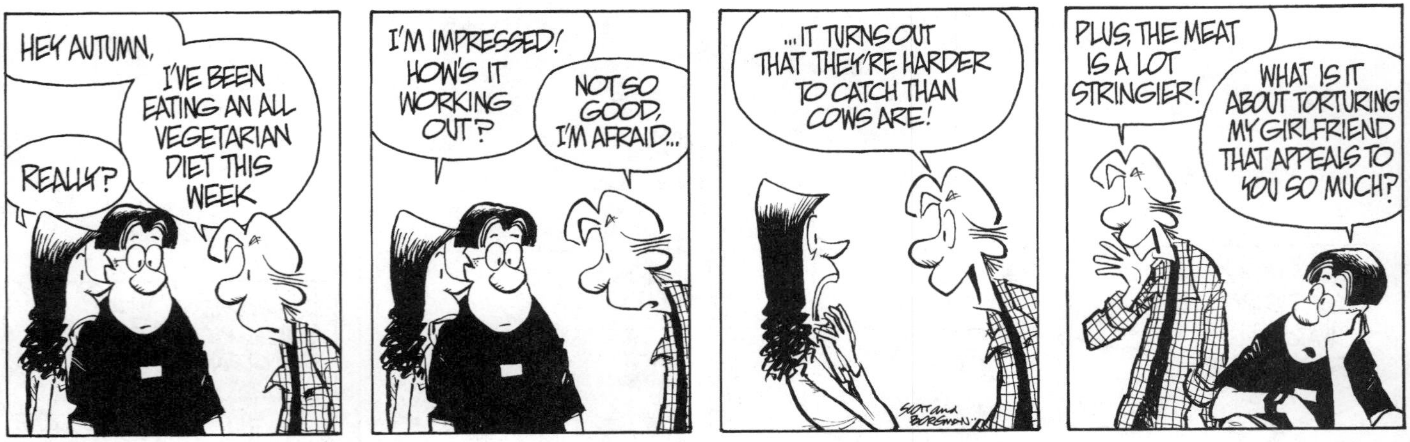
HEY AUTUMN,
I'VE BEEN EATING AN ALL VEGETARIAN DIET THIS WEEK
REALLY?
I'M IMPRESSED! HOW'S IT WORKING OUT?
NOT SO GOOD, I'M AFRAID...
...IT TURNS OUT THAT THEY'RE HARDER TO CATCH THAN COWS ARE!
SCOTT and BORGMAN
PLUS, THE MEAT IS A LOT STRINGIER!
WHAT IS IT ABOUT TORTURING MY GIRLFRIEND THAT APPEALS TO YOU SO MUCH?

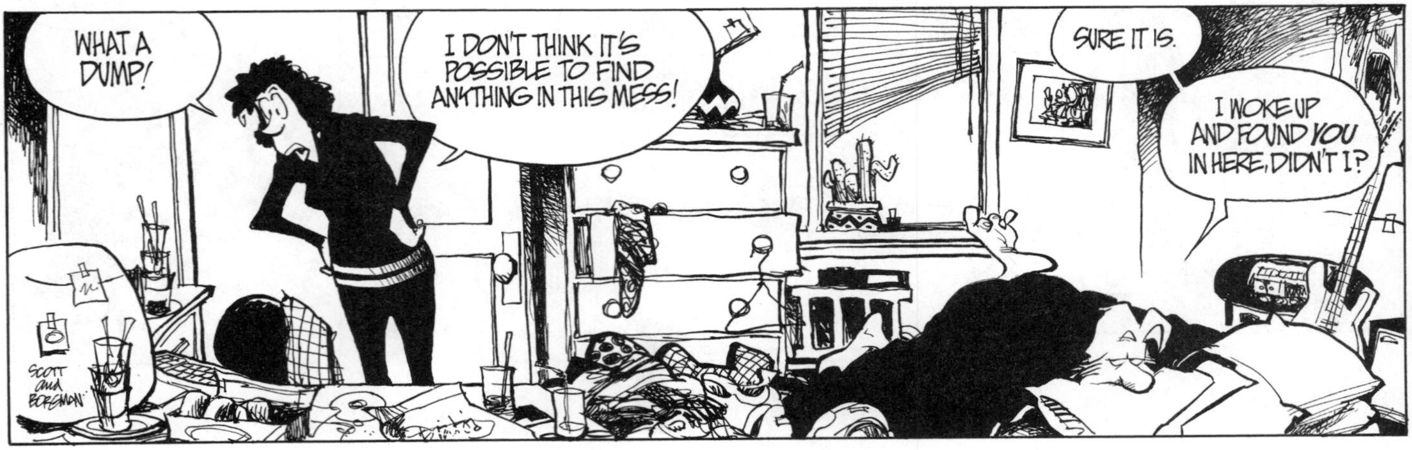
WHAT A DUMP!
I DON'T THINK IT'S POSSIBLE TO FIND ANYTHING IN THIS MESS!
SURE IT IS.
I WOKE UP AND FOUND *YOU* IN HERE, DIDN'T I?
SCOTT and BORGMAN

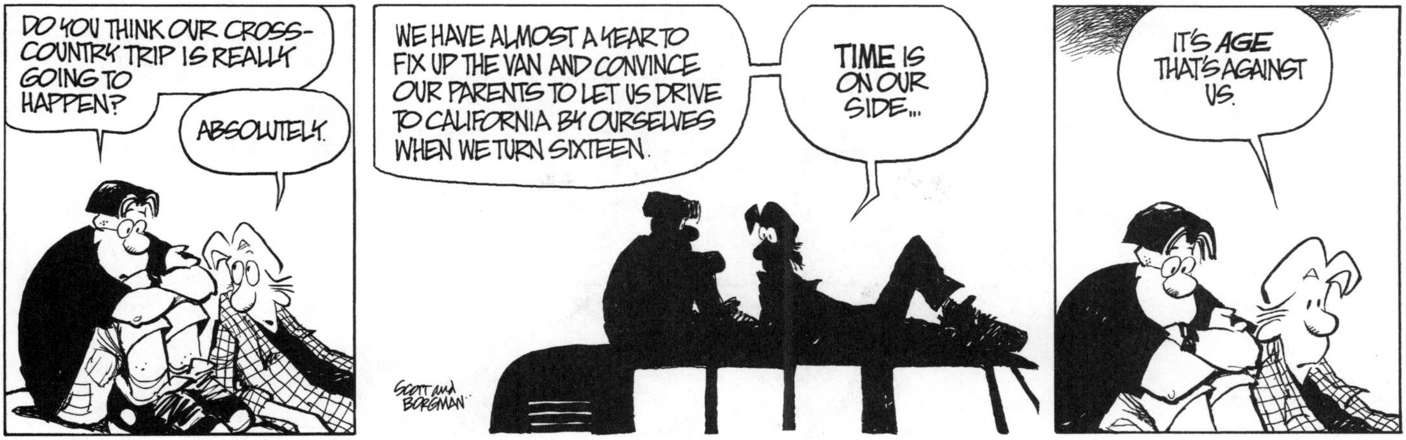
DO YOU THINK OUR CROSS-COUNTRY TRIP IS REALLY GOING TO HAPPEN?
ABSOLUTELY.
WE HAVE ALMOST A YEAR TO FIX UP THE VAN AND CONVINCE OUR PARENTS TO LET US DRIVE TO CALIFORNIA BY OURSELVES WHEN WE TURN SIXTEEN.
TIME IS ON OUR SIDE...
SCOTT AND BORGMAN
IT'S AGE THAT'S AGAINST US.

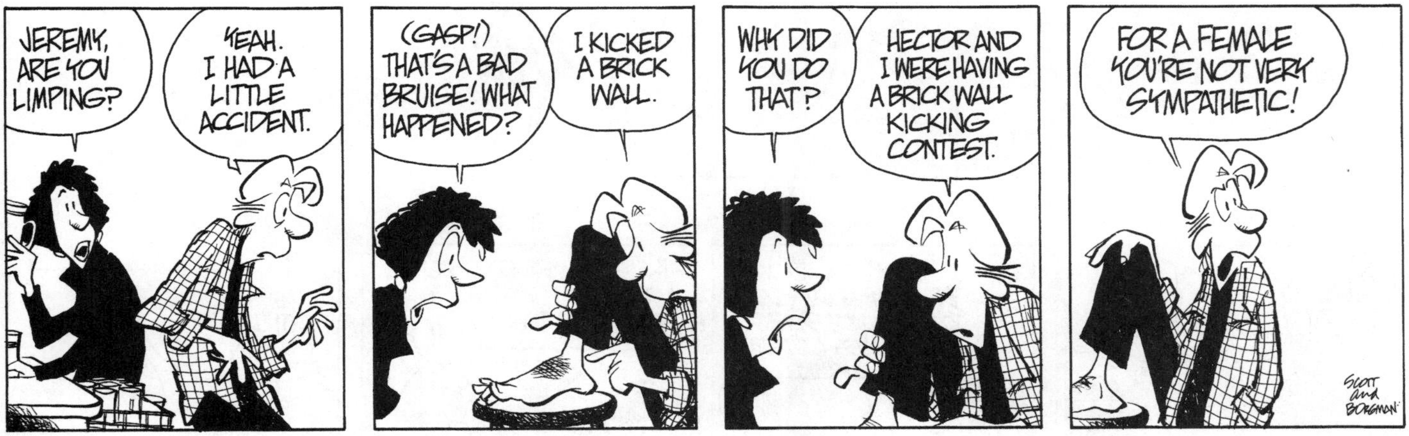
JEREMY, ARE YOU LIMPING?
YEAH. I HAD A LITTLE ACCIDENT.
(GASP!) THAT'S A BAD BRUISE! WHAT HAPPENED?
I KICKED A BRICK WALL.
WHY DID YOU DO THAT?
HECTOR AND I WERE HAVING A BRICK WALL KICKING CONTEST.
FOR A FEMALE YOU'RE NOT VERY SYMPATHETIC!
SCOTT AND BORGMAN

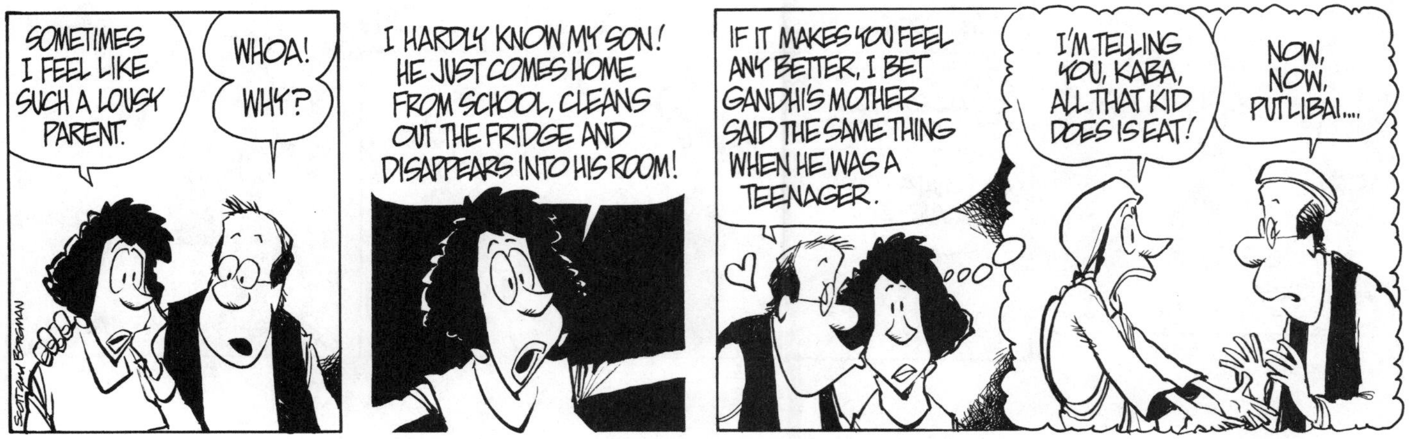
SOMETIMES I FEEL LIKE SUCH A LOUSY PARENT.
WHOA! WHY?
SCOTT AND BORGMAN
I HARDLY KNOW MY SON! HE JUST COMES HOME FROM SCHOOL, CLEANS OUT THE FRIDGE AND DISAPPEARS INTO HIS ROOM!
IF IT MAKES YOU FEEL ANY BETTER, I BET GANDHI'S MOTHER SAID THE SAME THING WHEN HE WAS A TEENAGER.
I'M TELLING YOU, KABA, ALL THAT KID DOES IS EAT!
NOW, NOW, PUTLIBAI....

Zits
by JERRY SCOTT and JIM BORGMAN

NICE SHIRT
THANKS, SARA
GIVE ME
UM—
THIS ISN'T A CRITICISM, BUT IF THAT'S SUPPOSED TO BE A PEACE SYMBOL, SOMEBODY GOOFED.
HUH?
GIVE ME
THAT'S THE MERCEDES-BENZ LOGO... THE PEACE SYMBOL GOES LIKE THIS.
HUH.
SO, WHILE IT'S INTENDED TO CALL FOR PEACE, TECHNICALLY YOU'RE WALKING AROUND IN A SHIRT THAT'S DEMANDING A LUXURY CAR.
GIVE ME
SCOTT and BORGMAN
SO, IF IT WORKS, EITHER WAY I WIN.
LIKE I SAID, IT'S NOT A CRITICISM.
GIVE ME

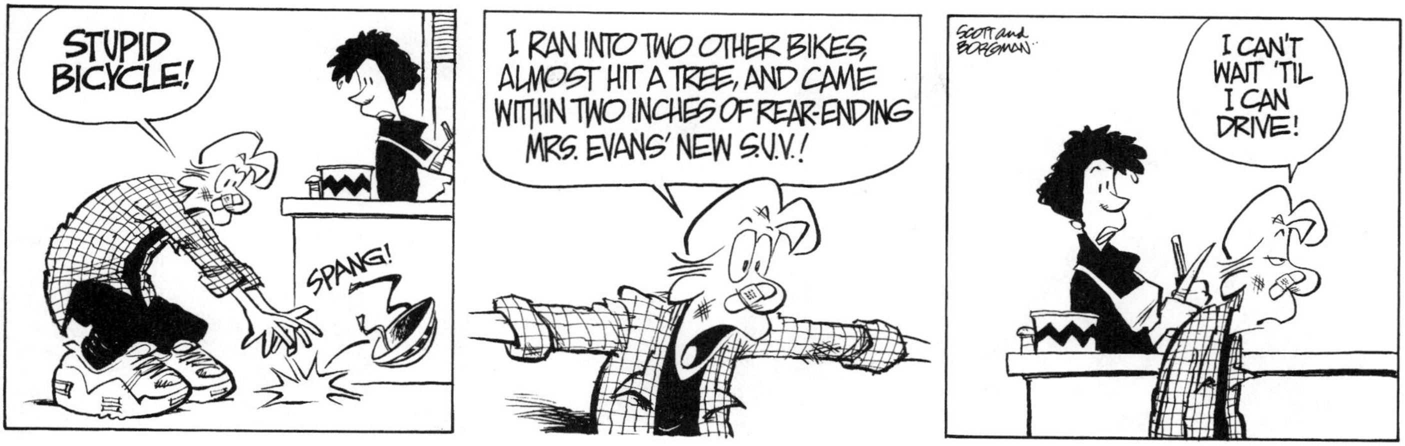
STUPID BICYCLE!
SPANG!
I RAN INTO TWO OTHER BIKES, ALMOST HIT A TREE, AND CAME WITHIN TWO INCHES OF REAR-ENDING MRS. EVANS' NEW S.U.V.!
SCOTT and BORGMAN
I CAN'T WAIT 'TIL I CAN DRIVE!

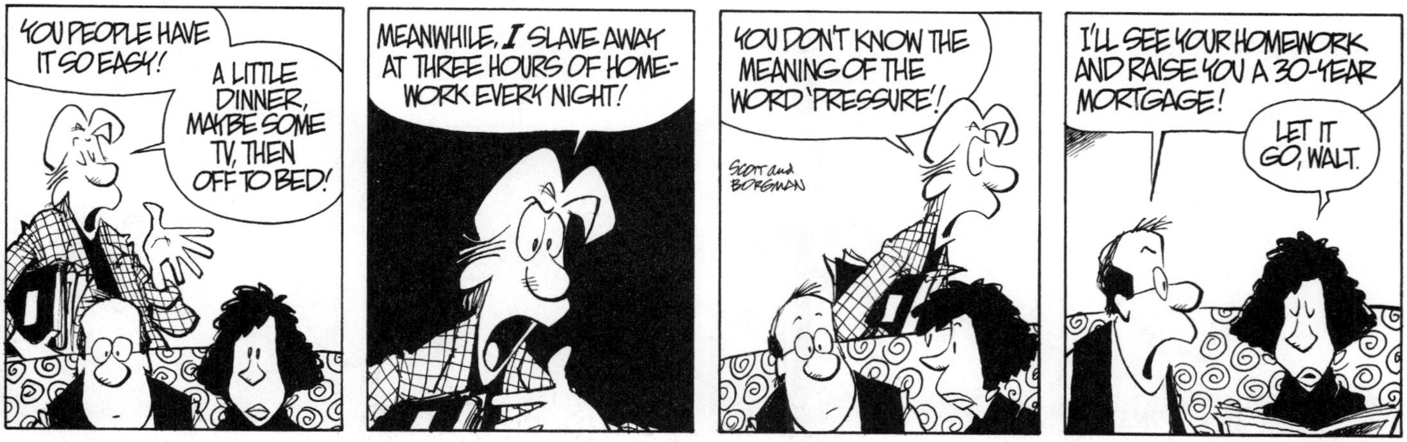
YOU PEOPLE HAVE IT SO EASY!
A LITTLE DINNER, MAYBE SOME TV, THEN OFF TO BED!
MEANWHILE, *I* SLAVE AWAY AT THREE HOURS OF HOME-WORK EVERY NIGHT!
YOU DON'T KNOW THE MEANING OF THE WORD 'PRESSURE'!
SCOTT and BORGMAN
I'LL SEE YOUR HOMEWORK AND RAISE YOU A 30-YEAR MORTGAGE!
LET IT GO, WALT.

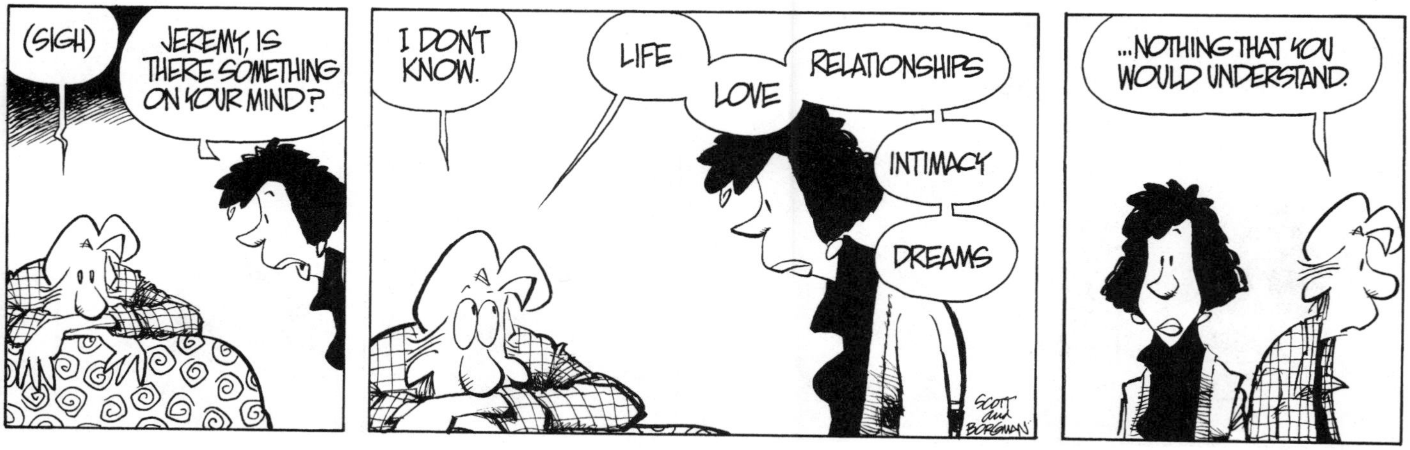
(SIGH)
JEREMY, IS THERE SOMETHING ON YOUR MIND?
I DON'T KNOW.
LIFE
LOVE
RELATIONSHIPS
INTIMACY
DREAMS
SCOTT and BORGMAN
...NOTHING THAT YOU WOULD UNDERSTAND.

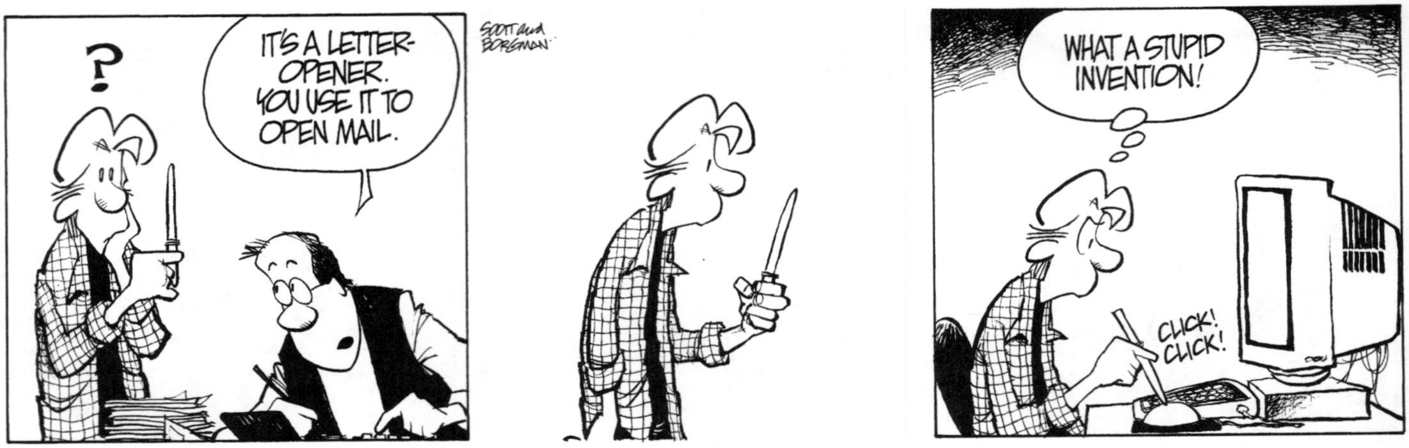
?
IT'S A LETTER-OPENER. YOU USE IT TO OPEN MAIL.
SCOTT and BORGMAN
WHAT A STUPID INVENTION!
CLICK! CLICK!

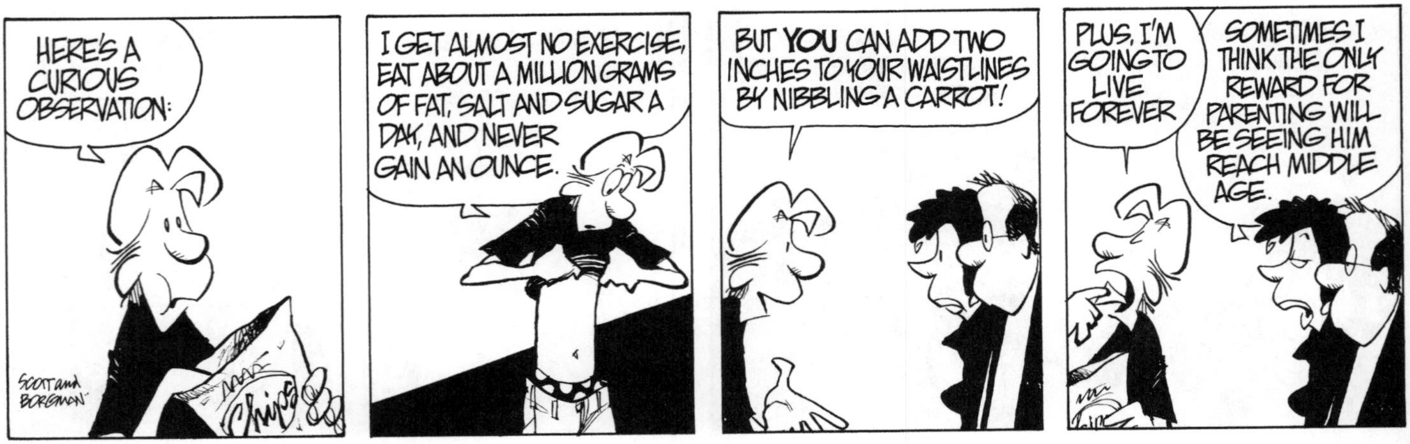
HERE'S A CURIOUS OBSERVATION:
SCOTT and BORGMAN
I GET ALMOST NO EXERCISE, EAT ABOUT A MILLION GRAMS OF FAT, SALT AND SUGAR A DAY, AND NEVER GAIN AN OUNCE.
BUT **YOU** CAN ADD TWO INCHES TO YOUR WAISTLINES BY NIBBLING A CARROT!
PLUS, I'M GOING TO LIVE FOREVER
SOMETIMES I THINK THE ONLY REWARD FOR PARENTING WILL BE SEEING HIM REACH MIDDLE AGE.

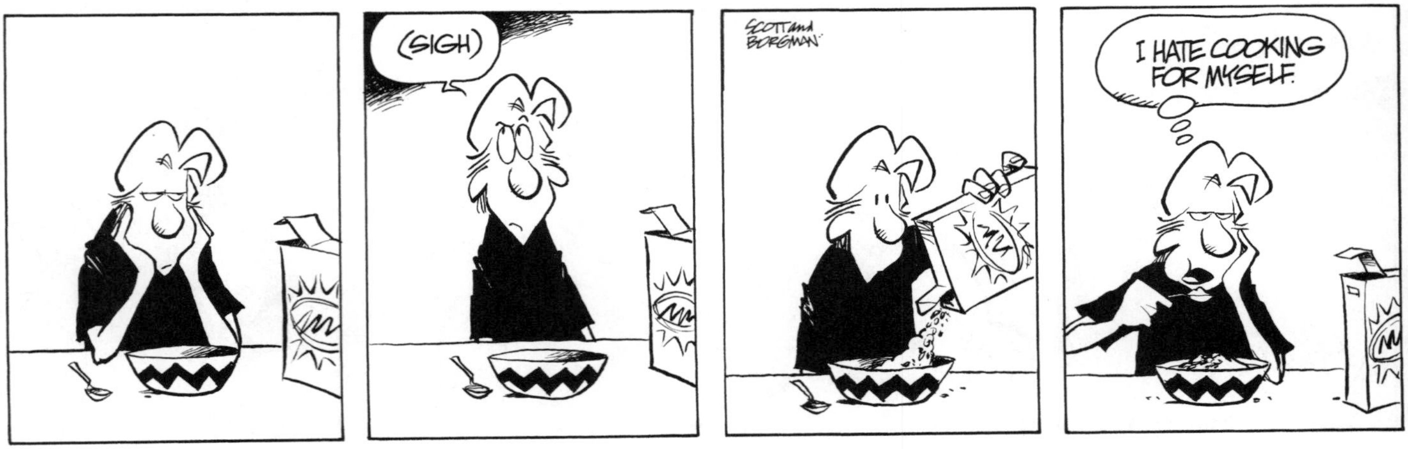
(SIGH)
SCOTT and BORGMAN
I HATE COOKING FOR MYSELF.

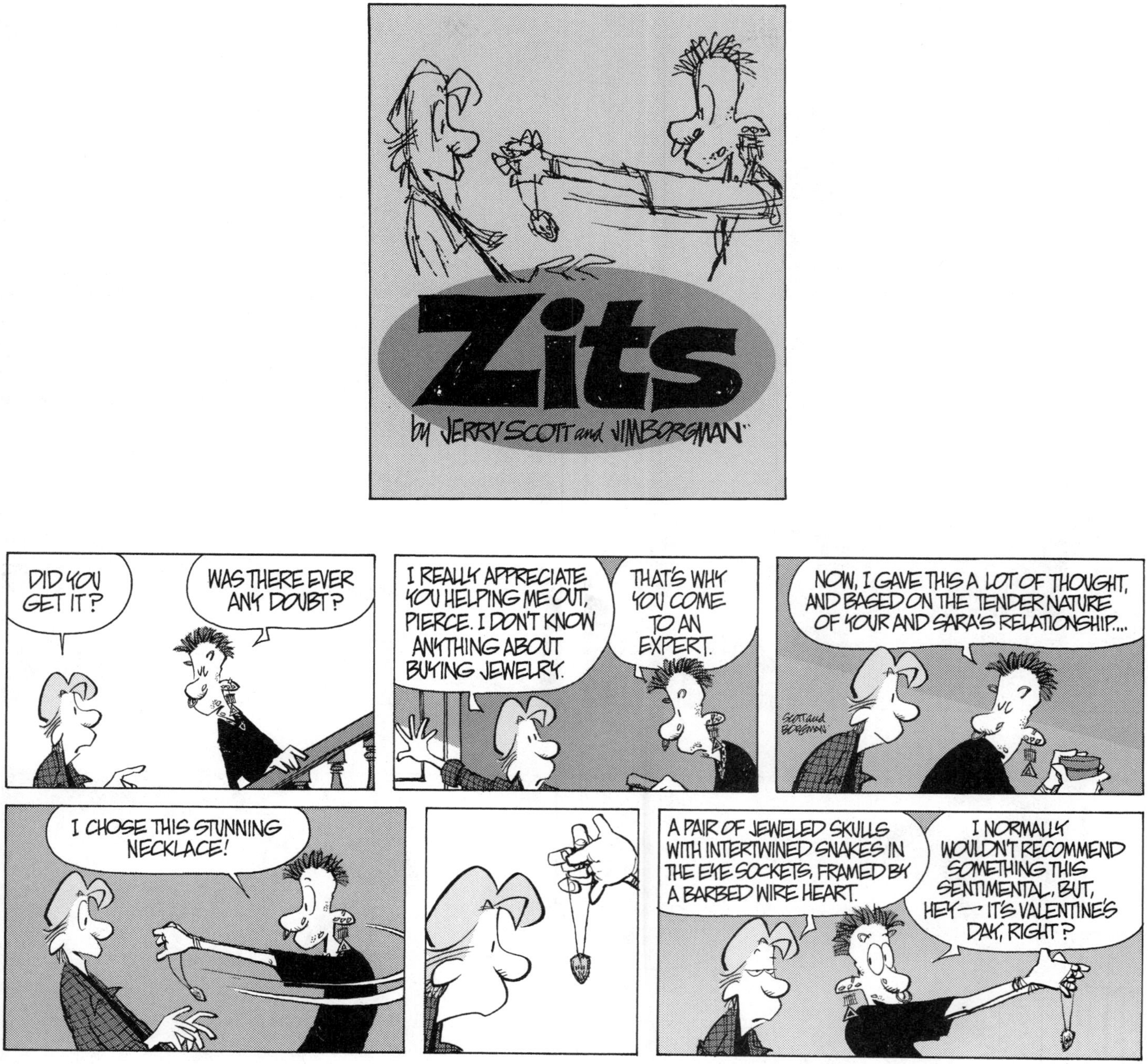
Zits
by JERRY SCOTT and JIM BORGMAN
DID YOU GET IT?
WAS THERE EVER ANY DOUBT?
I REALLY APPRECIATE YOU HELPING ME OUT, PIERCE. I DON'T KNOW ANYTHING ABOUT BUYING JEWELRY.
THAT'S WHY YOU COME TO AN EXPERT.
NOW, I GAVE THIS A LOT OF THOUGHT, AND BASED ON THE TENDER NATURE OF YOUR AND SARA'S RELATIONSHIP....
SCOTT and BORGMAN
I CHOSE THIS STUNNING NECKLACE!
A PAIR OF JEWELED SKULLS WITH INTERTWINED SNAKES IN THE EYE SOCKETS, FRAMED BY A BARBED WIRE HEART.
I NORMALLY WOULDN'T RECOMMEND SOMETHING THIS SENTIMENTAL, BUT, HEY— IT'S VALENTINE'S DAY, RIGHT?

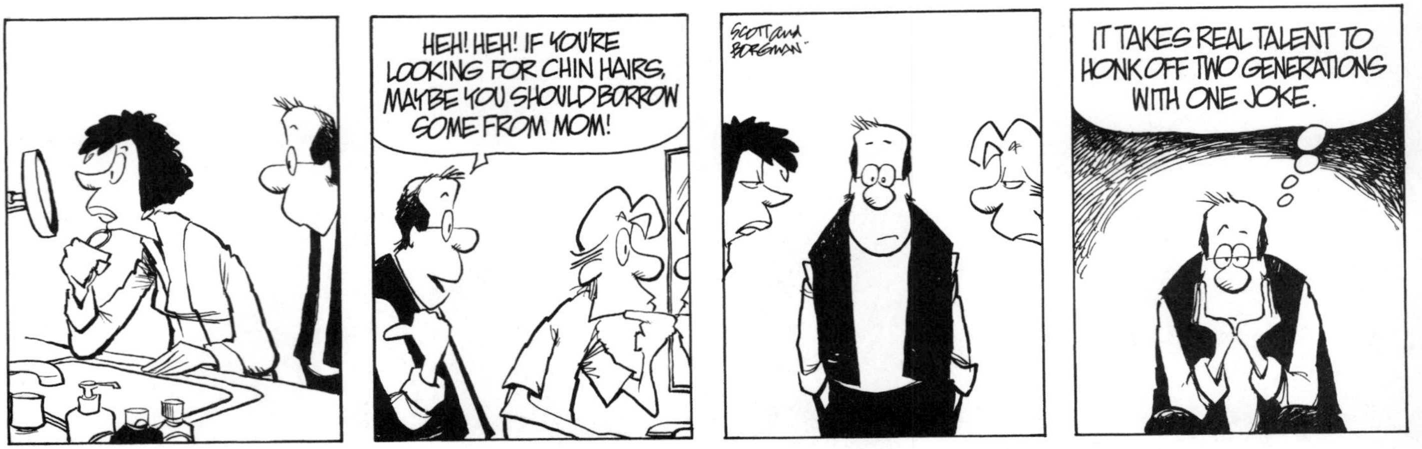
HEH! HEH! IF YOU'RE LOOKING FOR CHIN HAIRS, MAYBE YOU SHOULD BORROW SOME FROM MOM!
SCOTT and BORGMAN
IT TAKES REAL TALENT TO HONK OFF TWO GENERATIONS WITH ONE JOKE.

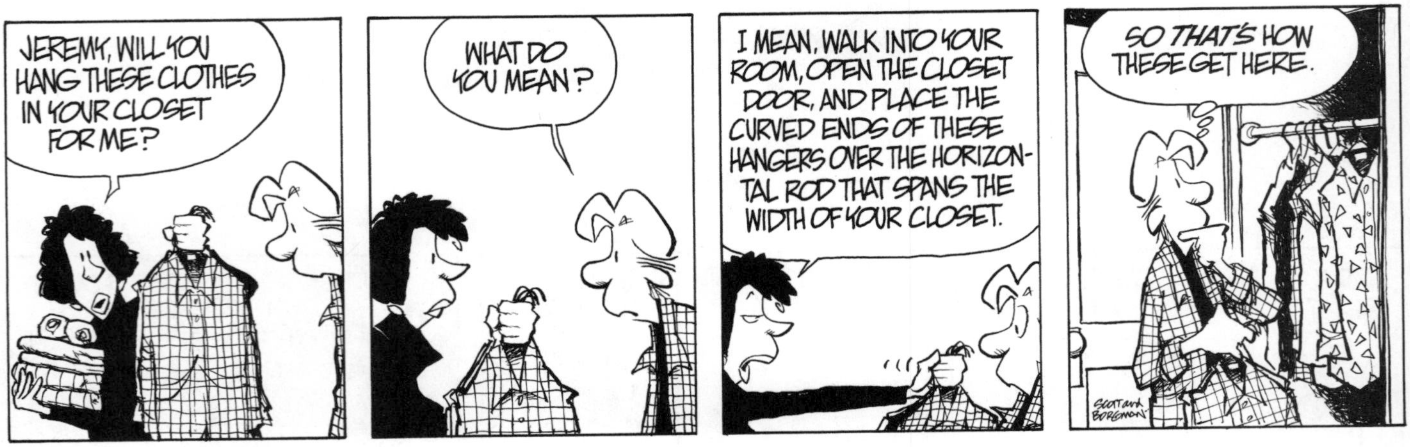
JEREMY, WILL YOU HANG THESE CLOTHES IN YOUR CLOSET FOR ME?
WHAT DO YOU MEAN?
I MEAN, WALK INTO YOUR ROOM, OPEN THE CLOSET DOOR, AND PLACE THE CURVED ENDS OF THESE HANGERS OVER THE HORIZONTAL ROD THAT SPANS THE WIDTH OF YOUR CLOSET.
SO *THAT'S* HOW THESE GET HERE.
SCOTT and BORGMAN

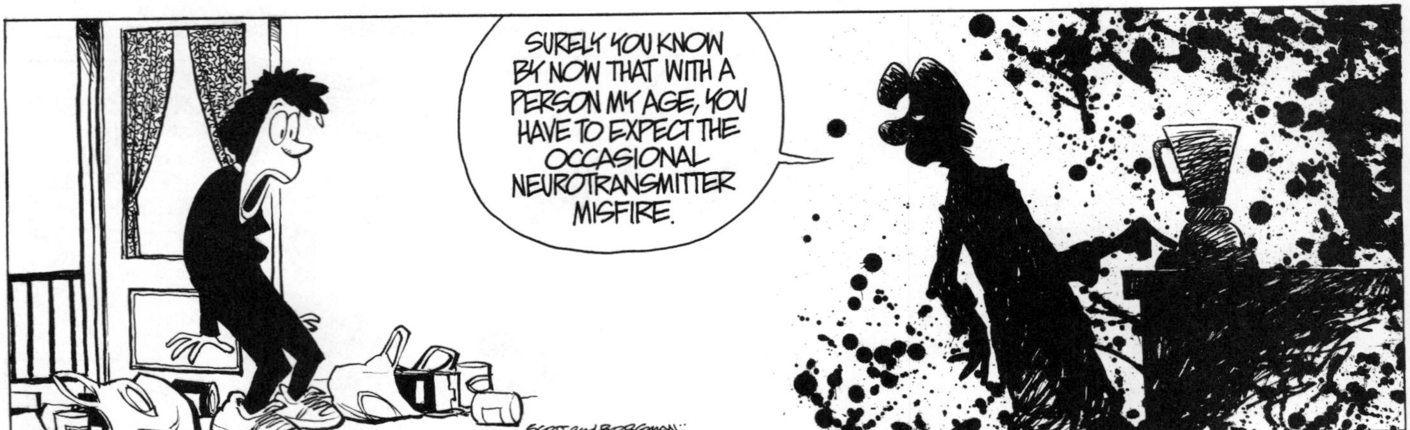
SURELY YOU KNOW BY NOW THAT WITH A PERSON MY AGE, YOU HAVE TO EXPECT THE OCCASIONAL NEUROTRANSMITTER MISFIRE.
SCOTT and BORGMAN

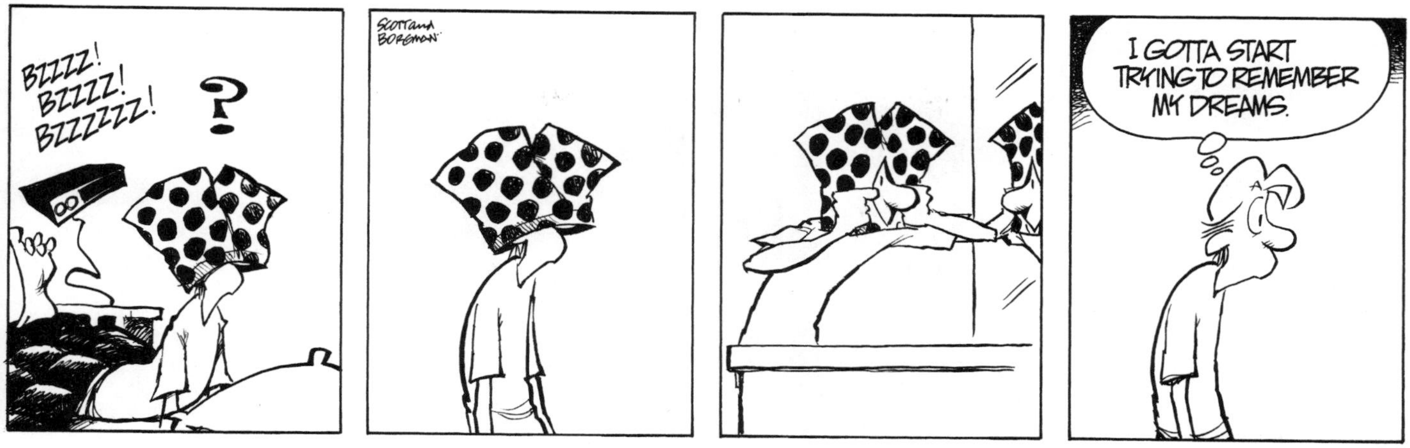
BZZZZ! BZZZZ! BZZZZZZ!
?
SCOTT and BORGMAN
I GOTTA START TRYING TO REMEMBER MY DREAMS.

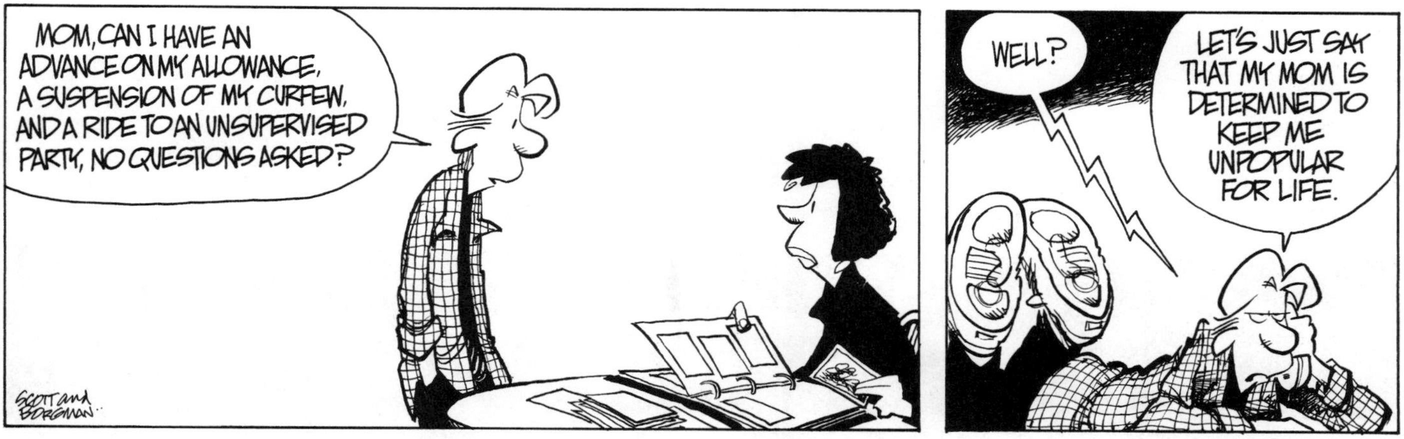
MOM, CAN I HAVE AN ADVANCE ON MY ALLOWANCE, A SUSPENSION OF MY CURFEW, AND A RIDE TO AN UNSUPERVISED PARTY, NO QUESTIONS ASKED?
SCOTT and BORGMAN
WELL?
LET'S JUST SAY THAT MY MOM IS DETERMINED TO KEEP ME UNPOPULAR FOR LIFE.

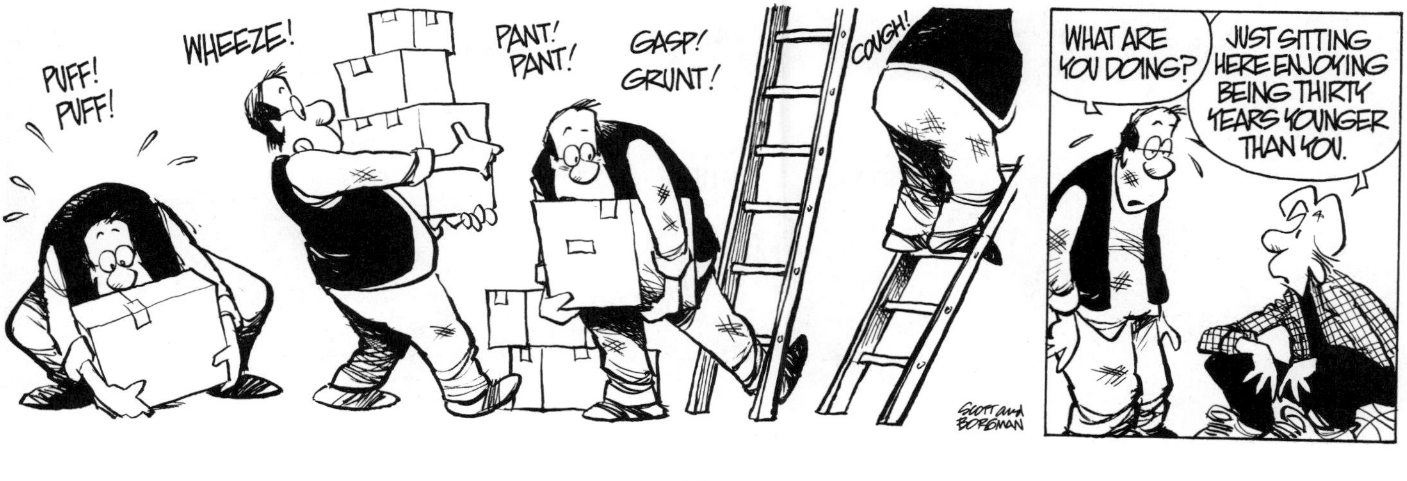
PUFF! PUFF!
WHEEZE!
PANT! PANT!
GASP! GRUNT!
COUGH!
SCOTT and BORGMAN
WHAT ARE YOU DOING?
JUST SITTING HERE ENJOYING BEING THIRTY YEARS YOUNGER THAN YOU.

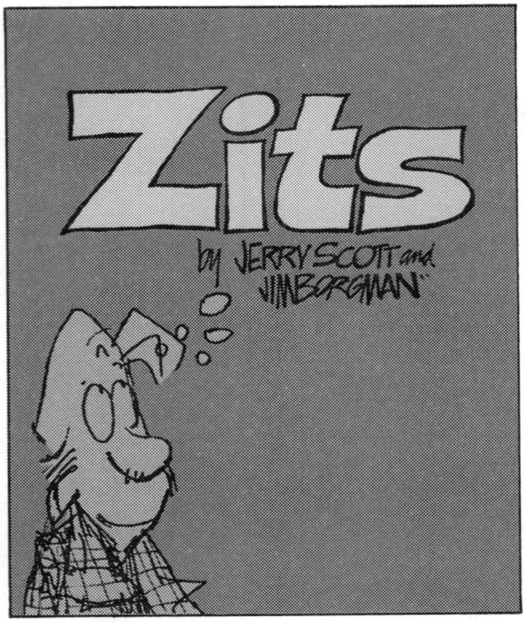
Zits
by JERRY SCOTT and JIM BORGMAN

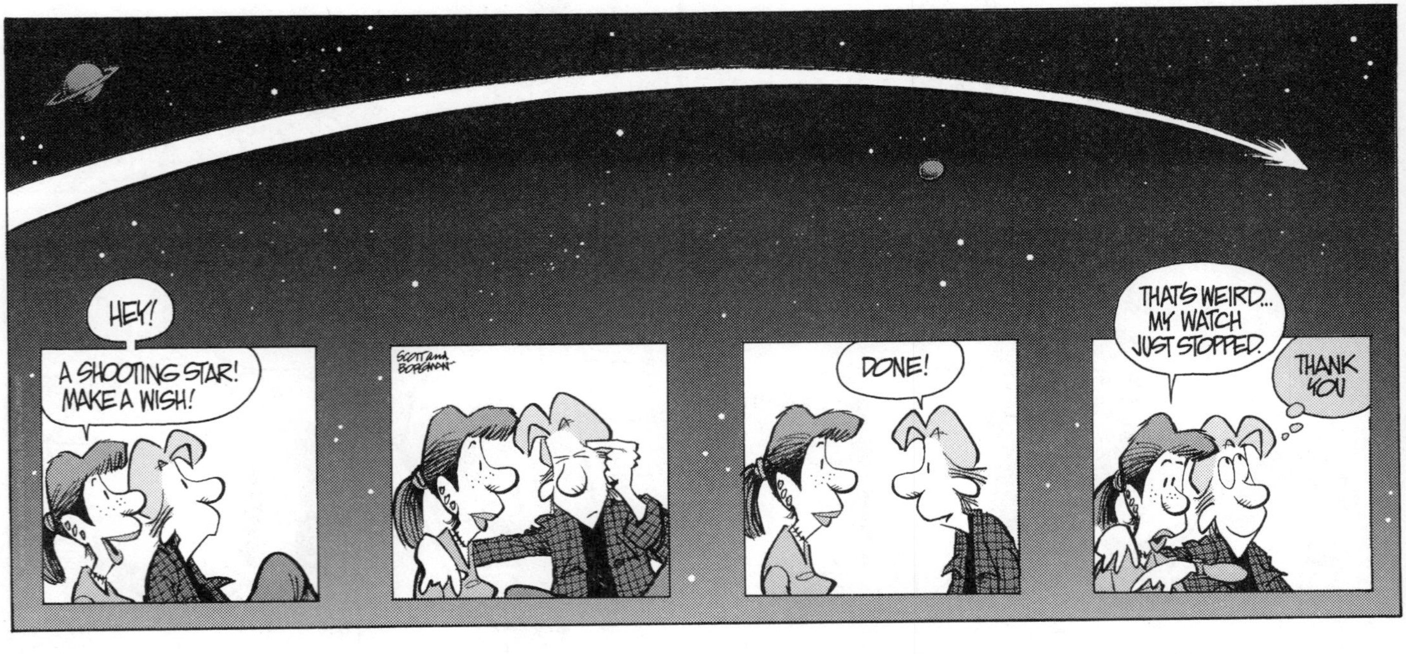
HEY!
A SHOOTING STAR! MAKE A WISH!
DONE!
THAT'S WEIRD... MY WATCH JUST STOPPED.
THANK YOU

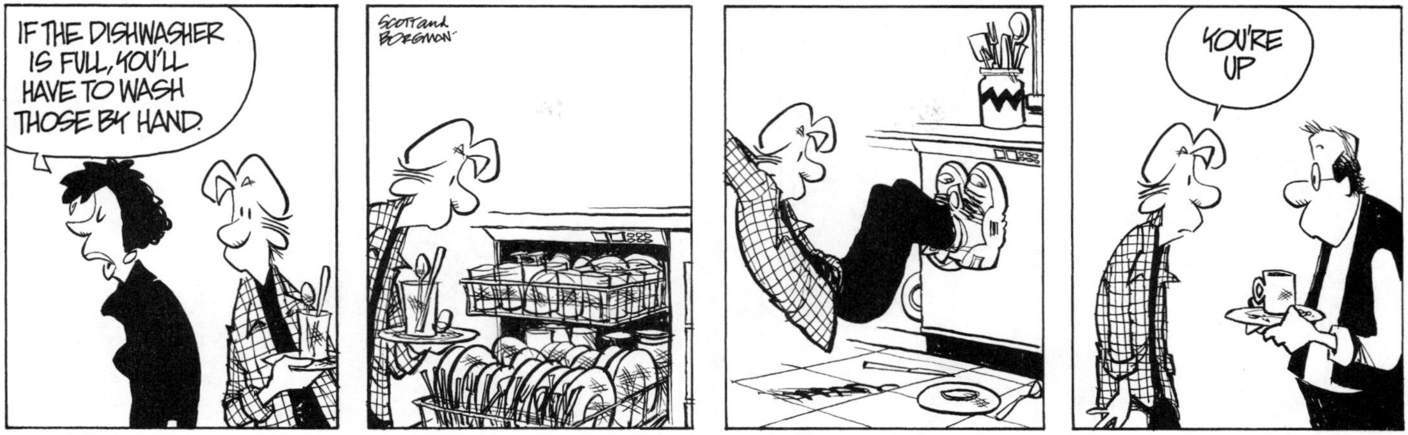
IF THE DISHWASHER IS FULL, YOU'LL HAVE TO WASH THOSE BY HAND.
SCOTT and BORGMAN
YOU'RE UP

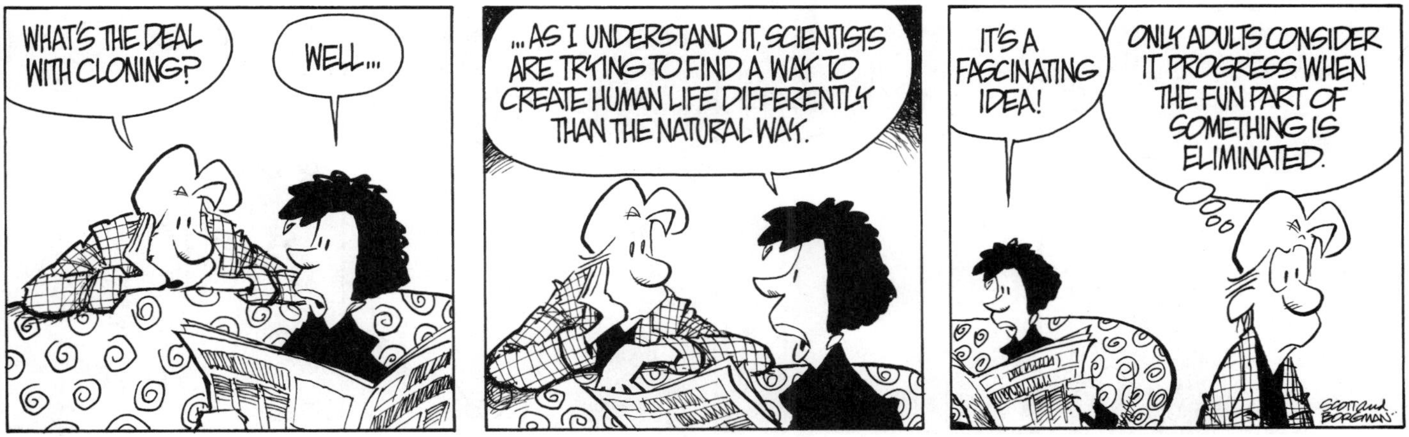
WHAT'S THE DEAL WITH CLONING?
WELL...
...AS I UNDERSTAND IT, SCIENTISTS ARE TRYING TO FIND A WAY TO CREATE HUMAN LIFE DIFFERENTLY THAN THE NATURAL WAY.
IT'S A FASCINATING IDEA!
ONLY ADULTS CONSIDER IT PROGRESS WHEN THE FUN PART OF SOMETHING IS ELIMINATED.
SCOTT and BORGMAN

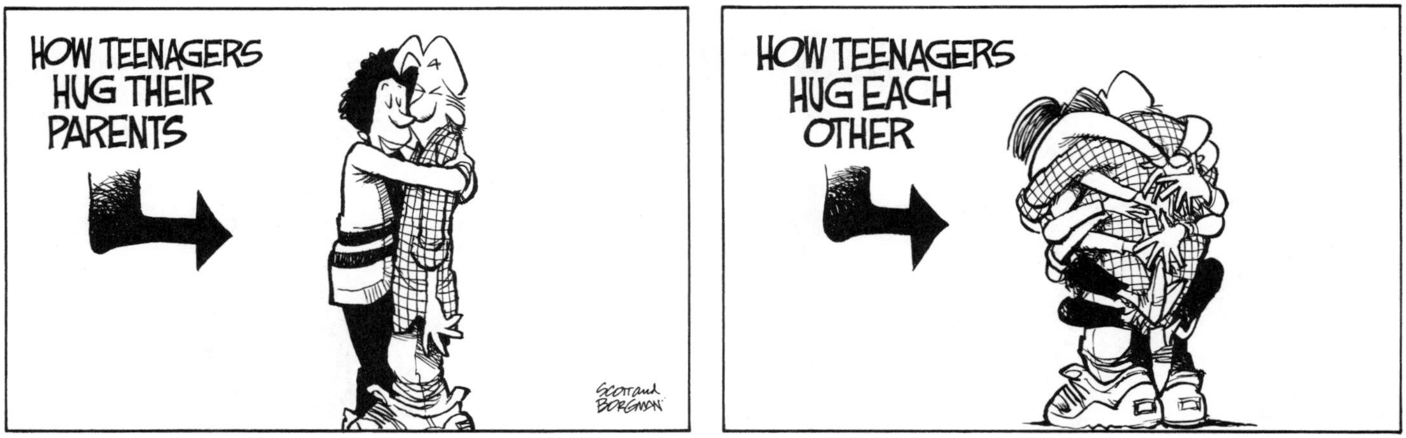
HOW TEENAGERS HUG THEIR PARENTS
SCOTT and BORGMAN
HOW TEENAGERS HUG EACH OTHER

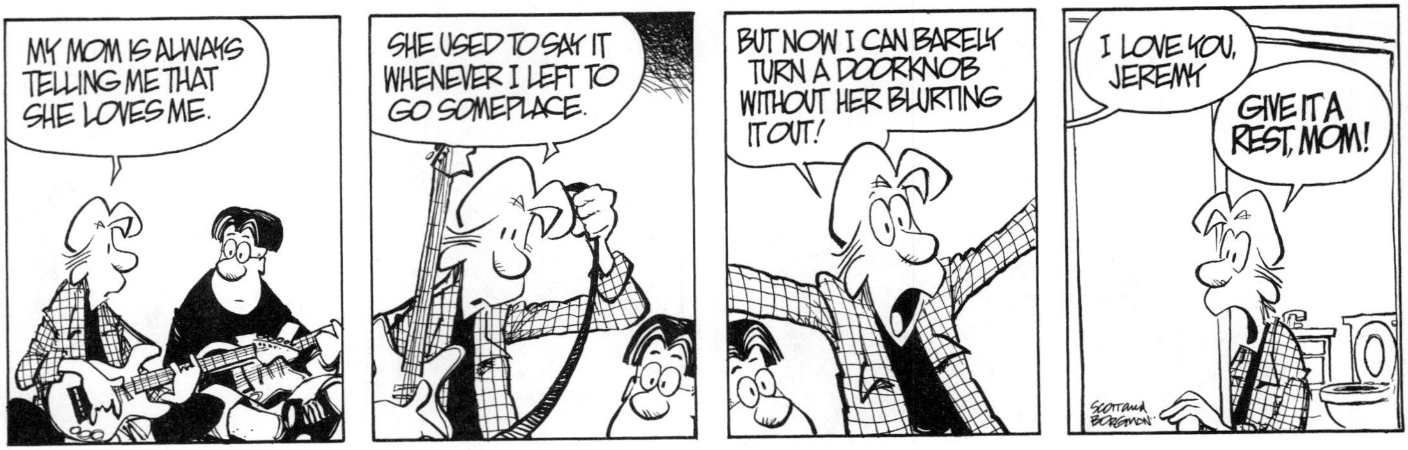
MY MOM IS ALWAYS TELLING ME THAT SHE LOVES ME.
SHE USED TO SAY IT WHENEVER I LEFT TO GO SOMEPLACE.
BUT NOW I CAN BARELY TURN A DOORKNOB WITHOUT HER BLURTING IT OUT!
I LOVE YOU, JEREMY
GIVE IT A REST, MOM!
SCOTT and BORGMAN

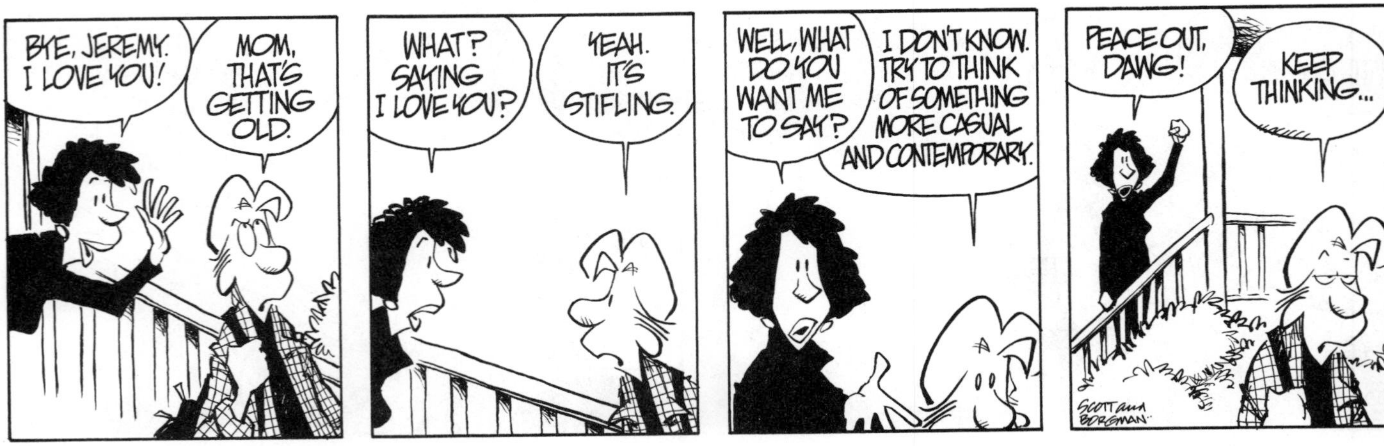
BYE, JEREMY. I LOVE YOU!
MOM, THAT'S GETTING OLD.
WHAT? SAYING I LOVE YOU?
YEAH. IT'S STIFLING.
WELL, WHAT DO YOU WANT ME TO SAY?
I DON'T KNOW. TRY TO THINK OF SOMETHING MORE CASUAL AND CONTEMPORARY.
PEACE OUT, DAWG!
KEEP THINKING...
SCOTT and BORGMAN

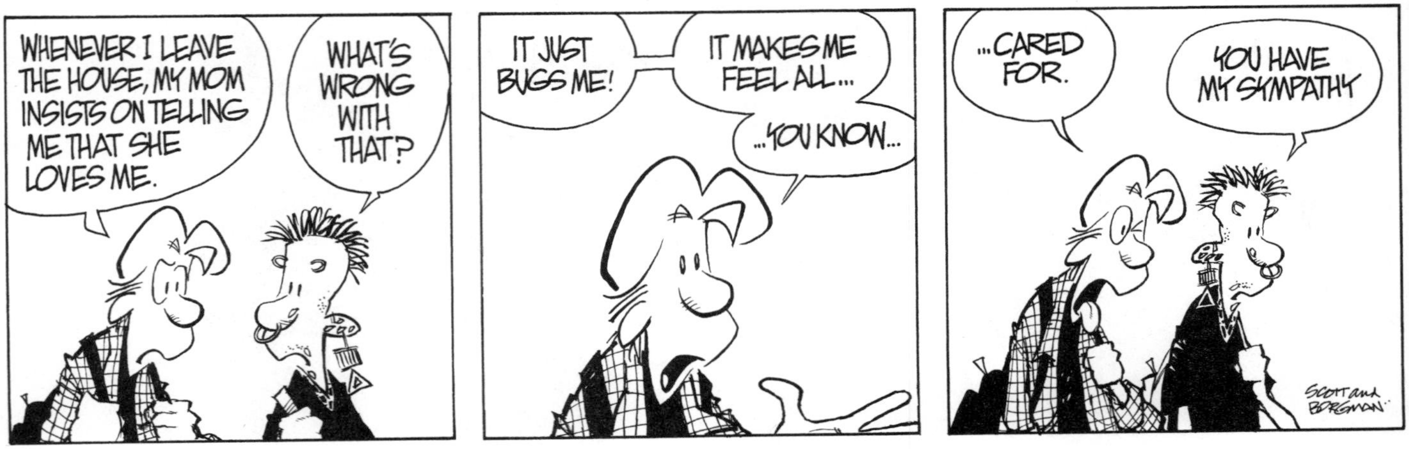
WHENEVER I LEAVE THE HOUSE, MY MOM INSISTS ON TELLING ME THAT SHE LOVES ME.
WHAT'S WRONG WITH THAT?
IT JUST BUGS ME!
IT MAKES ME FEEL ALL...
...YOU KNOW...
...CARED FOR.
YOU HAVE MY SYMPATHY
SCOTT and BORGMAN

Zits
JERRY SCOTT and JIM BORGMAN

AHEM!
SMILE! FIRST IMPRESSIONS ARE IMPORTANT!
SHOW INITIATIVE!
STRIVE FOR EXCELLENCE, NOT PERFECTION!
ONE GOOD TURN DESERVES ANOTHER!
CHASTITY IS A VIRTUE!
LOOK PEOPLE IN THE EYE WHEN YOU SPEAK!
AND SHE WONDERS WHY MY POSTURE IS SO BAD SOMETIMES.
GOOD WORK IS ITS OWN REWARD!
IS THAT THE ONLY SHIRT YOU OWN?
WHEN YOU'RE INTERESTED IN PEOPLE, PEOPLE ARE INTERESTED IN YOU.
WHATEVER YOU DO, DON'T SCOWL LIKE THAT!
THE EARLY BIRD CATCHES THE WORM
THERE WILL BE PLENTY OF TIME FOR ROMANCE AFTER YOU'RE MARRIED.
WHY CAN'T YOU BE MORE LIKE YOUR BROTHER?
YOU CAN ALWAYS DO BETTER.
THE HARDER YOU WORK, THE LUCKIER YOU BECOME!
SCOTT and BORGMAN

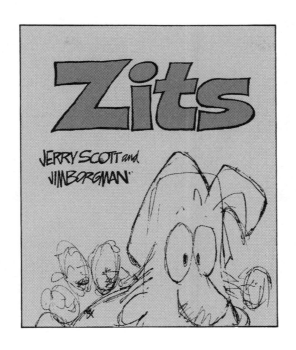

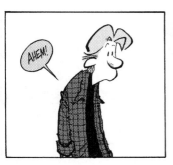

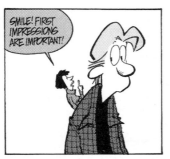

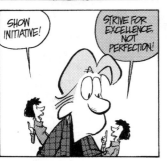

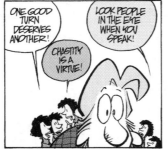

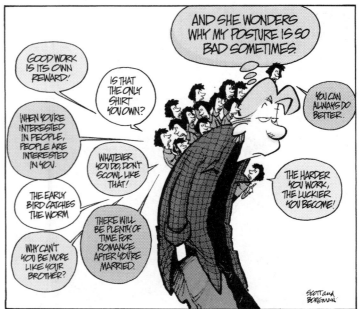

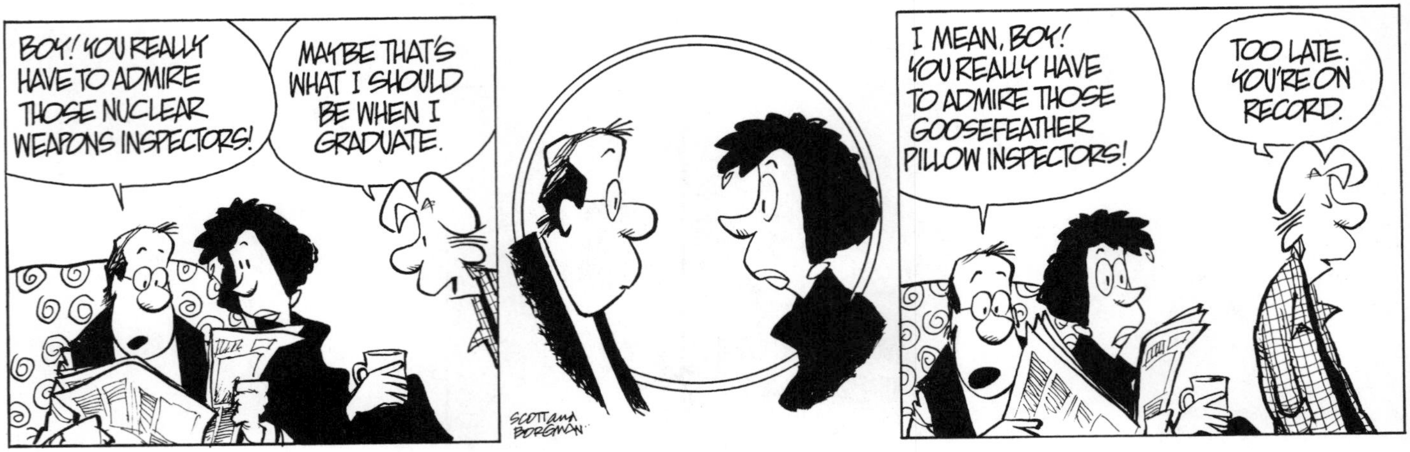
BOY! YOU REALLY HAVE TO ADMIRE THOSE NUCLEAR WEAPONS INSPECTORS!
MAYBE THAT'S WHAT I SHOULD BE WHEN I GRADUATE.
SCOTT and BORGMAN
I MEAN, BOY! YOU REALLY HAVE TO ADMIRE THOSE GOOSEFEATHER PILLOW INSPECTORS!
TOO LATE. YOU'RE ON RECORD.

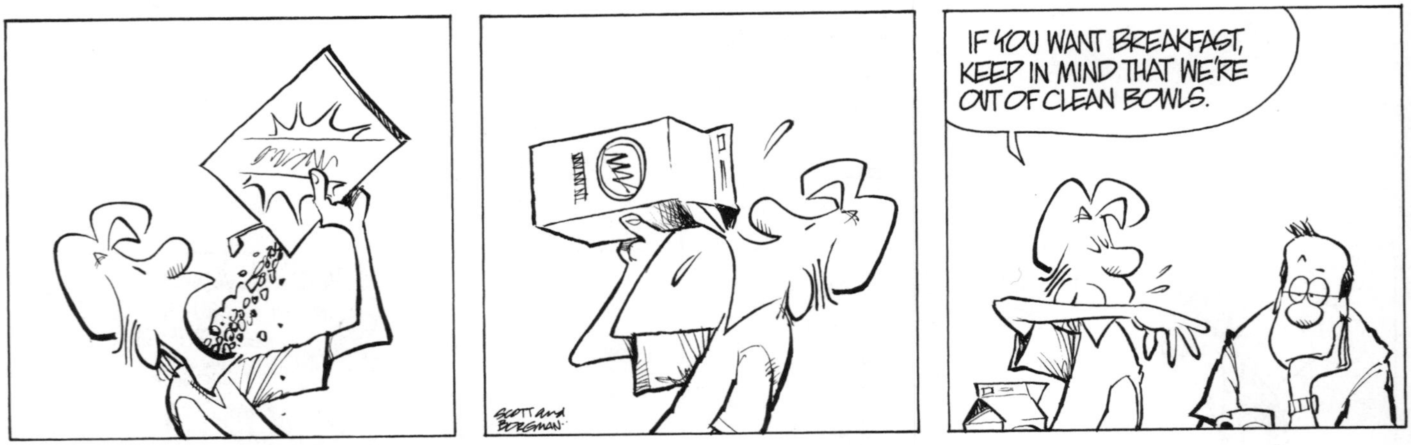
SCOTT and BORGMAN
IF YOU WANT BREAKFAST, KEEP IN MIND THAT WE'RE OUT OF CLEAN BOWLS.

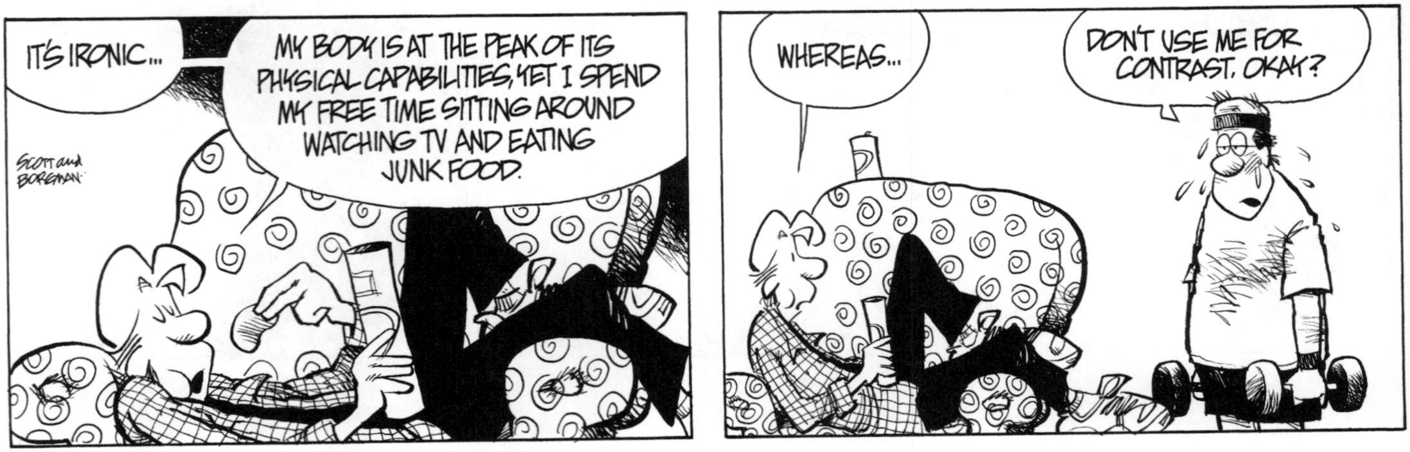
IT'S IRONIC...
SCOTT and BORGMAN
MY BODY IS AT THE PEAK OF ITS PHYSICAL CAPABILITIES, YET I SPEND MY FREE TIME SITTING AROUND WATCHING TV AND EATING JUNK FOOD.
WHEREAS...
DON'T USE ME FOR CONTRAST, OKAY?

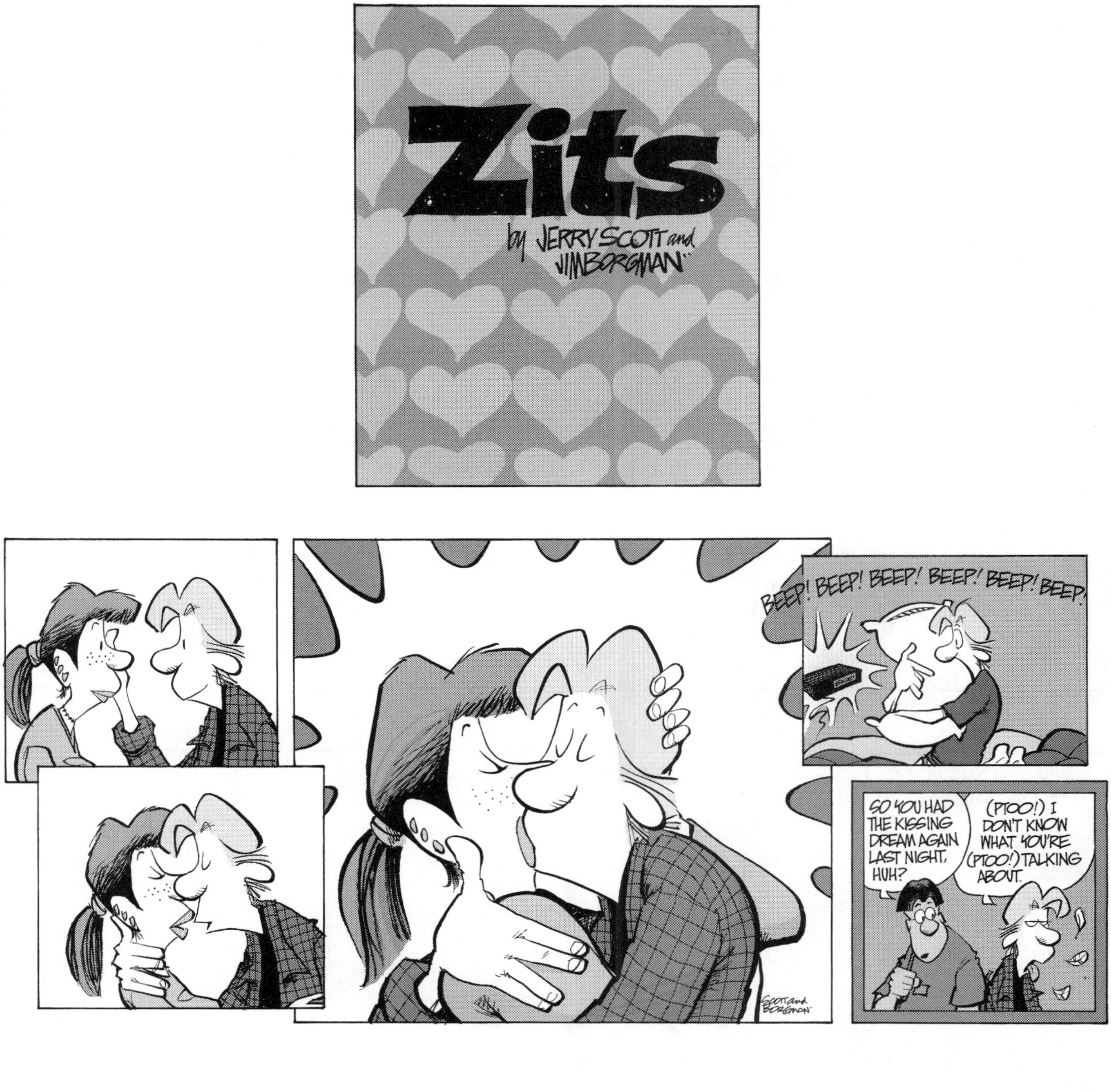
Zits
by JERRY SCOTT and JIM BORGMAN
BEEP! BEEP! BEEP! BEEP! BEEP! BEEP!
SO YOU HAD THE KISSING DREAM AGAIN LAST NIGHT, HUH?
(PTOO!) I DON'T KNOW WHAT YOU'RE (PTOO!) TALKING ABOUT.
SCOTT and BORGMAN

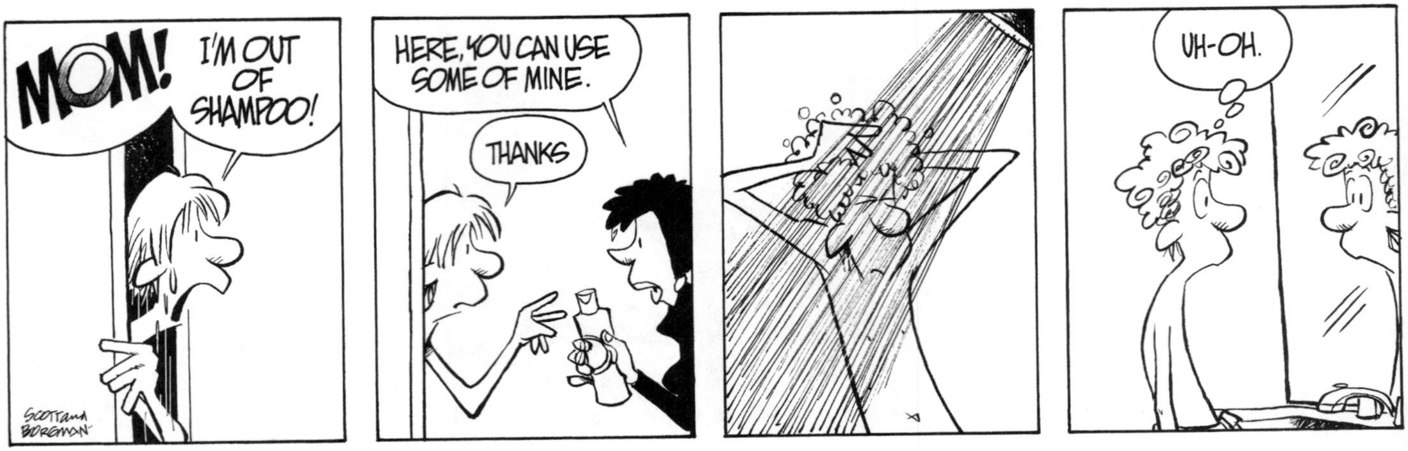
MOM! I'M OUT OF SHAMPOO!
HERE, YOU CAN USE SOME OF MINE.
THANKS
UH-OH.

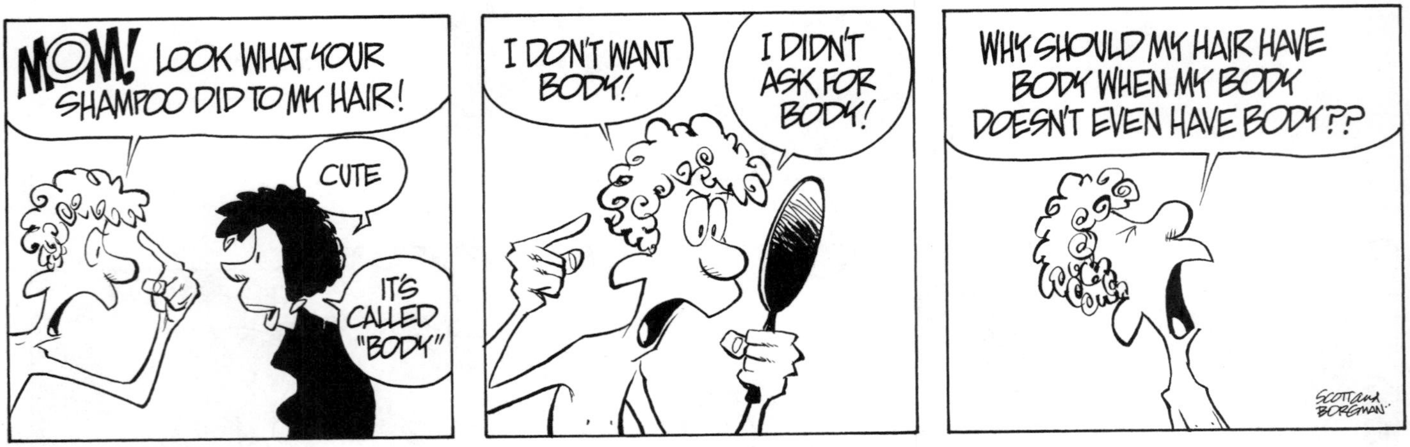
MOM! LOOK WHAT YOUR SHAMPOO DID TO MY HAIR!
CUTE
IT'S CALLED "BODY"
I DON'T WANT BODY!
I DIDN'T ASK FOR BODY!
WHY SHOULD MY HAIR HAVE BODY WHEN MY BODY DOESN'T EVEN HAVE BODY??

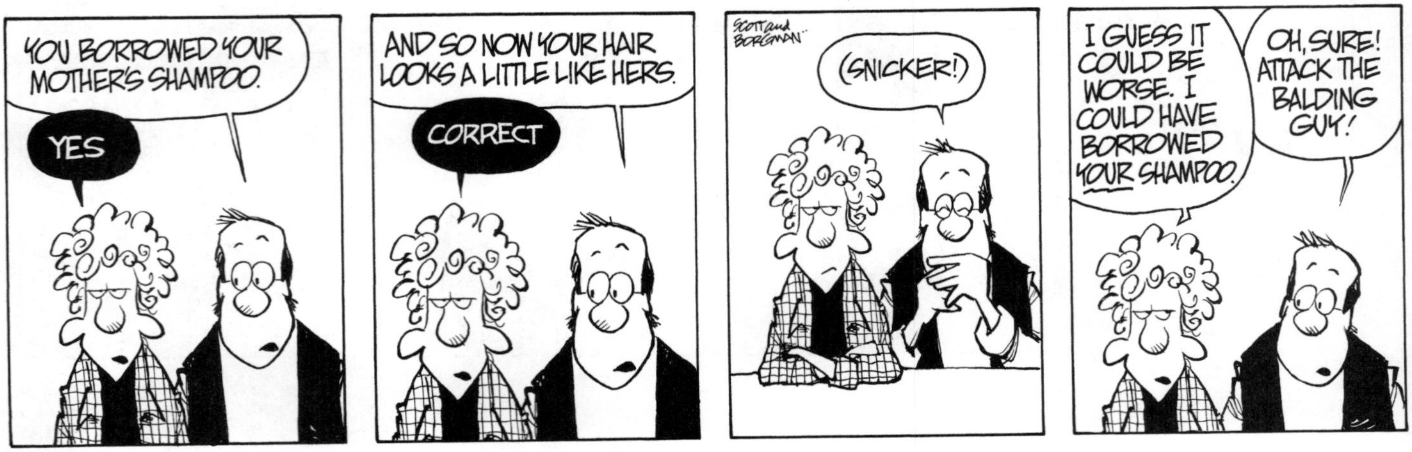
YOU BORROWED YOUR MOTHER'S SHAMPOO.
YES
AND SO NOW YOUR HAIR LOOKS A LITTLE LIKE HERS.
CORRECT
(SNICKER!)
I GUESS IT COULD BE WORSE. I COULD HAVE BORROWED YOUR SHAMPOO.
OH, SURE! ATTACK THE BALDING GUY!

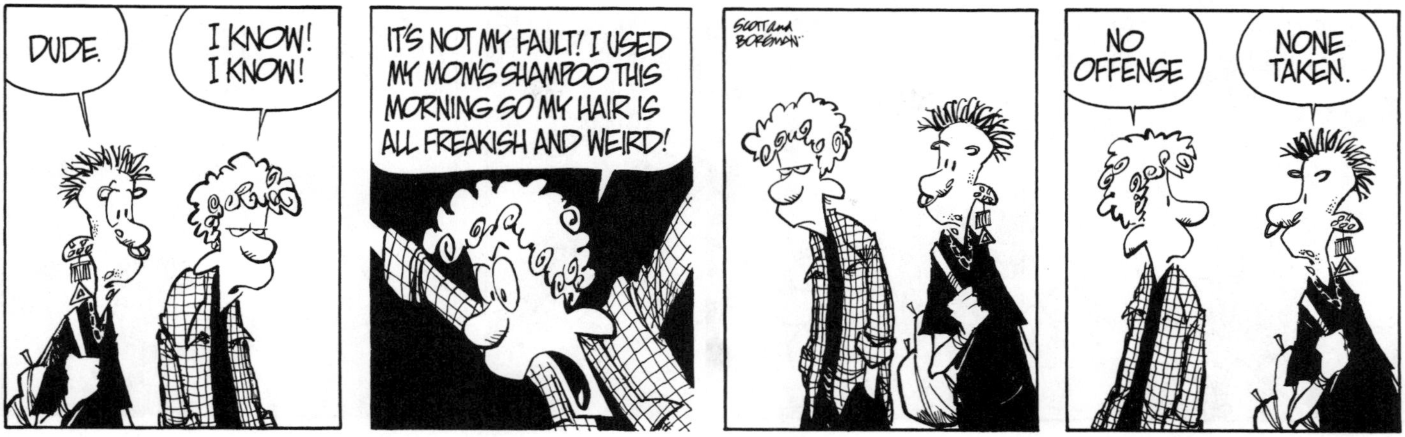
DUDE.
I KNOW! I KNOW!
IT'S NOT MY FAULT! I USED MY MOM'S SHAMPOO THIS MORNING SO MY HAIR IS ALL FREAKISH AND WEIRD!
NO OFFENSE
NONE TAKEN.

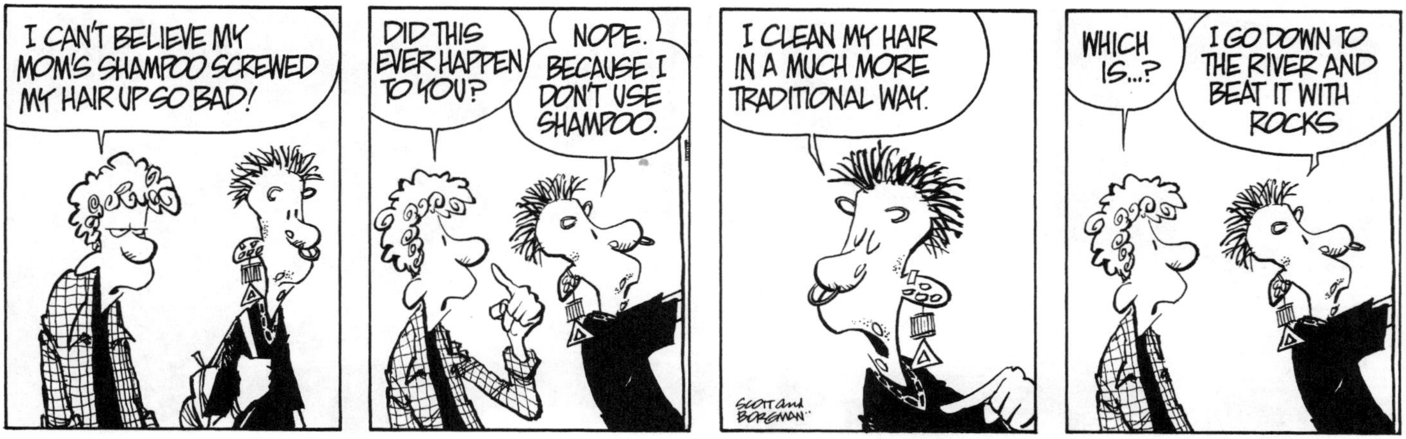
I CAN'T BELIEVE MY MOM'S SHAMPOO SCREWED MY HAIR UP SO BAD!
DID THIS EVER HAPPEN TO YOU?
NOPE. BECAUSE I DON'T USE SHAMPOO.
I CLEAN MY HAIR IN A MUCH MORE TRADITIONAL WAY.
WHICH IS...?
I GO DOWN TO THE RIVER AND BEAT IT WITH ROCKS

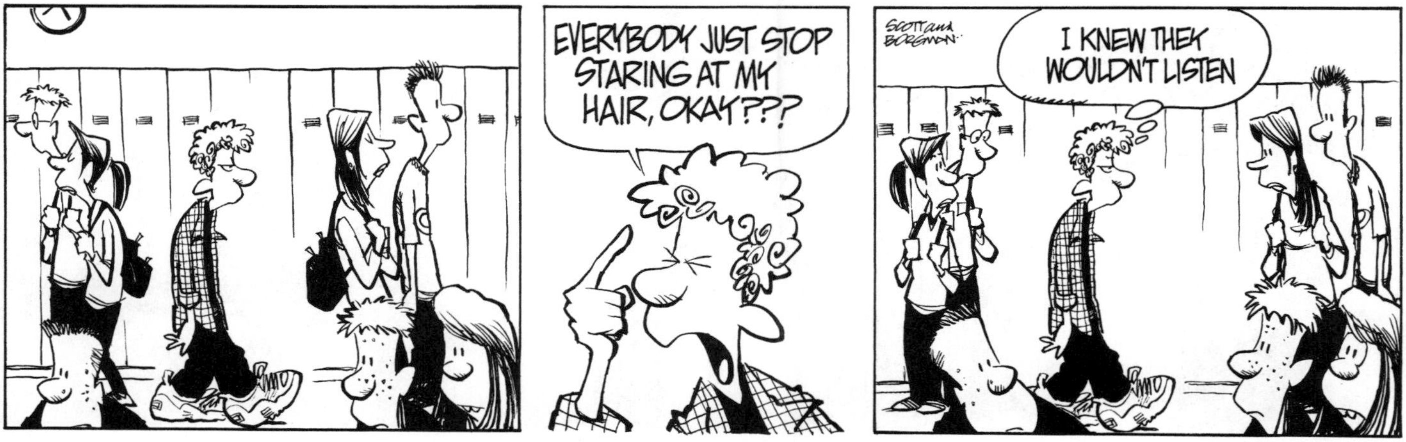
EVERYBODY JUST STOP STARING AT MY HAIR, OKAY???
I KNEW THEY WOULDN'T LISTEN

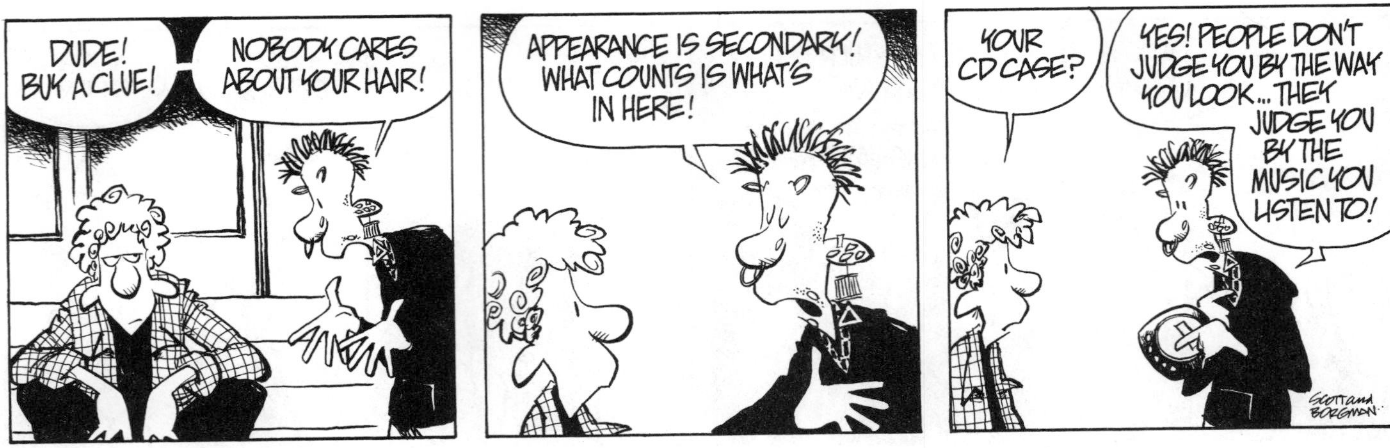
DUDE! BUY A CLUE!
NOBODY CARES ABOUT YOUR HAIR!
APPEARANCE IS SECONDARY! WHAT COUNTS IS WHAT'S IN HERE!
YOUR CD CASE?
YES! PEOPLE DON'T JUDGE YOU BY THE WAY YOU LOOK... THEY JUDGE YOU BY THE MUSIC YOU LISTEN TO!
SCOTT and BORGMAN

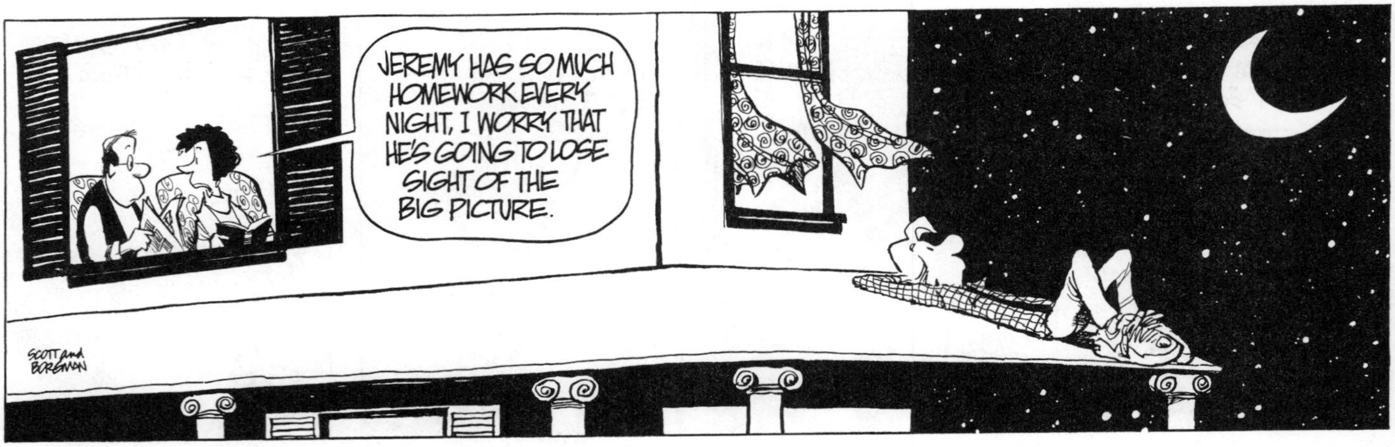
SCOTT and BORGMAN
JEREMY HAS SO MUCH HOMEWORK EVERY NIGHT, I WORRY THAT HE'S GOING TO LOSE SIGHT OF THE BIG PICTURE.

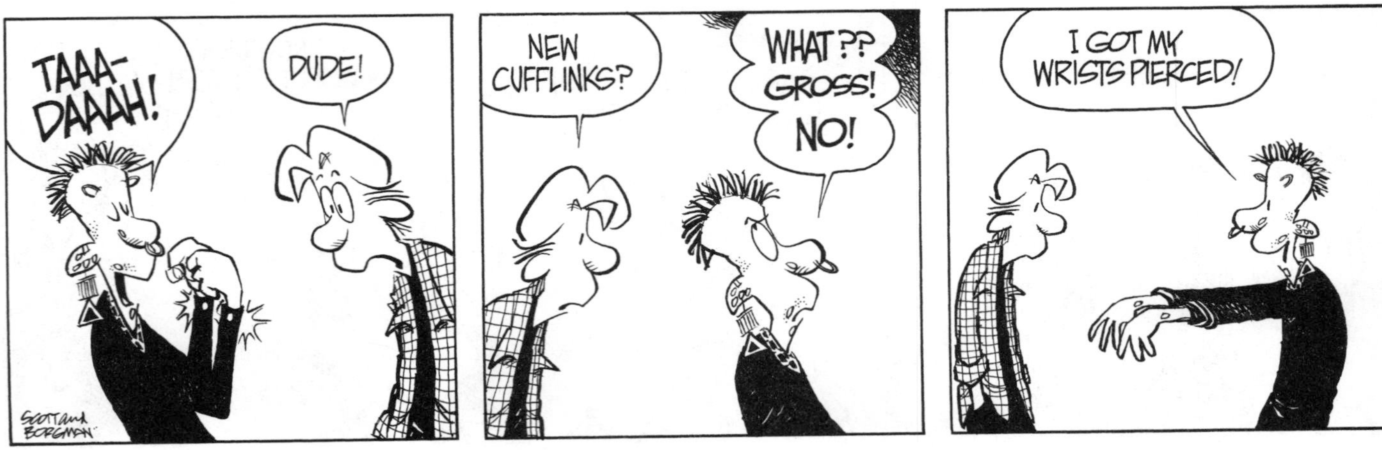
TAAA-DAAAH!
DUDE!
SCOTT and BORGMAN
NEW CUFFLINKS?
WHAT?? GROSS! NO!
I GOT MY WRISTS PIERCED!

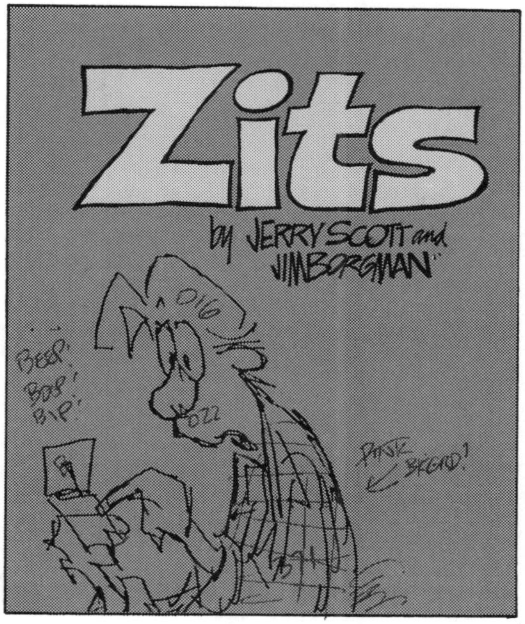
Zits
by JERRY SCOTT and JIM BORGMAN
BEEP!
BIP!

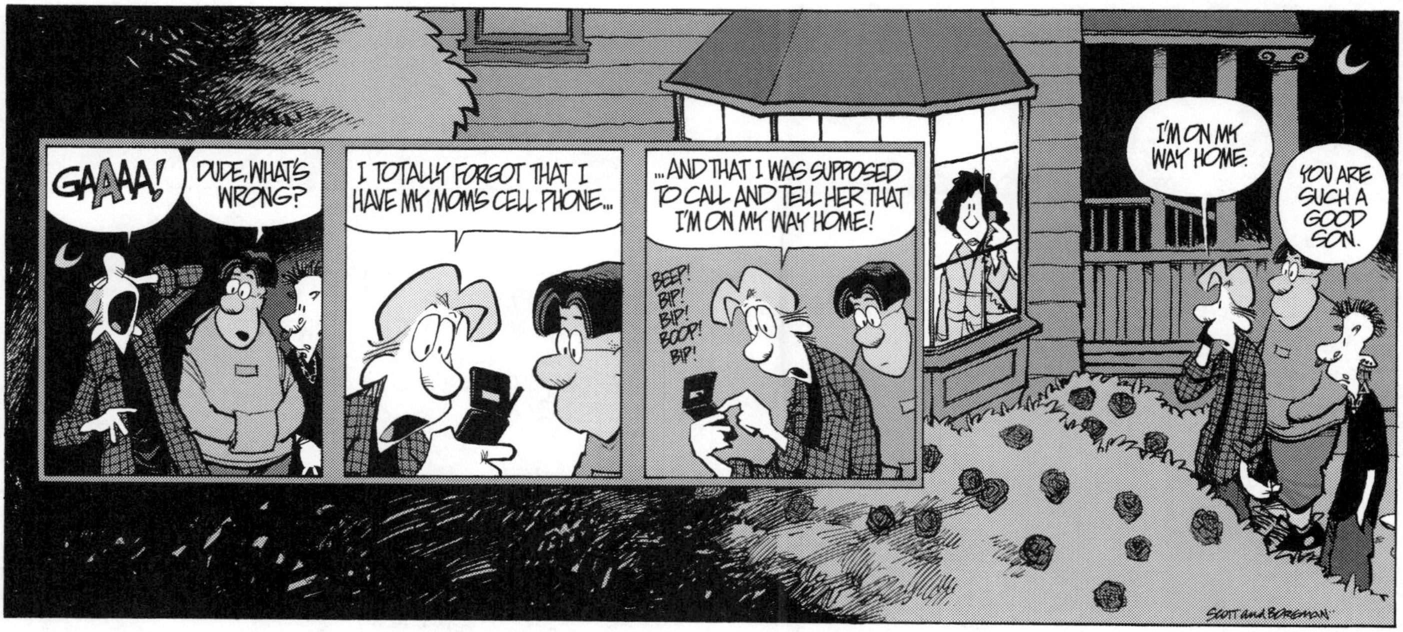
GAAAA!
DUDE, WHAT'S WRONG?
I TOTALLY FORGOT THAT I HAVE MY MOM'S CELL PHONE...
...AND THAT I WAS SUPPOSED TO CALL AND TELL HER THAT I'M ON MY WAY HOME!
BEEP! BIP! BIP! BOOP! BIP!
I'M ON MY WAY HOME.
YOU ARE SUCH A GOOD SON.
SCOTT and BORGMAN

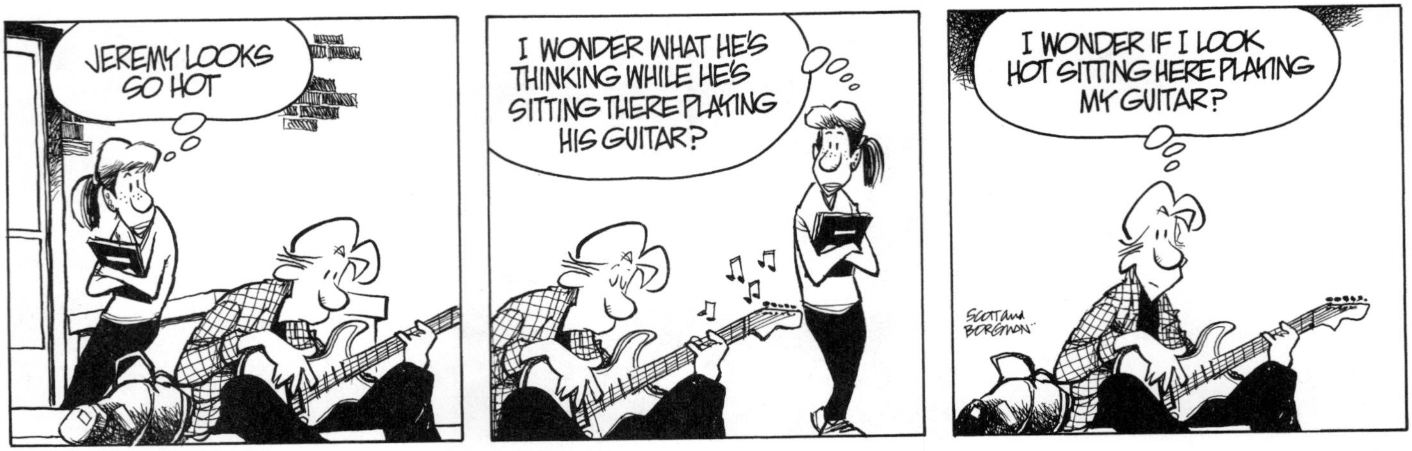
JEREMY LOOKS SO HOT
I WONDER WHAT HE'S THINKING WHILE HE'S SITTING THERE PLAYING HIS GUITAR?
I WONDER IF I LOOK HOT SITTING HERE PLAYING MY GUITAR?
SCOTT AND BORGMAN

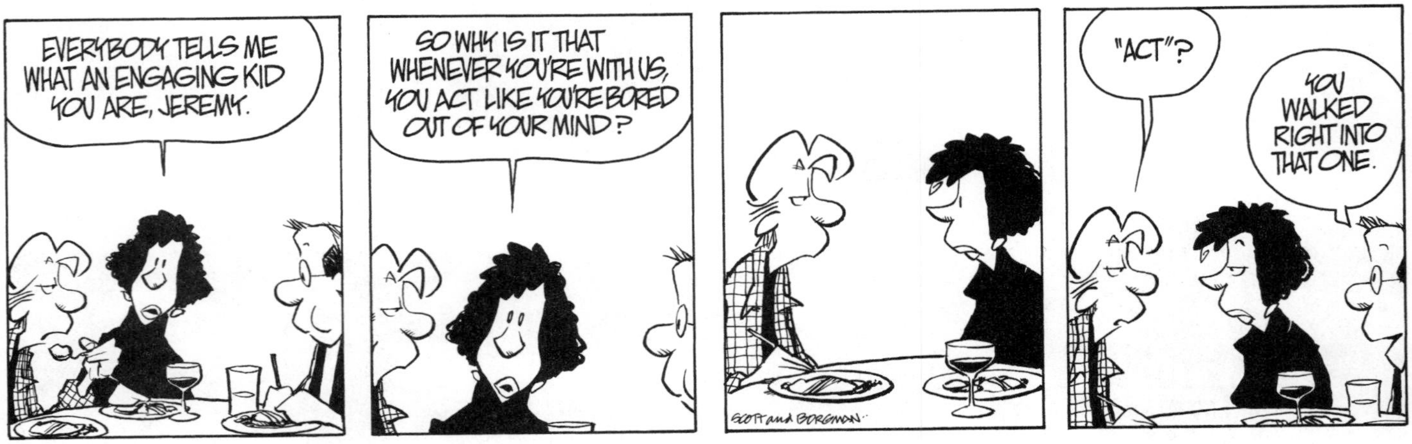
EVERYBODY TELLS ME WHAT AN ENGAGING KID YOU ARE, JEREMY.
SO WHY IS IT THAT WHENEVER YOU'RE WITH US, YOU ACT LIKE YOU'RE BORED OUT OF YOUR MIND?
SCOTT AND BORGMAN
"ACT"?
YOU WALKED RIGHT INTO THAT ONE.

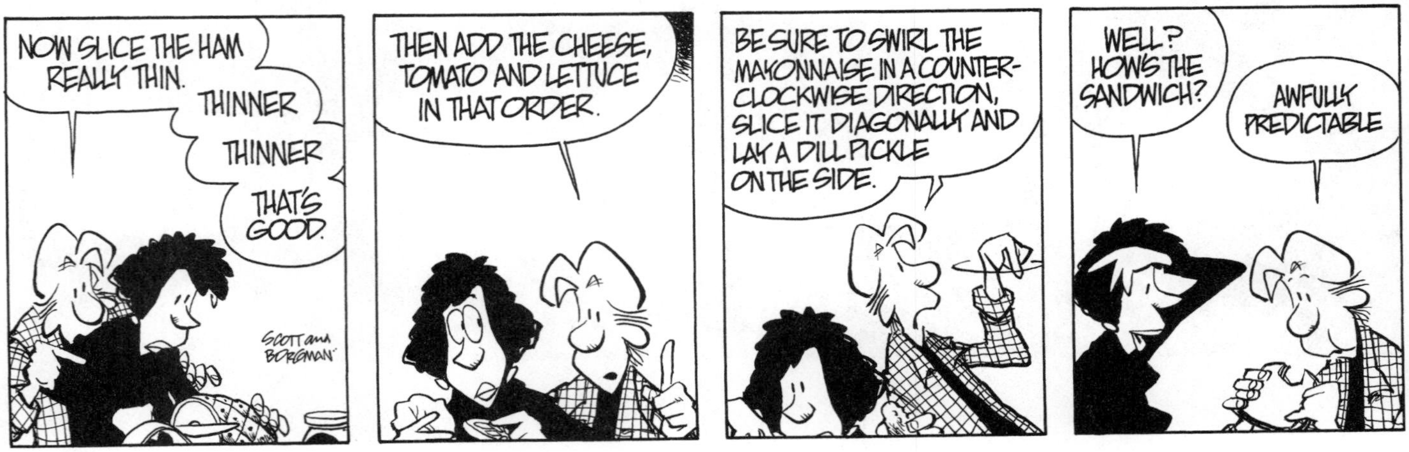
NOW SLICE THE HAM REALLY THIN.
THINNER
THINNER
THAT'S GOOD.
SCOTT AND BORGMAN
THEN ADD THE CHEESE, TOMATO AND LETTUCE IN THAT ORDER.
BE SURE TO SWIRL THE MAYONNAISE IN A COUNTER-CLOCKWISE DIRECTION, SLICE IT DIAGONALLY AND LAY A DILL PICKLE ON THE SIDE.
WELL? HOW'S THE SANDWICH?
AWFULLY PREDICTABLE

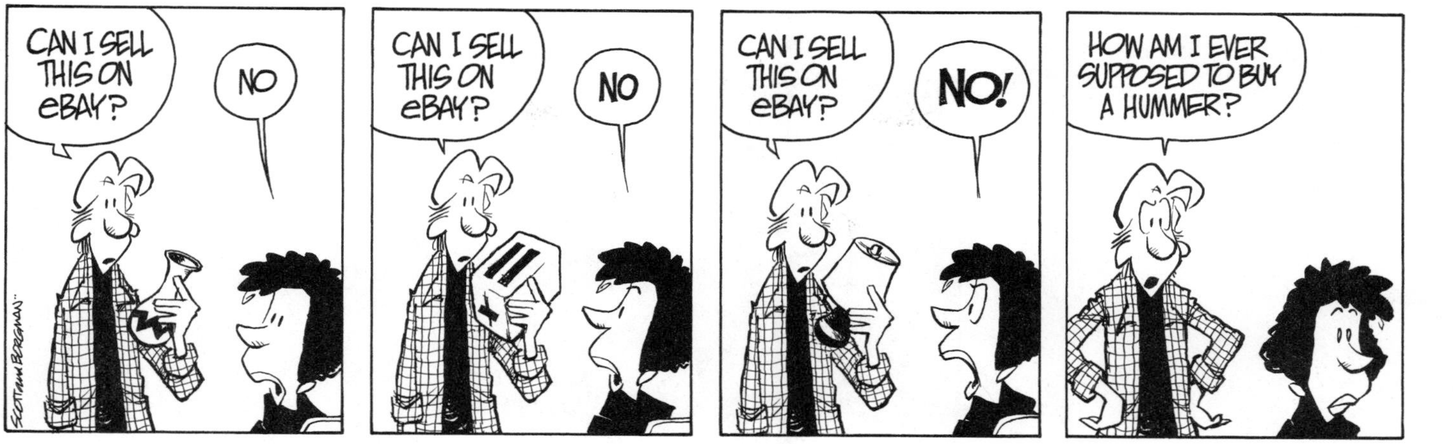
CAN I SELL THIS ON eBAY?
NO
CAN I SELL THIS ON eBAY?
NO
CAN I SELL THIS ON eBAY?
NO!
HOW AM I EVER SUPPOSED TO BUY A HUMMER?
SCOTT and BORGMAN

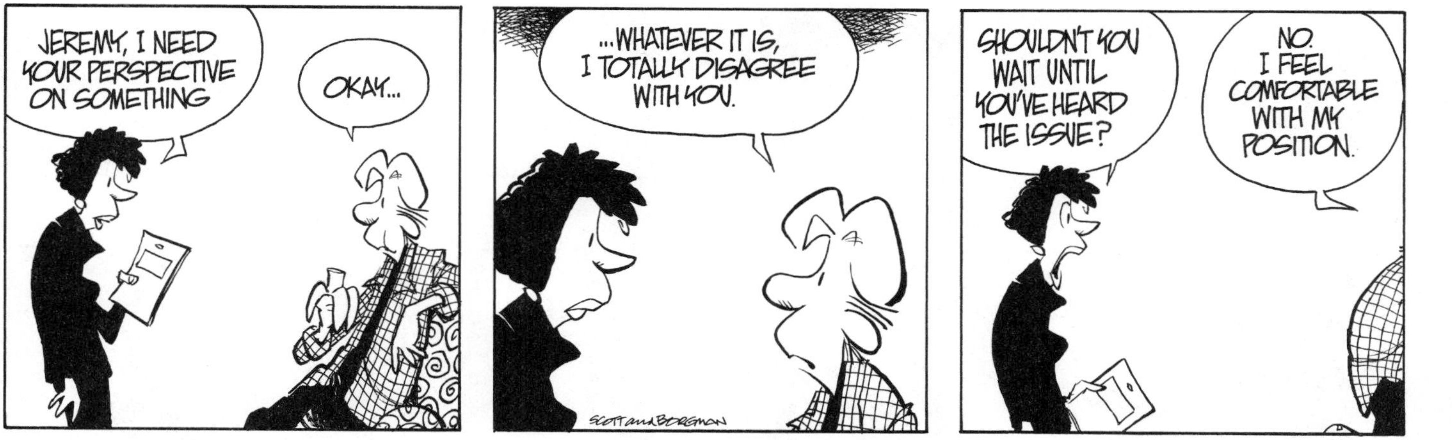
JEREMY, I NEED YOUR PERSPECTIVE ON SOMETHING
OKAY...
...WHATEVER IT IS, I TOTALLY DISAGREE WITH YOU.
SCOTT and BORGMAN
SHOULDN'T YOU WAIT UNTIL YOU'VE HEARD THE ISSUE?
NO. I FEEL COMFORTABLE WITH MY POSITION.

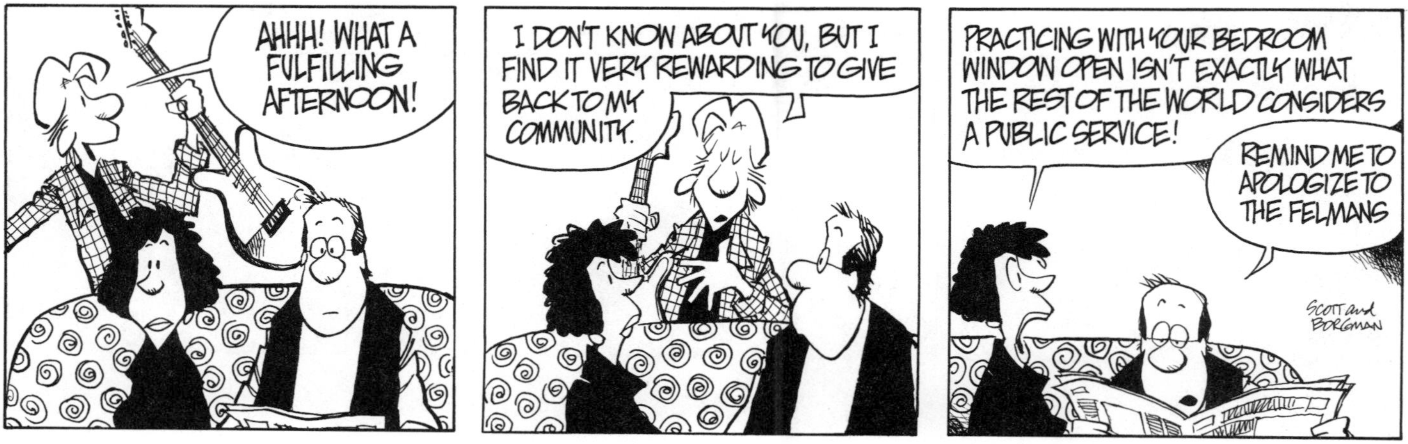
AHHH! WHAT A FULFILLING AFTERNOON!
I DON'T KNOW ABOUT YOU, BUT I FIND IT VERY REWARDING TO GIVE BACK TO MY COMMUNITY.
PRACTICING WITH YOUR BEDROOM WINDOW OPEN ISN'T EXACTLY WHAT THE REST OF THE WORLD CONSIDERS A PUBLIC SERVICE!
REMIND ME TO APOLOGIZE TO THE FELMANS
SCOTT and BORGMAN

Zits
by
JERRY SCOTT and
JIM BORGMAN

MOM, CAN I SAY ★@#*?
NOT IN THIS HOUSE
WHY NOT?
BECAUSE IT'S UGLY.
WHAT ABOUT #★?
NO
*!@★?
JEREMY!
MOM! THEY SAY THIS STUFF ON TV ALL THE TIME!
WELL, THIS ISN'T TV, IT'S OUR HOME! AND IN OUR HOME WE DON'T USE PROFANITY!
I'M THE ONLY GUY I KNOW WITH A LESS COLORFUL VOCABULARY THAN BEETLE BAILEY.
SCOTT and BORGMAN

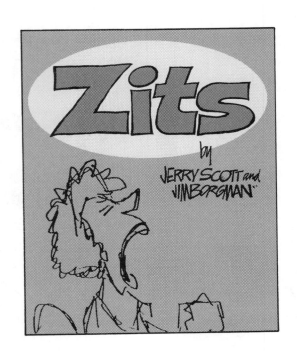

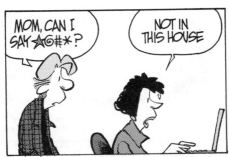

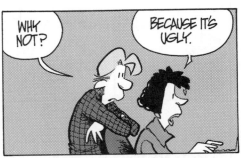

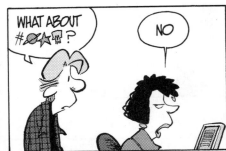

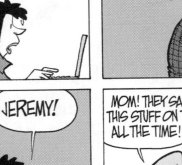

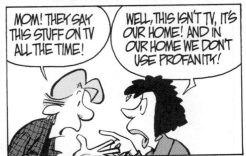

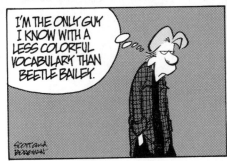

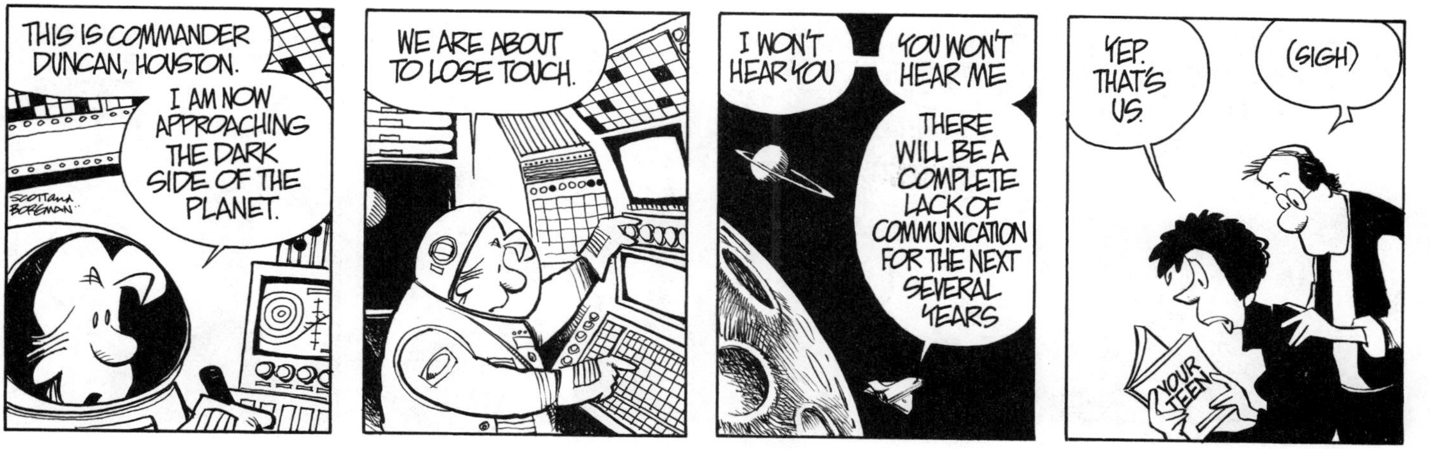
THIS IS COMMANDER DUNCAN, HOUSTON.
I AM NOW APPROACHING THE DARK SIDE OF THE PLANET.
SCOTT and BORGMAN
WE ARE ABOUT TO LOSE TOUCH.
I WON'T HEAR YOU
YOU WON'T HEAR ME
THERE WILL BE A COMPLETE LACK OF COMMUNICATION FOR THE NEXT SEVERAL YEARS
YEP. THAT'S US.
(SIGH)
YOUR TEEN

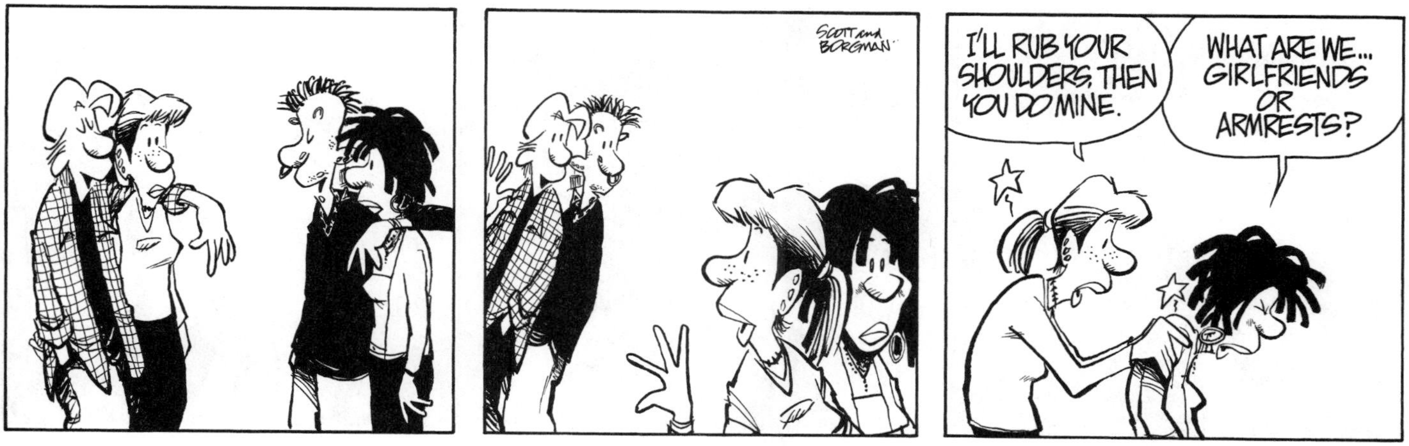
SCOTT and BORGMAN
I'LL RUB YOUR SHOULDERS, THEN YOU DO MINE.
WHAT ARE WE... GIRLFRIENDS OR ARMRESTS?

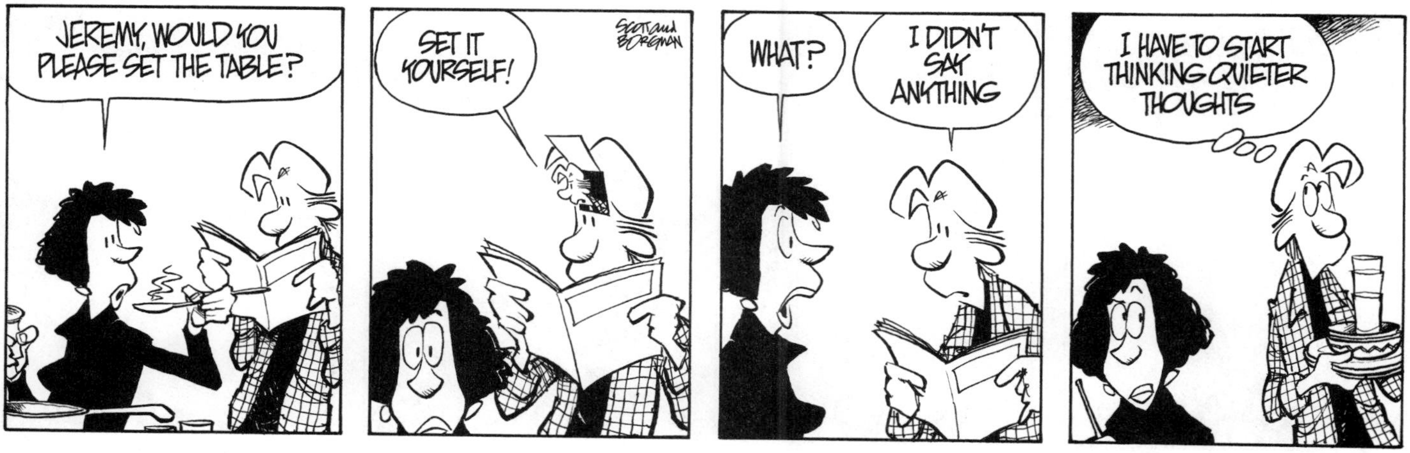
JEREMY, WOULD YOU PLEASE SET THE TABLE?
SET IT YOURSELF!
SCOTT and BORGMAN
WHAT?
I DIDN'T SAY ANYTHING
I HAVE TO START THINKING QUIETER THOUGHTS

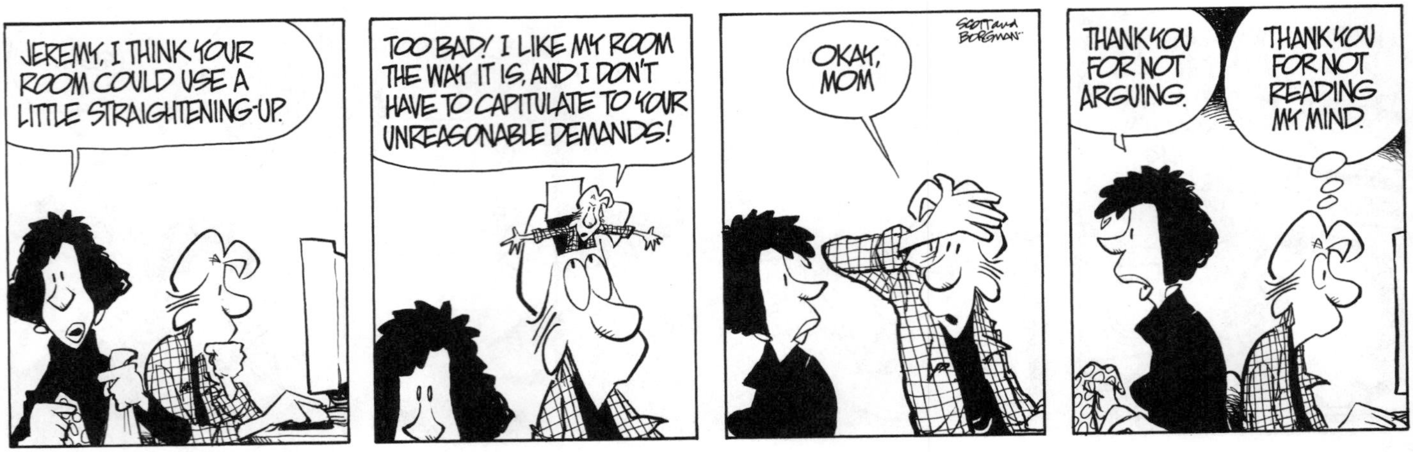
JEREMY, I THINK YOUR ROOM COULD USE A LITTLE STRAIGHTENING-UP.
TOO BAD! I LIKE MY ROOM THE WAY IT IS, AND I DON'T HAVE TO CAPITULATE TO YOUR UNREASONABLE DEMANDS!
OKAY, MOM
THANK YOU FOR NOT ARGUING.
THANK YOU FOR NOT READING MY MIND.

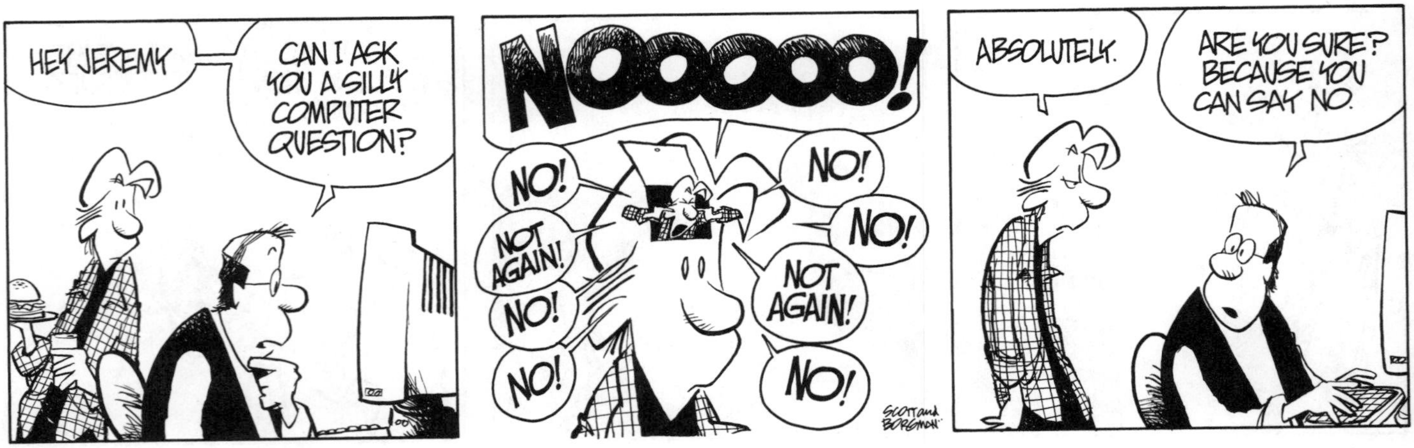
HEY JEREMY
CAN I ASK YOU A SILLY COMPUTER QUESTION?
NOOOOOO!
NO!
NOT AGAIN!
NO!
NO!
NO!
NO!
NOT AGAIN!
NO!
ABSOLUTELY.
ARE YOU SURE? BECAUSE YOU CAN SAY NO.

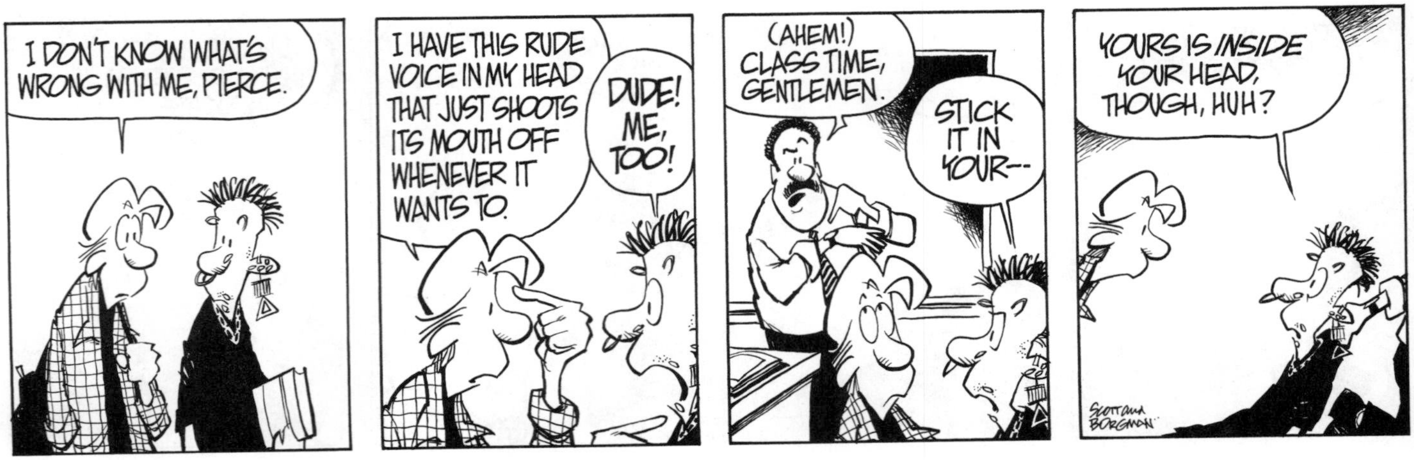
I DON'T KNOW WHAT'S WRONG WITH ME, PIERCE.
I HAVE THIS RUDE VOICE IN MY HEAD THAT JUST SHOOTS ITS MOUTH OFF WHENEVER IT WANTS TO.
DUDE! ME, TOO!
(AHEM!) CLASS TIME, GENTLEMEN.
STICK IT IN YOUR--
YOURS IS *INSIDE* YOUR HEAD, THOUGH, HUH?

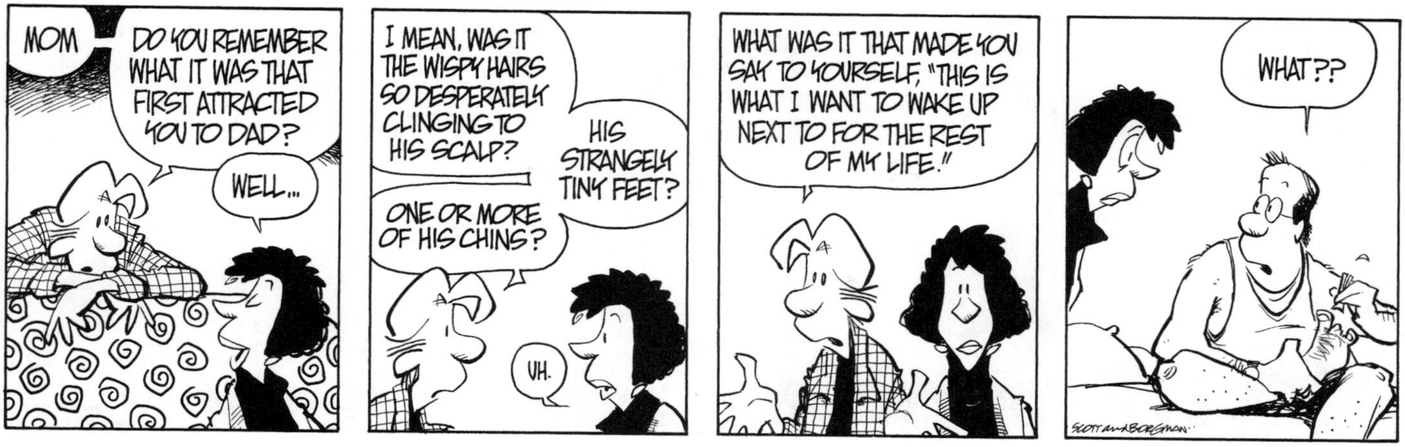
MOM
DO YOU REMEMBER WHAT IT WAS THAT FIRST ATTRACTED YOU TO DAD?
WELL...
I MEAN, WAS IT THE WISPY HAIRS SO DESPERATELY CLINGING TO HIS SCALP?
HIS STRANGELY TINY FEET?
ONE OR MORE OF HIS CHINS?
UH.
WHAT WAS IT THAT MADE YOU SAY TO YOURSELF, "THIS IS WHAT I WANT TO WAKE UP NEXT TO FOR THE REST OF MY LIFE."
WHAT??

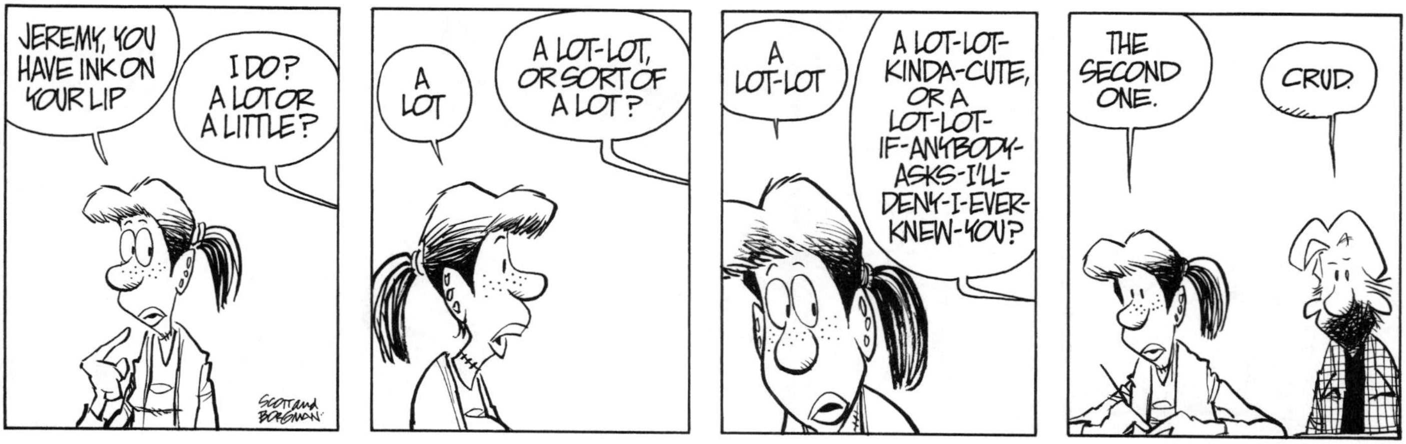
JEREMY, YOU HAVE INK ON YOUR LIP
I DO? A LOT OR A LITTLE?
A LOT
A LOT-LOT, OR SORT OF A LOT?
A LOT-LOT
A LOT-LOT-KINDA-CUTE, OR A LOT-LOT-IF-ANYBODY-ASKS-I'LL-DENY-I-EVER-KNEW-YOU?
THE SECOND ONE.
CRUD.

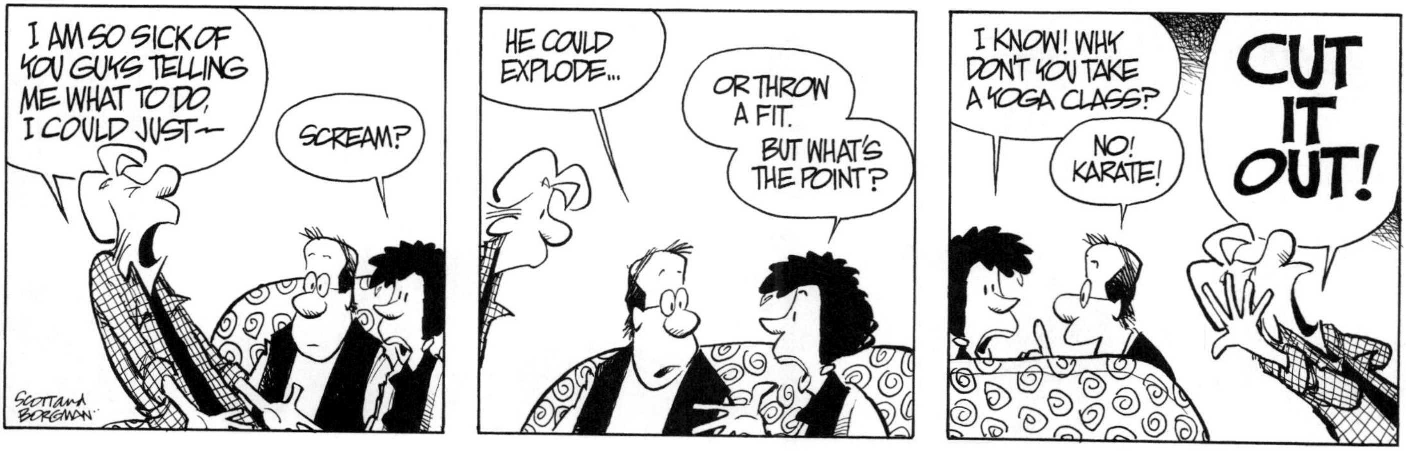
I AM SO SICK OF YOU GUYS TELLING ME WHAT TO DO, I COULD JUST--
SCREAM?
HE COULD EXPLODE...
OR THROW A FIT.
BUT WHAT'S THE POINT?
I KNOW! WHY DON'T YOU TAKE A YOGA CLASS?
NO! KARATE!
CUT IT OUT!

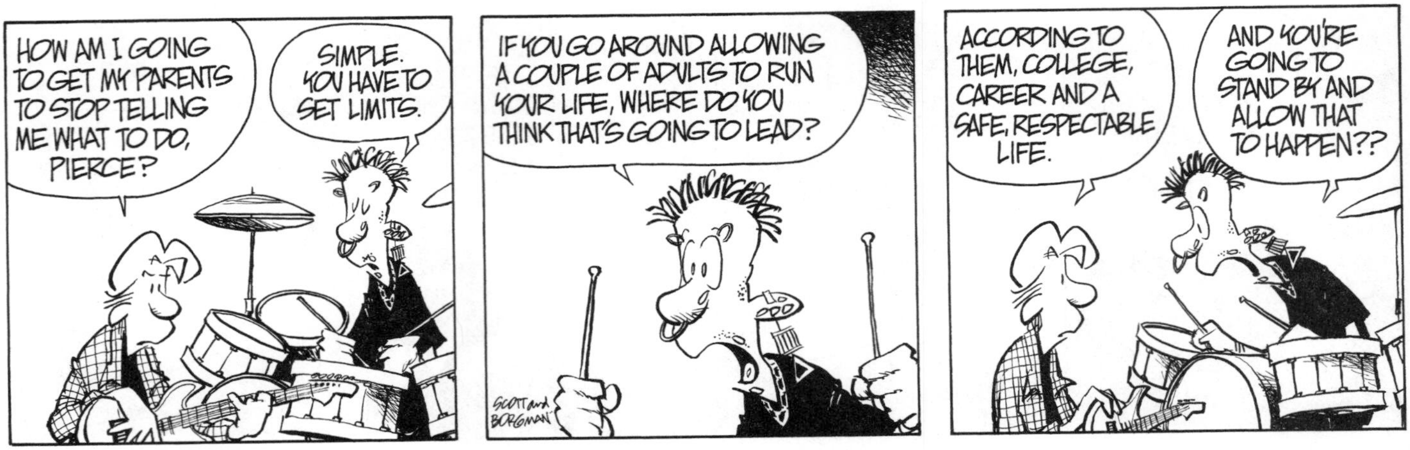
HOW AM I GOING TO GET MY PARENTS TO STOP TELLING ME WHAT TO DO, PIERCE?
SIMPLE. YOU HAVE TO SET LIMITS.
IF YOU GO AROUND ALLOWING A COUPLE OF ADULTS TO RUN YOUR LIFE, WHERE DO YOU THINK THAT'S GOING TO LEAD?
SCOTT and BORGMAN
ACCORDING TO THEM, COLLEGE, CAREER AND A SAFE, RESPECTABLE LIFE.
AND YOU'RE GOING TO STAND BY AND ALLOW THAT TO HAPPEN??

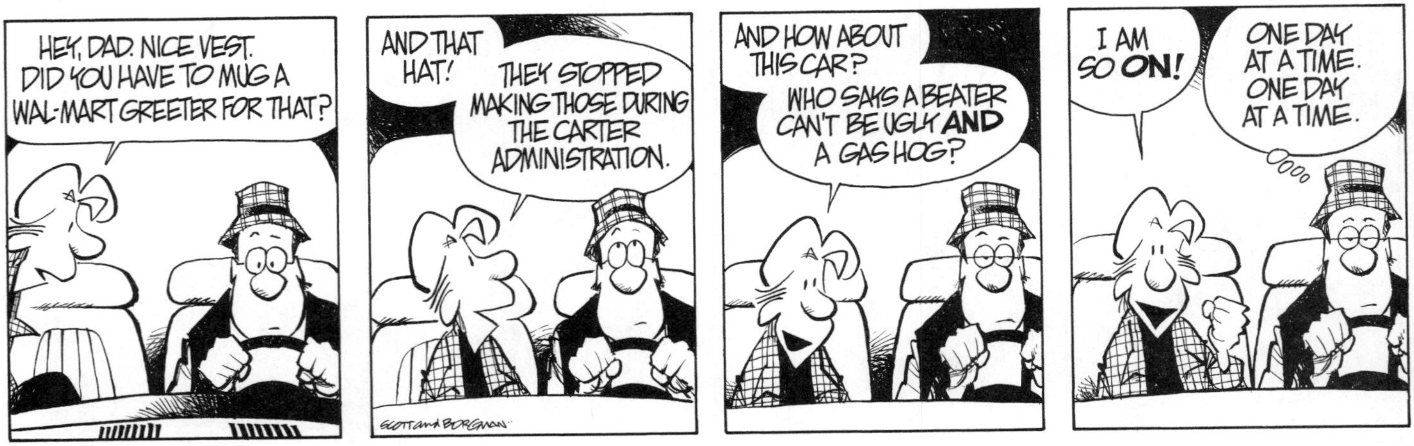
HEY, DAD. NICE VEST. DID YOU HAVE TO MUG A WAL-MART GREETER FOR THAT?
AND THAT HAT!
THEY STOPPED MAKING THOSE DURING THE CARTER ADMINISTRATION.
SCOTT and BORGMAN
AND HOW ABOUT THIS CAR?
WHO SAYS A BEATER CAN'T BE UGLY AND A GAS HOG?
I AM SO ON!
ONE DAY AT A TIME. ONE DAY AT A TIME.

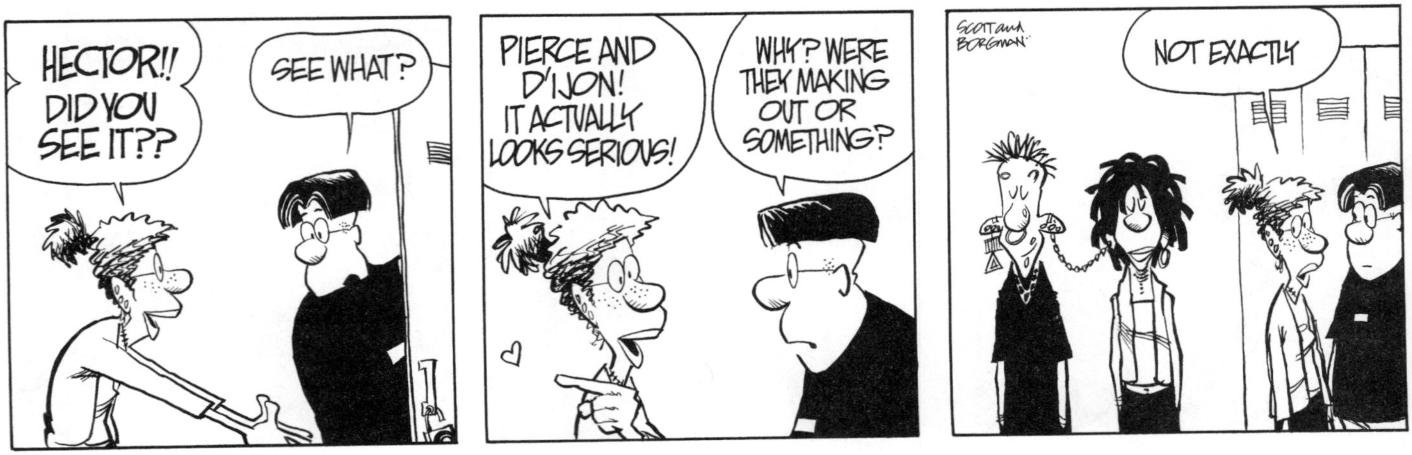
HECTOR!! DID YOU SEE IT??
SEE WHAT?
PIERCE AND D'IJON! IT ACTUALLY LOOKS SERIOUS!
WHY? WERE THEY MAKING OUT OR SOMETHING?
SCOTT and BORGMAN
NOT EXACTLY

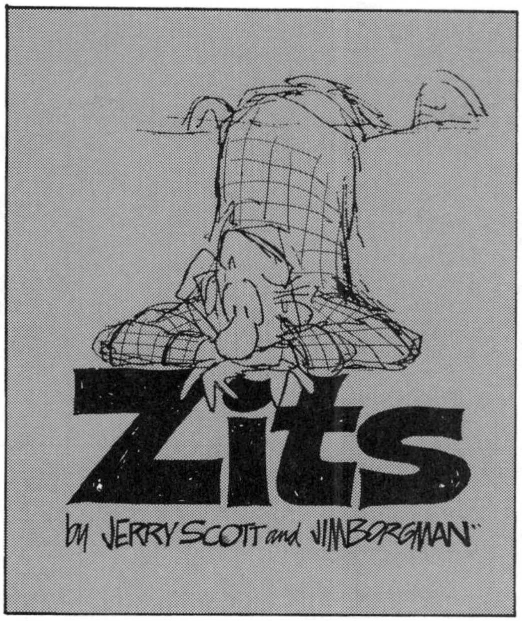
Zits
by JERRY SCOTT and JIM BORGMAN

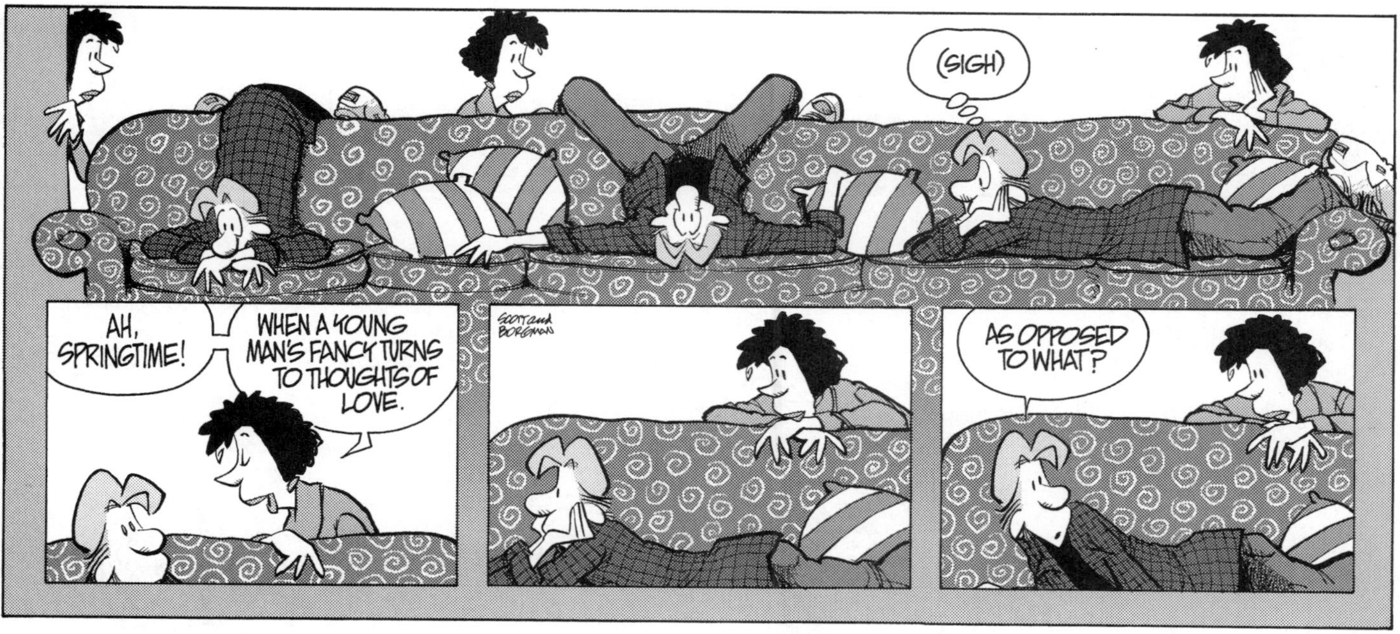
(SIGH)
AH, SPRINGTIME!
WHEN A YOUNG MAN'S FANCY TURNS TO THOUGHTS OF LOVE.
SCOTT and BORGMAN
AS OPPOSED TO WHAT?

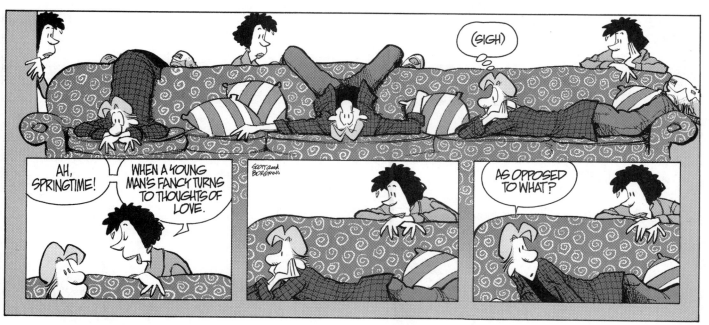

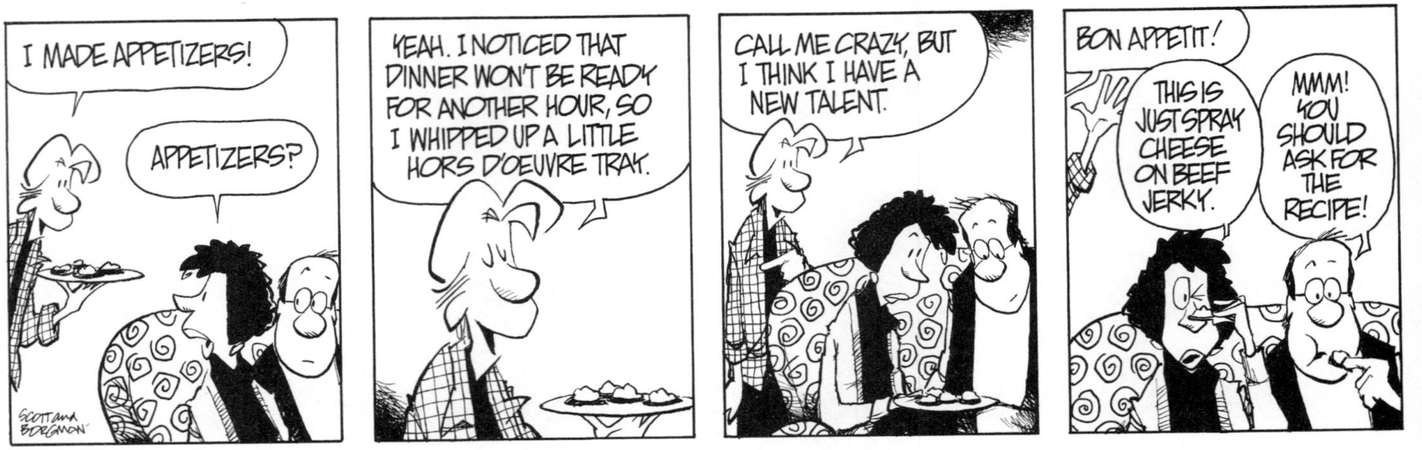
I MADE APPETIZERS!
APPETIZERS?
SCOTT and BORGMAN
YEAH. I NOTICED THAT DINNER WON'T BE READY FOR ANOTHER HOUR, SO I WHIPPED UP A LITTLE HORS D'OEUVRE TRAY.
CALL ME CRAZY, BUT I THINK I HAVE A NEW TALENT.
BON APPETIT!
THIS IS JUST SPRAY CHEESE ON BEEF JERKY.
MMM! YOU SHOULD ASK FOR THE RECIPE!

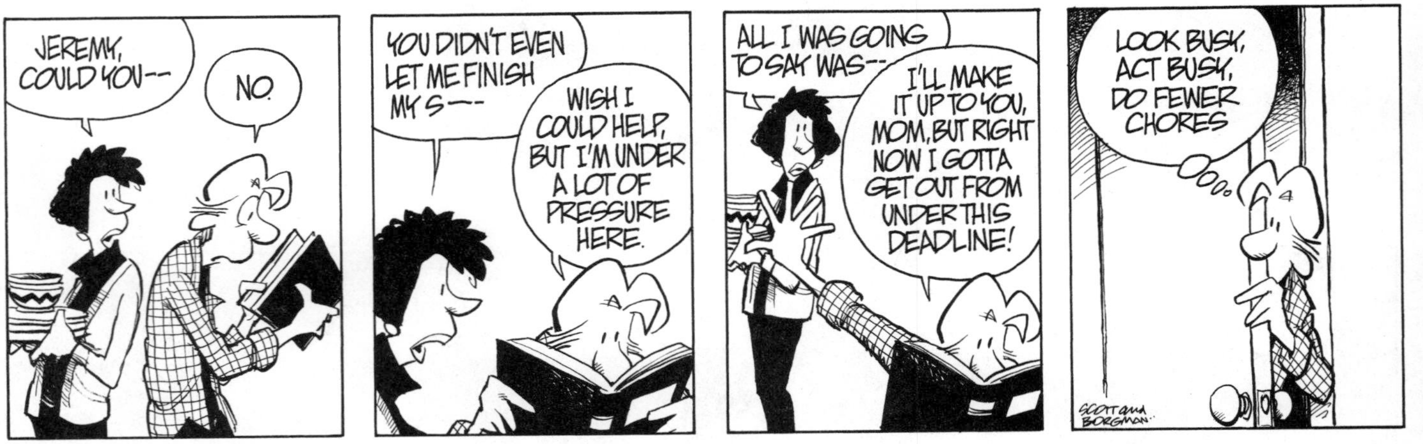
JEREMY, COULD YOU--
NO.
YOU DIDN'T EVEN LET ME FINISH MY S---
WISH I COULD HELP, BUT I'M UNDER A LOT OF PRESSURE HERE.
ALL I WAS GOING TO SAY WAS--
I'LL MAKE IT UP TO YOU, MOM, BUT RIGHT NOW I GOTTA GET OUT FROM UNDER THIS DEADLINE!
LOOK BUSY, ACT BUSY, DO FEWER CHORES
SCOTT and BORGMAN

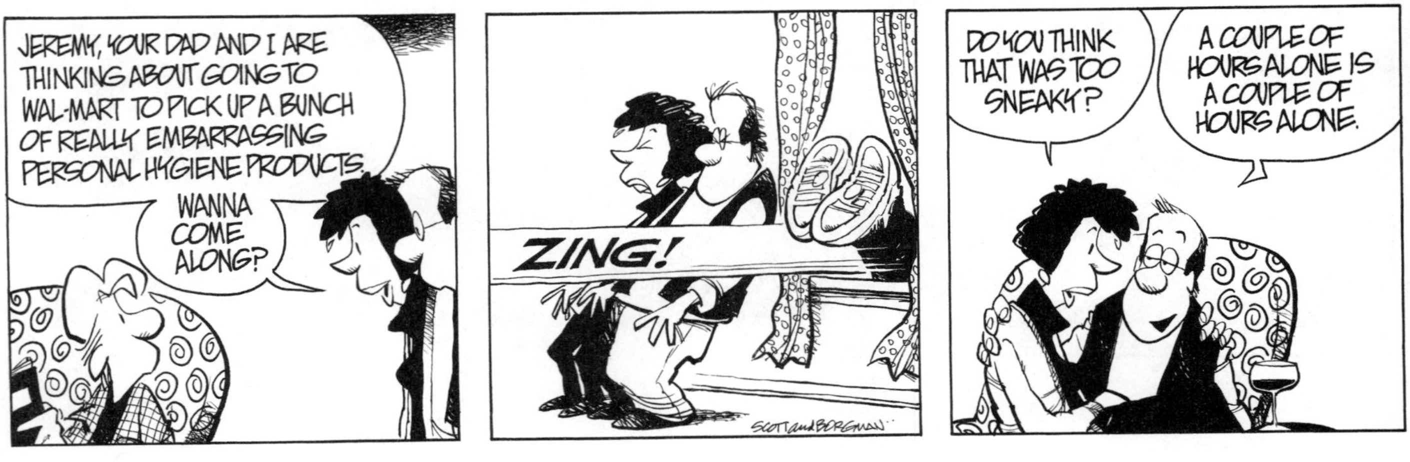
JEREMY, YOUR DAD AND I ARE THINKING ABOUT GOING TO WAL-MART TO PICK UP A BUNCH OF REALLY EMBARRASSING PERSONAL HYGIENE PRODUCTS.
WANNA COME ALONG?
ZING!
SCOTT and BORGMAN
DO YOU THINK THAT WAS TOO SNEAKY?
A COUPLE OF HOURS ALONE IS A COUPLE OF HOURS ALONE.

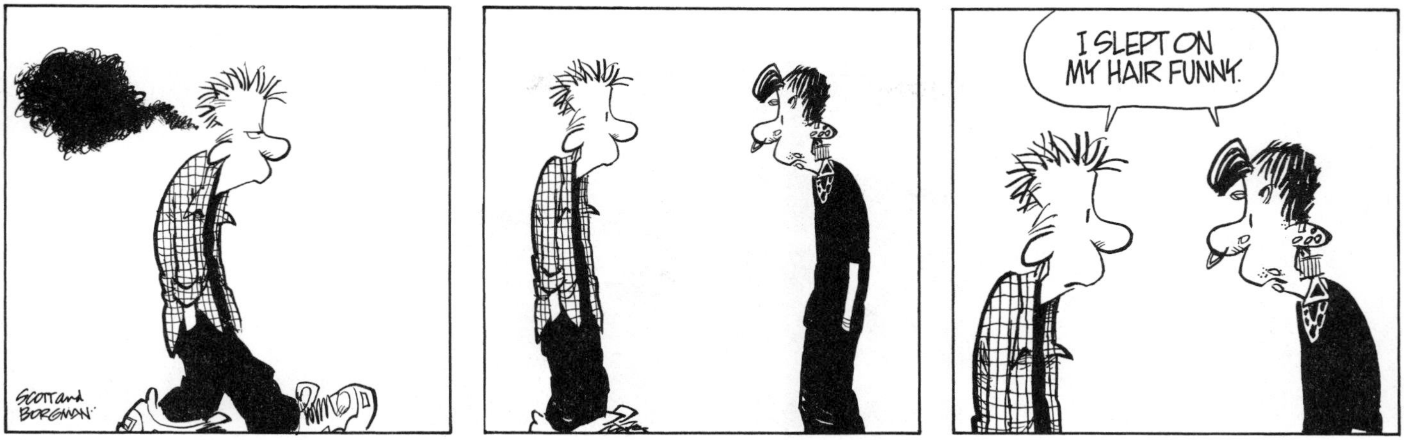
I SLEPT ON MY HAIR FUNNY.

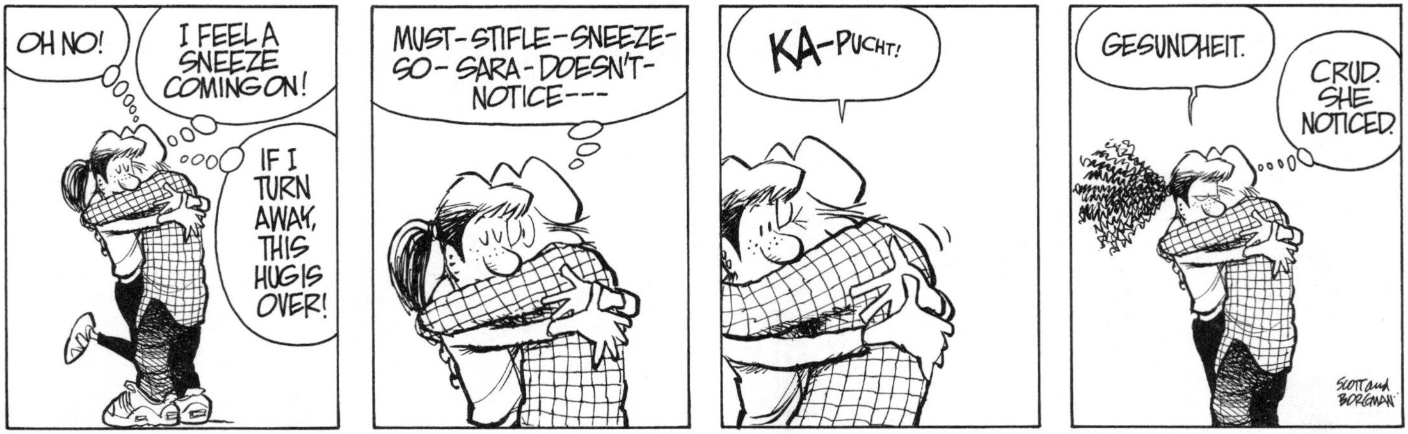
OH NO!
I FEEL A SNEEZE COMING ON!
IF I TURN AWAY, THIS HUG IS OVER!
MUST-STIFLE-SNEEZE-SO-SARA-DOESN'T-NOTICE---
KA-PUCHT!
GESUNDHEIT.
CRUD. SHE NOTICED.

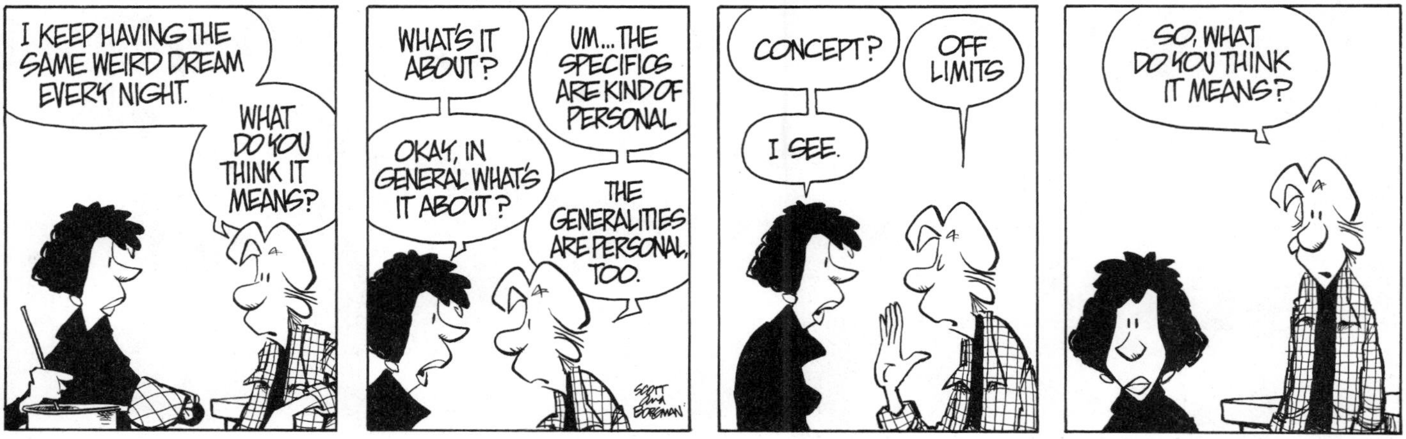
I KEEP HAVING THE SAME WEIRD DREAM EVERY NIGHT.
WHAT DO YOU THINK IT MEANS?
WHAT'S IT ABOUT?
UM... THE SPECIFICS ARE KIND OF PERSONAL
OKAY, IN GENERAL WHAT'S IT ABOUT?
THE GENERALITIES ARE PERSONAL, TOO.
CONCEPT?
OFF LIMITS
I SEE.
SO, WHAT DO YOU THINK IT MEANS?

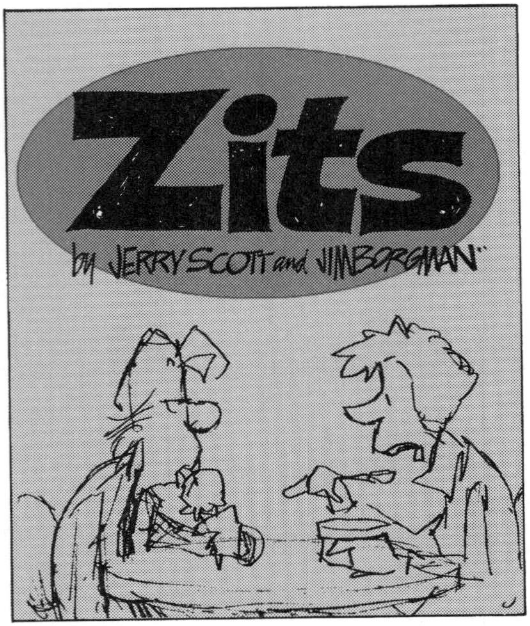
Zits
by JERRY SCOTT and JIM BORGMAN

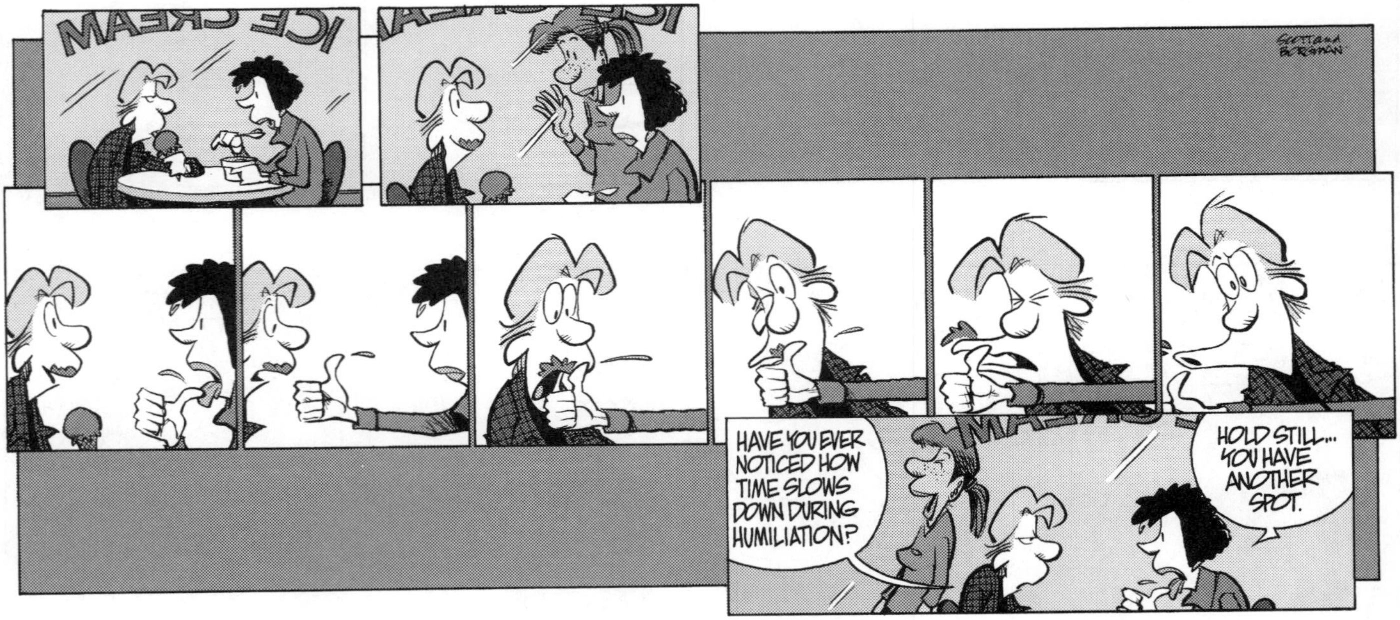
HAVE YOU EVER NOTICED HOW TIME SLOWS DOWN DURING HUMILIATION?
HOLD STILL... YOU HAVE ANOTHER SPOT.

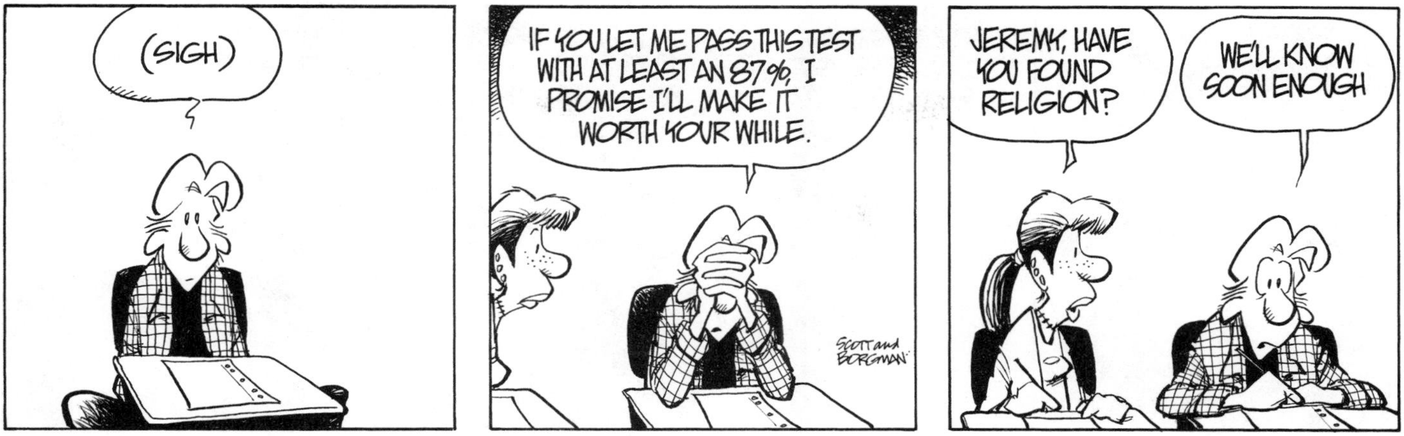
(SIGH)
IF YOU LET ME PASS THIS TEST WITH AT LEAST AN 87%, I PROMISE I'LL MAKE IT WORTH YOUR WHILE.
SCOTT and BORGMAN
JEREMY, HAVE YOU FOUND RELIGION?
WE'LL KNOW SOON ENOUGH

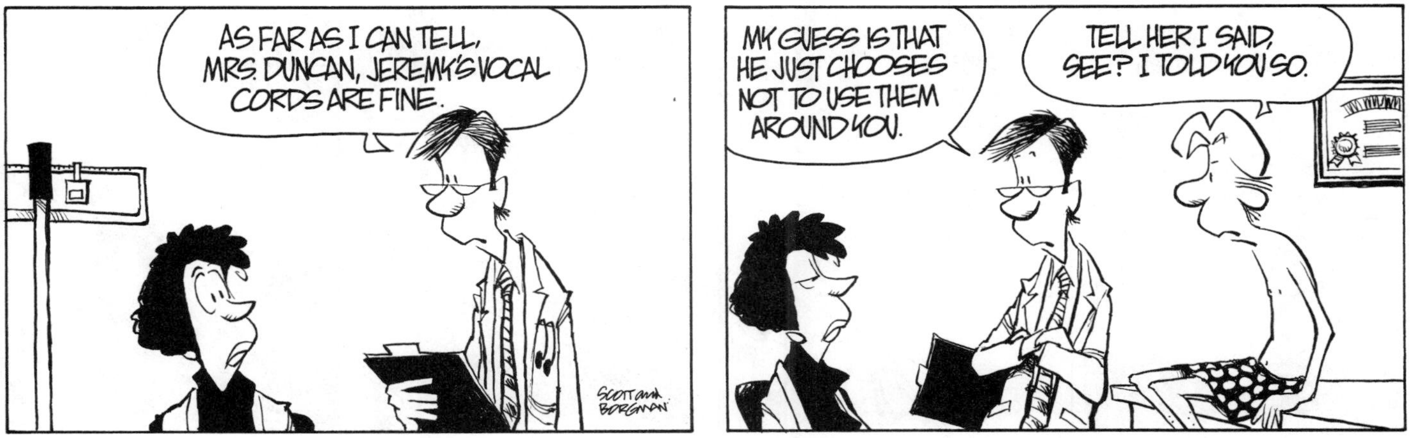
AS FAR AS I CAN TELL, MRS. DUNCAN, JEREMY'S VOCAL CORDS ARE FINE.
SCOTT and BORGMAN
MY GUESS IS THAT HE JUST CHOOSES NOT TO USE THEM AROUND YOU.
TELL HER I SAID, SEE? I TOLD YOU SO.

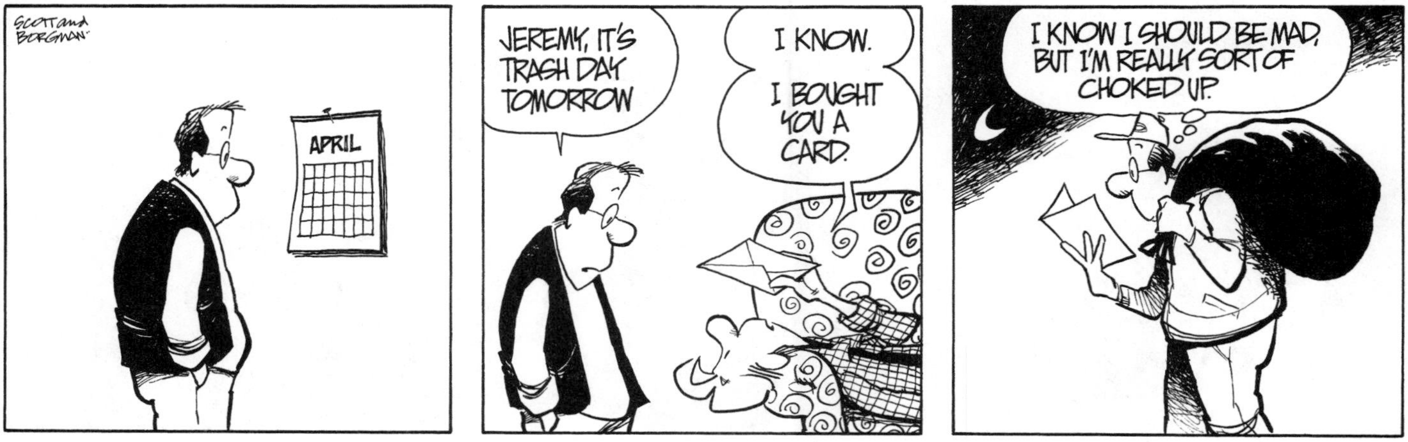
SCOTT and BORGMAN
APRIL
JEREMY, IT'S TRASH DAY TOMORROW
I KNOW.
I BOUGHT YOU A CARD.
I KNOW I SHOULD BE MAD, BUT I'M REALLY SORT OF CHOKED UP.

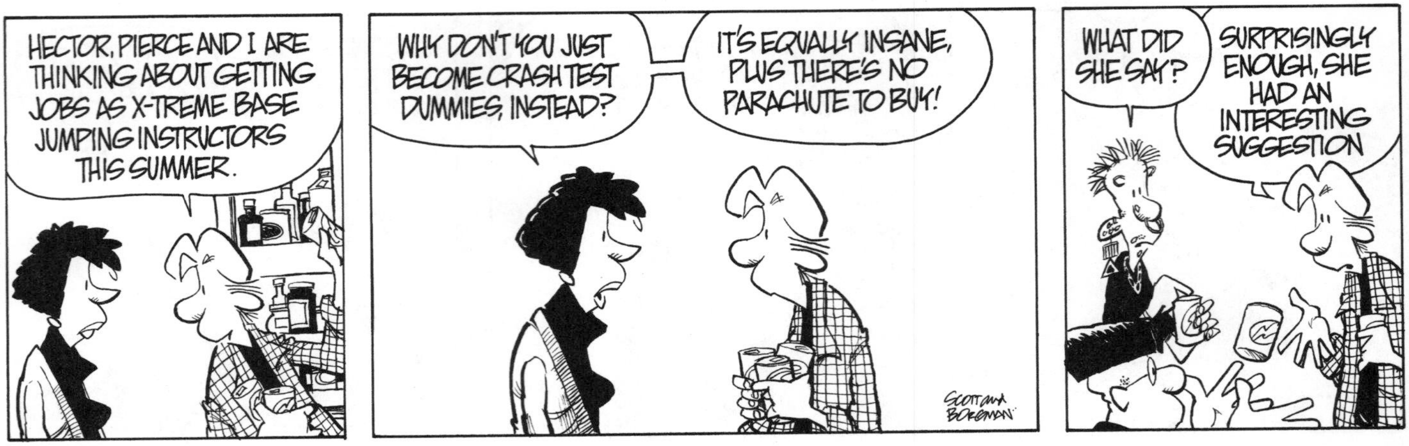
HECTOR, PIERCE AND I ARE THINKING ABOUT GETTING JOBS AS X-TREME BASE JUMPING INSTRUCTORS THIS SUMMER.
WHY DON'T YOU JUST BECOME CRASH TEST DUMMIES, INSTEAD?
IT'S EQUALLY INSANE, PLUS THERE'S NO PARACHUTE TO BUY!
WHAT DID SHE SAY?
SURPRISINGLY ENOUGH, SHE HAD AN INTERESTING SUGGESTION

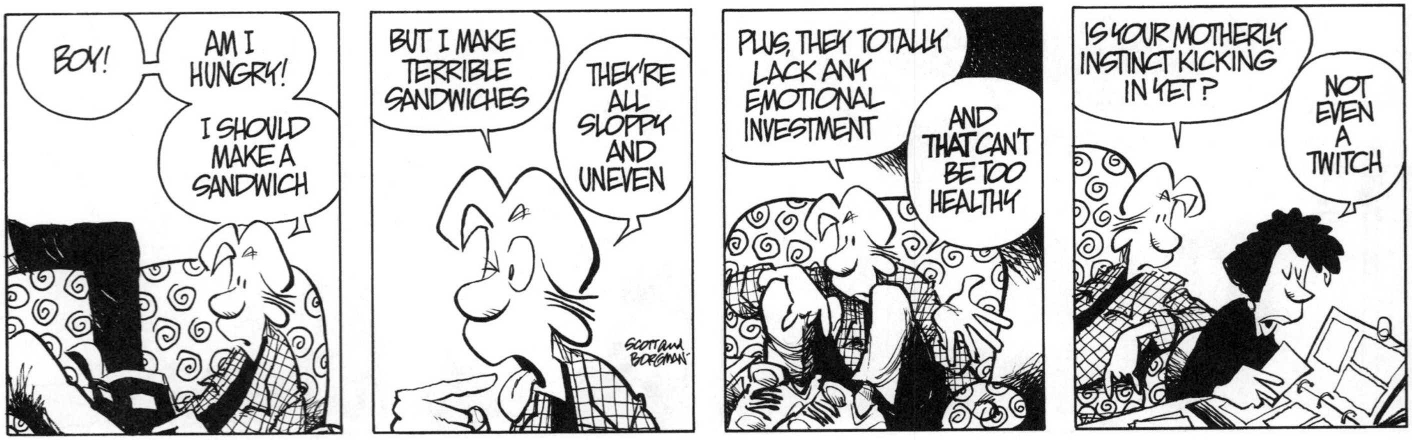
BOY!
AM I HUNGRY!
I SHOULD MAKE A SANDWICH
BUT I MAKE TERRIBLE SANDWICHES
THEY'RE ALL SLOPPY AND UNEVEN
PLUS, THEY TOTALLY LACK ANY EMOTIONAL INVESTMENT
AND THAT CAN'T BE TOO HEALTHY
IS YOUR MOTHERLY INSTINCT KICKING IN YET?
NOT EVEN A TWITCH

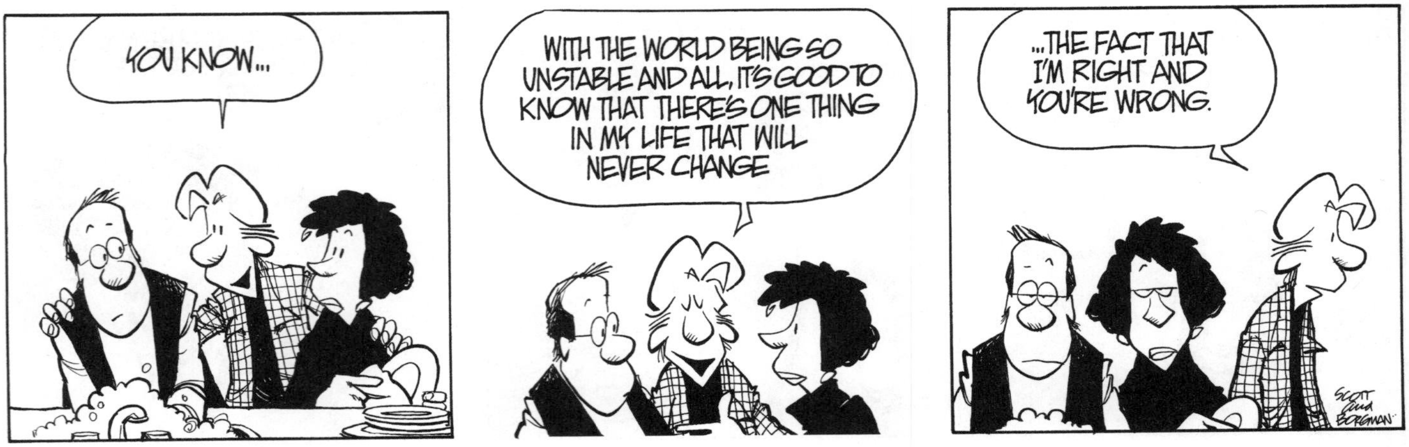
YOU KNOW...
WITH THE WORLD BEING SO UNSTABLE AND ALL, IT'S GOOD TO KNOW THAT THERE'S ONE THING IN MY LIFE THAT WILL NEVER CHANGE
...THE FACT THAT I'M RIGHT AND YOU'RE WRONG.

Zits
by
JERRY SCOTT and JIM BORGMAN

DO YOU HAVE ANY HOMEWORK TONIGHT, JEREMY?
SOME.

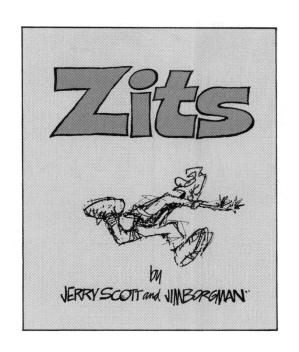

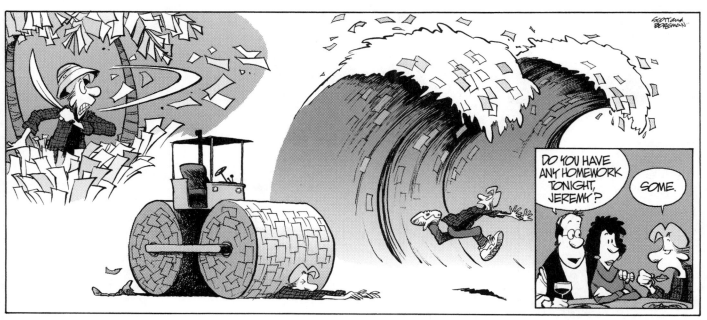

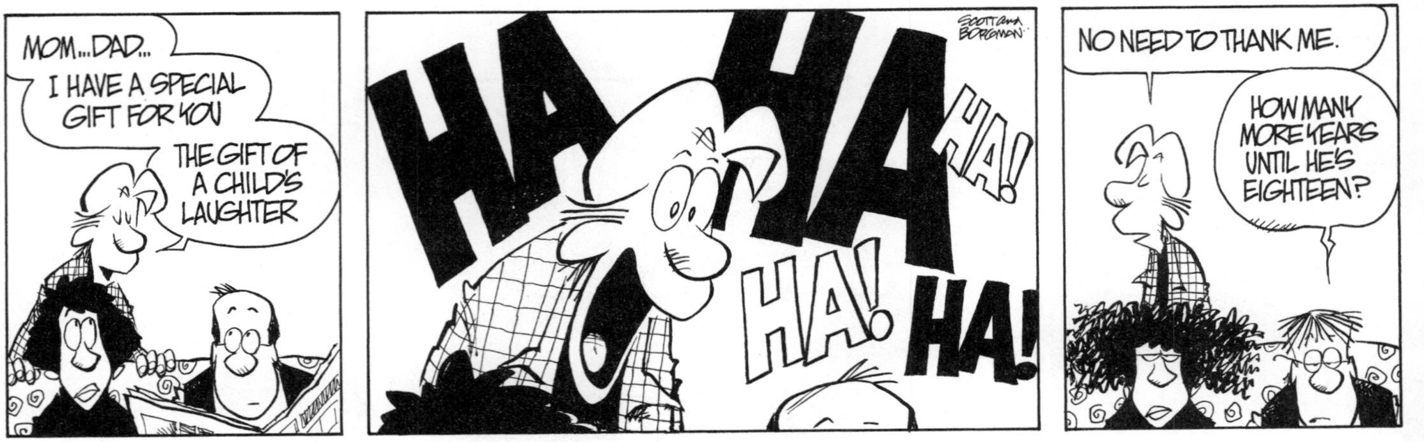
MOM...DAD...
I HAVE A SPECIAL GIFT FOR YOU
THE GIFT OF A CHILD'S LAUGHTER
SCOTT and BORGMAN
HA HA HA! HA! HA! HA!
NO NEED TO THANK ME.
HOW MANY MORE YEARS UNTIL HE'S EIGHTEEN?

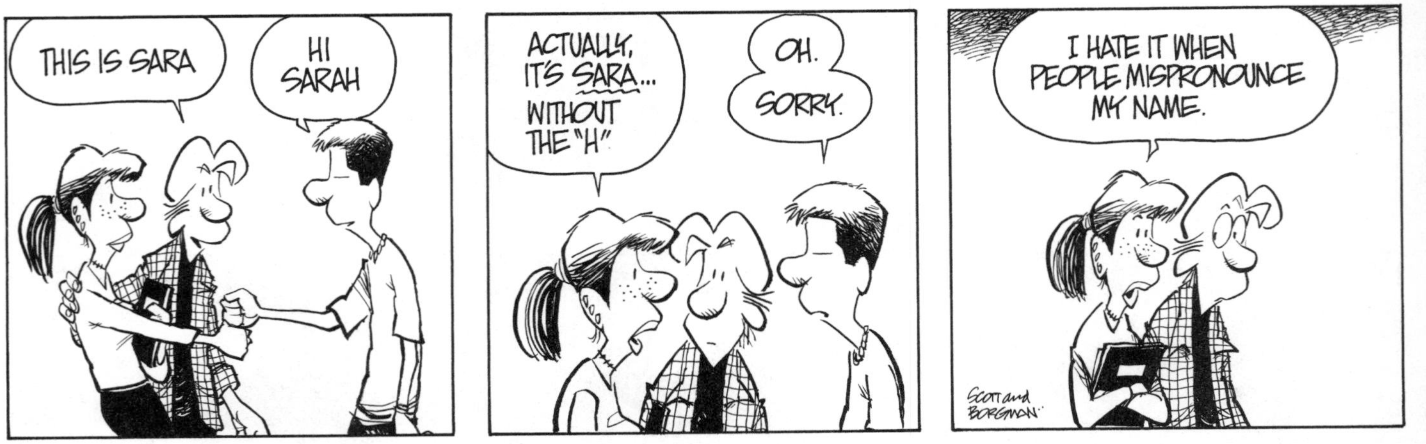
THIS IS SARA
HI SARAH
ACTUALLY, IT'S SARA... WITHOUT THE "H"
OH.
SORRY.
I HATE IT WHEN PEOPLE MISPRONOUNCE MY NAME.
SCOTT and BORGMAN

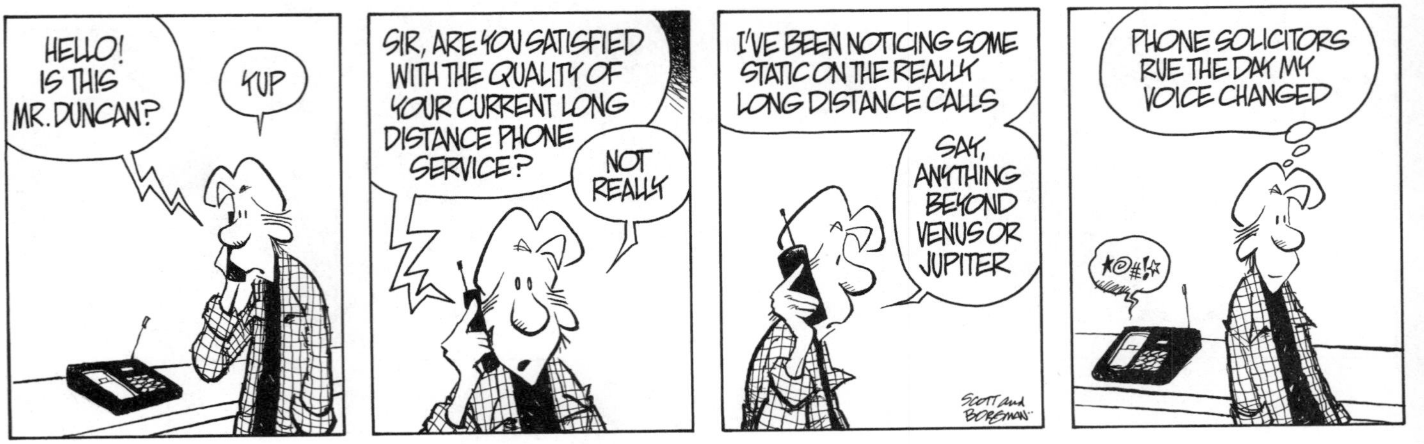
HELLO! IS THIS MR. DUNCAN?
YUP
SIR, ARE YOU SATISFIED WITH THE QUALITY OF YOUR CURRENT LONG DISTANCE PHONE SERVICE?
NOT REALLY
I'VE BEEN NOTICING SOME STATIC ON THE REALLY LONG DISTANCE CALLS
SAY, ANYTHING BEYOND VENUS OR JUPITER
SCOTT and BORGMAN
PHONE SOLICITORS RUE THE DAY MY VOICE CHANGED
*@#!☆

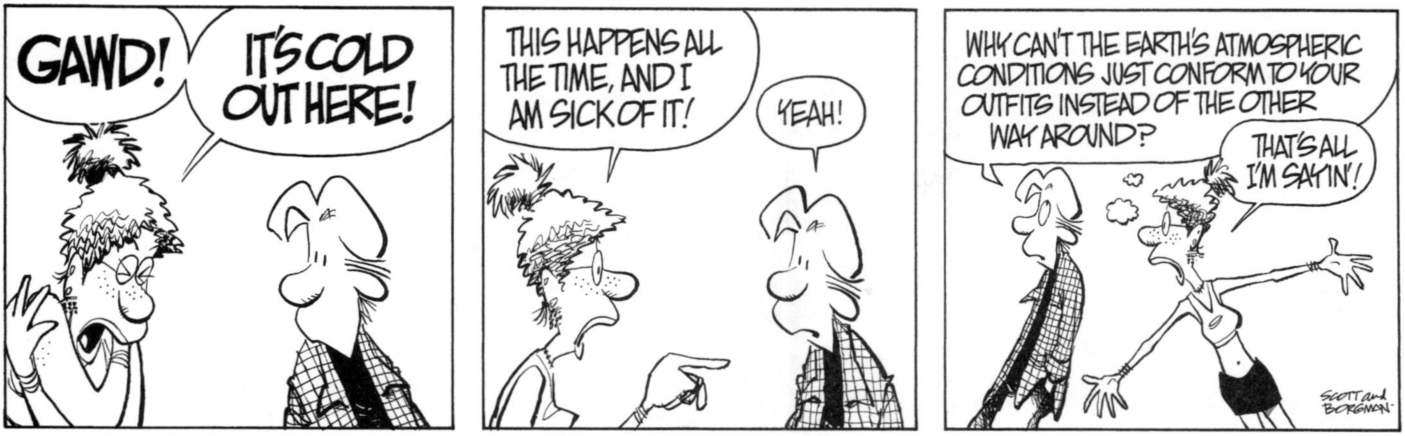
GAWD!
IT'S COLD OUT HERE!
THIS HAPPENS ALL THE TIME, AND I AM SICK OF IT!
YEAH!
WHY CAN'T THE EARTH'S ATMOSPHERIC CONDITIONS JUST CONFORM TO YOUR OUTFITS INSTEAD OF THE OTHER WAY AROUND?
THAT'S ALL I'M SAYIN'!
SCOTT and BORGMAN

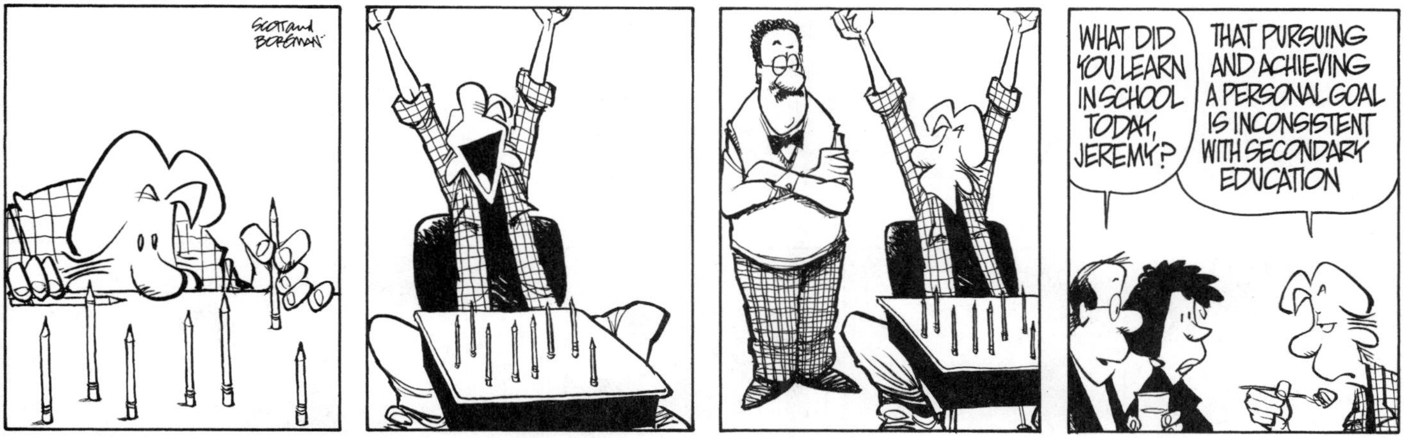
SCOTT and BORGMAN
WHAT DID YOU LEARN IN SCHOOL TODAY, JEREMY?
THAT PURSUING AND ACHIEVING A PERSONAL GOAL IS INCONSISTENT WITH SECONDARY EDUCATION

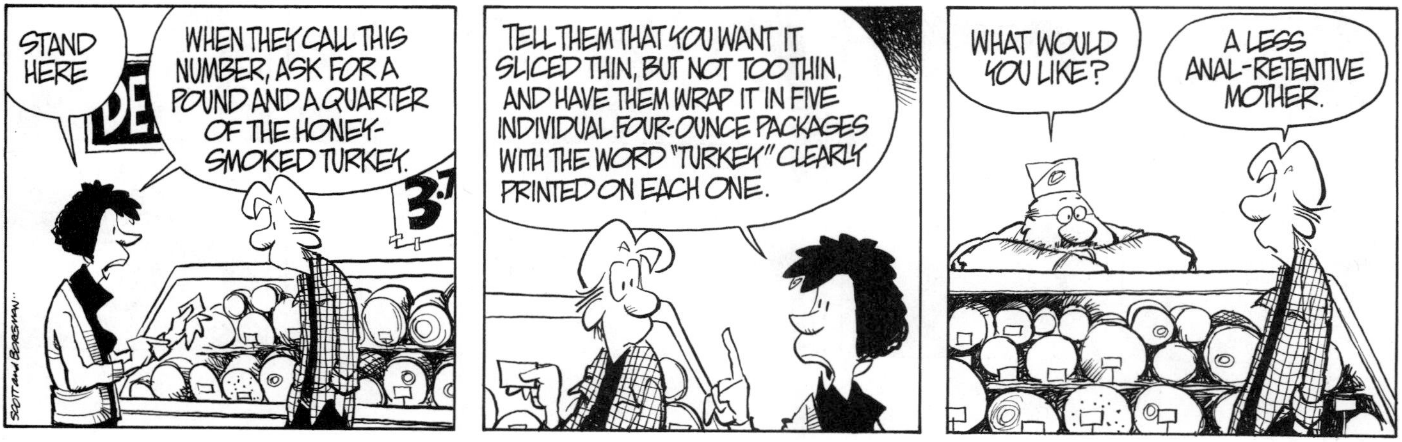
STAND HERE
WHEN THEY CALL THIS NUMBER, ASK FOR A POUND AND A QUARTER OF THE HONEY-SMOKED TURKEY.
SCOTT and BORGMAN
TELL THEM THAT YOU WANT IT SLICED THIN, BUT NOT TOO THIN, AND HAVE THEM WRAP IT IN FIVE INDIVIDUAL FOUR-OUNCE PACKAGES WITH THE WORD "TURKEY" CLEARLY PRINTED ON EACH ONE.
WHAT WOULD YOU LIKE?
A LESS ANAL-RETENTIVE MOTHER.

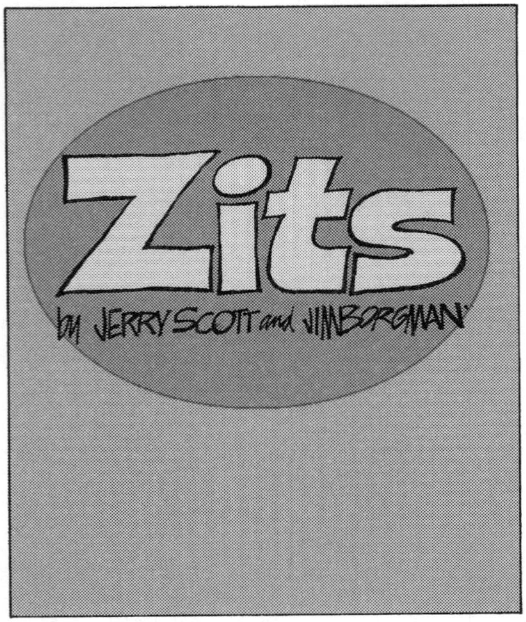
Zits
by JERRY SCOTT and JIM BORGMAN

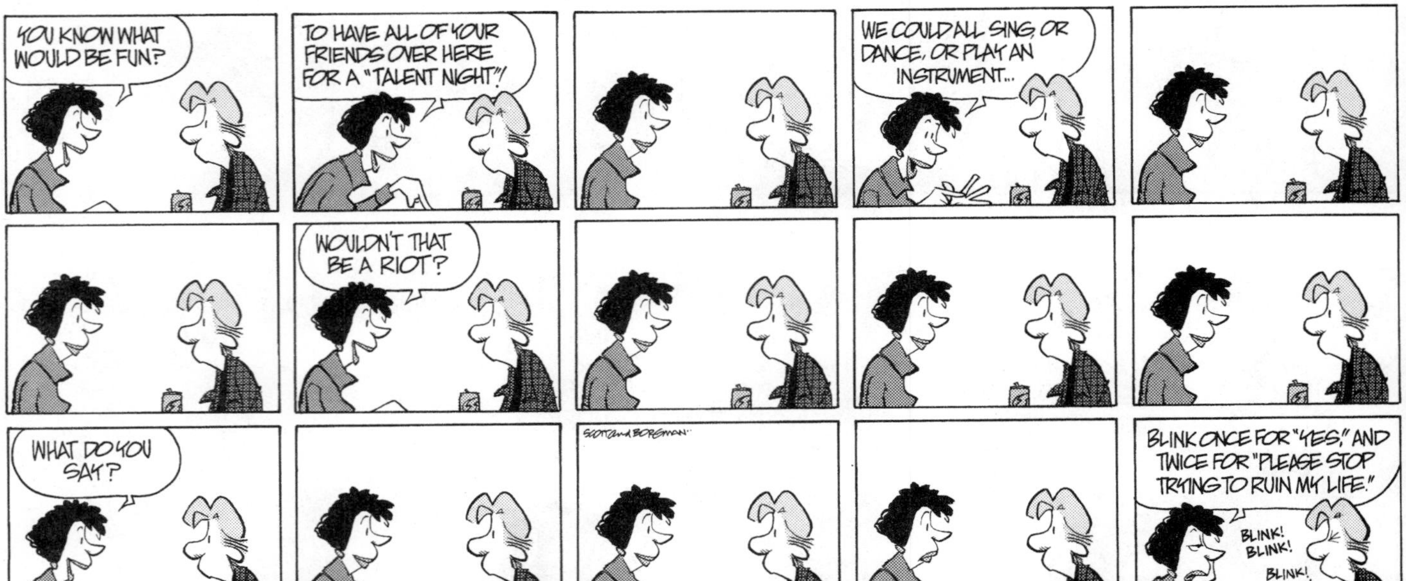
YOU KNOW WHAT WOULD BE FUN?
TO HAVE ALL OF YOUR FRIENDS OVER HERE FOR A "TALENT NIGHT"!
WE COULD ALL SING, OR DANCE, OR PLAY AN INSTRUMENT...
WOULDN'T THAT BE A RIOT?
WHAT DO YOU SAY?
BLINK ONCE FOR "YES," AND TWICE FOR "PLEASE STOP TRYING TO RUIN MY LIFE."
BLINK! BLINK!
BLINK! BLINK!

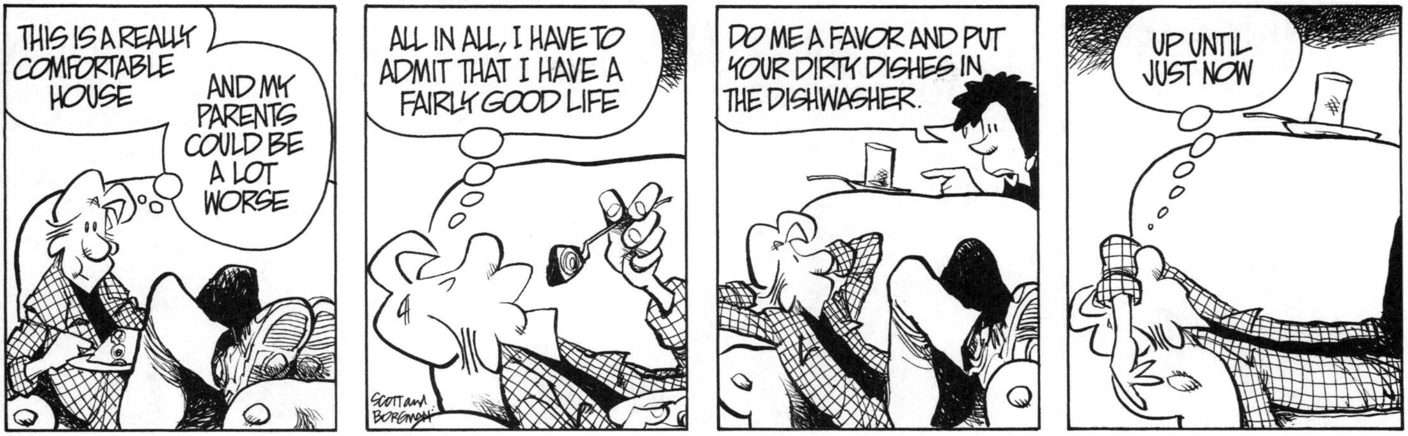
THIS IS A REALLY COMFORTABLE HOUSE
AND MY PARENTS COULD BE A LOT WORSE
ALL IN ALL, I HAVE TO ADMIT THAT I HAVE A FAIRLY GOOD LIFE
SCOTT and BORGMAN
DO ME A FAVOR AND PUT YOUR DIRTY DISHES IN THE DISHWASHER.
UP UNTIL JUST NOW

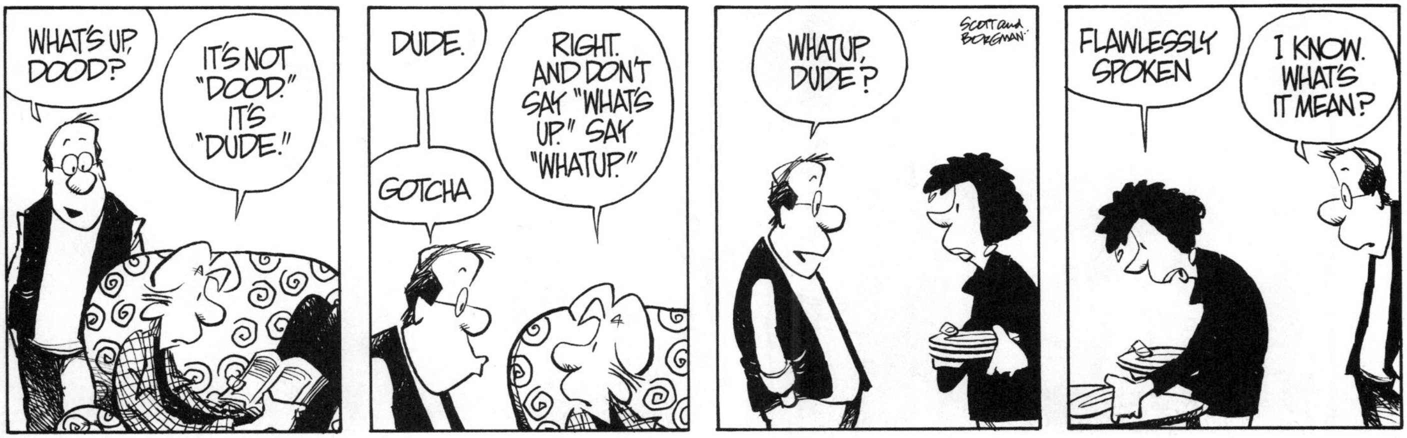
WHAT'S UP, DOOD?
IT'S NOT "DOOD." IT'S "DUDE."
DUDE.
GOTCHA
RIGHT. AND DON'T SAY "WHAT'S UP." SAY "WHATUP."
WHATUP, DUDE?
SCOTT and BORGMAN
FLAWLESSLY SPOKEN
I KNOW. WHAT'S IT MEAN?

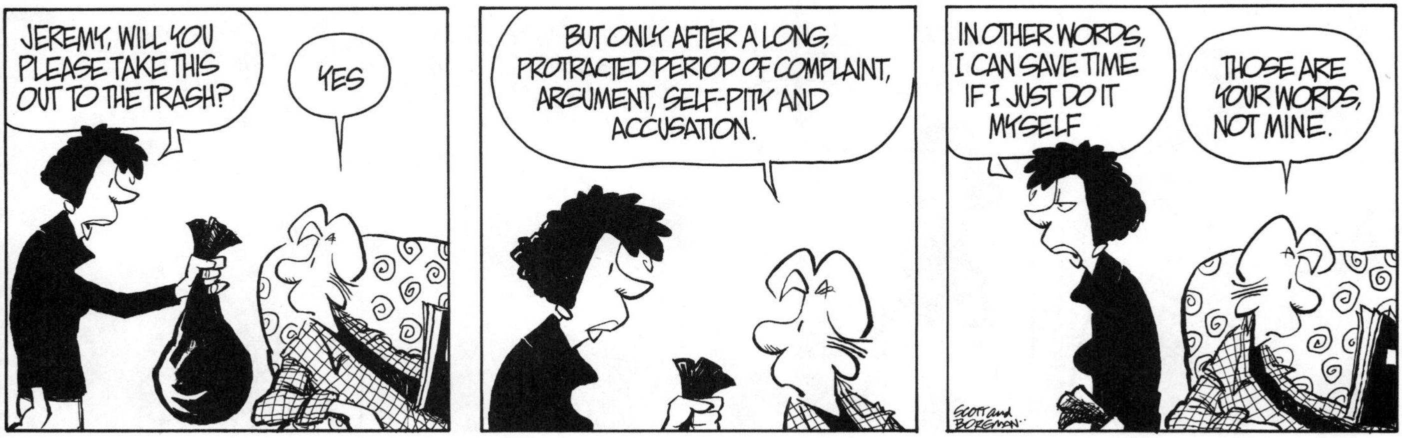
JEREMY, WILL YOU PLEASE TAKE THIS OUT TO THE TRASH?
YES
BUT ONLY AFTER A LONG, PROTRACTED PERIOD OF COMPLAINT, ARGUMENT, SELF-PITY AND ACCUSATION.
IN OTHER WORDS, I CAN SAVE TIME IF I JUST DO IT MYSELF
THOSE ARE YOUR WORDS, NOT MINE.
SCOTT and BORGMAN

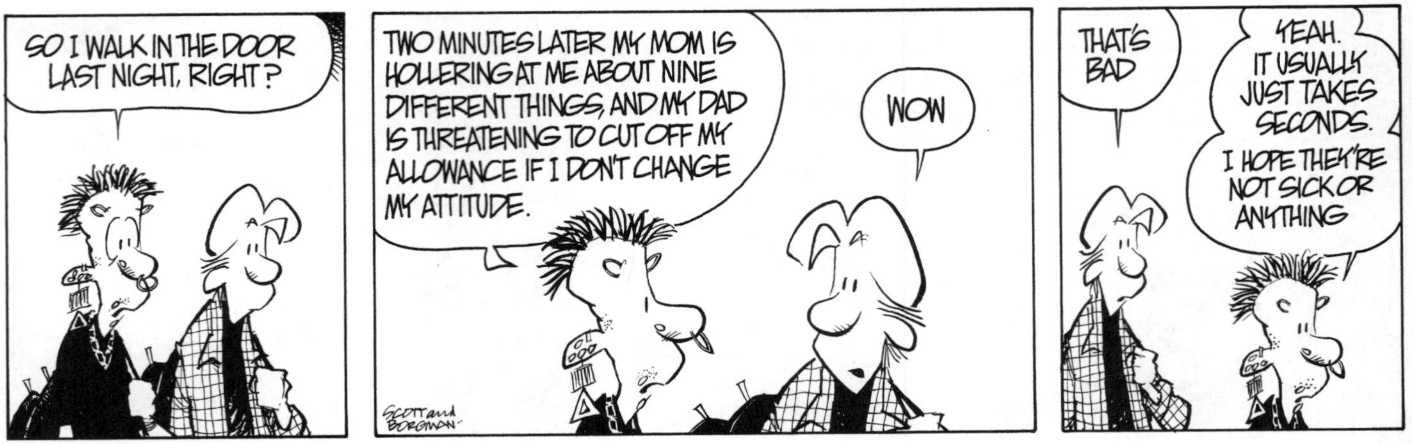
SO I WALK IN THE DOOR LAST NIGHT, RIGHT?
TWO MINUTES LATER MY MOM IS HOLLERING AT ME ABOUT NINE DIFFERENT THINGS, AND MY DAD IS THREATENING TO CUT OFF MY ALLOWANCE IF I DON'T CHANGE MY ATTITUDE.
WOW
THAT'S BAD
YEAH. IT USUALLY JUST TAKES SECONDS.
I HOPE THEY'RE NOT SICK OR ANYTHING

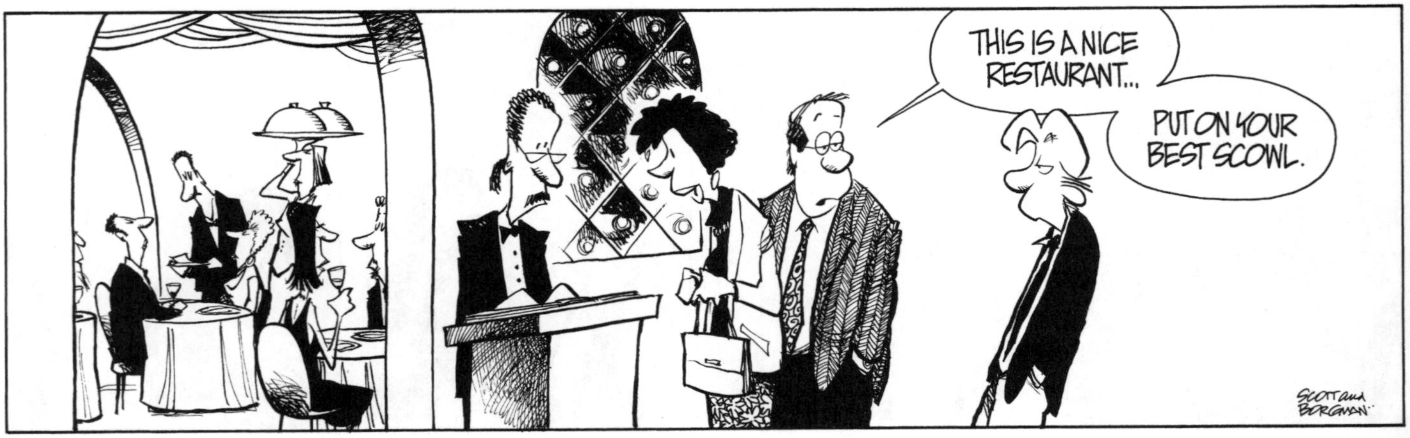
THIS IS A NICE RESTAURANT...
PUT ON YOUR BEST SCOWL.

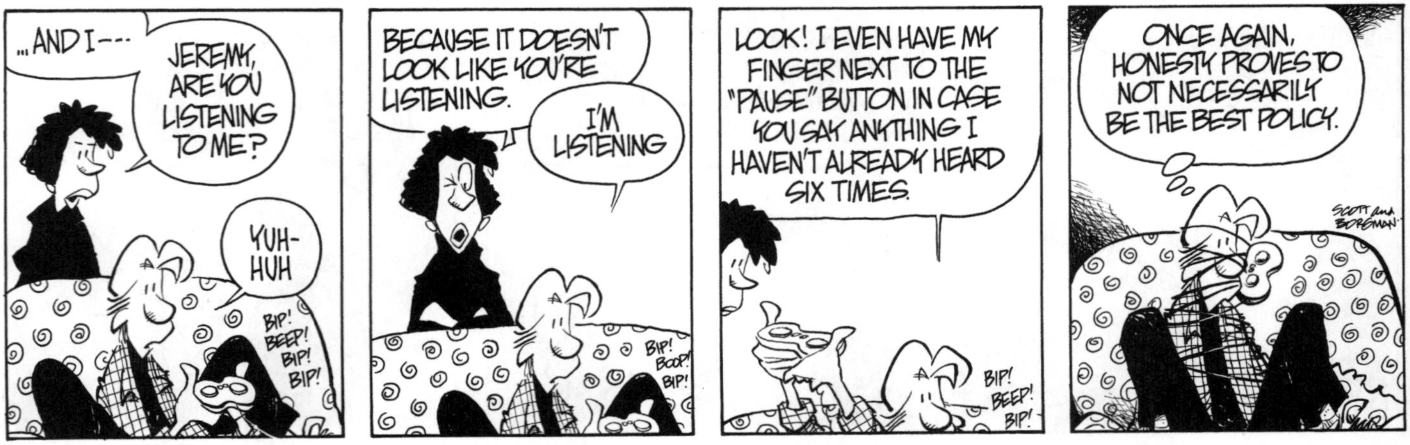
...AND I---
JEREMY, ARE YOU LISTENING TO ME?
YUH-HUH
BIP! BEEP! BIP! BIP!
BECAUSE IT DOESN'T LOOK LIKE YOU'RE LISTENING.
I'M LISTENING
BIP! BOOP! BIP!
LOOK! I EVEN HAVE MY FINGER NEXT TO THE "PAUSE" BUTTON IN CASE YOU SAY ANYTHING I HAVEN'T ALREADY HEARD SIX TIMES.
BIP! BEEP! BIP!
ONCE AGAIN, HONESTY PROVES TO NOT NECESSARILY BE THE BEST POLICY.

Zits
by JERRY SCOTT and JIM BORGMAN

MOM, I KNOW THAT YOU'RE NOT WILD ABOUT UNSUPERVISED PARTIES, BUT PIERCE AND I WERE THINKING ABOUT--
NO NO NO NO NO NO
BUT
YOU NEVER--
IT'S NOT--
WHY CAN'T I JUST--
SCOTT and BORGMAN
SHE'S THINKING ABOUT IT
YUH-HUH.

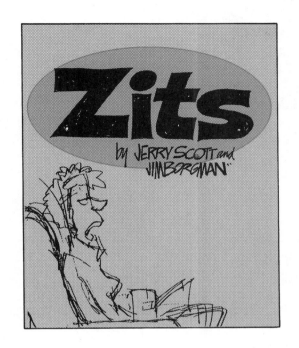

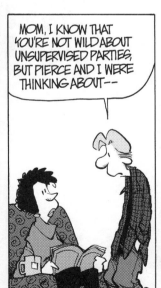

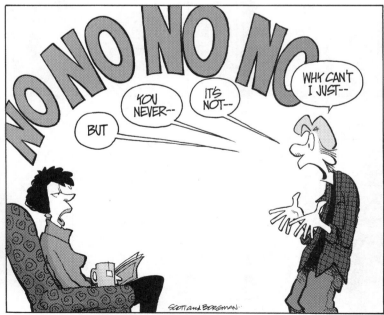

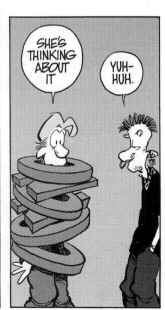

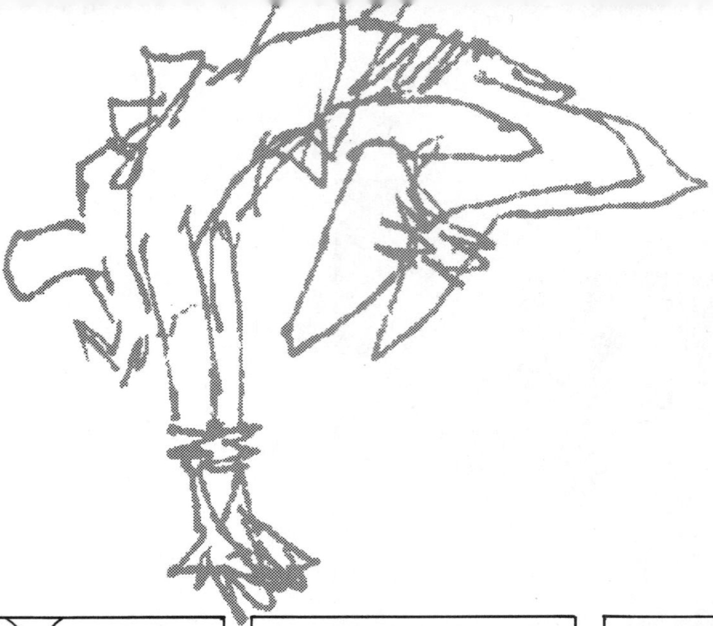

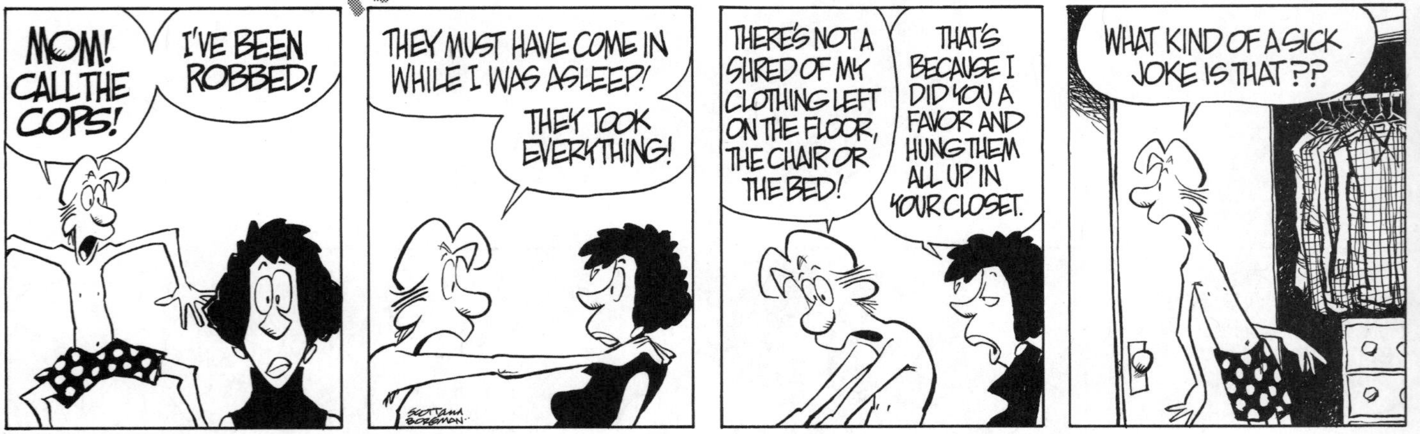

MOM! CALL THE COPS!
I'VE BEEN ROBBED!
THEY MUST HAVE COME IN WHILE I WAS ASLEEP!
THEY TOOK EVERYTHING!
THERE'S NOT A SHRED OF MY CLOTHING LEFT ON THE FLOOR, THE CHAIR OR THE BED!
THAT'S BECAUSE I DID YOU A FAVOR AND HUNG THEM ALL UP IN YOUR CLOSET.
WHAT KIND OF A SICK JOKE IS THAT??

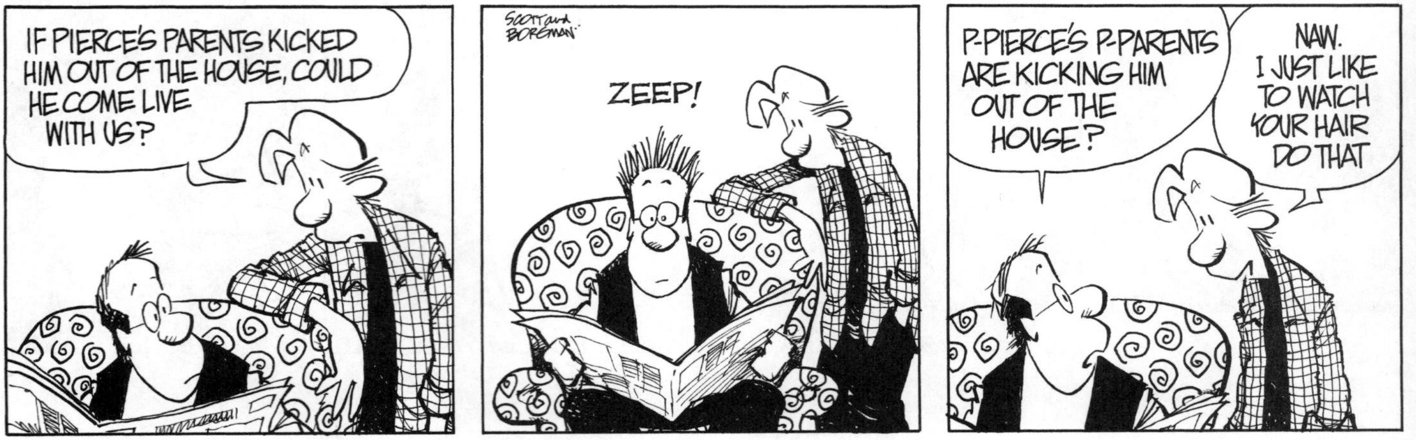

IF PIERCE'S PARENTS KICKED HIM OUT OF THE HOUSE, COULD HE COME LIVE WITH US?
ZEEP!
P-PIERCE'S P-PARENTS ARE KICKING HIM OUT OF THE HOUSE?
NAW. I JUST LIKE TO WATCH YOUR HAIR DO THAT

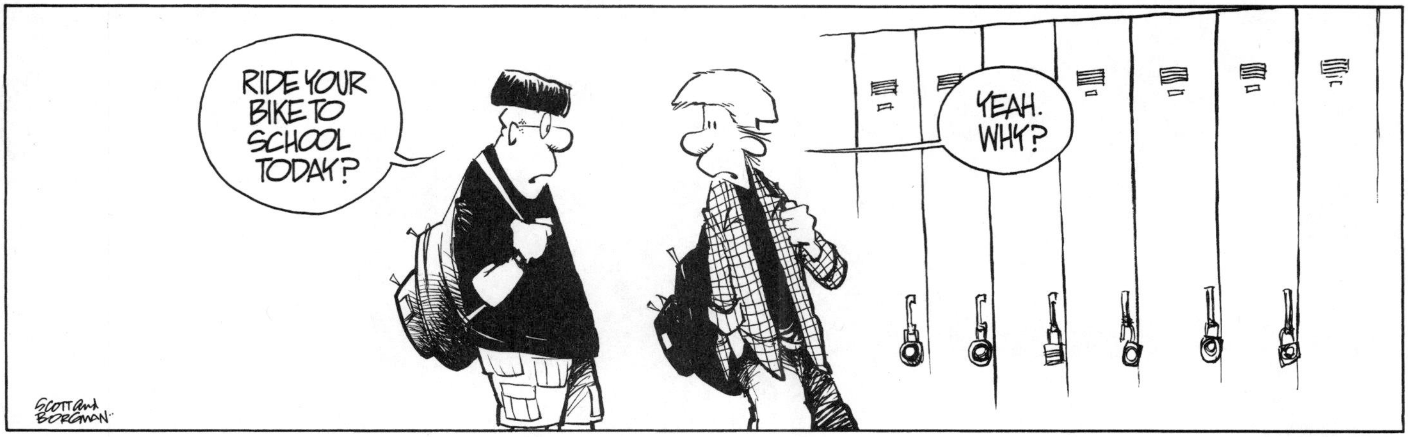
RIDE YOUR BIKE TO SCHOOL TODAY?
YEAH. WHY?
SCOTT and BORGMAN

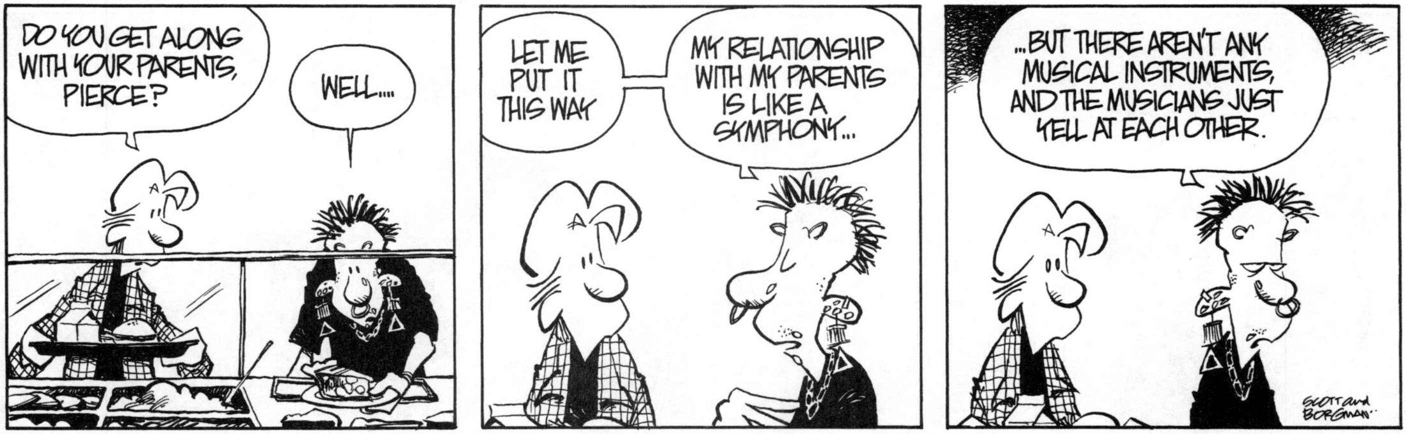
DO YOU GET ALONG WITH YOUR PARENTS, PIERCE?
WELL....
LET ME PUT IT THIS WAY
MY RELATIONSHIP WITH MY PARENTS IS LIKE A SYMPHONY...
...BUT THERE AREN'T ANY MUSICAL INSTRUMENTS, AND THE MUSICIANS JUST YELL AT EACH OTHER.
SCOTT and BORGMAN

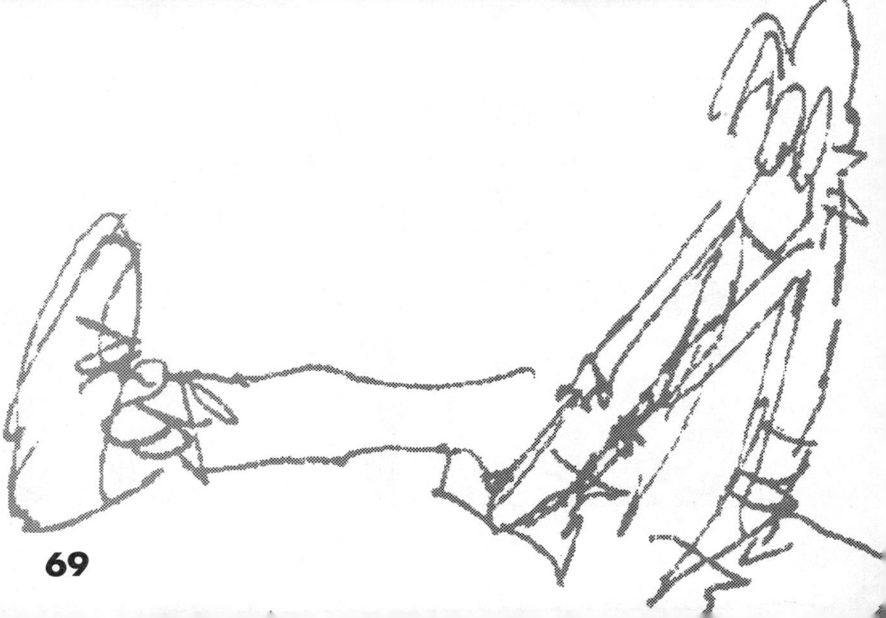

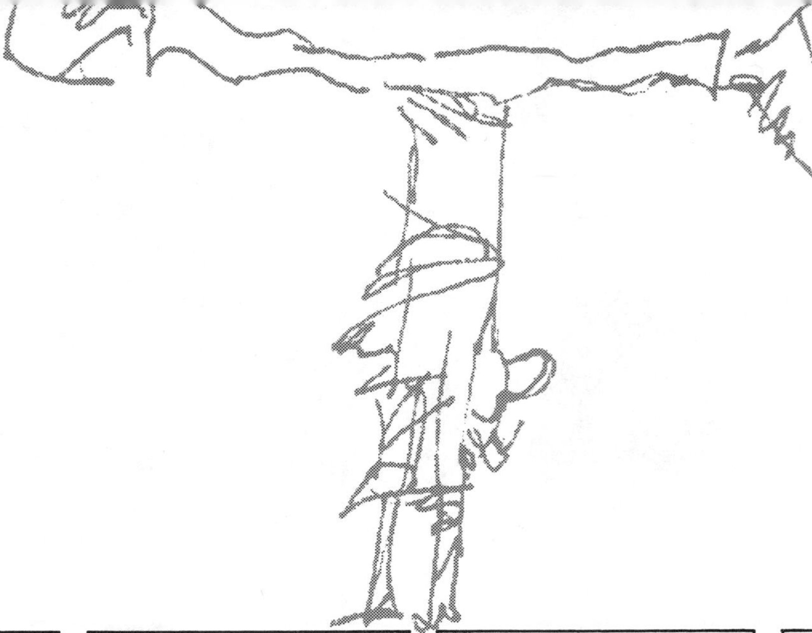

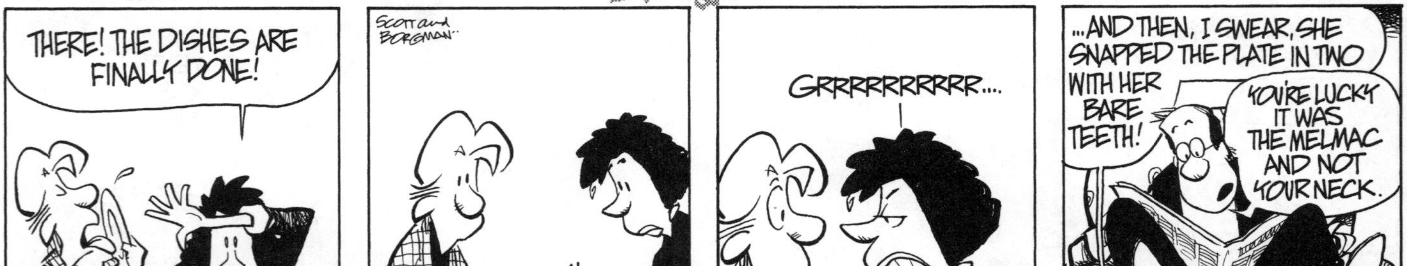

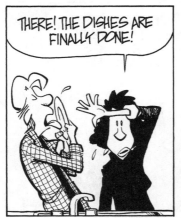

THERE! THE DISHES ARE FINALLY DONE!
SCOTT and BORGMAN
KLUNK!
GRRRRRRRRRR....
...AND THEN, I SWEAR, SHE SNAPPED THE PLATE IN TWO WITH HER BARE TEETH!
YOU'RE LUCKY IT WAS THE MELMAC AND NOT YOUR NECK.

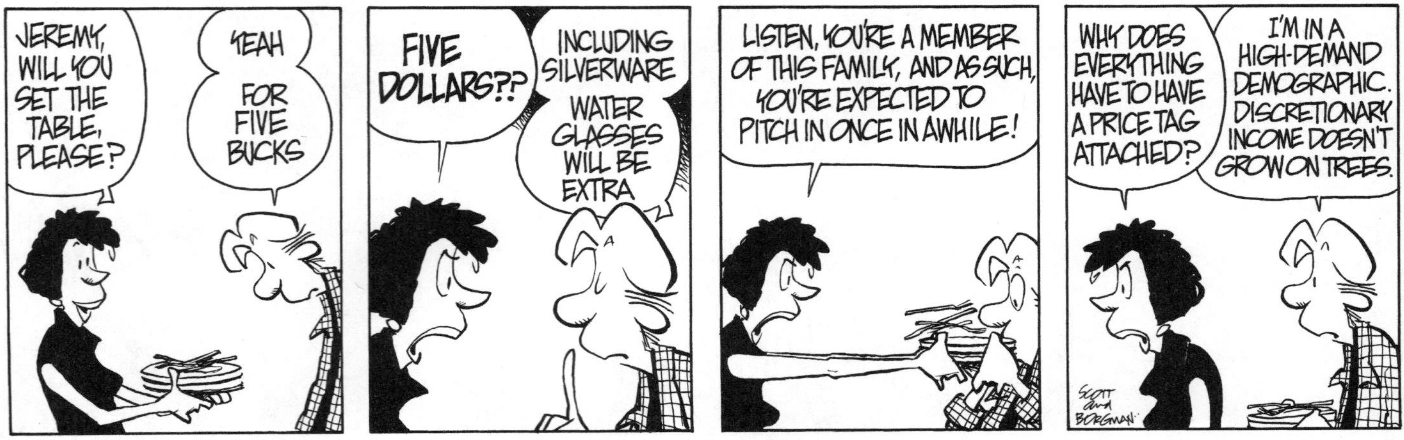

JEREMY, WILL YOU SET THE TABLE, PLEASE?
YEAH
FOR FIVE BUCKS
FIVE DOLLARS??
INCLUDING SILVERWARE
WATER GLASSES WILL BE EXTRA
LISTEN, YOU'RE A MEMBER OF THIS FAMILY, AND AS SUCH, YOU'RE EXPECTED TO PITCH IN ONCE IN AWHILE!
WHY DOES EVERYTHING HAVE TO HAVE A PRICE TAG ATTACHED?
I'M IN A HIGH-DEMAND DEMOGRAPHIC. DISCRETIONARY INCOME DOESN'T GROW ON TREES.
SCOTT and BORGMAN

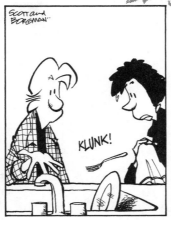

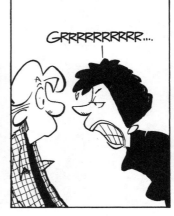

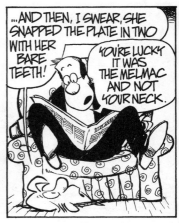

JERRY SCOTT and
JIM BORGMAN
Zits

TALK TO YOU LATER, DUDE.
LATER, JEREMY!
BYE
SEE YA, GUYS
BYE!
FOOM
I READ AN ARTICLE TODAY THAT SAID A TEENAGER'S SOCIAL LIFE AND HIS HOME LIFE ARE OFTEN WORLDS APART.
IF NOT LIGHT YEARS.

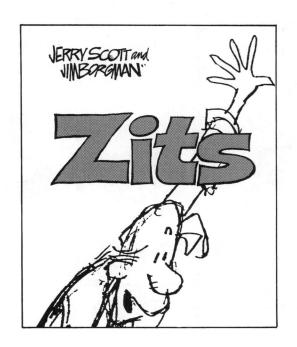

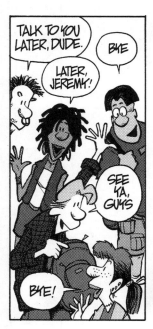

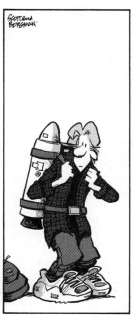

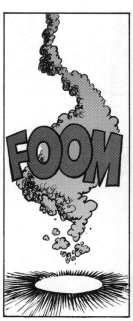

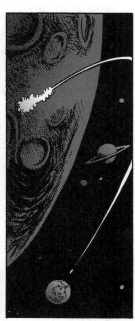

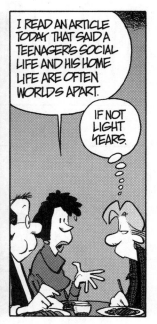

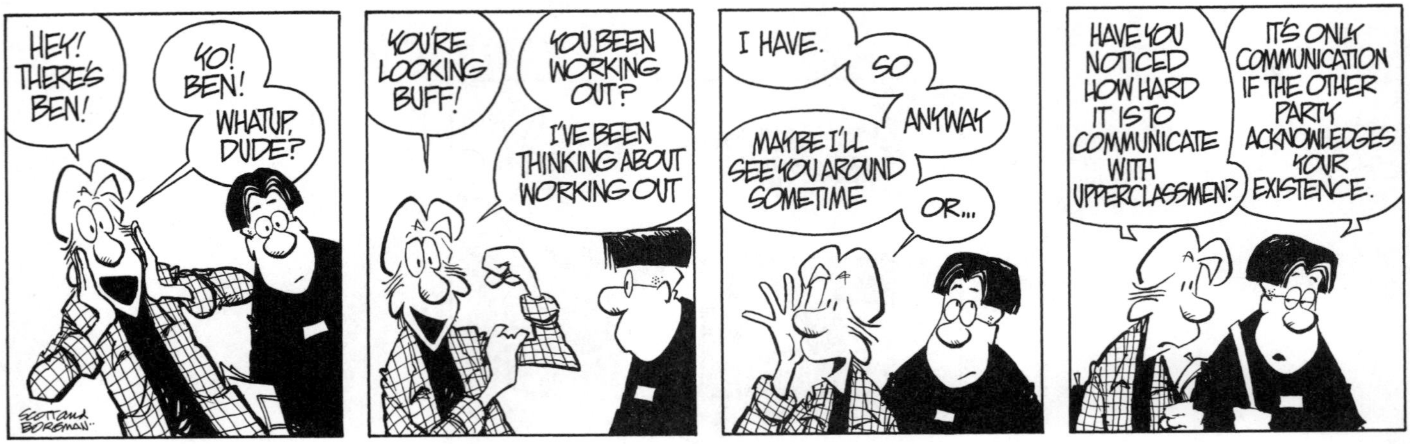
HEY! THERE'S BEN!
YO! BEN!
WHATUP, DUDE?
SCOTT and BORGMAN
YOU'RE LOOKING BUFF!
YOU BEEN WORKING OUT?
I'VE BEEN THINKING ABOUT WORKING OUT
I HAVE.
SO
ANYWAY
MAYBE I'LL SEE YOU AROUND SOMETIME
OR...
HAVE YOU NOTICED HOW HARD IT IS TO COMMUNICATE WITH UPPERCLASSMEN?
IT'S ONLY COMMUNICATION IF THE OTHER PARTY ACKNOWLEDGES YOUR EXISTENCE.

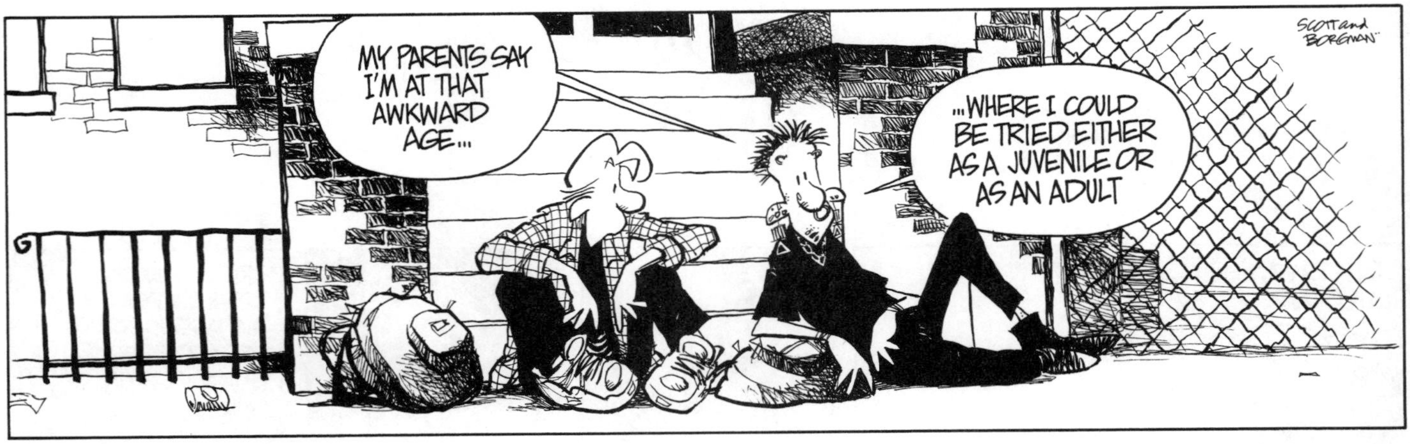
SCOTT and BORGMAN
MY PARENTS SAY I'M AT THAT AWKWARD AGE...
...WHERE I COULD BE TRIED EITHER AS A JUVENILE OR AS AN ADULT

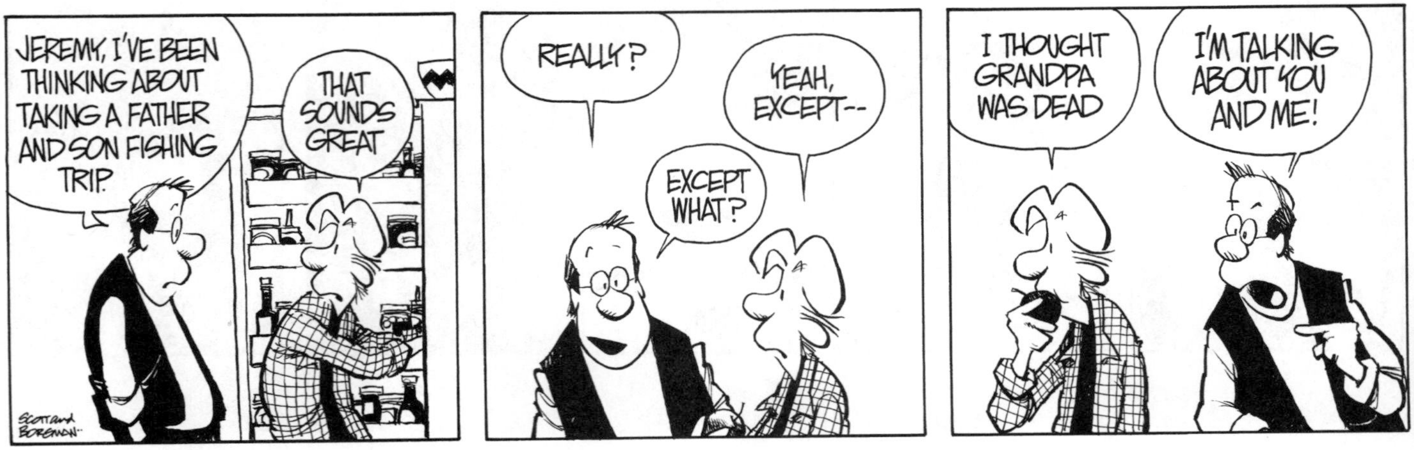
JEREMY, I'VE BEEN THINKING ABOUT TAKING A FATHER AND SON FISHING TRIP.
THAT SOUNDS GREAT
SCOTT and BORGMAN
REALLY?
YEAH, EXCEPT--
EXCEPT WHAT?
I THOUGHT GRANDPA WAS DEAD
I'M TALKING ABOUT YOU AND ME!

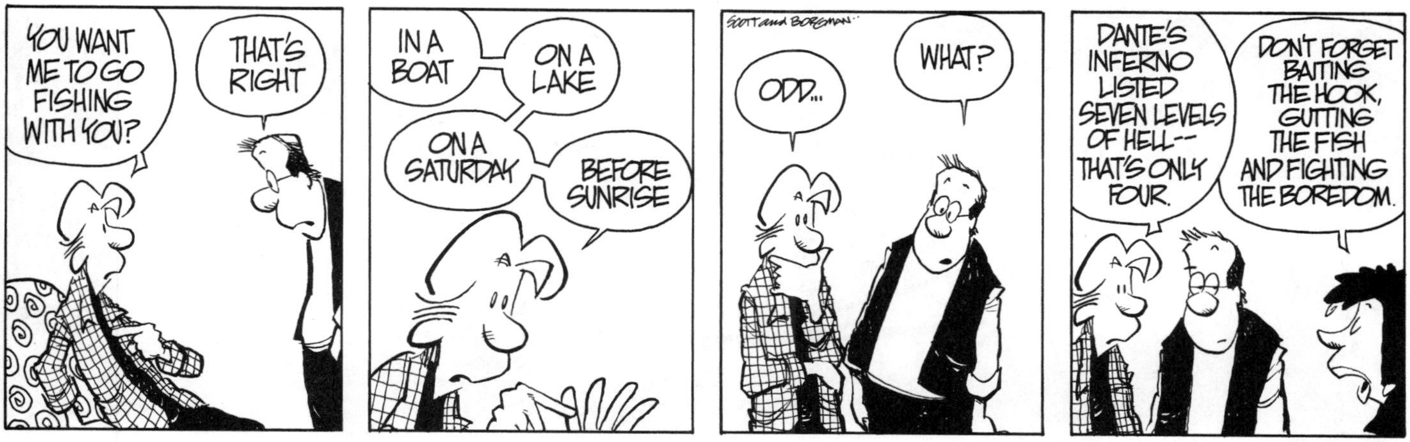
YOU WANT ME TO GO FISHING WITH YOU?
THAT'S RIGHT
IN A BOAT
ON A LAKE
ON A SATURDAY
BEFORE SUNRISE
SCOTT and BORGMAN
ODD...
WHAT?
DANTE'S INFERNO LISTED SEVEN LEVELS OF HELL-- THAT'S ONLY FOUR.
DON'T FORGET BAITING THE HOOK, GUTTING THE FISH AND FIGHTING THE BOREDOM.

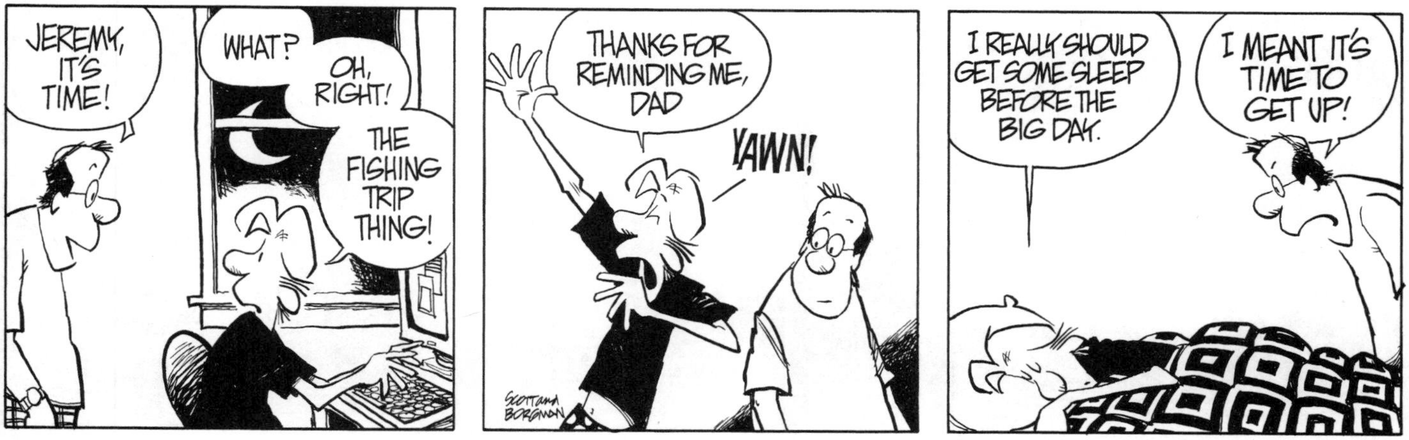
JEREMY, IT'S TIME!
WHAT?
OH, RIGHT!
THE FISHING TRIP THING!
THANKS FOR REMINDING ME, DAD
YAWN!
SCOTT and BORGMAN
I REALLY SHOULD GET SOME SLEEP BEFORE THE BIG DAY.
I MEANT IT'S TIME TO GET UP!

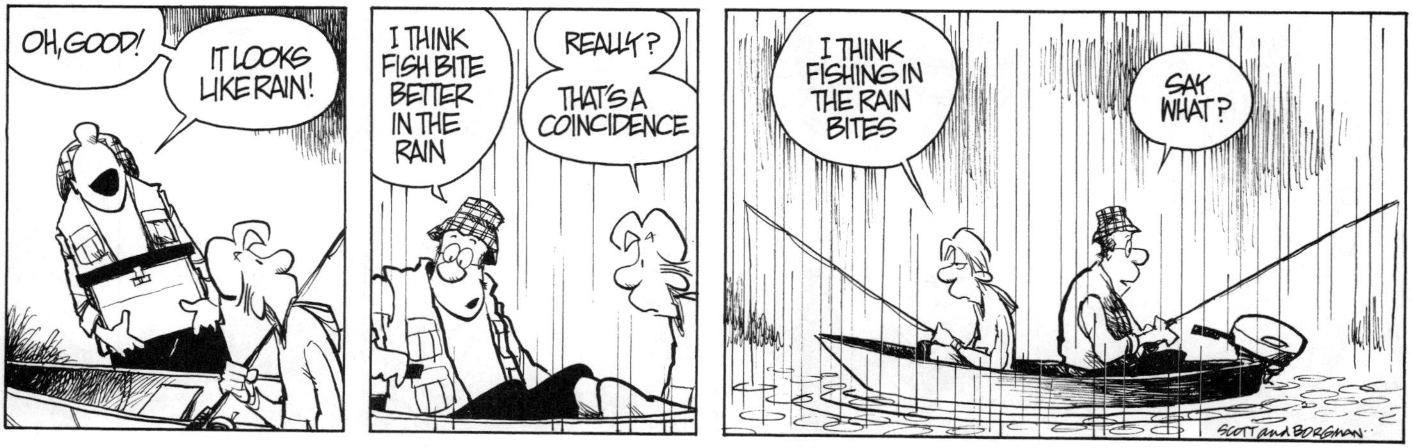
OH, GOOD!
IT LOOKS LIKE RAIN!
I THINK FISH BITE BETTER IN THE RAIN
REALLY?
THAT'S A COINCIDENCE
I THINK FISHING IN THE RAIN BITES
SAY WHAT?
SCOTT and BORGMAN

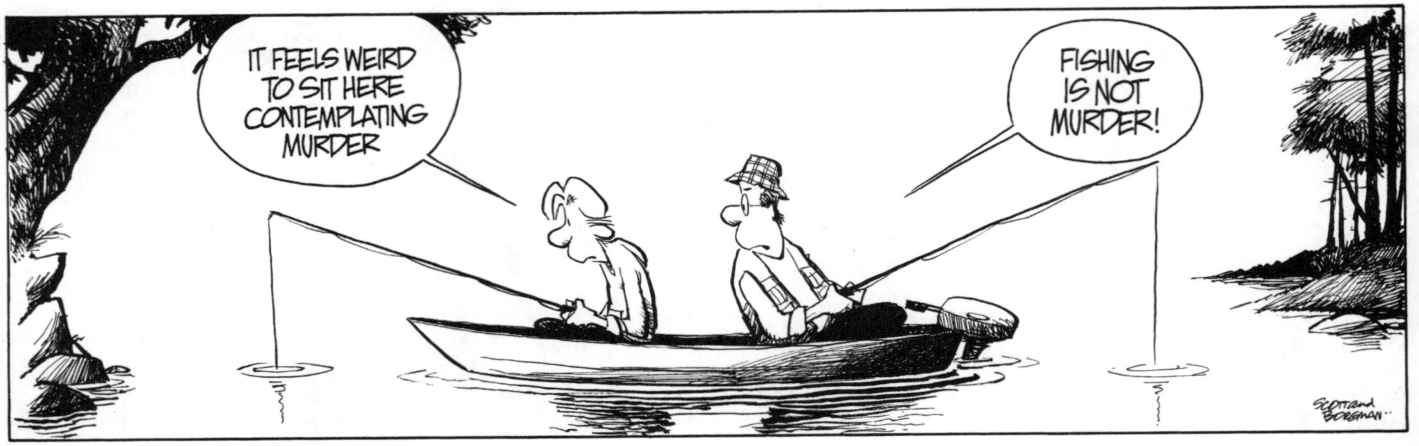
IT FEELS WEIRD TO SIT HERE CONTEMPLATING MURDER
FISHING IS NOT MURDER!
SCOTT and BORGMAN

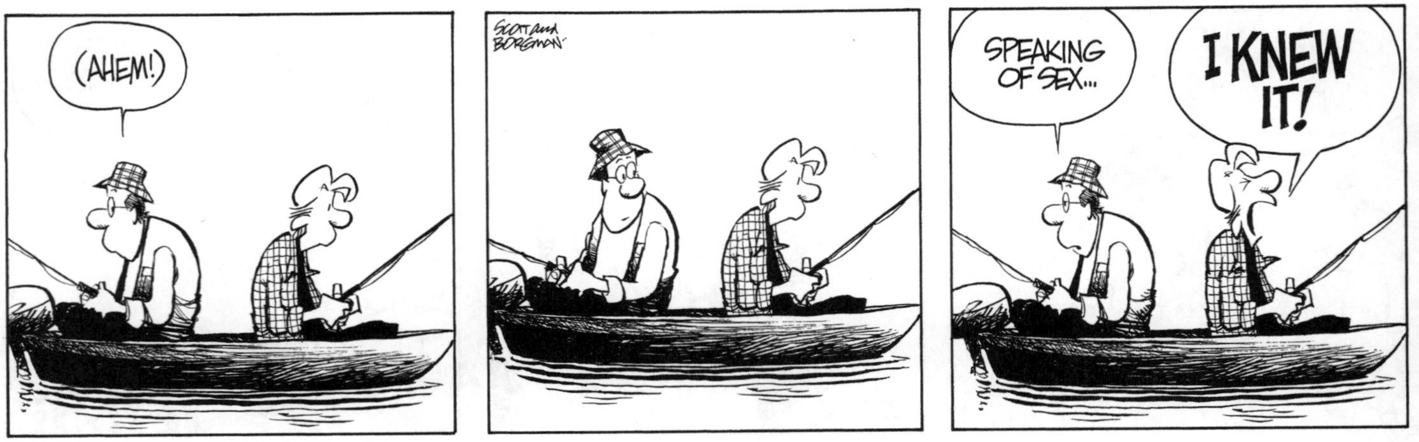
(AHEM!)
SCOTT and BORGMAN
SPEAKING OF SEX...
I KNEW IT!

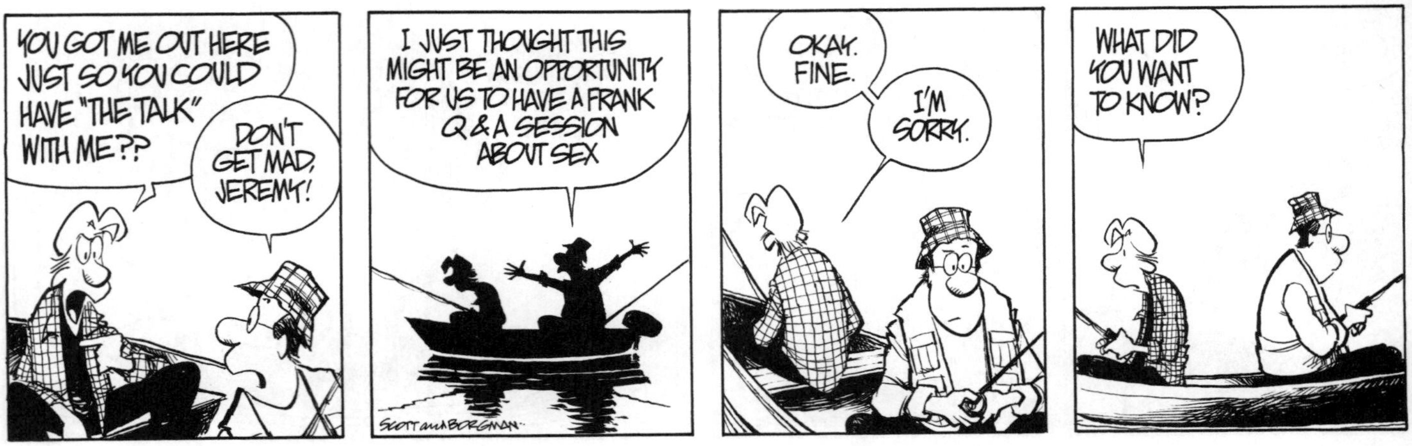
YOU GOT ME OUT HERE JUST SO YOU COULD HAVE "THE TALK" WITH ME??
DON'T GET MAD, JEREMY!
I JUST THOUGHT THIS MIGHT BE AN OPPORTUNITY FOR US TO HAVE A FRANK Q & A SESSION ABOUT SEX
SCOTT and BORGMAN
OKAY. FINE.
I'M SORRY.
WHAT DID YOU WANT TO KNOW?

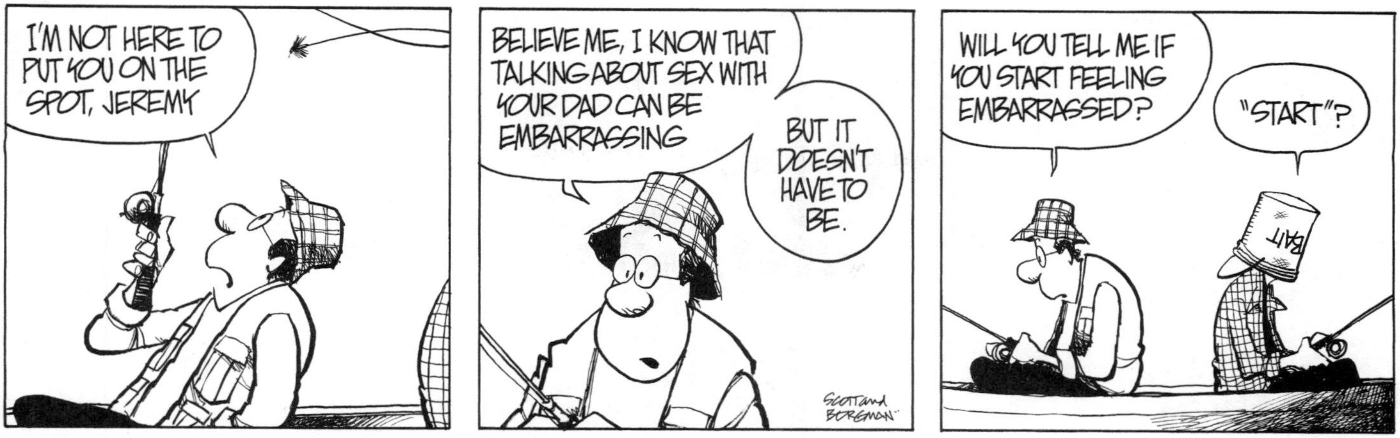
I'M NOT HERE TO PUT YOU ON THE SPOT, JEREMY
BELIEVE ME, I KNOW THAT TALKING ABOUT SEX WITH YOUR DAD CAN BE EMBARRASSING
BUT IT DOESN'T HAVE TO BE.
SCOTT AND BORGMAN
WILL YOU TELL ME IF YOU START FEELING EMBARRASSED?
"START"?
BAIT

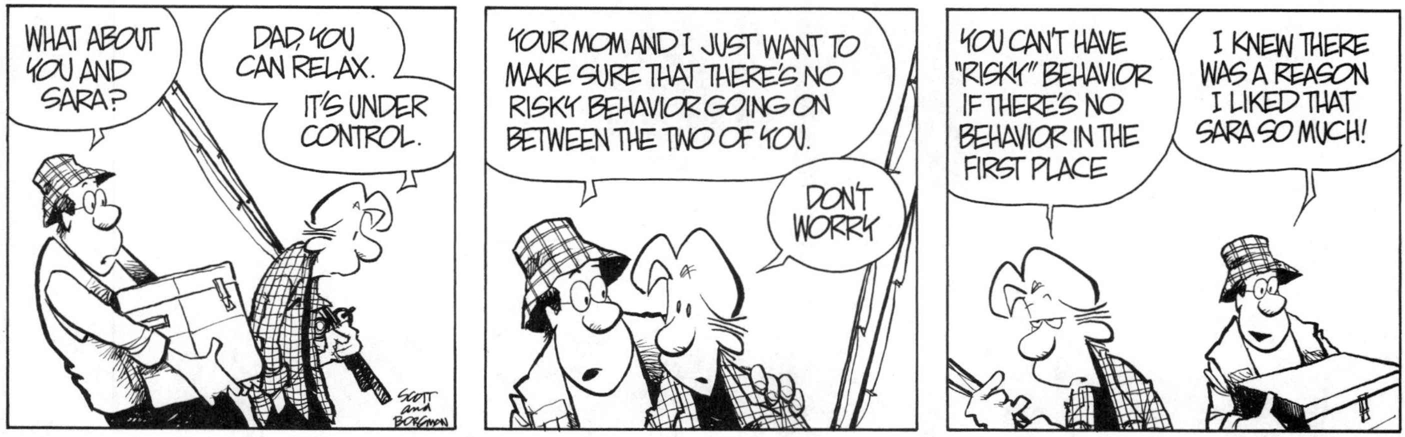
WHAT ABOUT YOU AND SARA?
DAD, YOU CAN RELAX.
IT'S UNDER CONTROL.
SCOTT AND BORGMAN
YOUR MOM AND I JUST WANT TO MAKE SURE THAT THERE'S NO RISKY BEHAVIOR GOING ON BETWEEN THE TWO OF YOU.
DON'T WORRY
YOU CAN'T HAVE "RISKY" BEHAVIOR IF THERE'S NO BEHAVIOR IN THE FIRST PLACE
I KNEW THERE WAS A REASON I LIKED THAT SARA SO MUCH!

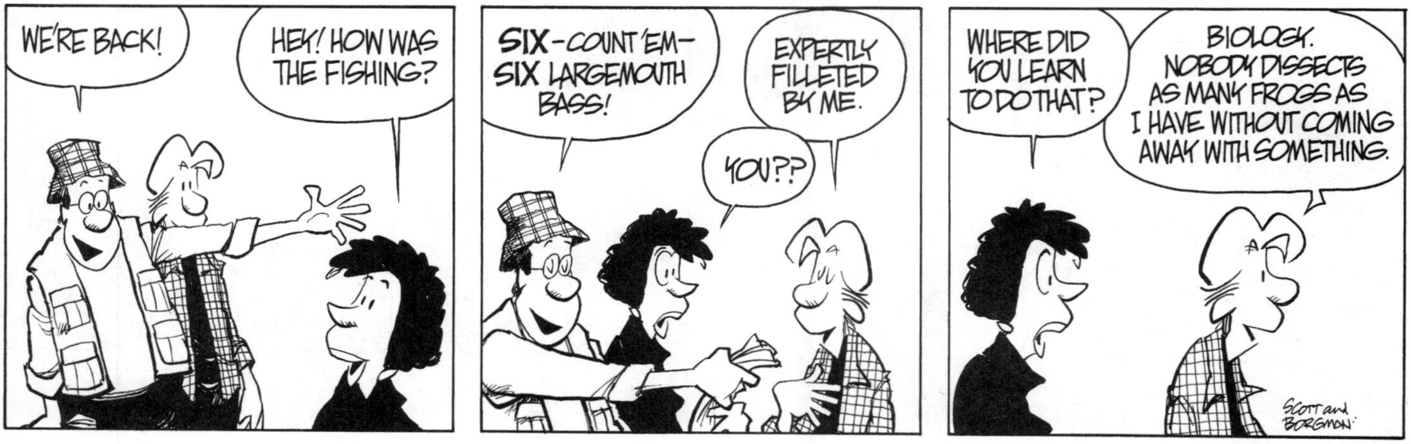
WE'RE BACK!
HEY! HOW WAS THE FISHING?
SIX-COUNT 'EM-SIX LARGEMOUTH BASS!
EXPERTLY FILLETED BY ME.
YOU??
WHERE DID YOU LEARN TO DO THAT?
BIOLOGY. NOBODY DISSECTS AS MANY FROGS AS I HAVE WITHOUT COMING AWAY WITH SOMETHING.
SCOTT AND BORGMAN

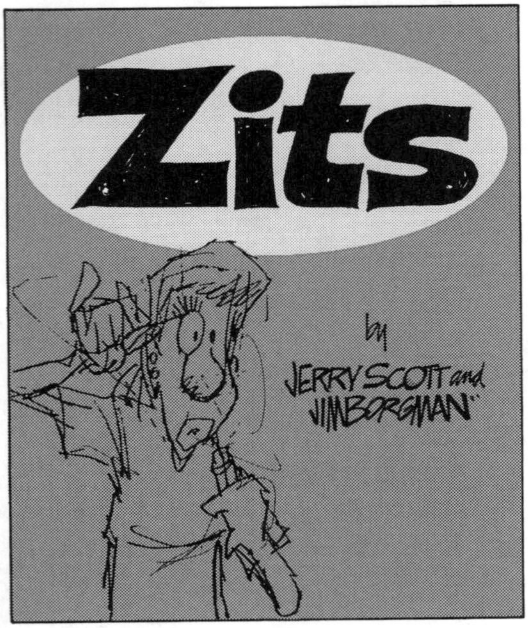
Zits
by
JERRY SCOTT and
JIM BORGMAN

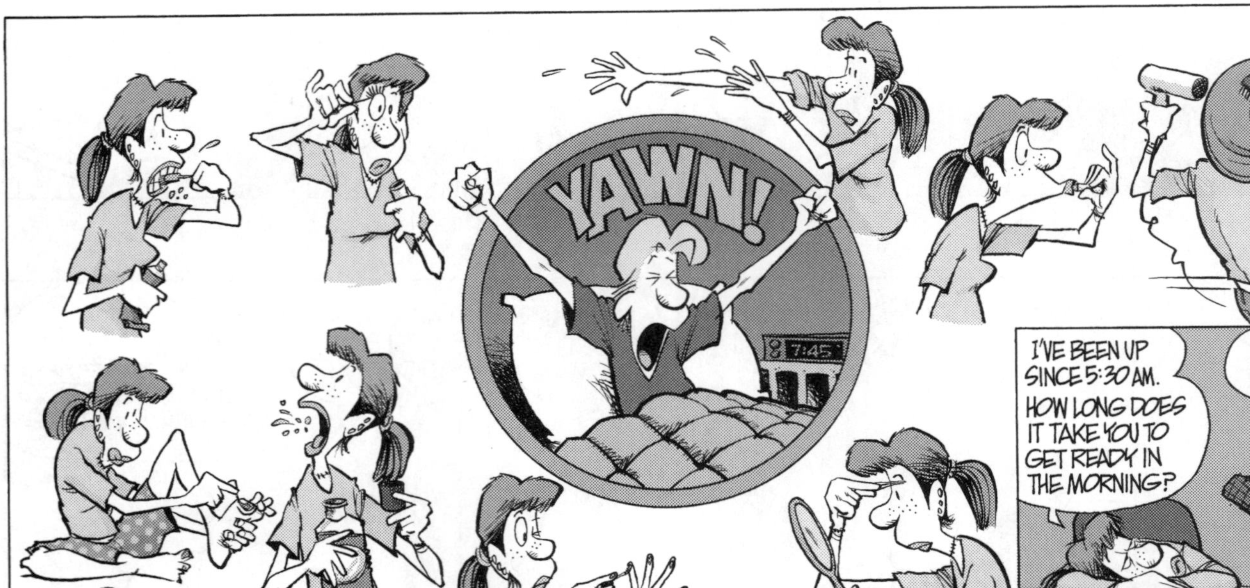
SCOTT and BORGMAN
YAWN!
7:45
I'VE BEEN UP SINCE 5:30 AM.
HOW LONG DOES IT TAKE YOU TO GET READY IN THE MORNING?
READY FOR WHAT?

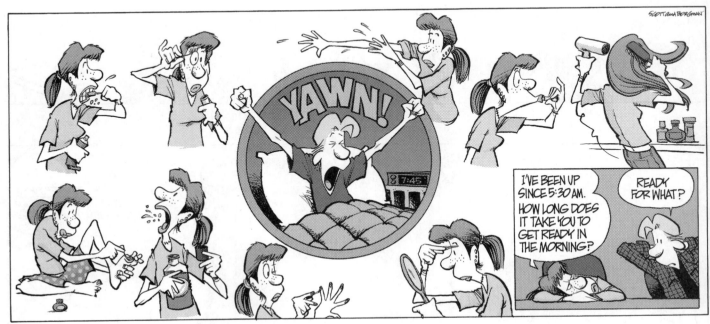

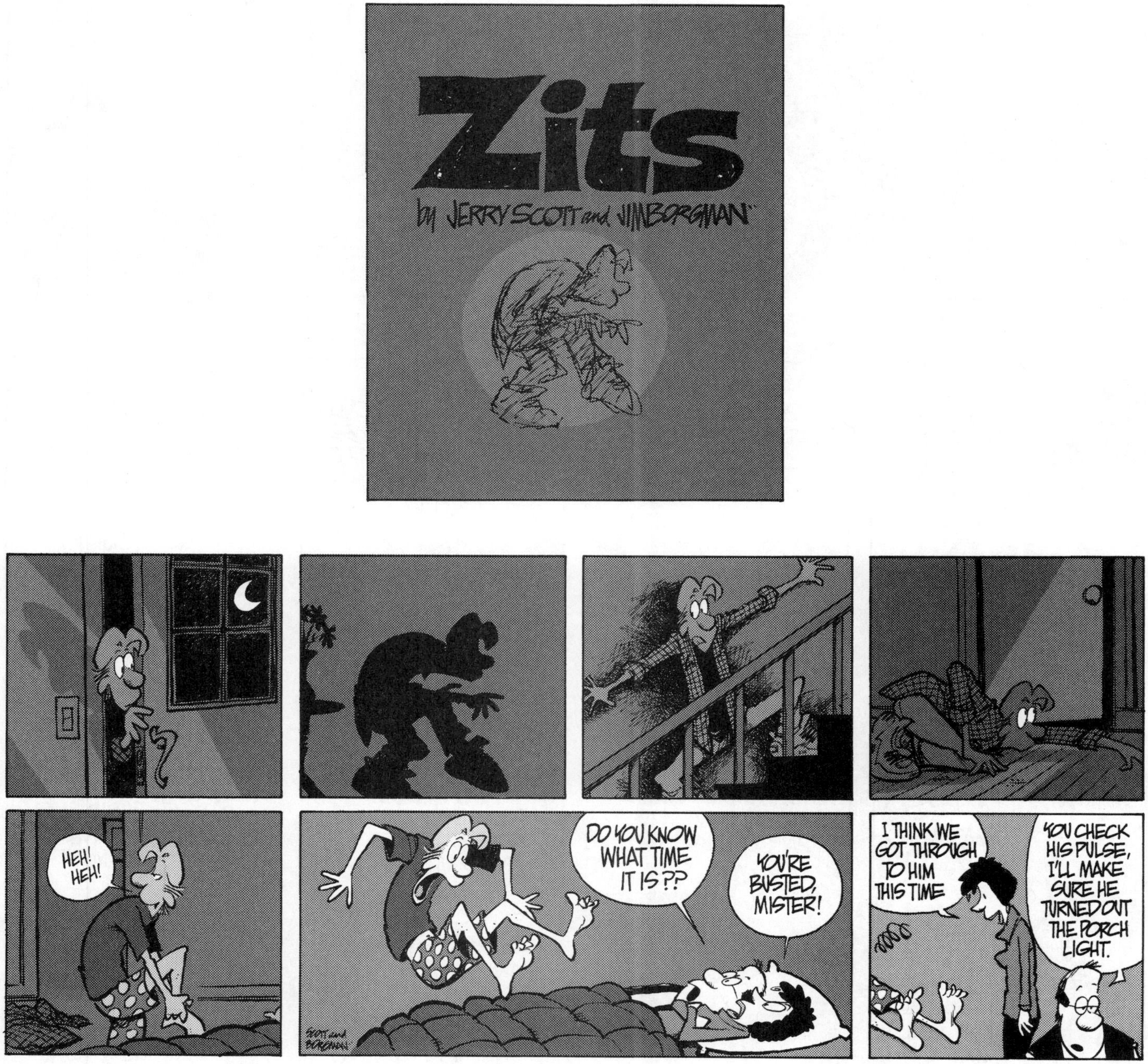
Zits
by JERRY SCOTT and JIM BORGMAN
HEH! HEH!
DO YOU KNOW WHAT TIME IT IS??
YOU'RE BUSTED, MISTER!
SCOTT and BORGMAN
I THINK WE GOT THROUGH TO HIM THIS TIME
YOU CHECK HIS PULSE, I'LL MAKE SURE HE TURNED OUT THE PORCH LIGHT.

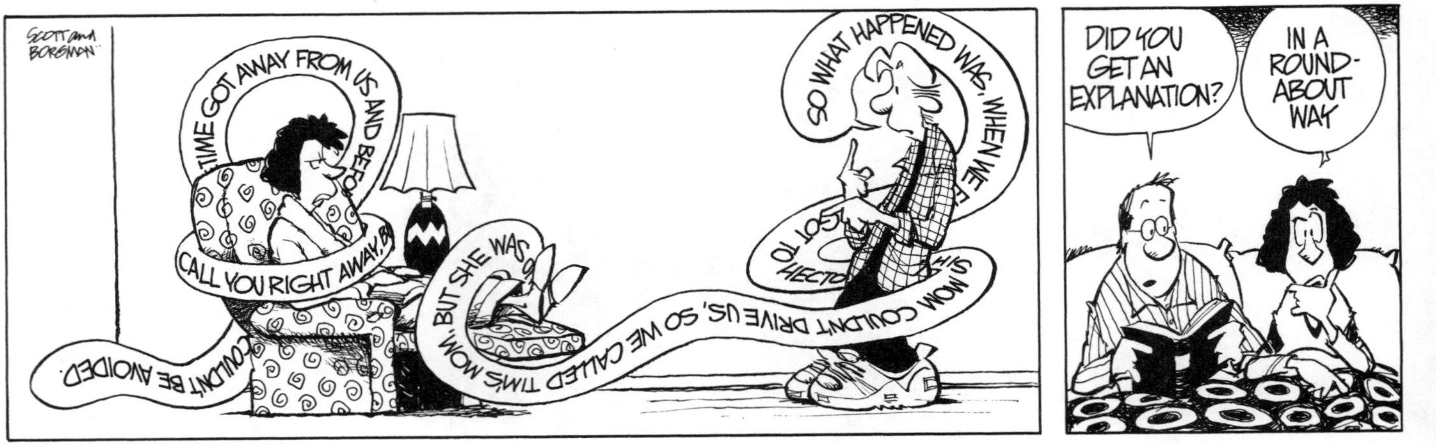
SCOTT and BORGMAN
SO WHAT HAPPENED WAS, WHEN WE
GOT TO
HECTO
HIS MOM COULDN'T DRIVE US, SO WE CALLED TIM'S MOM, BUT SHE WAS
TIME GOT AWAY FROM US AND BEFO
CALL YOU RIGHT AWAY, B
COULDN'T BE AVOIDED.
DID YOU GET AN EXPLANATION?
IN A ROUND-ABOUT WAY

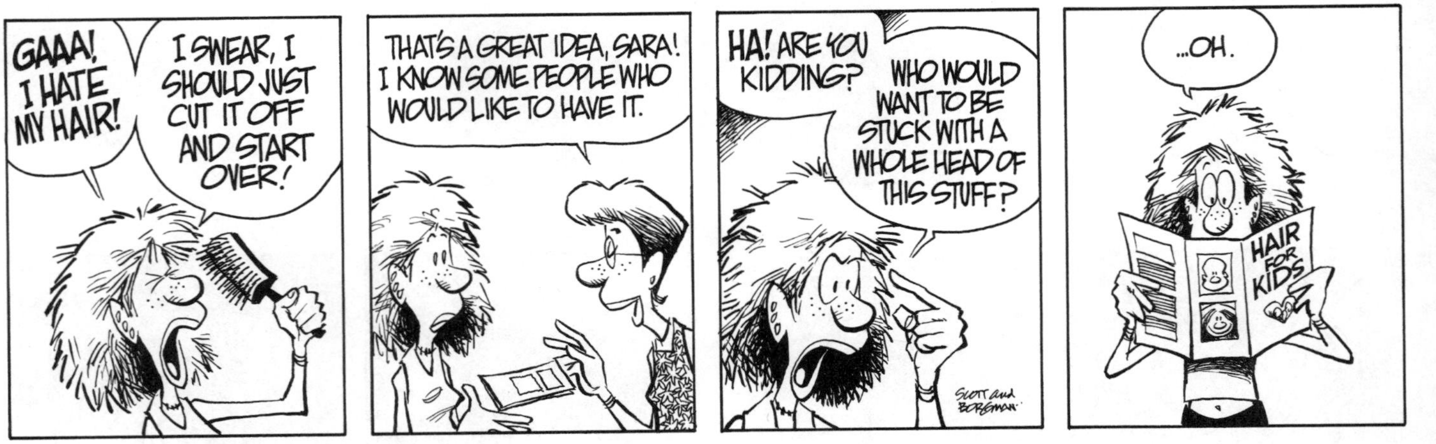
GAAA! I HATE MY HAIR!
I SWEAR, I SHOULD JUST CUT IT OFF AND START OVER!
THAT'S A GREAT IDEA, SARA! I KNOW SOME PEOPLE WHO WOULD LIKE TO HAVE IT.
HA! ARE YOU KIDDING?
WHO WOULD WANT TO BE STUCK WITH A WHOLE HEAD OF THIS STUFF?
SCOTT and BORGMAN
...OH.
HAIR FOR KIDS

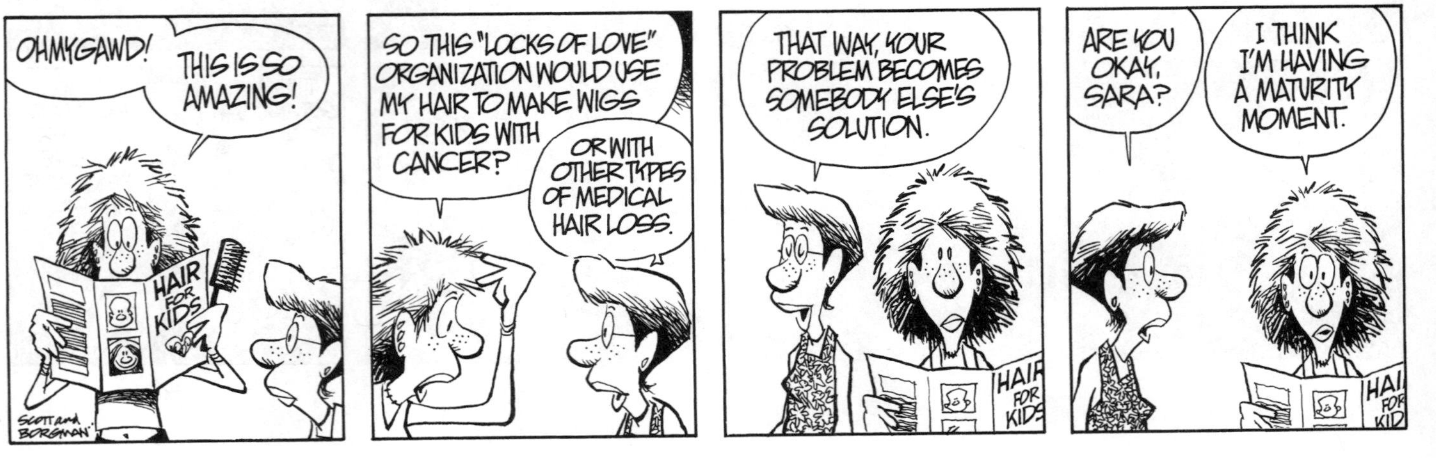
OHMYGAWD!
THIS IS SO AMAZING!
HAIR FOR KIDS
SCOTT and BORGMAN
SO THIS "LOCKS OF LOVE" ORGANIZATION WOULD USE MY HAIR TO MAKE WIGS FOR KIDS WITH CANCER?
OR WITH OTHER TYPES OF MEDICAL HAIR LOSS.
THAT WAY, YOUR PROBLEM BECOMES SOMEBODY ELSE'S SOLUTION.
ARE YOU OKAY, SARA?
I THINK I'M HAVING A MATURITY MOMENT.

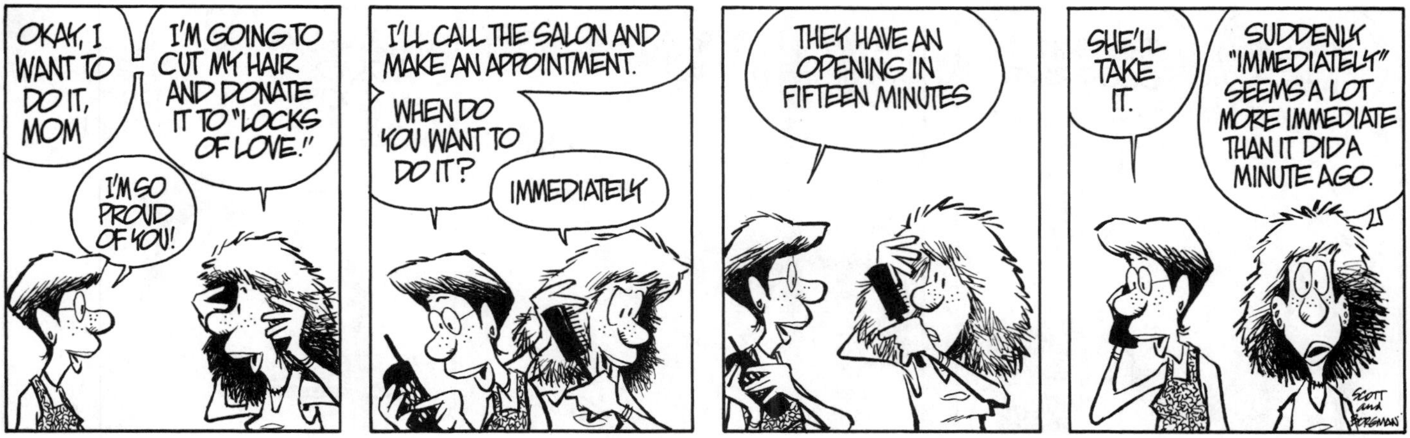
OKAY, I WANT TO DO IT, MOM
I'M GOING TO CUT MY HAIR AND DONATE IT TO "LOCKS OF LOVE."
I'M SO PROUD OF YOU!
I'LL CALL THE SALON AND MAKE AN APPOINTMENT.
WHEN DO YOU WANT TO DO IT?
IMMEDIATELY
THEY HAVE AN OPENING IN FIFTEEN MINUTES
SHE'LL TAKE IT.
SUDDENLY "IMMEDIATELY" SEEMS A LOT MORE IMMEDIATE THAN IT DID A MINUTE AGO.
SCOTT and BORGMAN

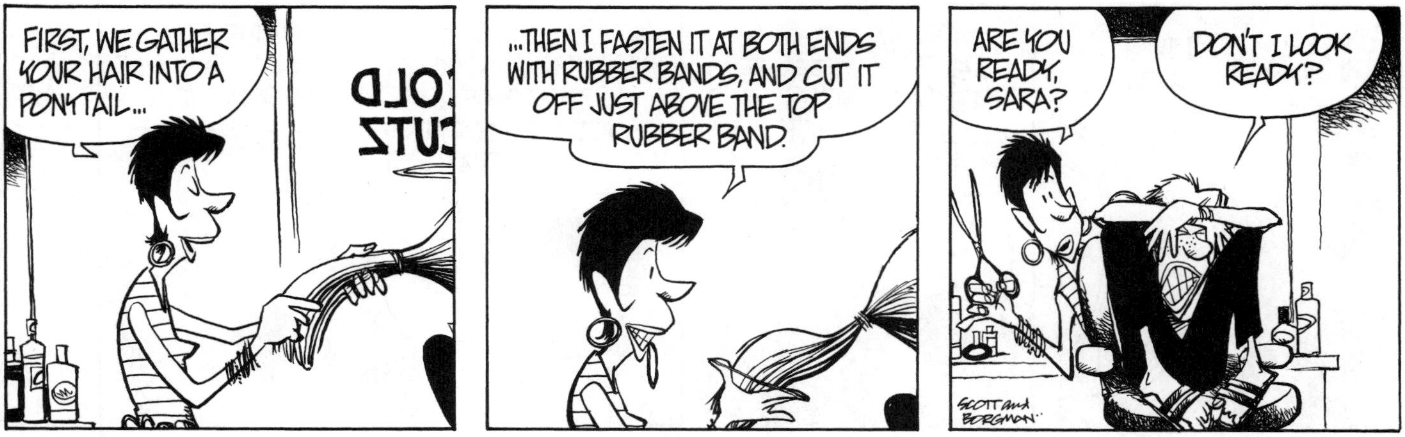
FIRST, WE GATHER YOUR HAIR INTO A PONYTAIL...
...THEN I FASTEN IT AT BOTH ENDS WITH RUBBER BANDS, AND CUT IT OFF JUST ABOVE THE TOP RUBBER BAND.
ARE YOU READY, SARA?
DON'T I LOOK READY?
SCOTT and BORGMAN

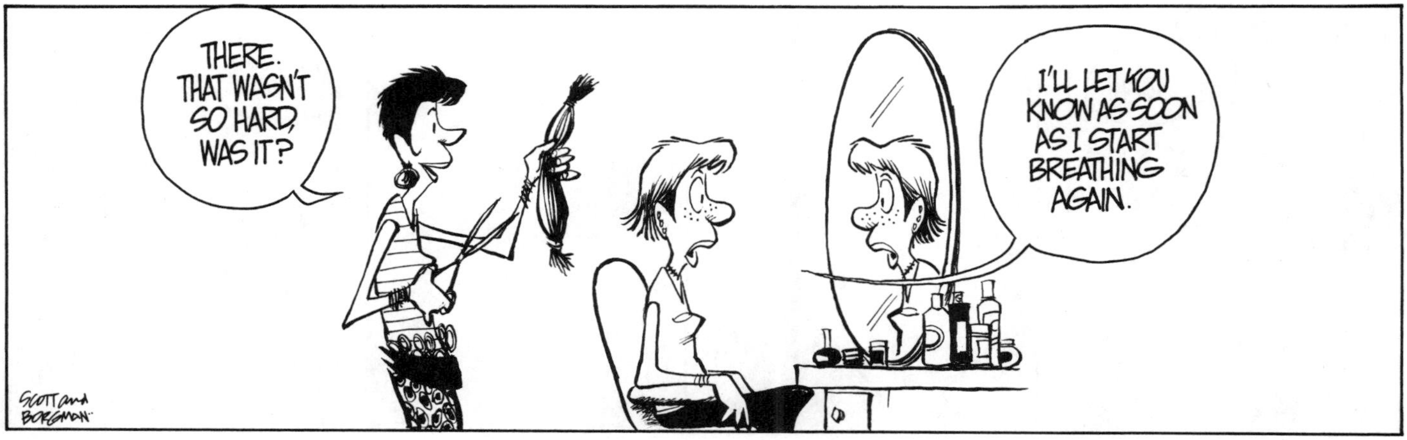
THERE. THAT WASN'T SO HARD, WAS IT?
I'LL LET YOU KNOW AS SOON AS I START BREATHING AGAIN.
SCOTT and BORGMAN

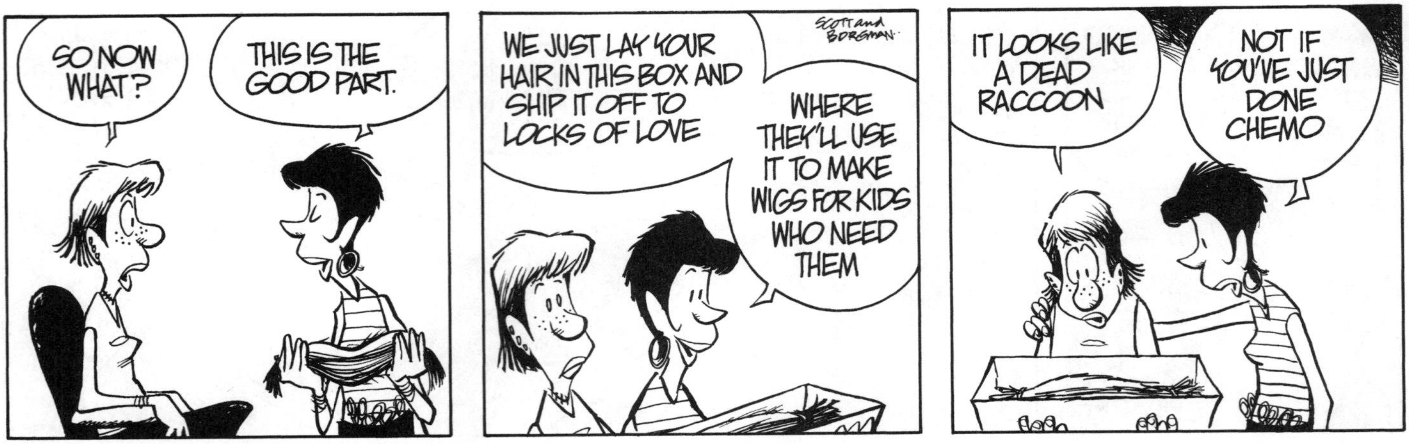
SO NOW WHAT?
THIS IS THE GOOD PART.
SCOTT and BORGMAN
WE JUST LAY YOUR HAIR IN THIS BOX AND SHIP IT OFF TO LOCKS OF LOVE
WHERE THEY'LL USE IT TO MAKE WIGS FOR KIDS WHO NEED THEM
IT LOOKS LIKE A DEAD RACCOON
NOT IF YOU'VE JUST DONE CHEMO

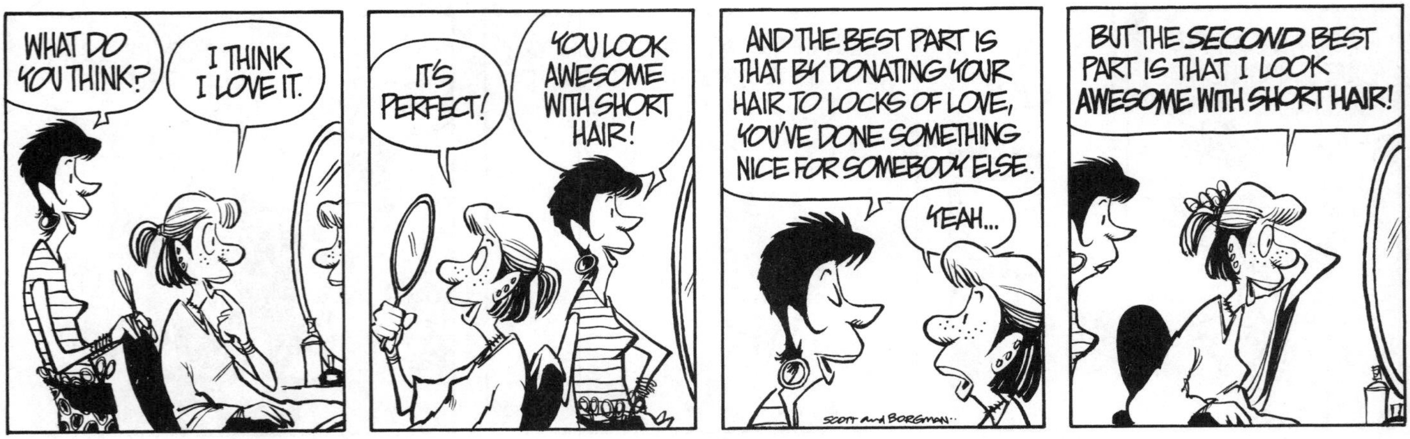
WHAT DO YOU THINK?
I THINK I LOVE IT.
IT'S PERFECT!
YOU LOOK AWESOME WITH SHORT HAIR!
AND THE BEST PART IS THAT BY DONATING YOUR HAIR TO LOCKS OF LOVE, YOU'VE DONE SOMETHING NICE FOR SOMEBODY ELSE.
YEAH...
SCOTT and BORGMAN
BUT THE *SECOND* BEST PART IS THAT I LOOK **AWESOME WITH SHORT HAIR!**

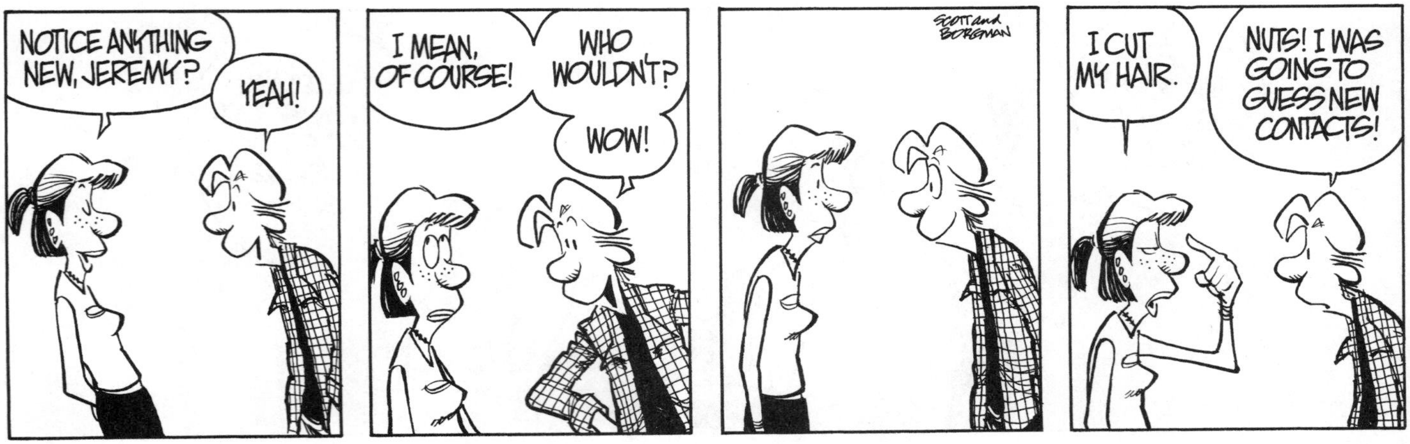
NOTICE ANYTHING NEW, JEREMY?
YEAH!
I MEAN, OF COURSE!
WHO WOULDN'T?
WOW!
SCOTT and BORGMAN
I CUT MY HAIR.
NUTS! I WAS GOING TO GUESS NEW CONTACTS!

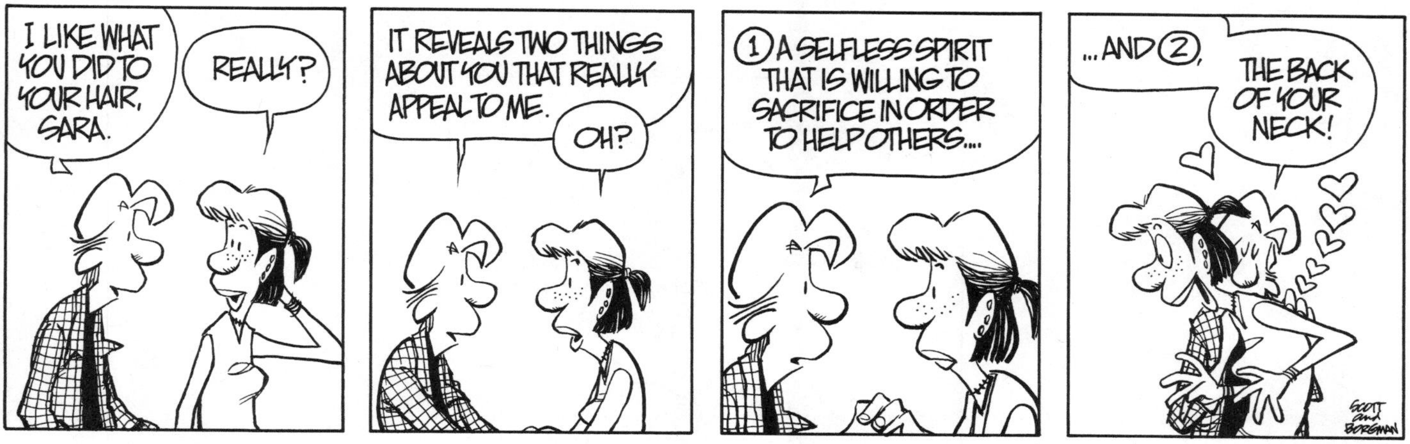
I LIKE WHAT YOU DID TO YOUR HAIR, SARA.
REALLY?
IT REVEALS TWO THINGS ABOUT YOU THAT REALLY APPEAL TO ME.
OH?
1 A SELFLESS SPIRIT THAT IS WILLING TO SACRIFICE IN ORDER TO HELP OTHERS....
...AND 2,
THE BACK OF YOUR NECK!
SCOTT and BORGMAN

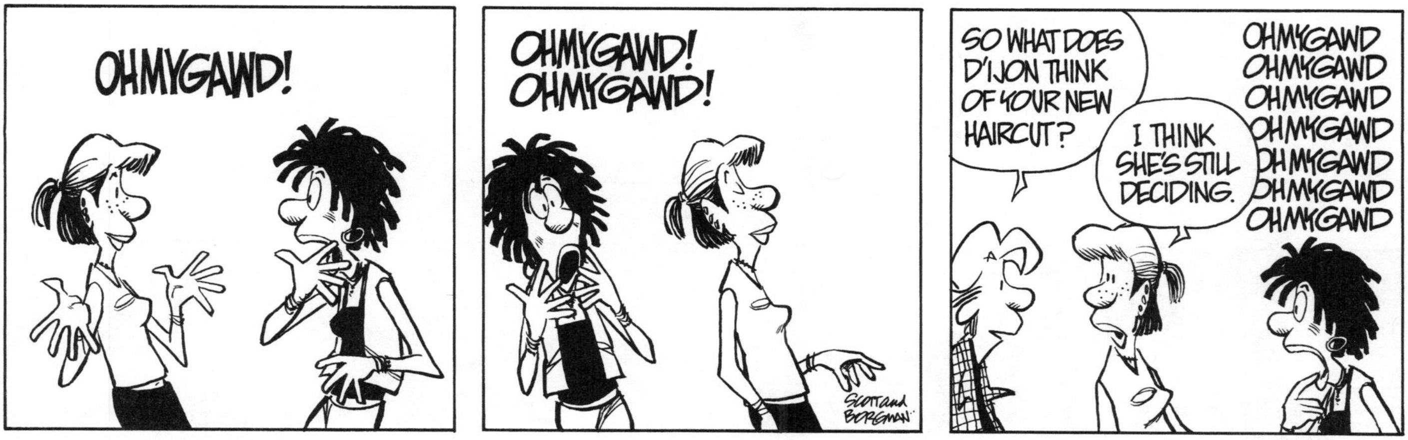
OHMYGAWD!
OHMYGAWD! OHMYGAWD!
SCOTT and BORGMAN
SO WHAT DOES D'IJON THINK OF YOUR NEW HAIRCUT?
I THINK SHE'S STILL DECIDING.
OHMYGAWD OHMYGAWD OHMYGAWD OHMYGAWD OHMYGAWD OHMYGAWD OHMYGAWD

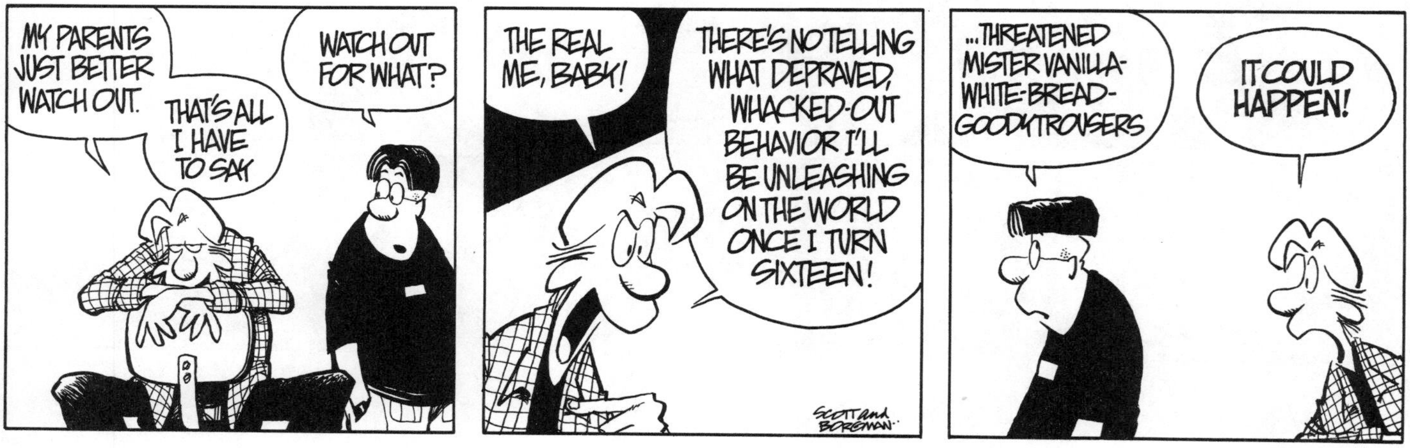
MY PARENTS JUST BETTER WATCH OUT.
THAT'S ALL I HAVE TO SAY.
WATCH OUT FOR WHAT?
THE REAL ME, BABY!
THERE'S NO TELLING WHAT DEPRAVED, WHACKED-OUT BEHAVIOR I'LL BE UNLEASHING ON THE WORLD ONCE I TURN SIXTEEN!
SCOTT and BORGMAN
...THREATENED MISTER VANILLA-WHITE-BREAD-GOODYTROUSERS
IT COULD HAPPEN!

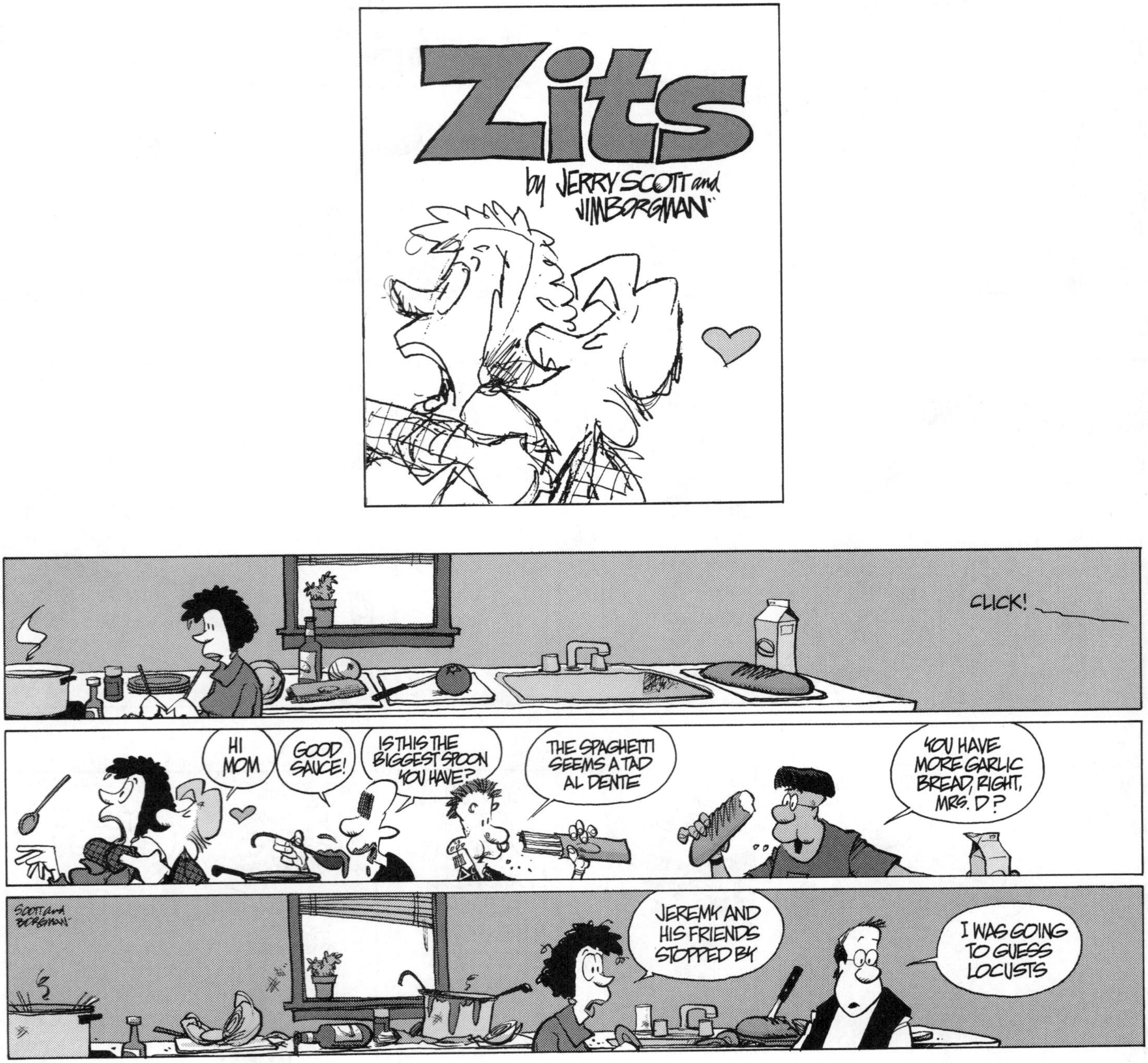
Zits
by JERRY SCOTT and JIM BORGMAN
CLICK!
HI MOM
GOOD SAUCE!
IS THIS THE BIGGEST SPOON YOU HAVE?
THE SPAGHETTI SEEMS A TAD AL DENTE
YOU HAVE MORE GARLIC BREAD, RIGHT, MRS. D?
SCOTT and BORGMAN
JEREMY AND HIS FRIENDS STOPPED BY
I WAS GOING TO GUESS LOCUSTS

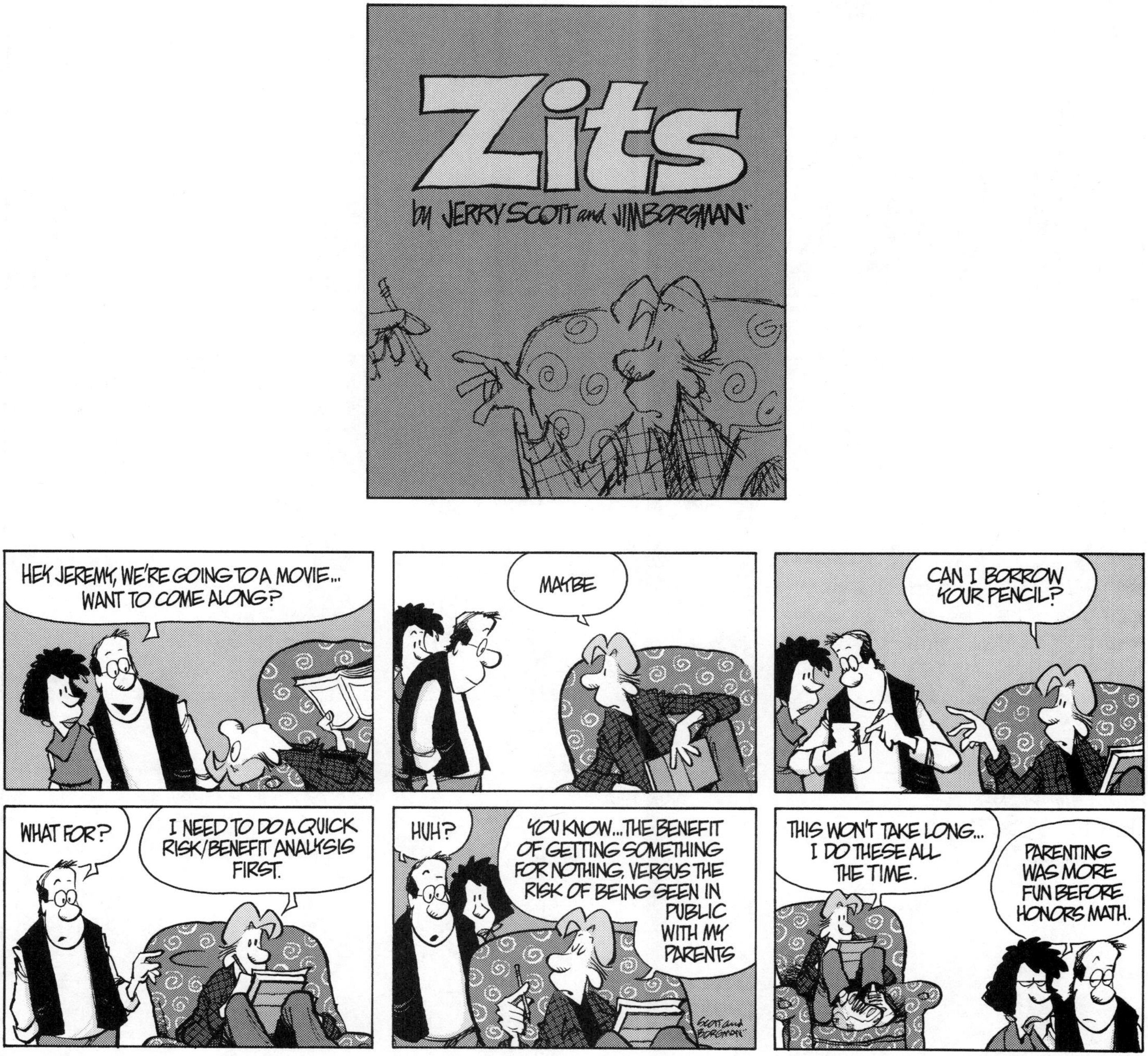
Zits
by JERRY SCOTT and JIM BORGMAN
HEY JEREMY, WE'RE GOING TO A MOVIE... WANT TO COME ALONG?
MAYBE
CAN I BORROW YOUR PENCIL?
WHAT FOR?
I NEED TO DO A QUICK RISK/BENEFIT ANALYSIS FIRST.
HUH?
YOU KNOW...THE BENEFIT OF GETTING SOMETHING FOR NOTHING, VERSUS THE RISK OF BEING SEEN IN PUBLIC WITH MY PARENTS
SCOTT and BORGMAN
THIS WON'T TAKE LONG... I DO THESE ALL THE TIME.
PARENTING WAS MORE FUN BEFORE HONORS MATH.

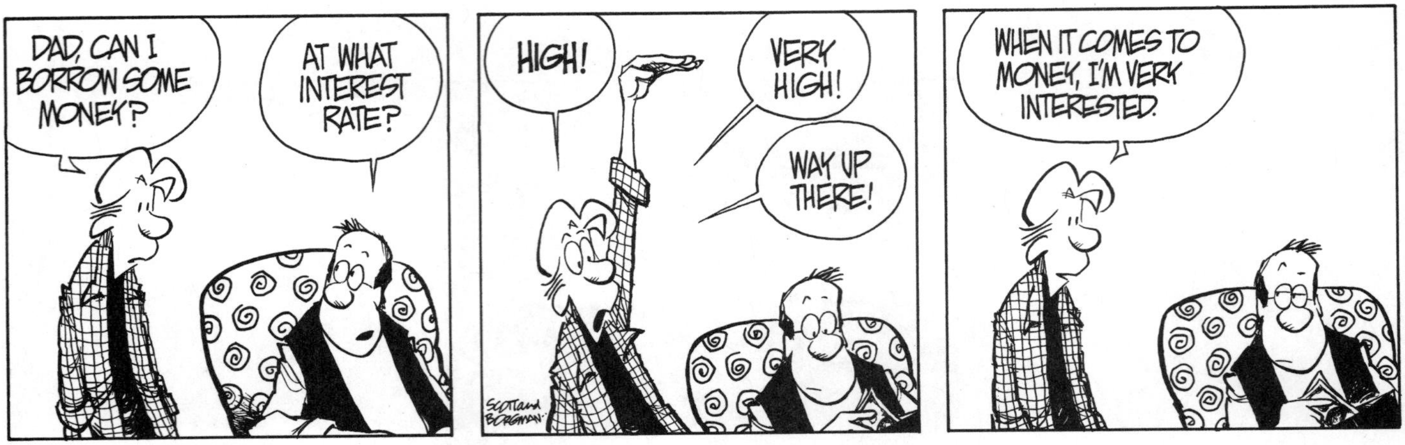
DAD, CAN I BORROW SOME MONEY?
AT WHAT INTEREST RATE?
HIGH!
VERY HIGH!
WAY UP THERE!
WHEN IT COMES TO MONEY, I'M VERY INTERESTED.

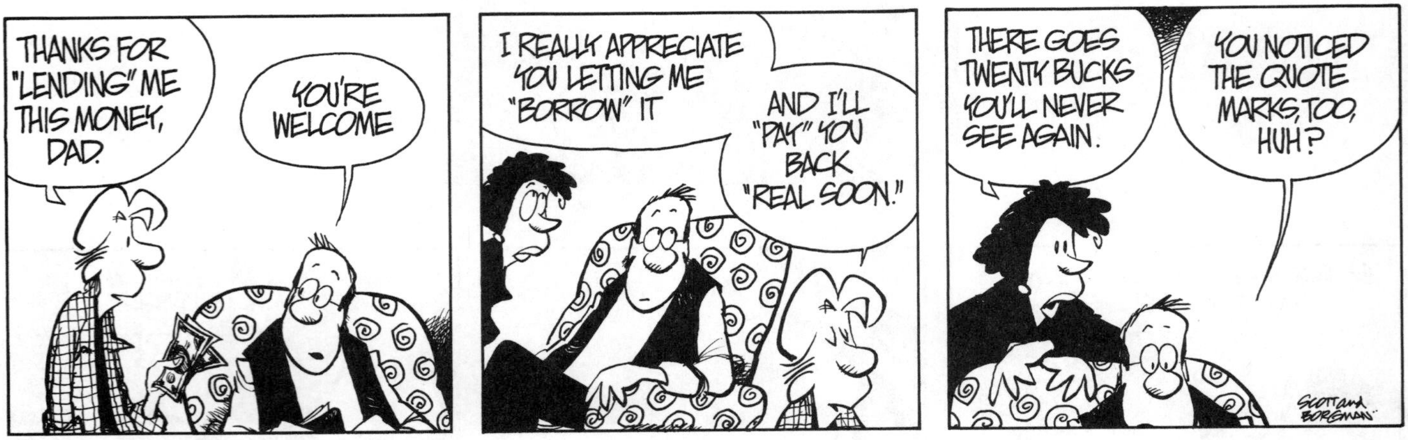
THANKS FOR "LENDING" ME THIS MONEY, DAD.
YOU'RE WELCOME
I REALLY APPRECIATE YOU LETTING ME "BORROW" IT
AND I'LL "PAY" YOU BACK "REAL SOON."
THERE GOES TWENTY BUCKS YOU'LL NEVER SEE AGAIN.
YOU NOTICED THE QUOTE MARKS, TOO, HUH?

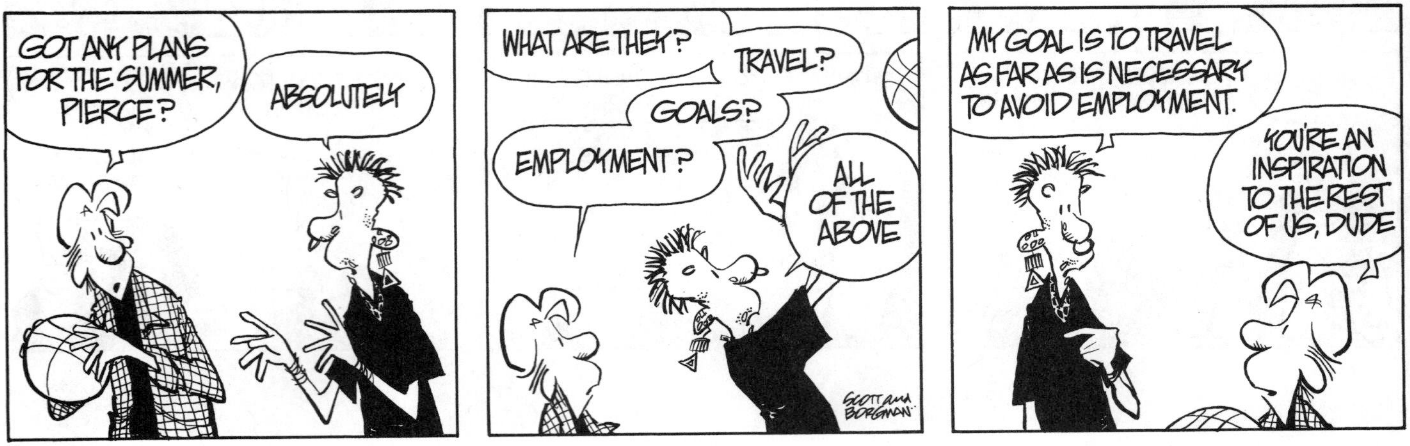
GOT ANY PLANS FOR THE SUMMER, PIERCE?
ABSOLUTELY
WHAT ARE THEY?
TRAVEL?
GOALS?
EMPLOYMENT?
ALL OF THE ABOVE
MY GOAL IS TO TRAVEL AS FAR AS IS NECESSARY TO AVOID EMPLOYMENT.
YOU'RE AN INSPIRATION TO THE REST OF US, DUDE

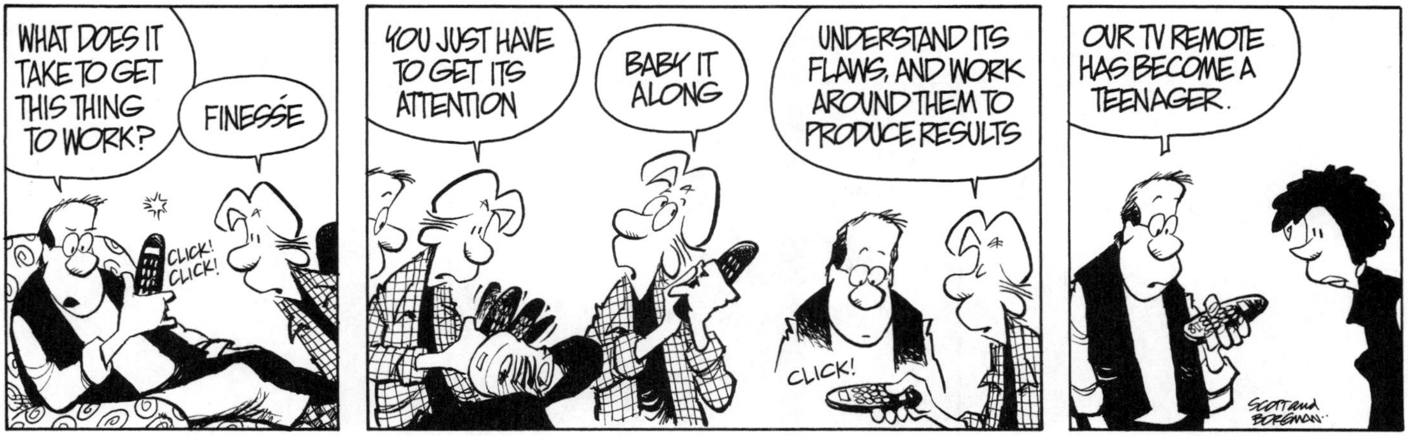
WHAT DOES IT TAKE TO GET THIS THING TO WORK?
CLICK! CLICK!
FINESSE
YOU JUST HAVE TO GET ITS ATTENTION
BABY IT ALONG
UNDERSTAND ITS FLAWS, AND WORK AROUND THEM TO PRODUCE RESULTS
CLICK!
OUR TV REMOTE HAS BECOME A TEENAGER.

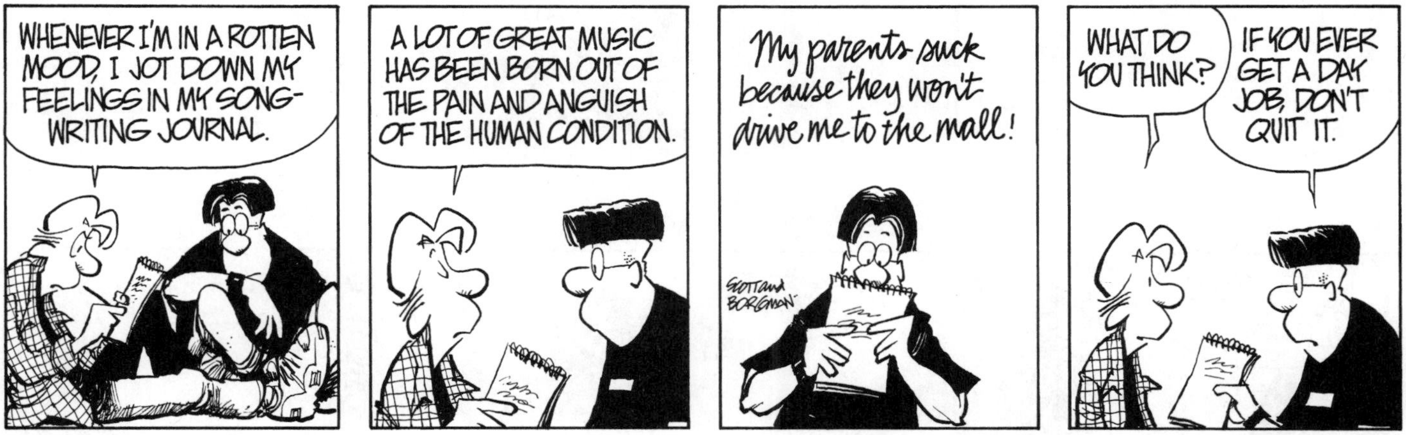
WHENEVER I'M IN A ROTTEN MOOD, I JOT DOWN MY FEELINGS IN MY SONG-WRITING JOURNAL.
A LOT OF GREAT MUSIC HAS BEEN BORN OUT OF THE PAIN AND ANGUISH OF THE HUMAN CONDITION.
My parents suck because they won't drive me to the mall!
WHAT DO YOU THINK?
IF YOU EVER GET A DAY JOB, DON'T QUIT IT.

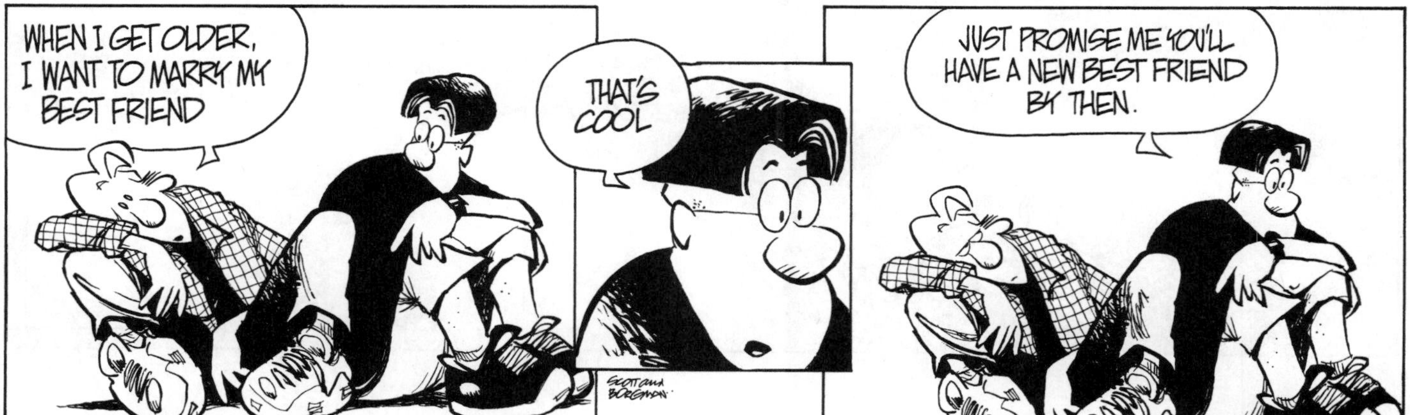
WHEN I GET OLDER, I WANT TO MARRY MY BEST FRIEND
THAT'S COOL
JUST PROMISE ME YOU'LL HAVE A NEW BEST FRIEND BY THEN.

Zits
by JERRY SCOTT and JIM BORGMAN

TELL ME A SECRET ABOUT YOURSELF, D'IJON
(GIGGLE!) YOU FIRST!
HMMM
LET'S SEE....
OKAY, HERE'S ONE
I'M SAVING MY NAVEL LINT IN HOPES THAT SOMEDAY MY WIFE WILL USE IT TO KNIT A SWEATER FOR OUR SON.
I'M HAVING PROBLEMS WITH INTIMACY.
FROM WHAT I HEAR, YOU'RE HAVING PROBLEMS WITH SANITY.
SCOTT and BORGMAN

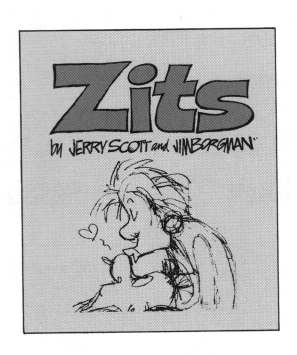

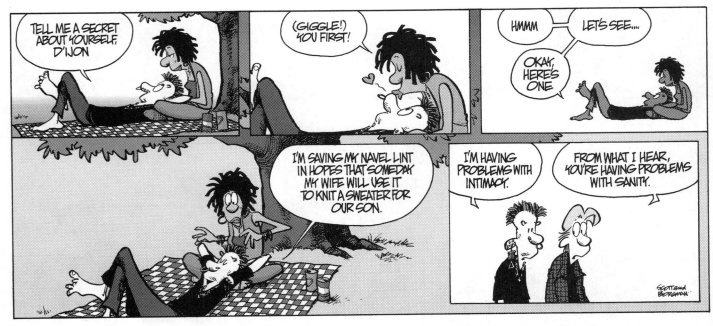

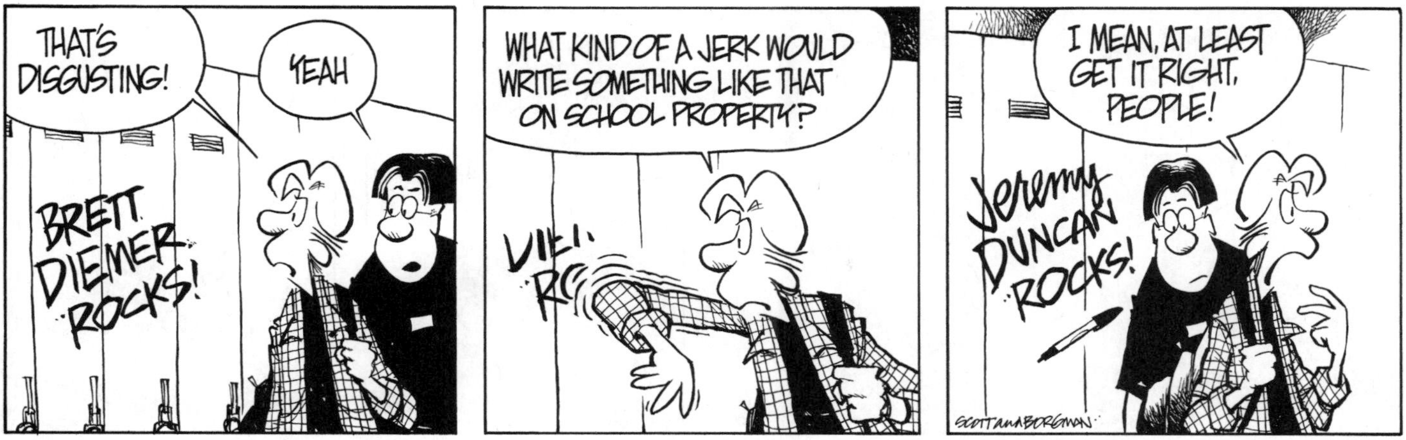
THAT'S DISGUSTING!
YEAH
BRETT DIEMER ROCKS!
WHAT KIND OF A JERK WOULD WRITE SOMETHING LIKE THAT ON SCHOOL PROPERTY?
I MEAN, AT LEAST GET IT RIGHT, PEOPLE!
Jeremy DUNCAN ROCKS!

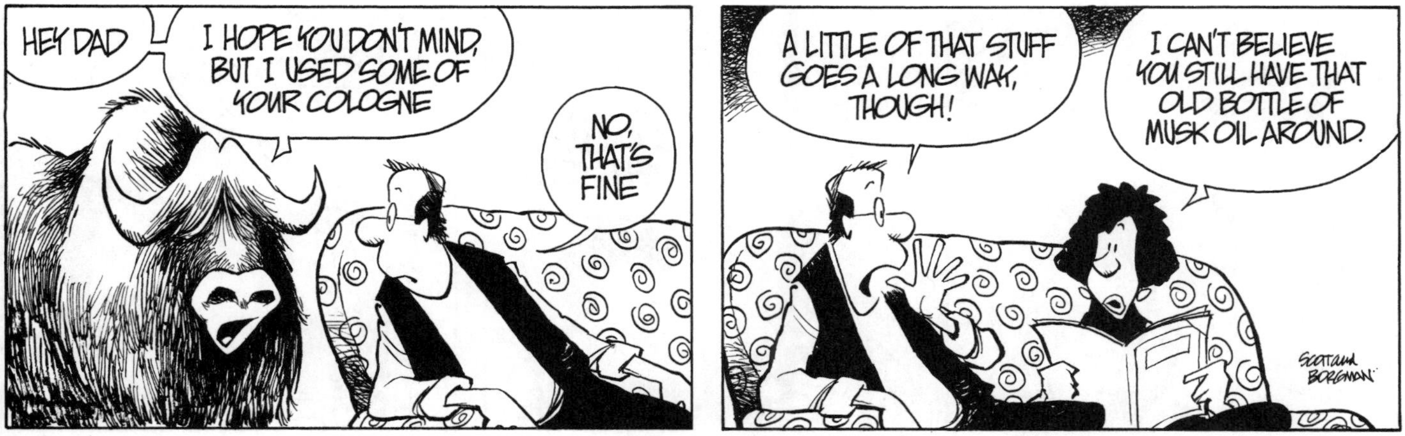
HEY DAD
I HOPE YOU DON'T MIND, BUT I USED SOME OF YOUR COLOGNE
NO, THAT'S FINE
A LITTLE OF THAT STUFF GOES A LONG WAY, THOUGH!
I CAN'T BELIEVE YOU STILL HAVE THAT OLD BOTTLE OF MUSK OIL AROUND.

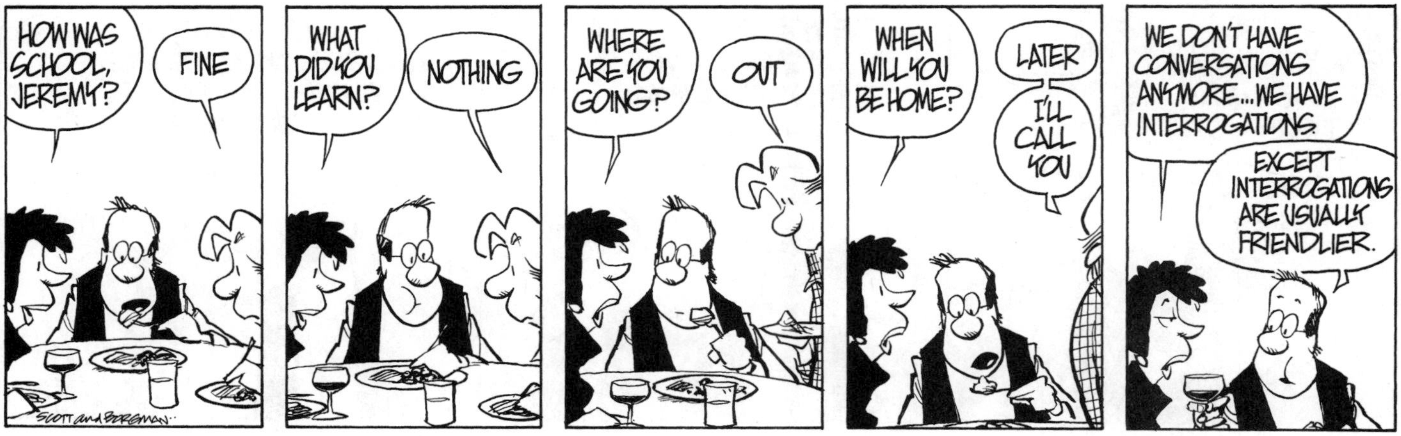
HOW WAS SCHOOL, JEREMY?
FINE
WHAT DID YOU LEARN?
NOTHING
WHERE ARE YOU GOING?
OUT
WHEN WILL YOU BE HOME?
LATER
I'LL CALL YOU
WE DON'T HAVE CONVERSATIONS ANYMORE... WE HAVE INTERROGATIONS.
EXCEPT INTERROGATIONS ARE USUALLY FRIENDLIER.

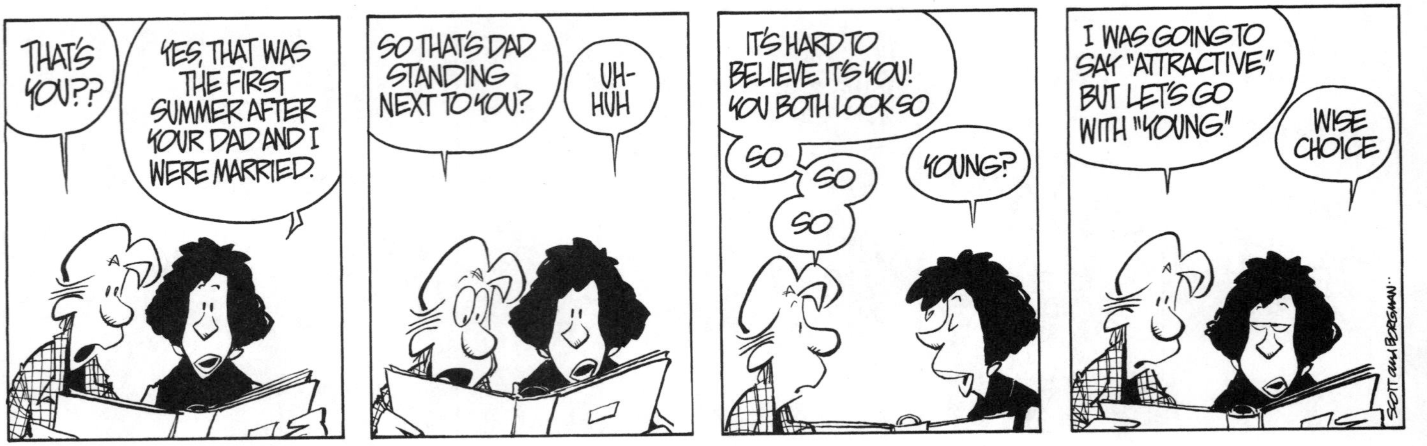
THAT'S YOU??
YES, THAT WAS THE FIRST SUMMER AFTER YOUR DAD AND I WERE MARRIED.
SO THAT'S DAD STANDING NEXT TO YOU?
UH-HUH
IT'S HARD TO BELIEVE IT'S YOU! YOU BOTH LOOK SO
SO
SO
SO
YOUNG?
I WAS GOING TO SAY "ATTRACTIVE," BUT LET'S GO WITH "YOUNG."
WISE CHOICE
SCOTT AND BORGMAN

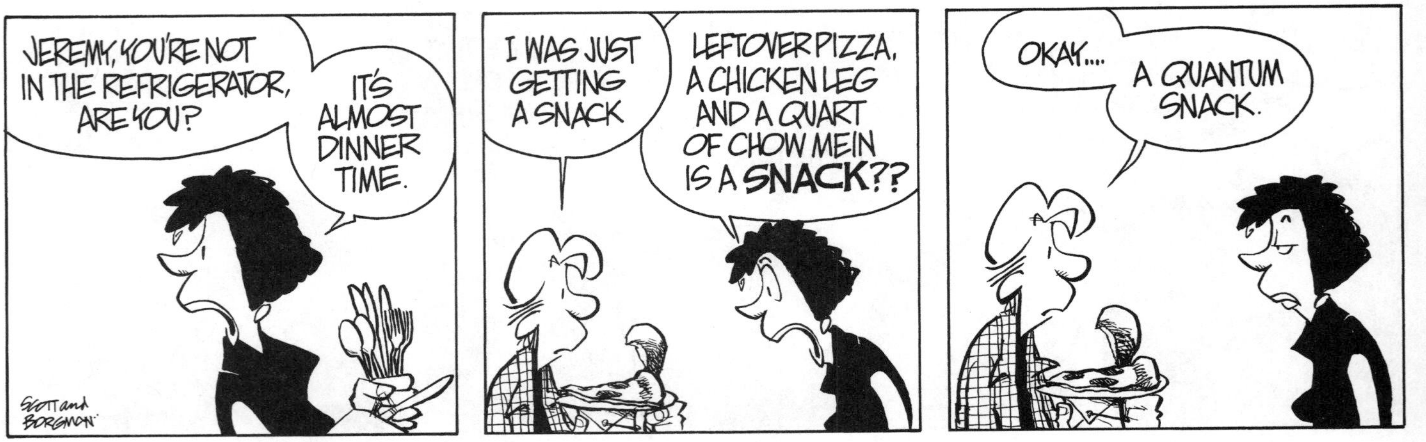
JEREMY, YOU'RE NOT IN THE REFRIGERATOR, ARE YOU?
IT'S ALMOST DINNER TIME.
SCOTT and BORGMAN
I WAS JUST GETTING A SNACK
LEFTOVER PIZZA, A CHICKEN LEG AND A QUART OF CHOW MEIN IS A SNACK??
OKAY....
A QUANTUM SNACK.

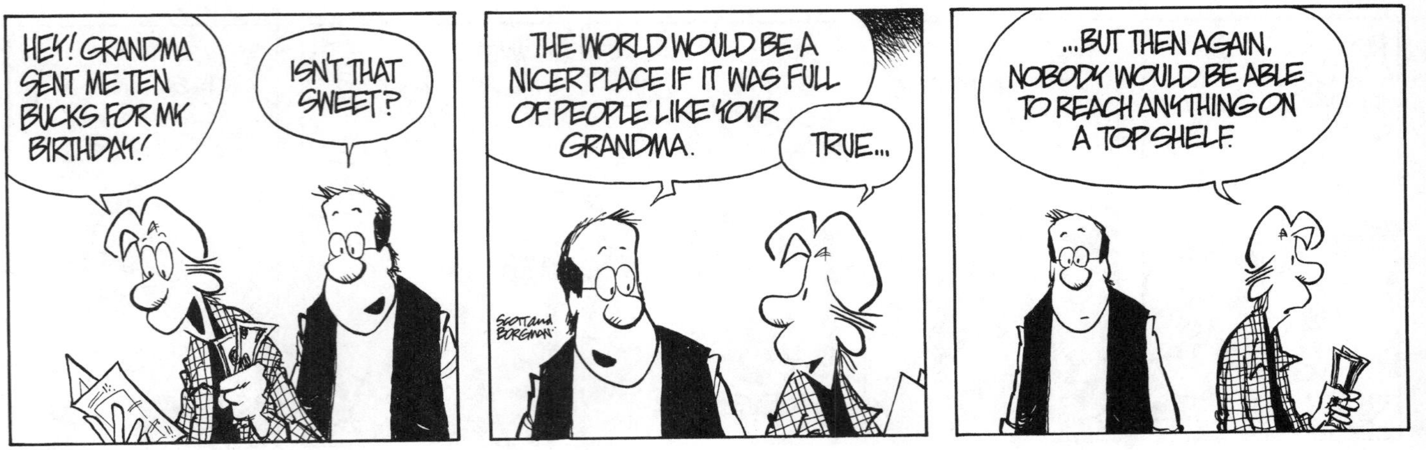
HEY! GRANDMA SENT ME TEN BUCKS FOR MY BIRTHDAY!
ISN'T THAT SWEET?
THE WORLD WOULD BE A NICER PLACE IF IT WAS FULL OF PEOPLE LIKE YOUR GRANDMA.
TRUE...
SCOTT and BORGMAN
...BUT THEN AGAIN, NOBODY WOULD BE ABLE TO REACH ANYTHING ON A TOP SHELF.

Zits
by
JERRY SCOTT and
JIM BORGMAN

JEREMY, I REALLY NEED YOUR OPINION ON SOMETHING.
I WANT YOU TO BE 100% HONEST WITH ME, OKAY?
I'M NOT LOOKING FOR MORAL SUPPORT, JUST HONESTY.
COMPLETE TOTAL HONESTY.
OKAY
HERE GOES
DOES MY HAIR LOOK BETTER UP, OR DOWN?
I DON'T KNOW. I HARDLY EVER LOOK AT YOU ABOVE THE NECK.
THERE'S HONESTY AND THEN THERE'S TRANSPARENCY

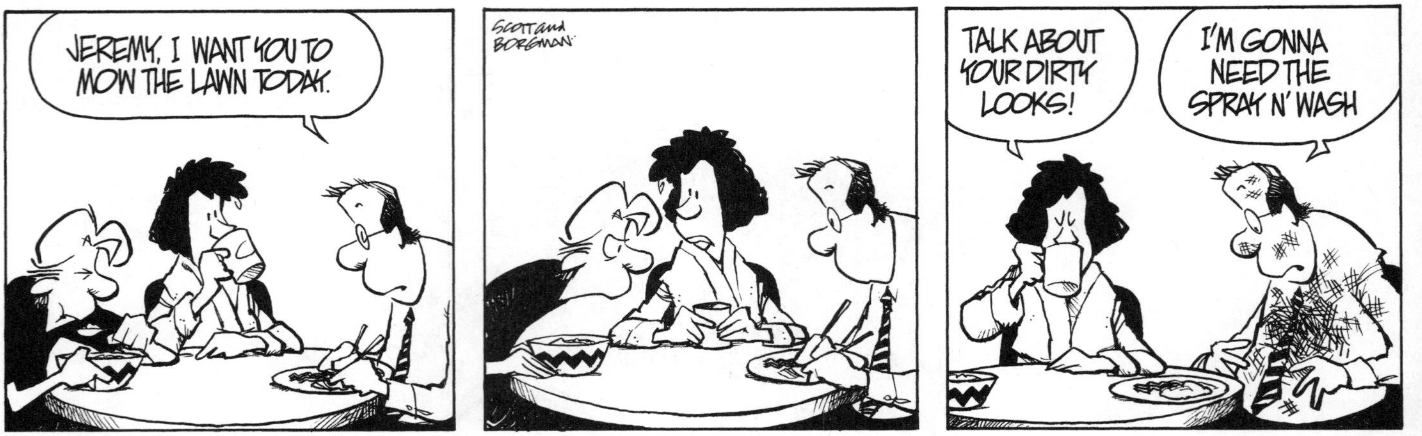
JEREMY, I WANT YOU TO MOW THE LAWN TODAY.
TALK ABOUT YOUR DIRTY LOOKS!
I'M GONNA NEED THE SPRAY N' WASH

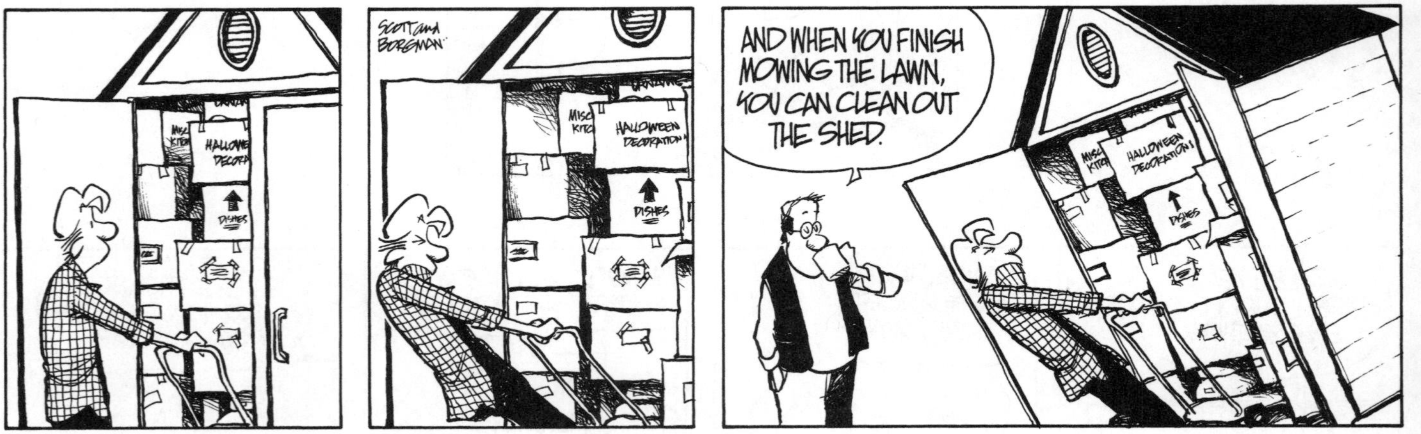
AND WHEN YOU FINISH MOWING THE LAWN, YOU CAN CLEAN OUT THE SHED.

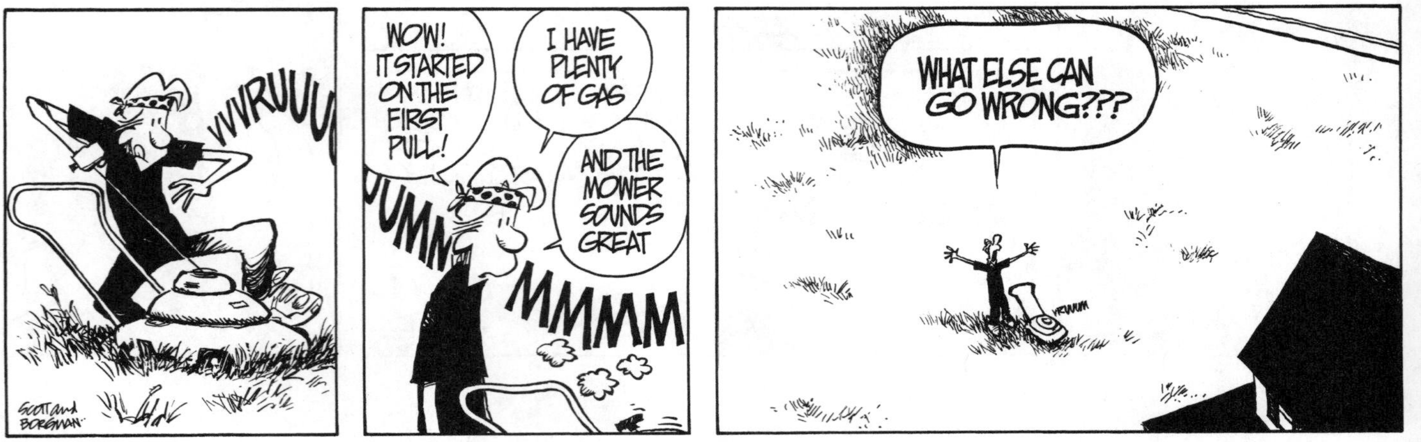
VVVRUUUU
UMM
WOW! IT STARTED ON THE FIRST PULL!
I HAVE PLENTY OF GAS
AND THE MOWER SOUNDS GREAT
MMMM
WHAT ELSE CAN GO WRONG???

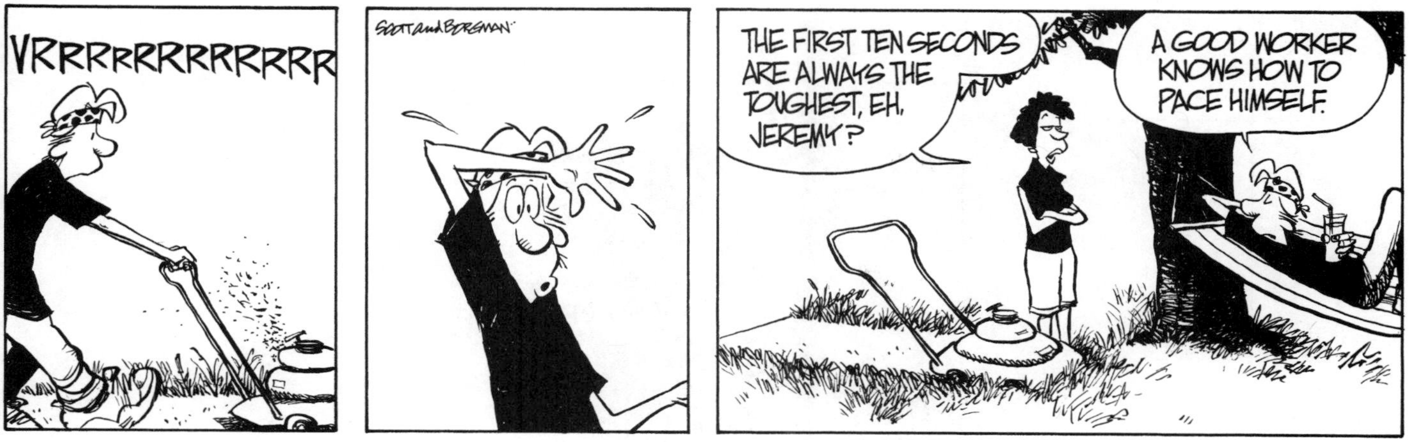
VRRRRRRRRRRRRR
SCOTT and BORGMAN
THE FIRST TEN SECONDS ARE ALWAYS THE TOUGHEST, EH, JEREMY?
A GOOD WORKER KNOWS HOW TO PACE HIMSELF.

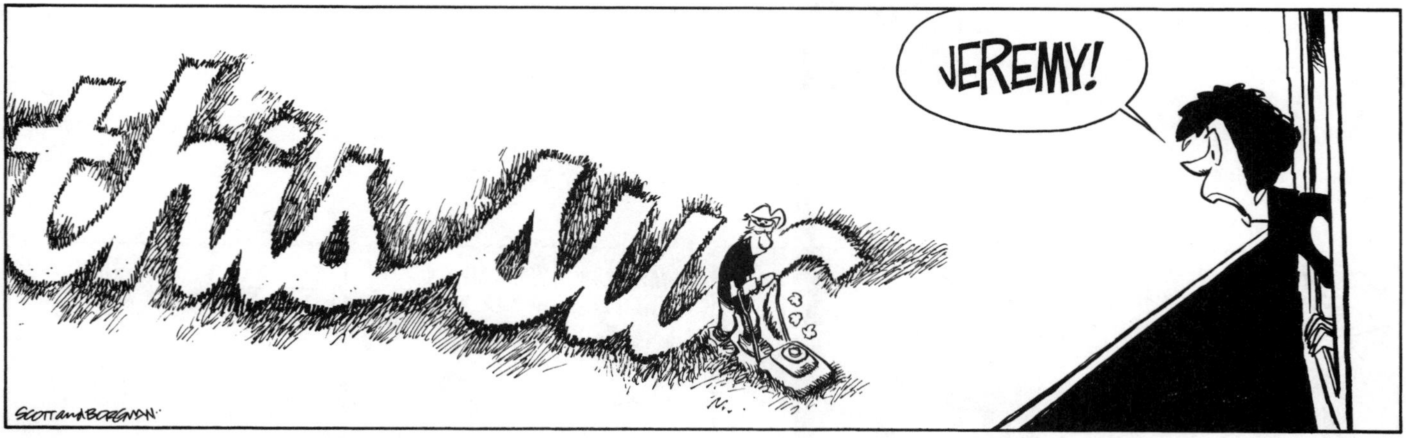
this su
JEREMY!
SCOTT and BORGMAN

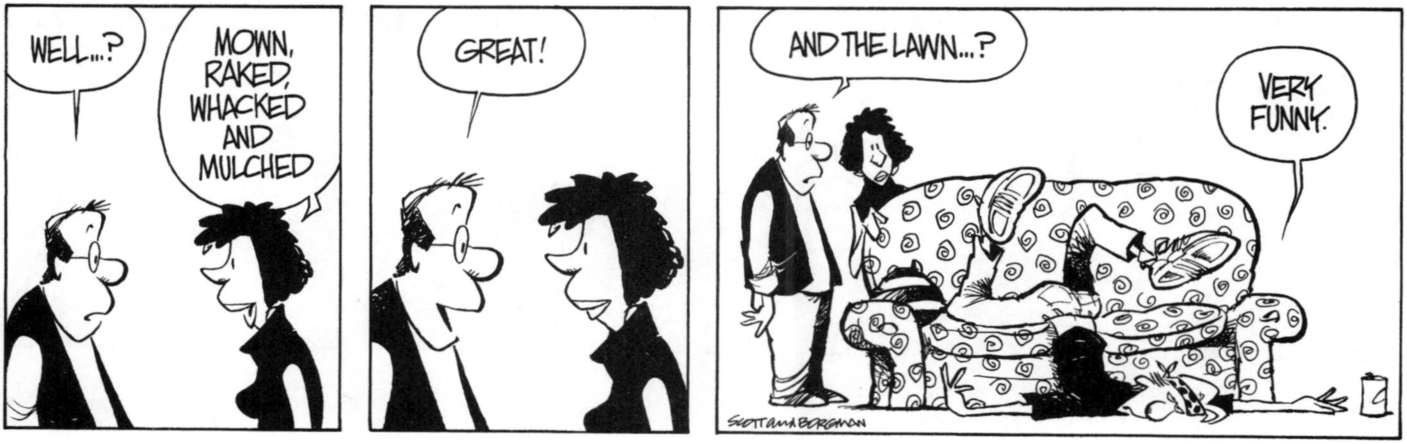
WELL...?
MOWN, RAKED, WHACKED AND MULCHED
GREAT!
AND THE LAWN...?
VERY FUNNY.
SCOTT and BORGMAN

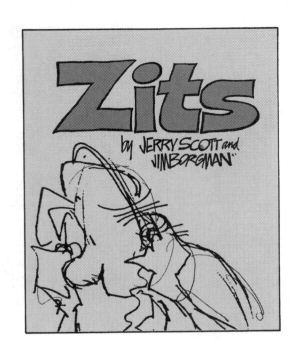

Zits by JERRY SCOTT and JIM BORGMAN

GOOD MORNING, JEREMY

HUH?

I SAID **GOOD MORNING!**

OH. HI.

WHY DO YOU WALK AROUND WITH THOSE THINGS ON YOUR HEAD ALL THE TIME?

SO I CAN LISTEN TO MUSIC, I GUESS

BUT **ALL** OF THE TIME?

YOU ACTUALLY ENJOY HAVING MUSIC CONSTANTLY PUMPED INTO YOUR EARS?

THINK OF ALL THE SOUNDS YOU'RE MISSING! ALL THE CONVERSATIONS YOU'RE OBLIVIOUS TO!

SCOTT and BORGMAN

WHY NOT JUST SAVE THE HEADPHONES FOR THOSE TIMES WHEN YOU WANT TO BLOCK OUT UNWANTED NOISE?

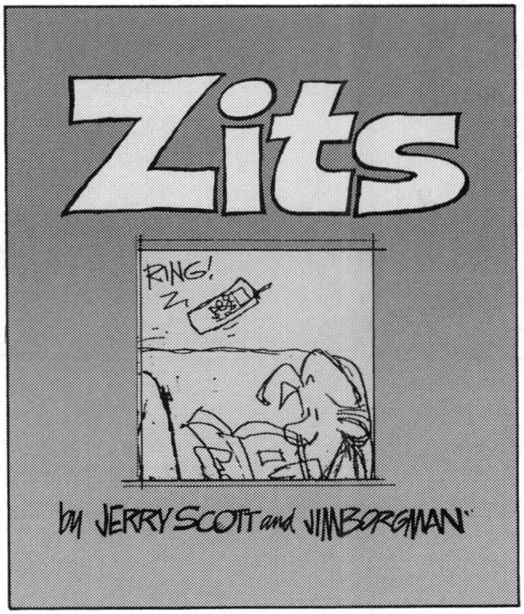
Zits
RING!
by JERRY SCOTT and JIM BORGMAN

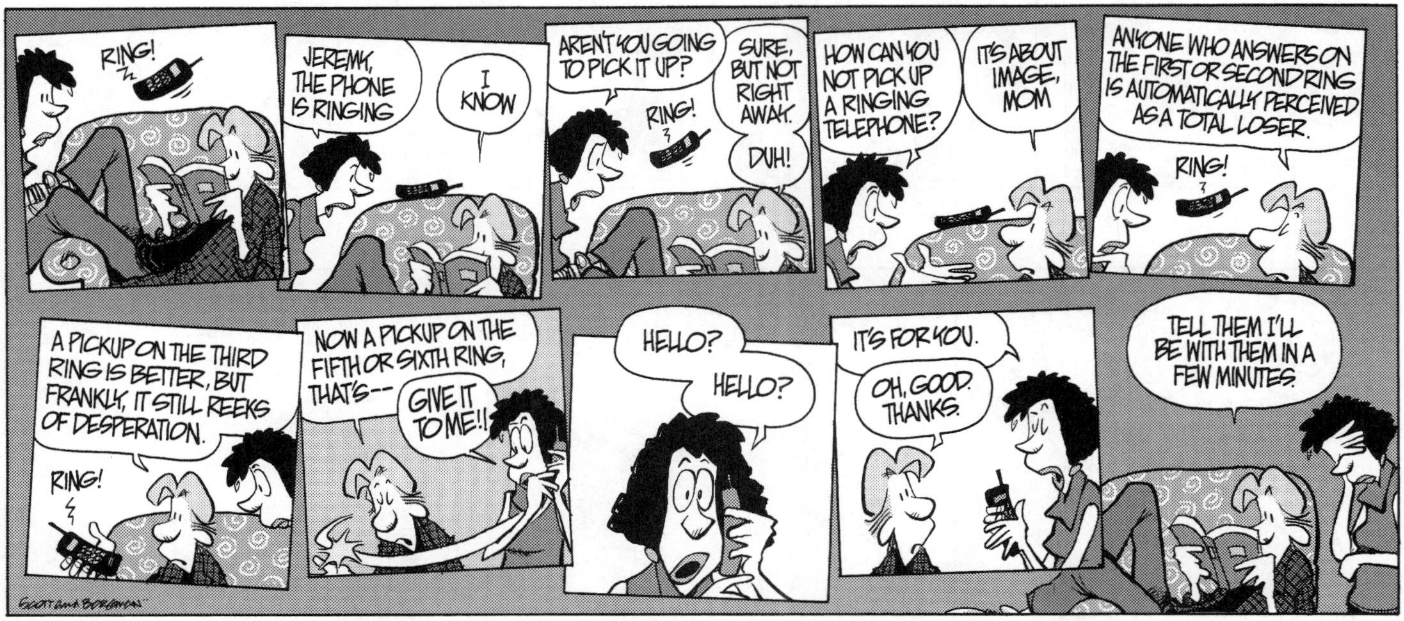
RING!
JEREMY, THE PHONE IS RINGING
I KNOW
AREN'T YOU GOING TO PICK IT UP?
RING!
SURE, BUT NOT RIGHT AWAY.
DUH!
HOW CAN YOU NOT PICK UP A RINGING TELEPHONE?
IT'S ABOUT IMAGE, MOM
ANYONE WHO ANSWERS ON THE FIRST OR SECOND RING IS AUTOMATICALLY PERCEIVED AS A TOTAL LOSER.
RING!
A PICKUP ON THE THIRD RING IS BETTER, BUT FRANKLY, IT STILL REEKS OF DESPERATION.
RING!
NOW A PICKUP ON THE FIFTH OR SIXTH RING, THAT'S--
GIVE IT TO ME!!
HELLO?
HELLO?
IT'S FOR YOU.
OH, GOOD. THANKS.
TELL THEM I'LL BE WITH THEM IN A FEW MINUTES.
SCOTT and BORGMAN

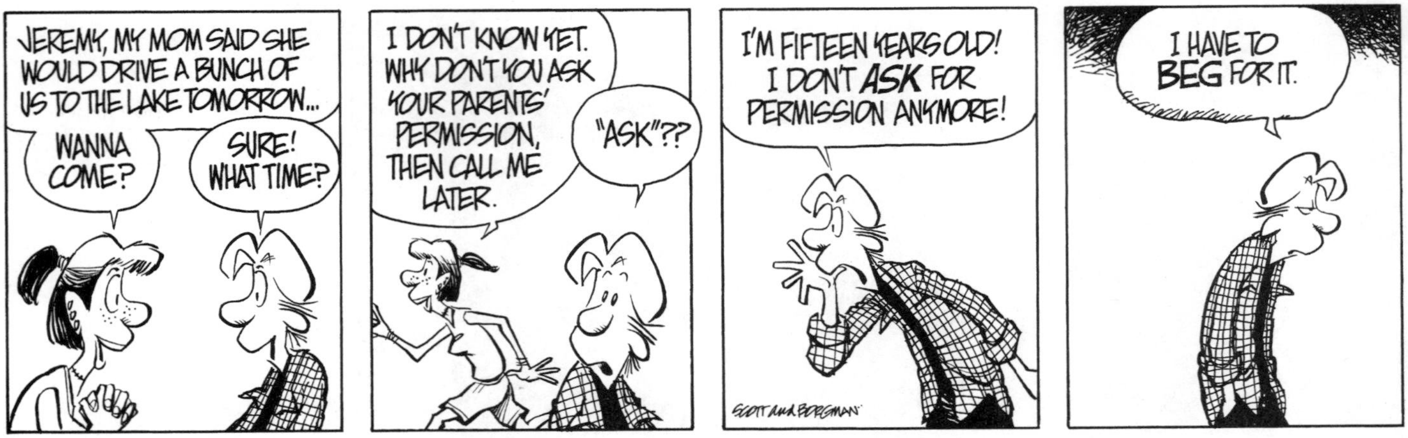
JEREMY, MY MOM SAID SHE WOULD DRIVE A BUNCH OF US TO THE LAKE TOMORROW...
WANNA COME?
SURE! WHAT TIME?
I DON'T KNOW YET. WHY DON'T YOU ASK YOUR PARENTS' PERMISSION, THEN CALL ME LATER.
"ASK"??
I'M FIFTEEN YEARS OLD! I DON'T **ASK** FOR PERMISSION ANYMORE!
SCOTT and BORGMAN
I HAVE TO **BEG** FOR IT.

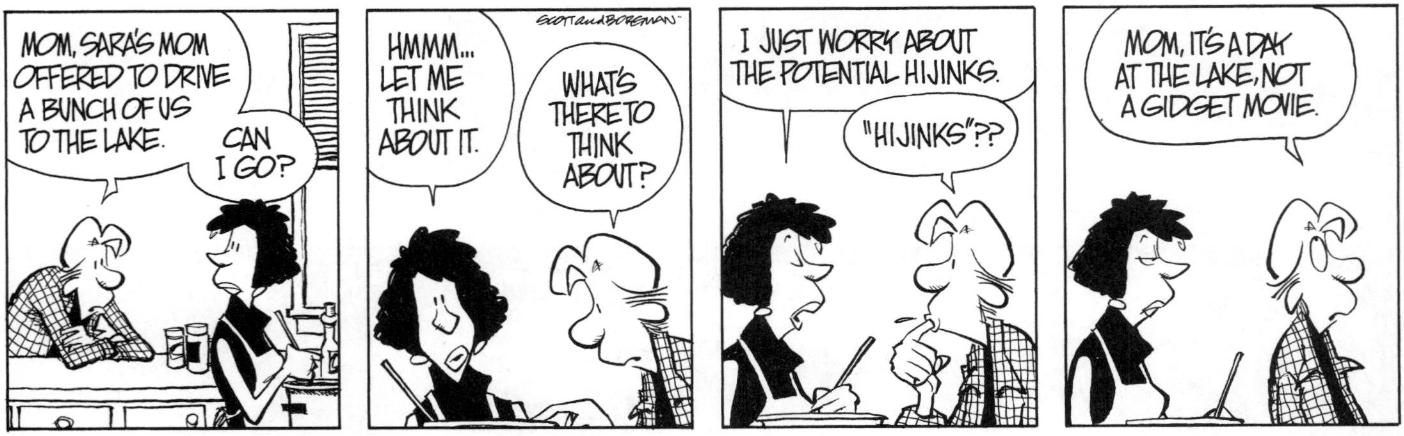
MOM, SARA'S MOM OFFERED TO DRIVE A BUNCH OF US TO THE LAKE.
CAN I GO?
SCOTT and BORGMAN
HMMM... LET ME THINK ABOUT IT.
WHAT'S THERE TO THINK ABOUT?
I JUST WORRY ABOUT THE POTENTIAL HIJINKS.
"HIJINKS"??
MOM, IT'S A DAY AT THE LAKE, NOT A GIDGET MOVIE.

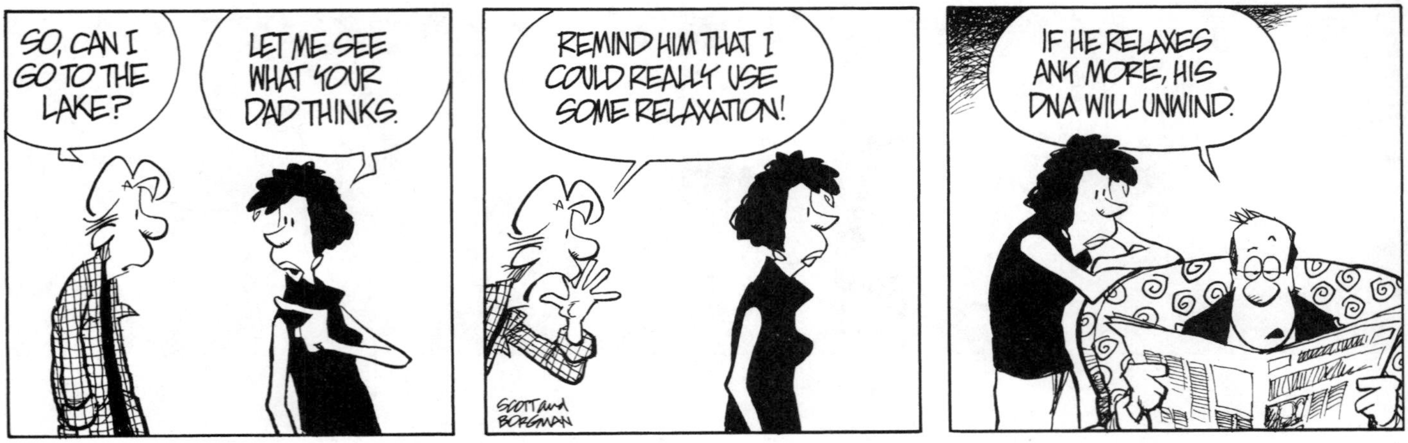
SO, CAN I GO TO THE LAKE?
LET ME SEE WHAT YOUR DAD THINKS.
REMIND HIM THAT I COULD REALLY USE SOME RELAXATION!
SCOTT and BORGMAN
IF HE RELAXES ANY MORE, HIS DNA WILL UNWIND.

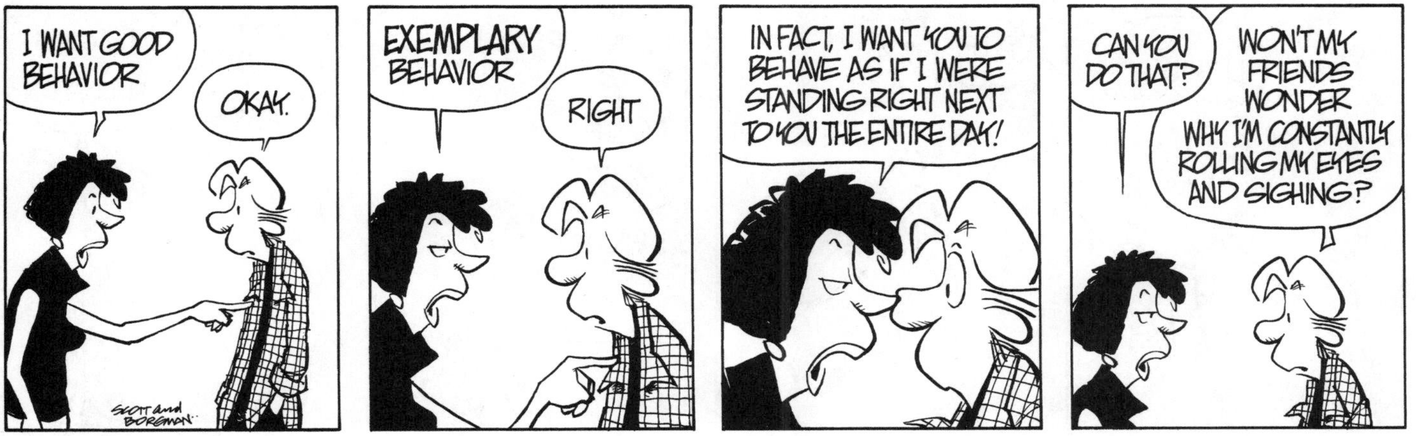
I WANT GOOD BEHAVIOR
OKAY.
SCOTT and BORGMAN
EXEMPLARY BEHAVIOR
RIGHT
IN FACT, I WANT YOU TO BEHAVE AS IF I WERE STANDING RIGHT NEXT TO YOU THE ENTIRE DAY!
CAN YOU DO THAT?
WON'T MY FRIENDS WONDER WHY I'M CONSTANTLY ROLLING MY EYES AND SIGHING?

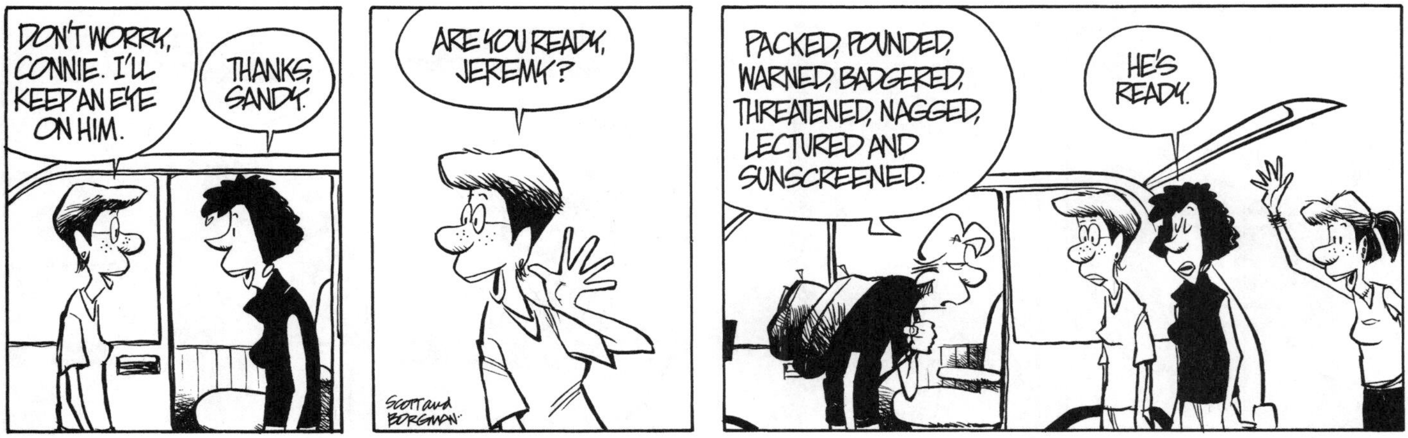
DON'T WORRY, CONNIE. I'LL KEEP AN EYE ON HIM.
THANKS, SANDY.
ARE YOU READY, JEREMY?
SCOTT and BORGMAN
PACKED, POUNDED, WARNED, BADGERED, THREATENED, NAGGED, LECTURED AND SUNSCREENED.
HE'S READY.

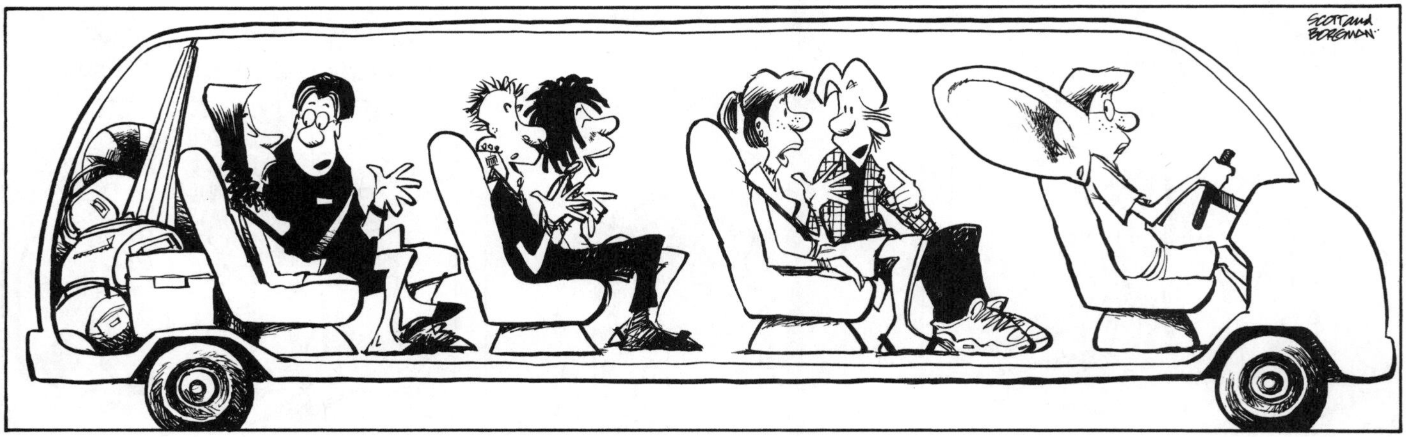
SCOTT and BORGMAN

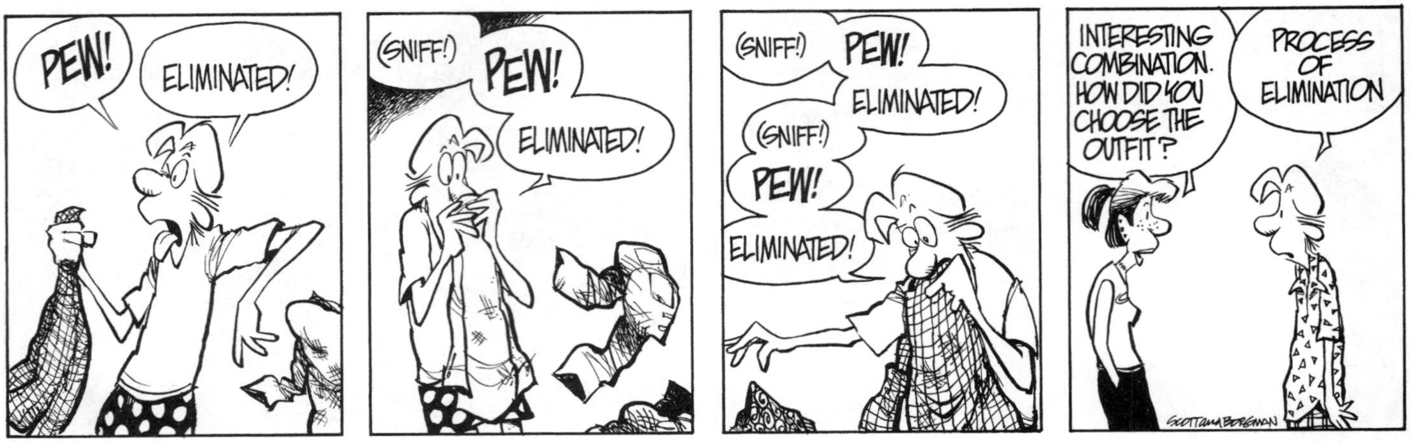
PEW!
ELIMINATED!
(SNIFF!)
PEW!
ELIMINATED!
(SNIFF!)
PEW!
ELIMINATED!
(SNIFF!)
PEW!
ELIMINATED!
INTERESTING COMBINATION. HOW DID YOU CHOOSE THE OUTFIT?
PROCESS OF ELIMINATION
SCOTT and BORGMAN

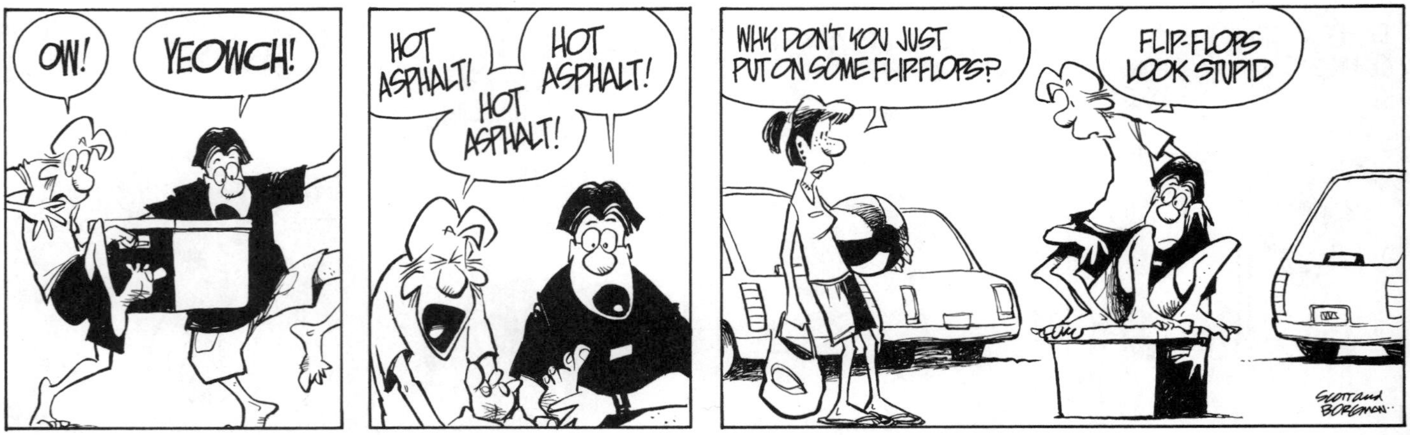
OW!
YEOWCH!
HOT ASPHALT!
HOT ASPHALT!
HOT ASPHALT!
WHY DON'T YOU JUST PUT ON SOME FLIP-FLOPS?
FLIP-FLOPS LOOK STUPID
SCOTT and BORGMAN

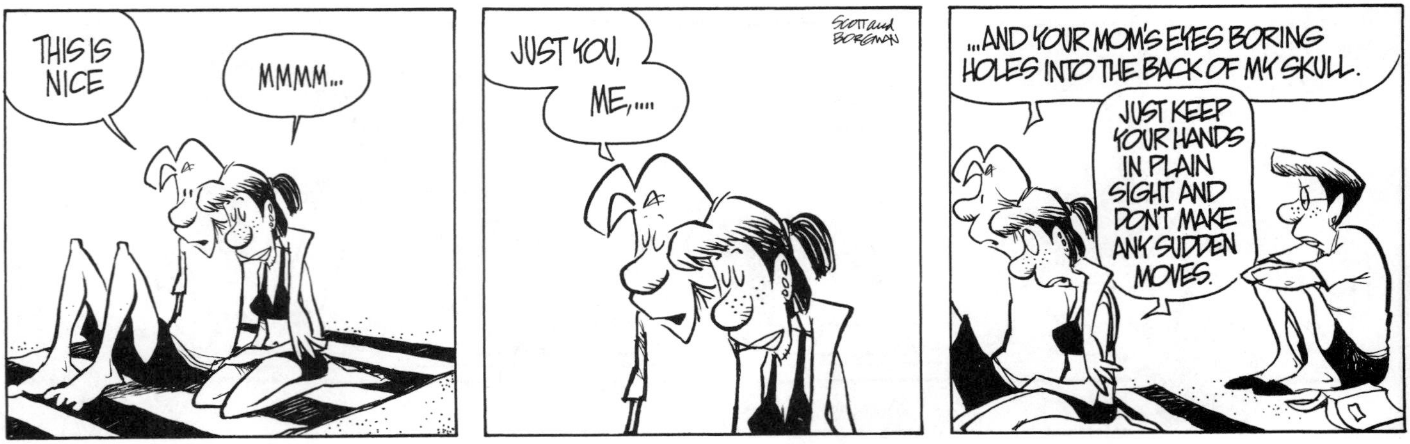
THIS IS NICE
MMMM...
JUST YOU,
ME,....
SCOTT and BORGMAN
...AND YOUR MOM'S EYES BORING HOLES INTO THE BACK OF MY SKULL.
JUST KEEP YOUR HANDS IN PLAIN SIGHT AND DON'T MAKE ANY SUDDEN MOVES.

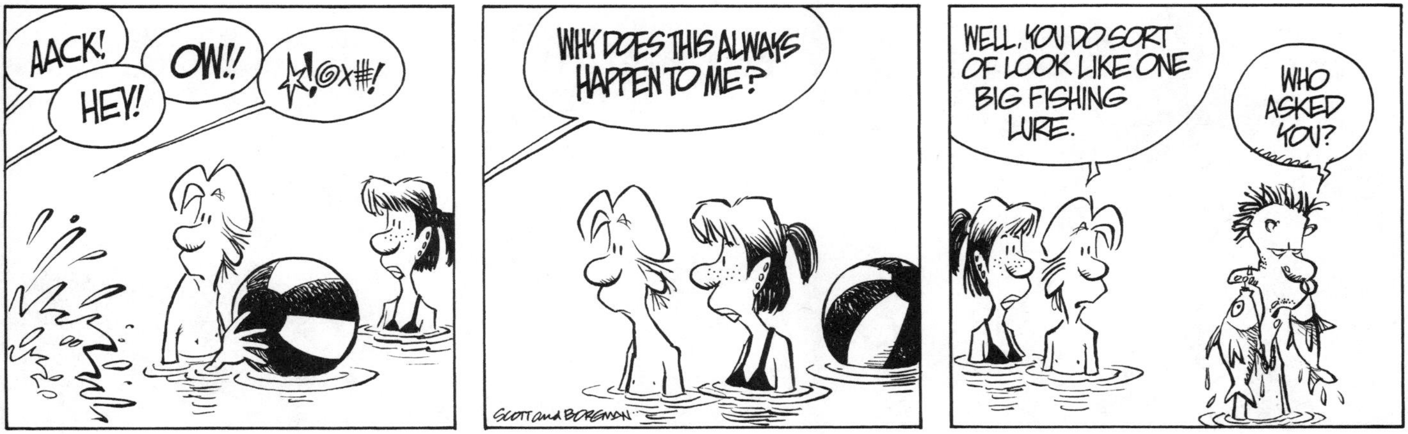
AACK!
HEY!
OW!!
WHY DOES THIS ALWAYS HAPPEN TO ME?
SCOTT and BORGMAN
WELL, YOU DO SORT OF LOOK LIKE ONE BIG FISHING LURE.
WHO ASKED YOU?

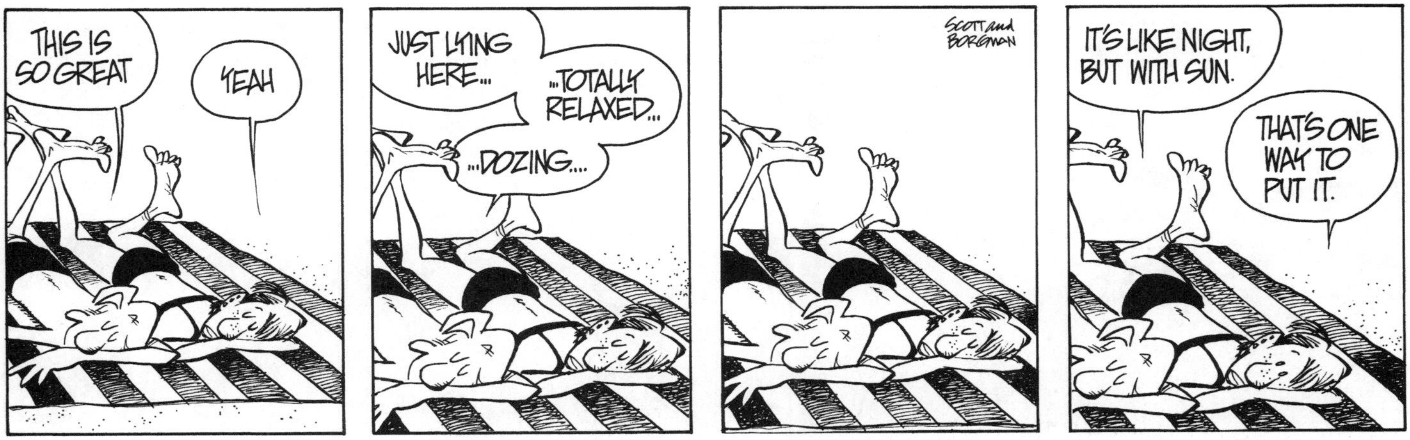
THIS IS SO GREAT
YEAH
JUST LYING HERE...
...TOTALLY RELAXED...
...DOZING....
SCOTT and BORGMAN
IT'S LIKE NIGHT, BUT WITH SUN.
THAT'S ONE WAY TO PUT IT.

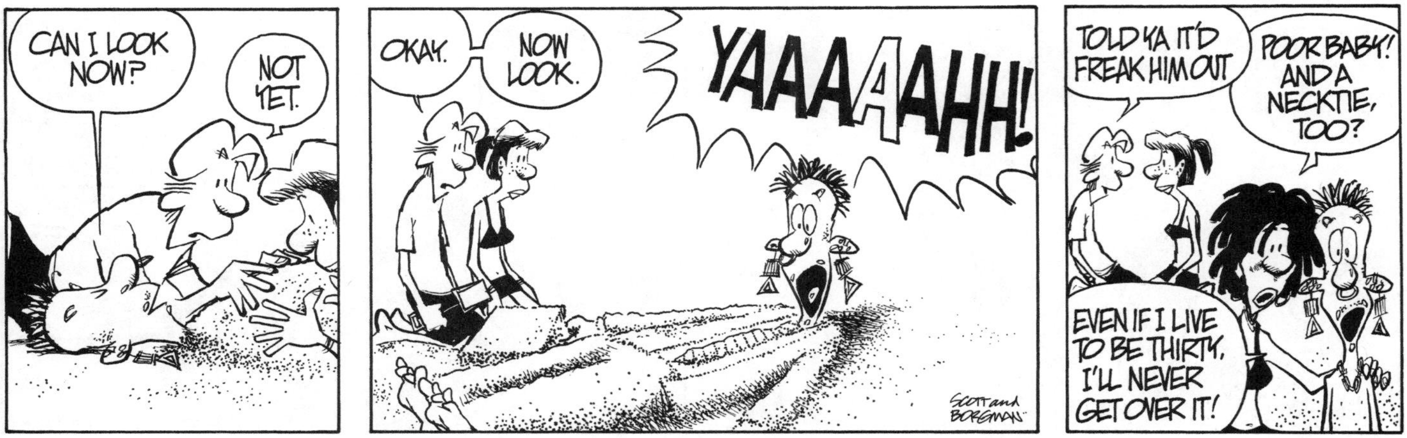
CAN I LOOK NOW?
NOT YET.
OKAY.
NOW LOOK.
YAAAAAHH!
SCOTT and BORGMAN
TOLD YA IT'D FREAK HIM OUT
POOR BABY! AND A NECKTIE, TOO?
EVEN IF I LIVE TO BE THIRTY, I'LL NEVER GET OVER IT!

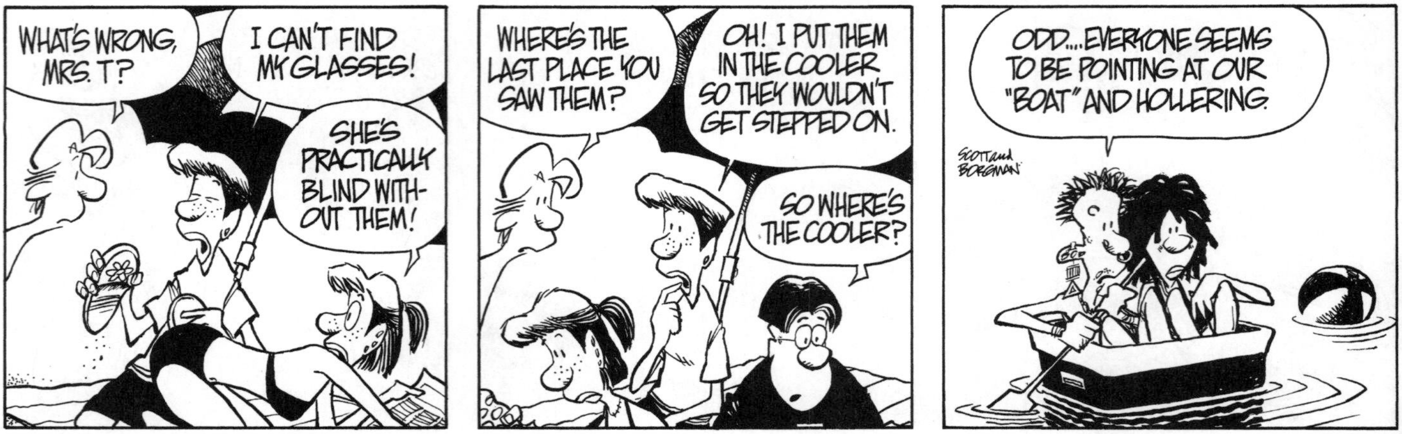
WHAT'S WRONG, MRS. T?
I CAN'T FIND MY GLASSES!
SHE'S PRACTICALLY BLIND WITH-OUT THEM!
WHERE'S THE LAST PLACE YOU SAW THEM?
OH! I PUT THEM IN THE COOLER SO THEY WOULDN'T GET STEPPED ON.
SO WHERE'S THE COOLER?
ODD.... EVERYONE SEEMS TO BE POINTING AT OUR "BOAT" AND HOLLERING.

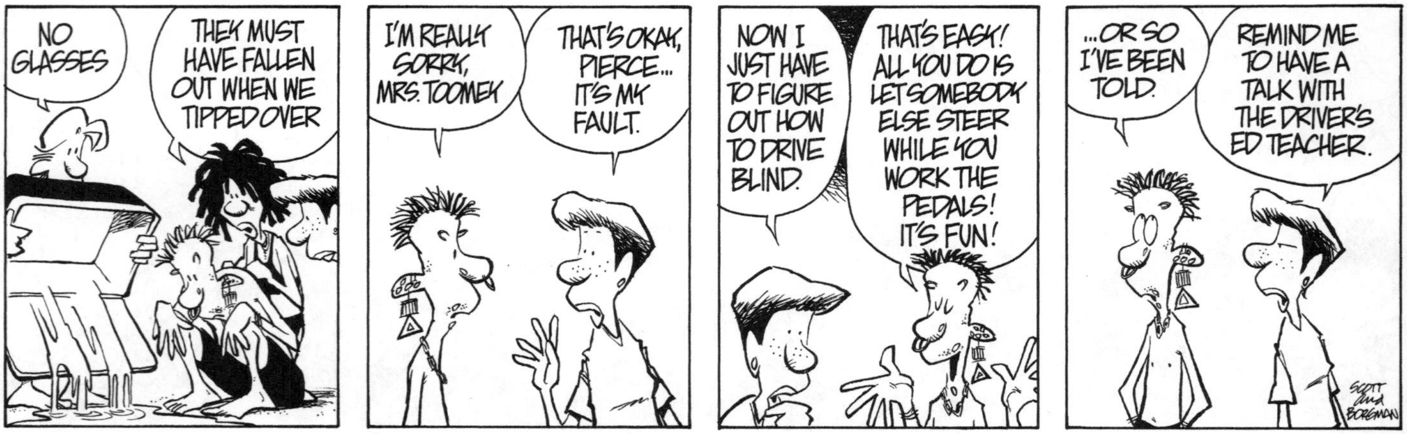
NO GLASSES
THEY MUST HAVE FALLEN OUT WHEN WE TIPPED OVER
I'M REALLY SORRY, MRS. TOOMEY
THAT'S OKAY, PIERCE... IT'S MY FAULT.
NOW I JUST HAVE TO FIGURE OUT HOW TO DRIVE BLIND.
THAT'S EASY! ALL YOU DO IS LET SOMEBODY ELSE STEER WHILE YOU WORK THE PEDALS! IT'S FUN!
...OR SO I'VE BEEN TOLD.
REMIND ME TO HAVE A TALK WITH THE DRIVER'S ED TEACHER.

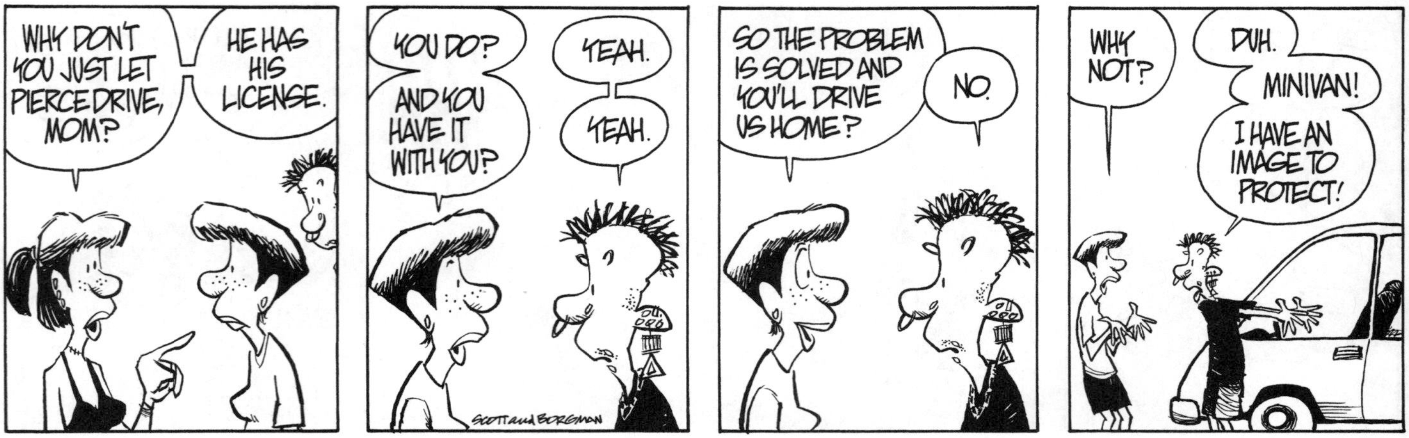
WHY DON'T YOU JUST LET PIERCE DRIVE, MOM?
HE HAS HIS LICENSE.
YOU DO?
YEAH.
AND YOU HAVE IT WITH YOU?
YEAH.
SO THE PROBLEM IS SOLVED AND YOU'LL DRIVE US HOME?
NO.
WHY NOT?
DUH.
MINIVAN!
I HAVE AN IMAGE TO PROTECT!

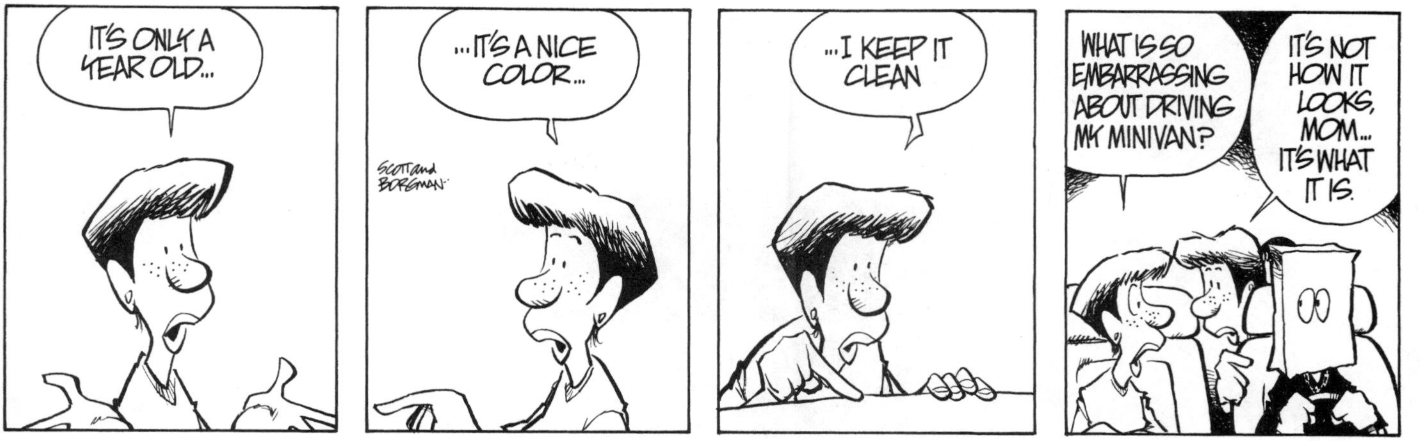

IT'S ONLY A YEAR OLD...
...IT'S A NICE COLOR...
...I KEEP IT CLEAN
WHAT IS SO EMBARRASSING ABOUT DRIVING MY MINIVAN?
IT'S NOT HOW IT LOOKS, MOM... IT'S WHAT IT IS.

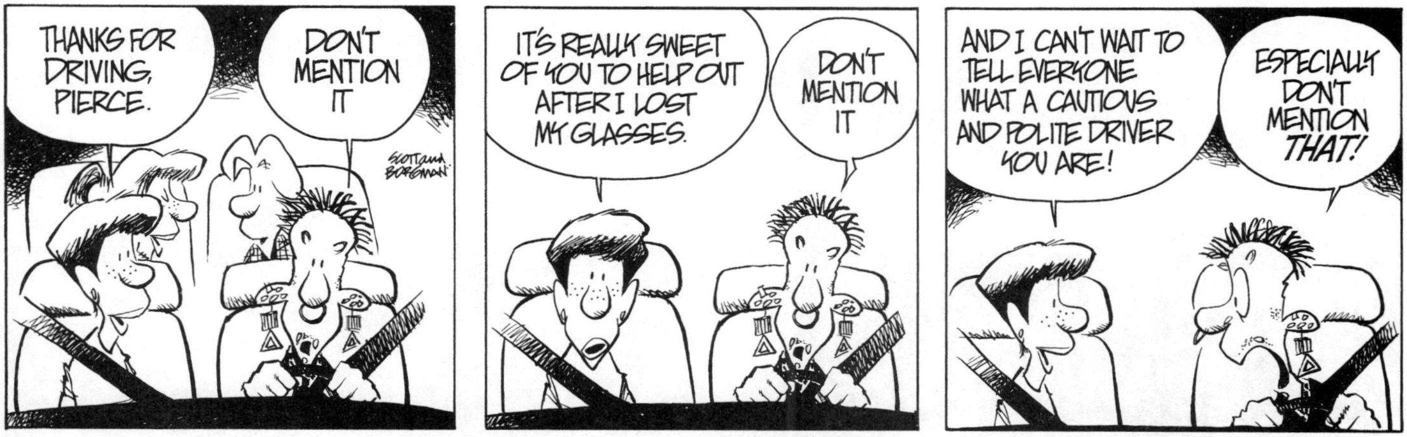

THANKS FOR DRIVING, PIERCE.
DON'T MENTION IT
IT'S REALLY SWEET OF YOU TO HELP OUT AFTER I LOST MY GLASSES.
DON'T MENTION IT
AND I CAN'T WAIT TO TELL EVERYONE WHAT A CAUTIOUS AND POLITE DRIVER YOU ARE!
ESPECIALLY DON'T MENTION THAT!

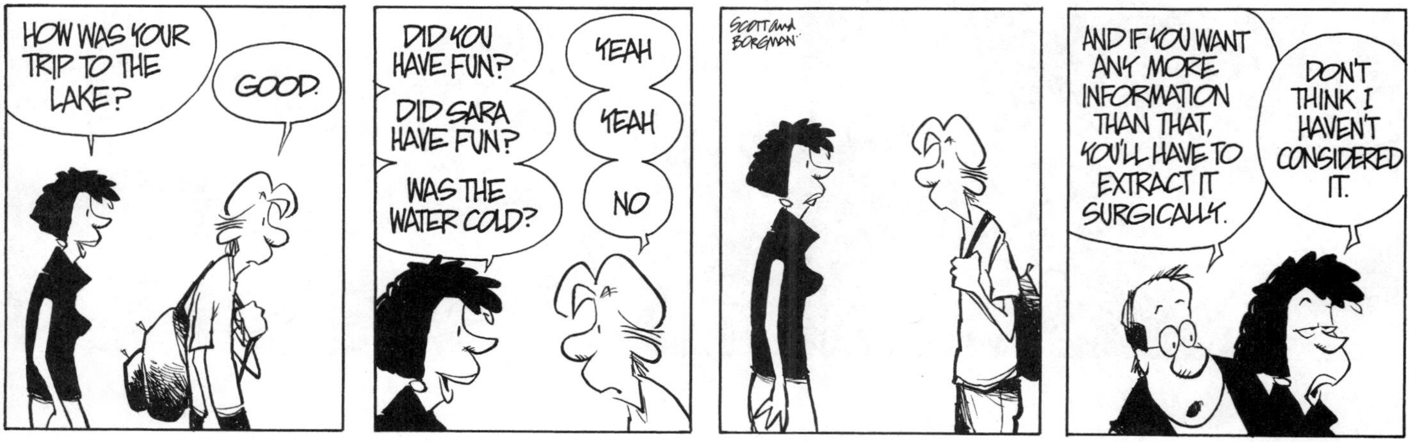

HOW WAS YOUR TRIP TO THE LAKE?
GOOD.
DID YOU HAVE FUN?
YEAH
DID SARA HAVE FUN?
YEAH
WAS THE WATER COLD?
NO
AND IF YOU WANT ANY MORE INFORMATION THAN THAT, YOU'LL HAVE TO EXTRACT IT SURGICALLY.
DON'T THINK I HAVEN'T CONSIDERED IT.

Zits
by JERRY SCOTT and JIM BORGMAN

GINGIVITIS
THIS IS WHERE I COME TO GET AWAY FROM IT ALL

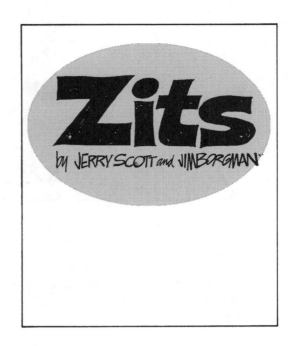

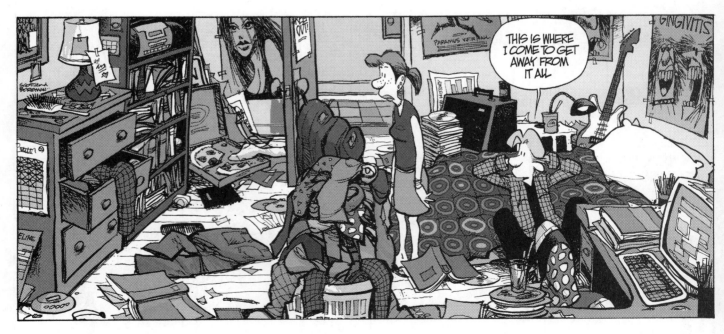

by
JERRY SCOTT and
JIM BORGMAN
Zits

SCOTT and BORGMAN
OKAY.
NOW LET'S TRY IT WHILE WE PLAY THE SONG.

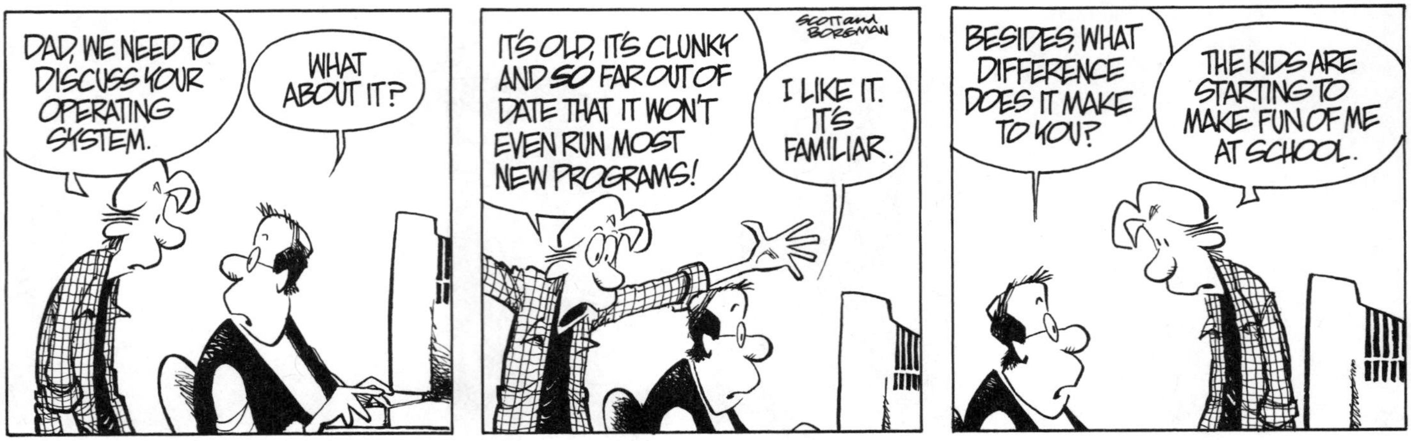
DAD, WE NEED TO DISCUSS YOUR OPERATING SYSTEM.
WHAT ABOUT IT?
IT'S OLD, IT'S CLUNKY AND *SO* FAR OUT OF DATE THAT IT WON'T EVEN RUN MOST NEW PROGRAMS!
I LIKE IT. IT'S FAMILIAR.
BESIDES, WHAT DIFFERENCE DOES IT MAKE TO YOU?
THE KIDS ARE STARTING TO MAKE FUN OF ME AT SCHOOL.
SCOTT and BORGMAN

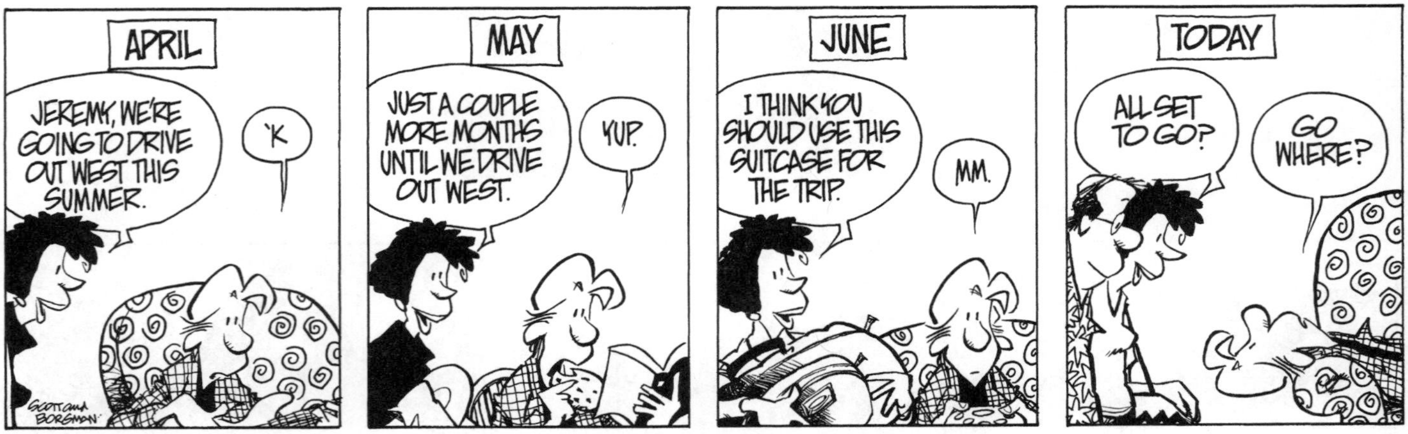
APRIL
JEREMY, WE'RE GOING TO DRIVE OUT WEST THIS SUMMER.
'K
MAY
JUST A COUPLE MORE MONTHS UNTIL WE DRIVE OUT WEST.
YUP.
JUNE
I THINK YOU SHOULD USE THIS SUITCASE FOR THE TRIP.
MM.
TODAY
ALL SET TO GO?
GO WHERE?
SCOTT and BORGMAN

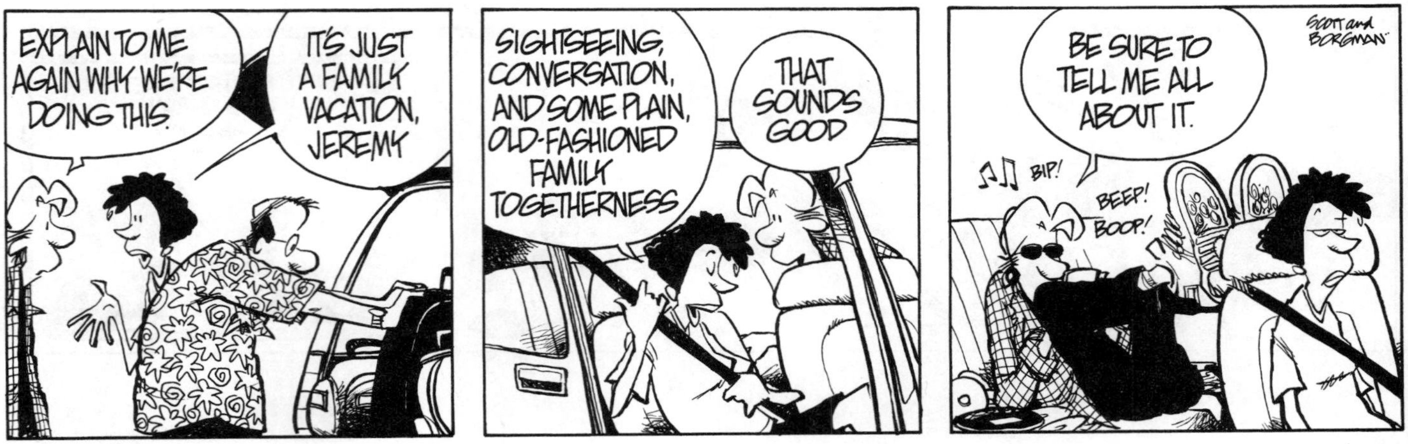
EXPLAIN TO ME AGAIN WHY WE'RE DOING THIS.
IT'S JUST A FAMILY VACATION, JEREMY
SIGHTSEEING, CONVERSATION, AND SOME PLAIN, OLD-FASHIONED FAMILY TOGETHERNESS
THAT SOUNDS GOOD
BE SURE TO TELL ME ALL ABOUT IT.
BIP!
BEEP!
BOOP!
SCOTT and BORGMAN

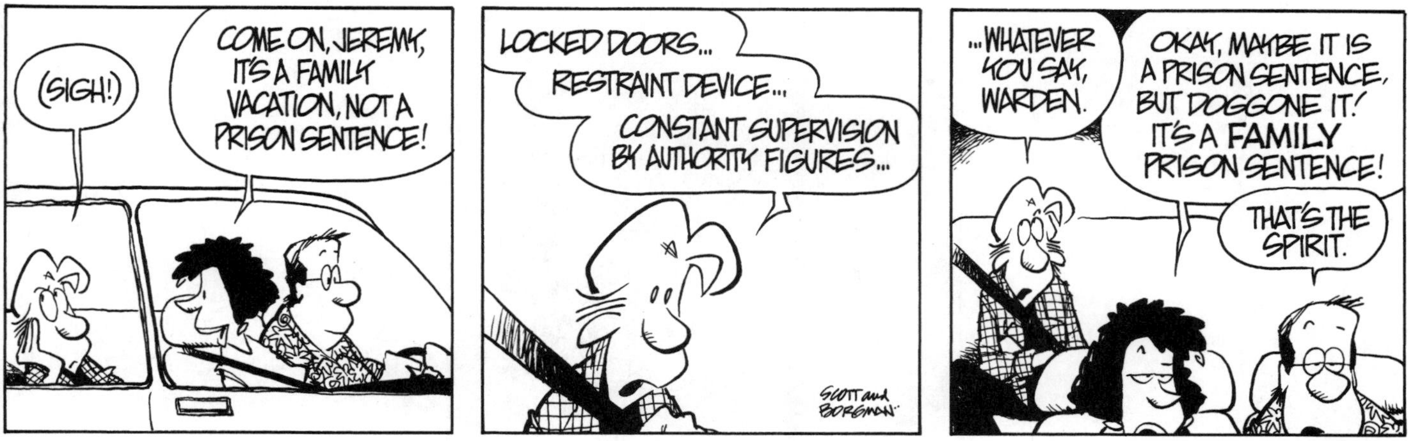
(SIGH!)
COME ON, JEREMY, IT'S A FAMILY VACATION, NOT A PRISON SENTENCE!
LOCKED DOORS...
RESTRAINT DEVICE...
CONSTANT SUPERVISION BY AUTHORITY FIGURES...
SCOTT and BORGMAN
...WHATEVER YOU SAY, WARDEN.
OKAY, MAYBE IT IS A PRISON SENTENCE, BUT DOGGONE IT! IT'S A FAMILY PRISON SENTENCE!
THAT'S THE SPIRIT.

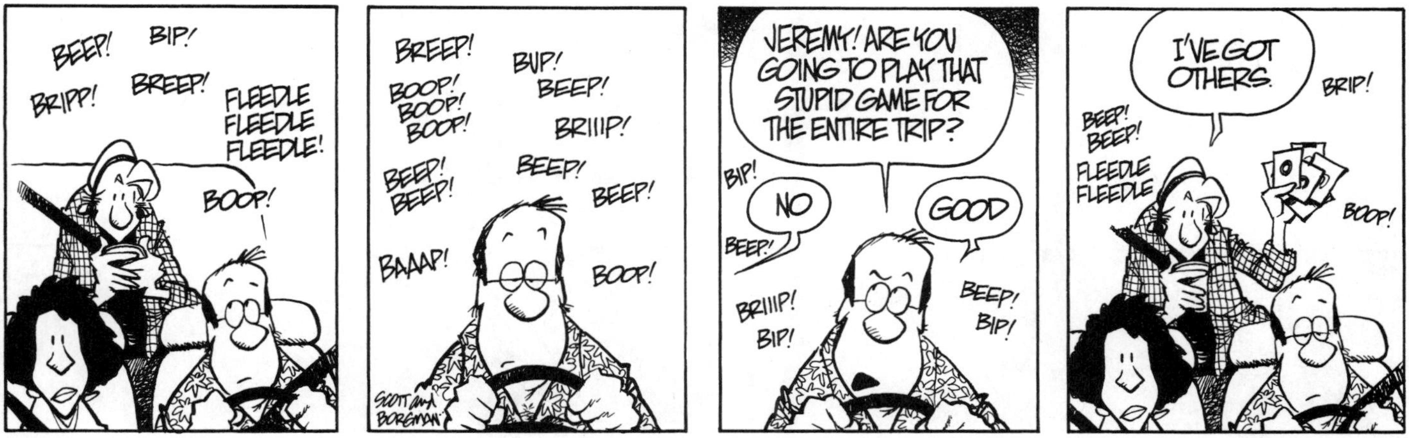
BEEP! BIP!
BRIPP! BREEP!
FLEEDLE FLEEDLE FLEEDLE!
BOOP!
BREEP! BUP! BEEP!
BOOP! BOOP! BOOP!
BRIIIP!
BEEP! BEEP!
BEEP! BEEP!
BAAAP! BOOP!
SCOTT and BORGMAN
JEREMY! ARE YOU GOING TO PLAY THAT STUPID GAME FOR THE ENTIRE TRIP?
BIP!
NO
BEEP!
GOOD
BRIIIP! BIP!
BEEP! BIP!
I'VE GOT OTHERS.
BRIP!
BEEP! BEEP!
FLEEDLE FLEEDLE
BOOP!

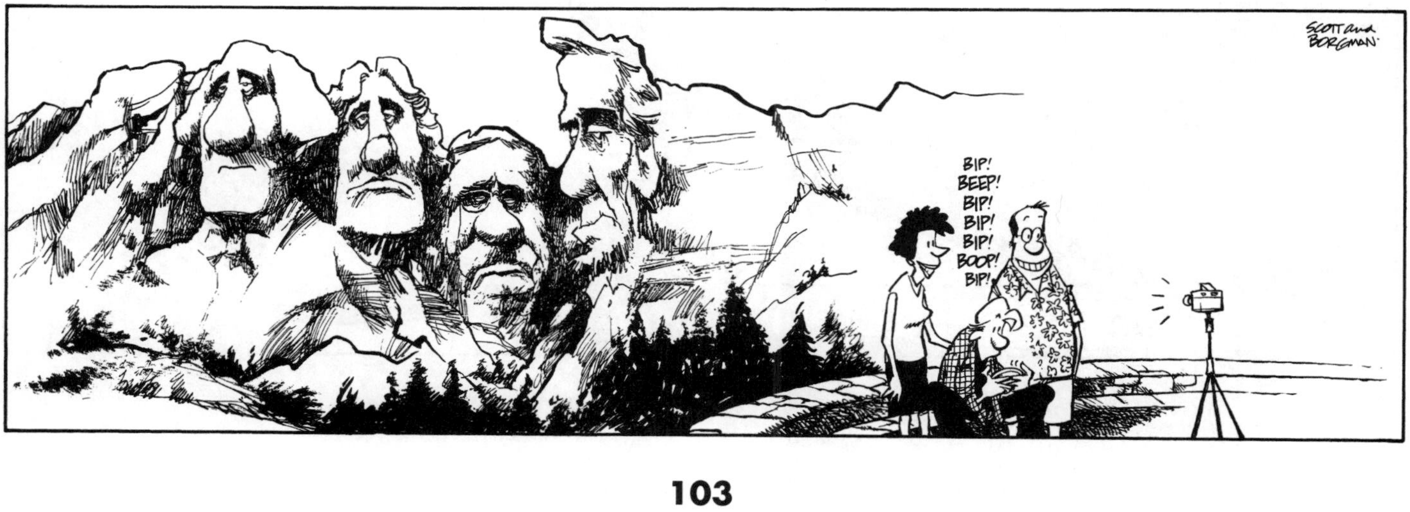
SCOTT and BORGMAN
BIP!
BEEP!
BIP!
BIP!
BIP!
BOOP!
BIP!

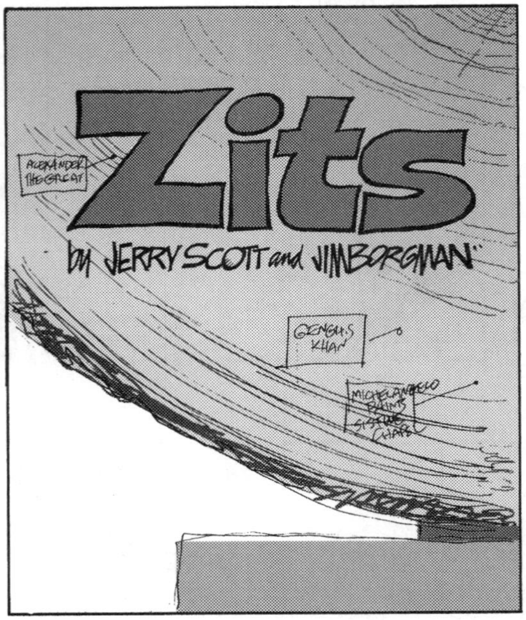
Zits
by JERRY SCOTT and JIM BORGMAN
ALEXANDER THE GREAT
GENGHIS KHAN
MICHELANGELO PAINTS SISTINE CHAPEL

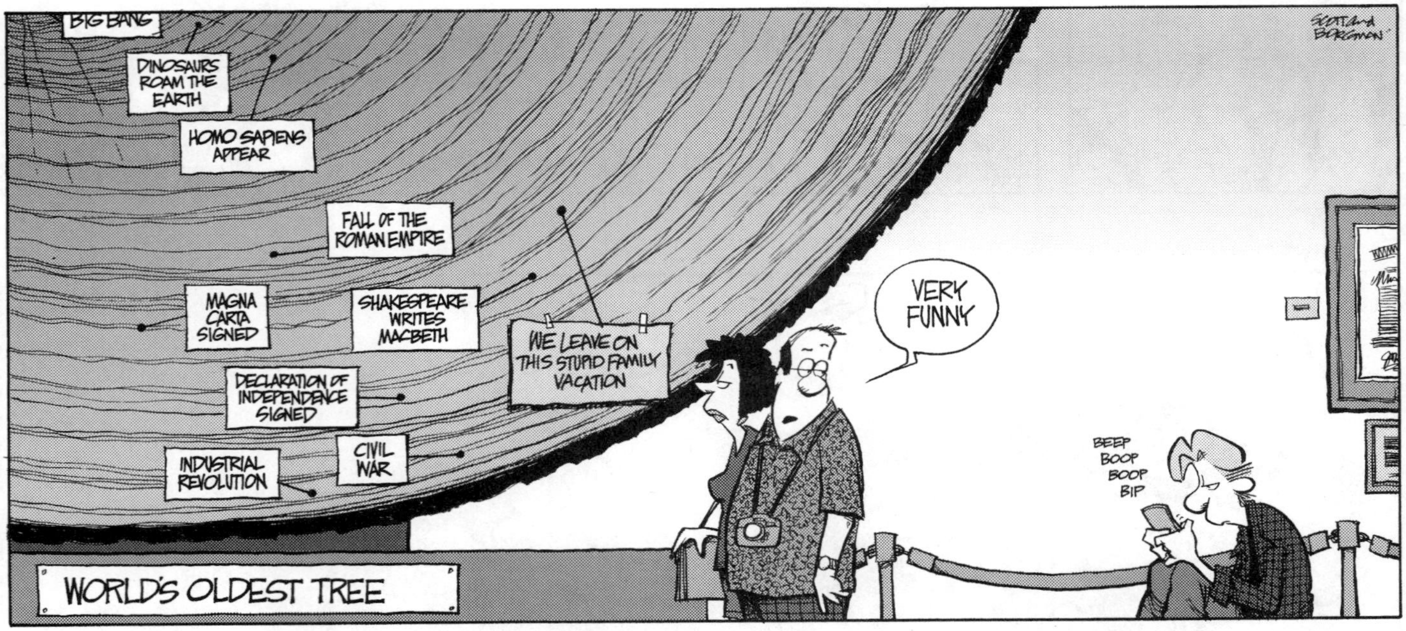
SCOTT and BORGMAN
BIG BANG
DINOSAURS ROAM THE EARTH
HOMO SAPIENS APPEAR
FALL OF THE ROMAN EMPIRE
MAGNA CARTA SIGNED
SHAKESPEARE WRITES MACBETH
WE LEAVE ON THIS STUPID FAMILY VACATION
DECLARATION OF INDEPENDENCE SIGNED
INDUSTRIAL REVOLUTION
CIVIL WAR
VERY FUNNY
BEEP BOOP BOOP BIP
WORLD'S OLDEST TREE

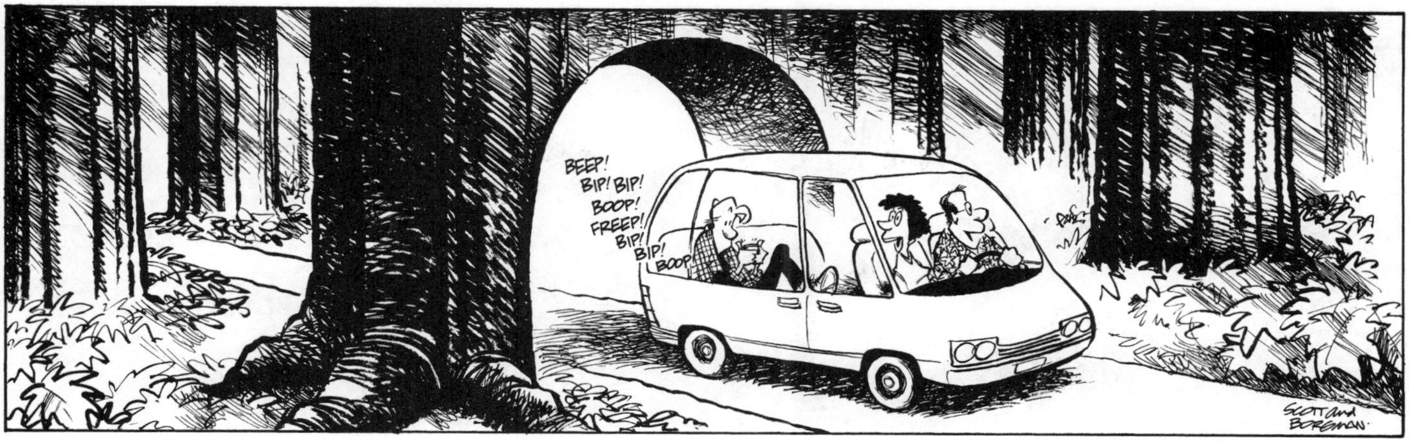
BEEP! BIP! BIP! BOOP! FREEP! BIP! BIP! BOOP
SCOTT and BORGMAN

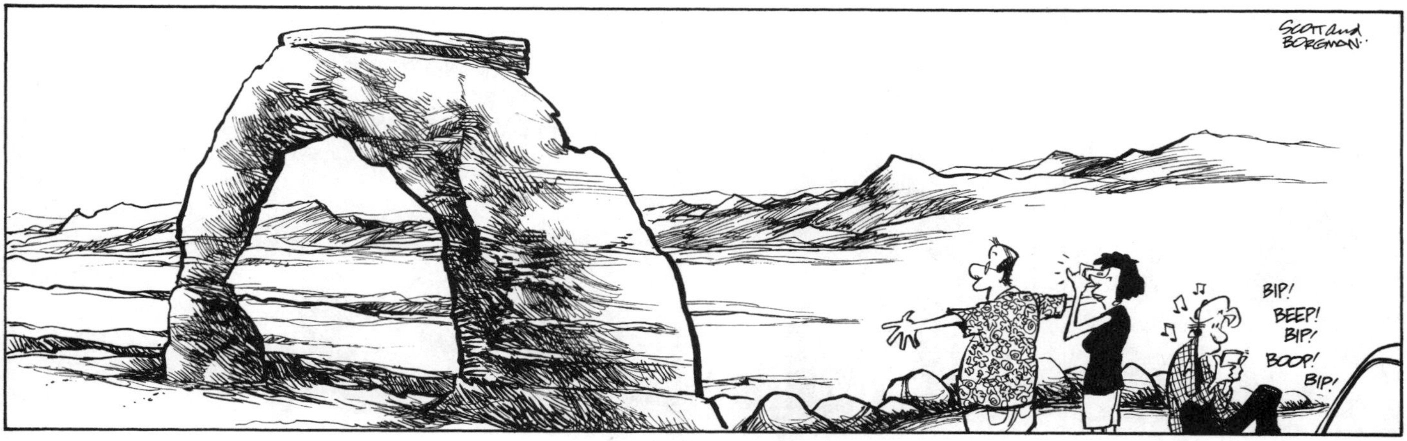
SCOTT and BORGMAN
BIP! BEEP! BIP! BOOP! BIP!

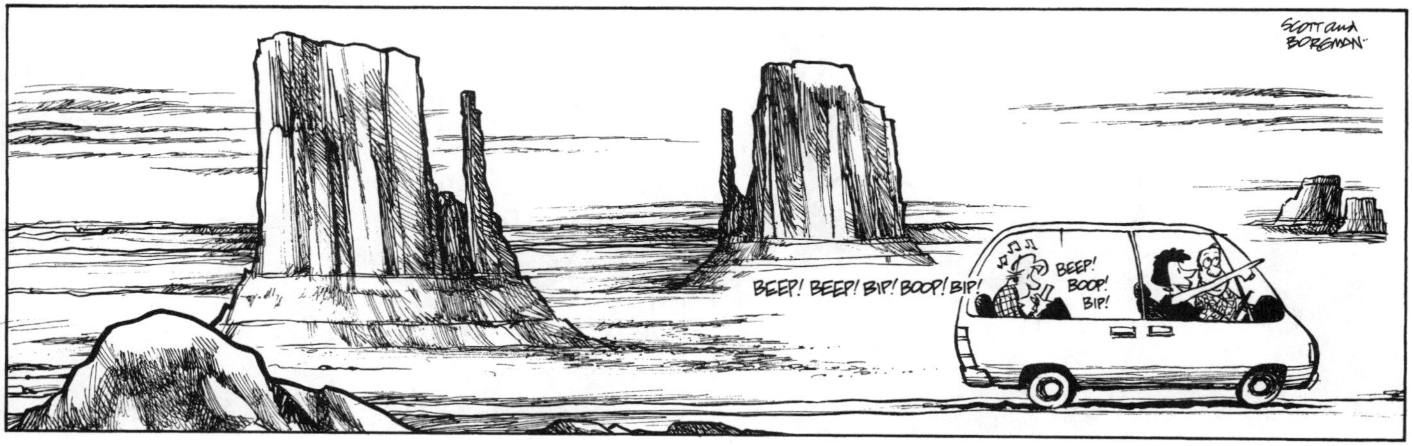
SCOTT and BORGMAN
BEEP! BEEP! BIP! BOOP! BIP!
BEEP! BOOP! BIP!

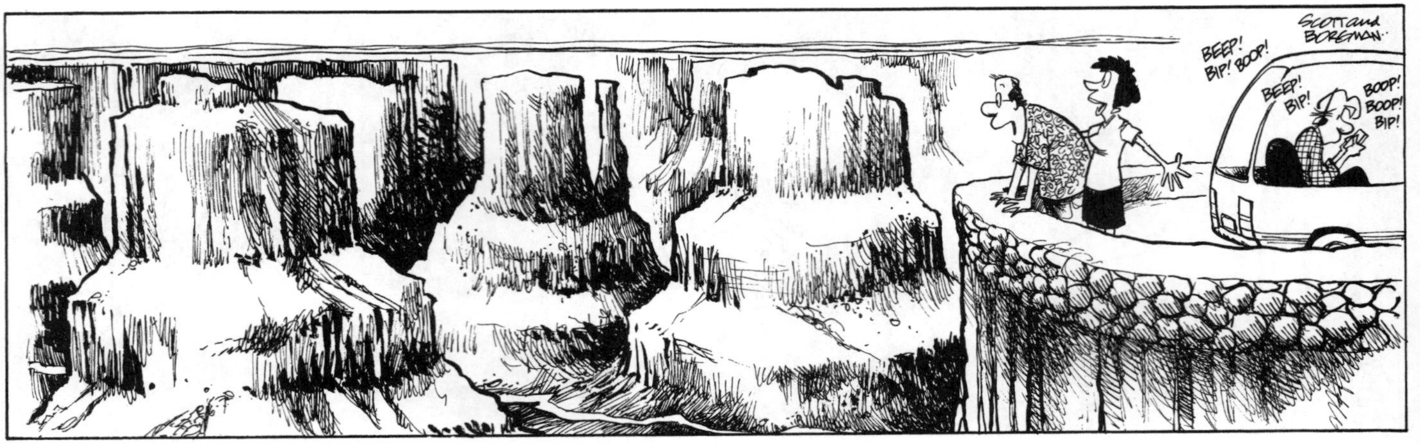
SCOTT and BORGMAN
BEEP! BIP! BOOP!
BEEP! BIP!
BOOP! BOOP! BIP!

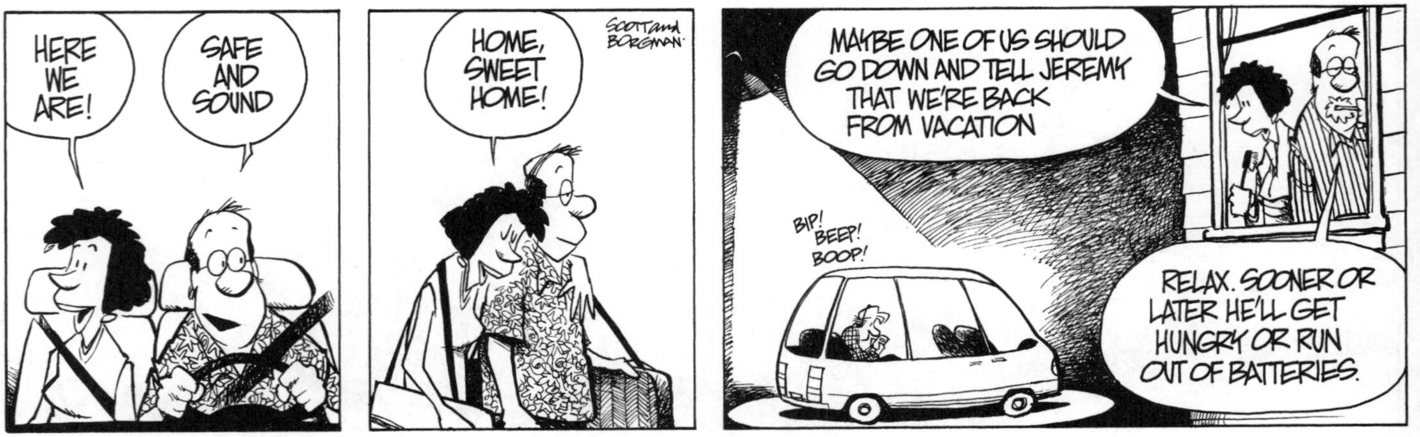
HERE WE ARE!
SAFE AND SOUND
SCOTT and BORGMAN
HOME, SWEET HOME!
MAYBE ONE OF US SHOULD GO DOWN AND TELL JEREMY THAT WE'RE BACK FROM VACATION
BIP! BEEP! BOOP!
RELAX. SOONER OR LATER HE'LL GET HUNGRY OR RUN OUT OF BATTERIES.

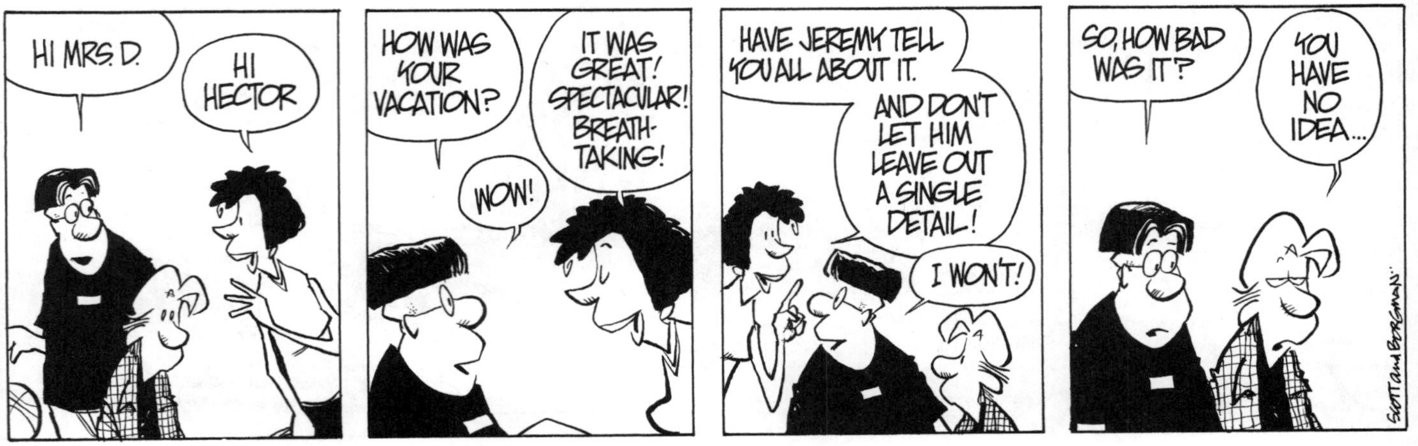
HI MRS. D.
HI HECTOR
HOW WAS YOUR VACATION?
IT WAS GREAT! SPECTACULAR! BREATH-TAKING!
WOW!
HAVE JEREMY TELL YOU ALL ABOUT IT.
AND DON'T LET HIM LEAVE OUT A SINGLE DETAIL!
I WON'T!
SO, HOW BAD WAS IT?
YOU HAVE NO IDEA...
SCOTT and BORGMAN

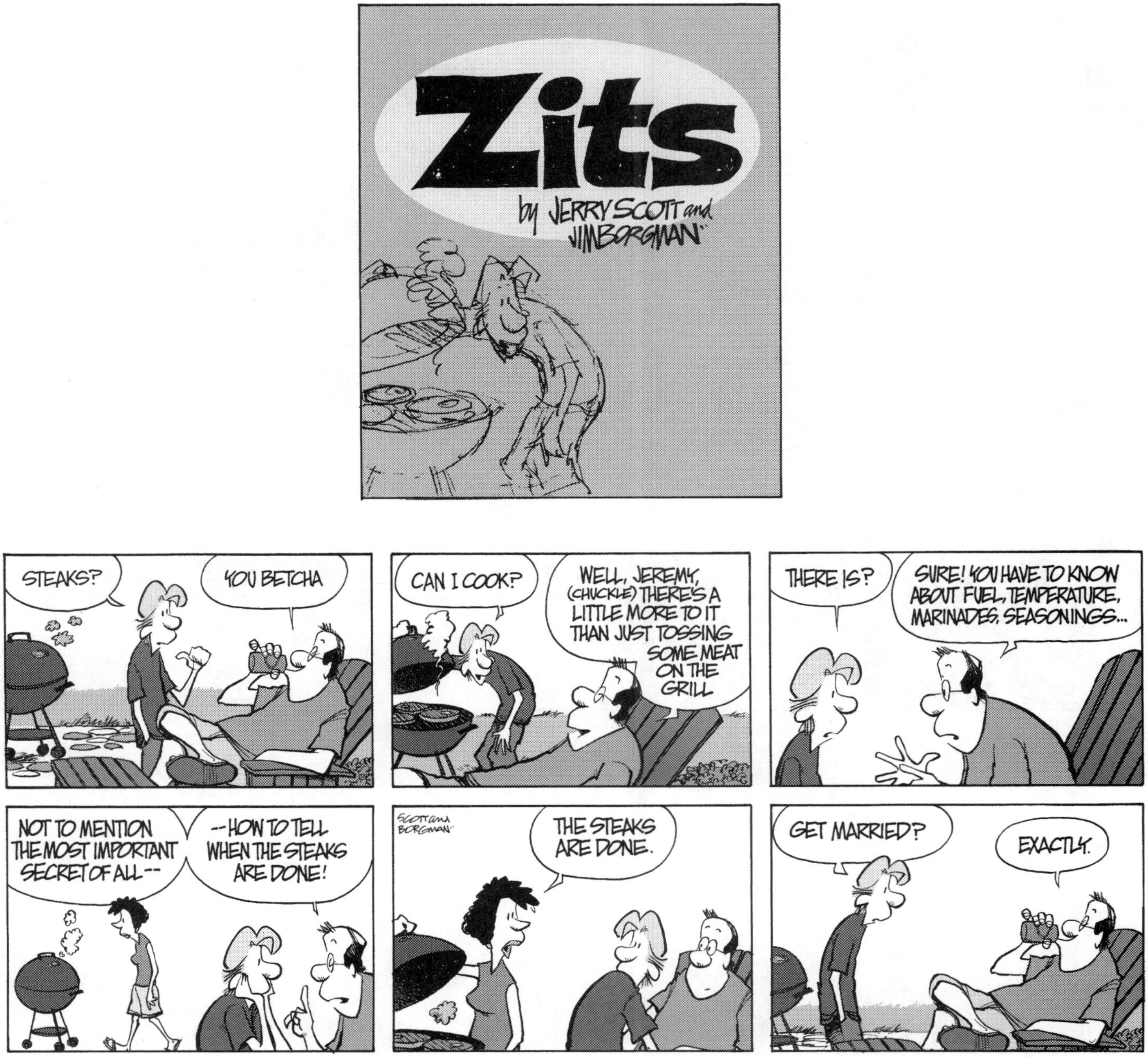
Zits
by JERRY SCOTT and JIM BORGMAN
STEAKS?
YOU BETCHA
CAN I COOK?
WELL, JEREMY, (CHUCKLE) THERE'S A LITTLE MORE TO IT THAN JUST TOSSING SOME MEAT ON THE GRILL
THERE IS?
SURE! YOU HAVE TO KNOW ABOUT FUEL, TEMPERATURE, MARINADES, SEASONINGS...
NOT TO MENTION THE MOST IMPORTANT SECRET OF ALL--
--HOW TO TELL WHEN THE STEAKS ARE DONE!
SCOTT and BORGMAN
THE STEAKS ARE DONE.
GET MARRIED?
EXACTLY.

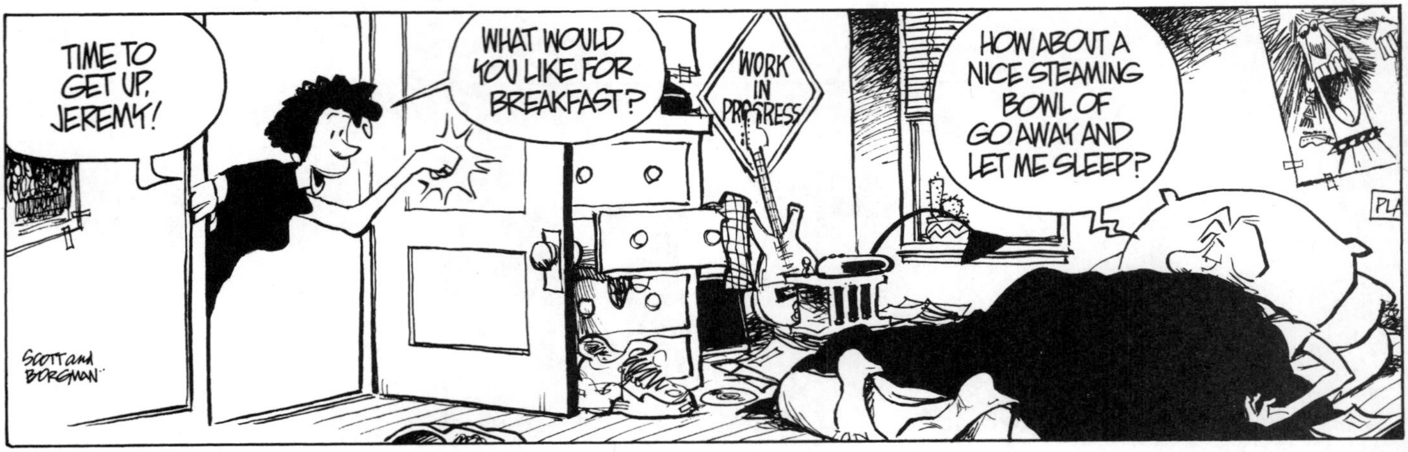
TIME TO GET UP, JEREMY!
WHAT WOULD YOU LIKE FOR BREAKFAST?
WORK IN PROGRESS
HOW ABOUT A NICE STEAMING BOWL OF GO AWAY AND LET ME SLEEP?
SCOTT and BORGMAN

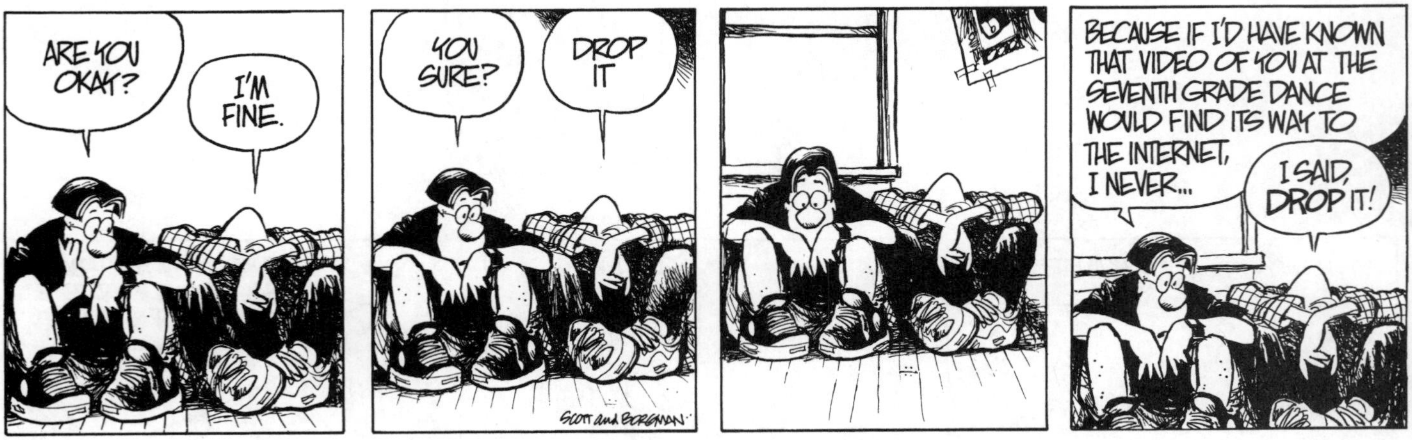
ARE YOU OKAY?
I'M FINE.
YOU SURE?
DROP IT
SCOTT and BORGMAN
BECAUSE IF I'D HAVE KNOWN THAT VIDEO OF YOU AT THE SEVENTH GRADE DANCE WOULD FIND ITS WAY TO THE INTERNET, I NEVER...
I SAID, DROP IT!

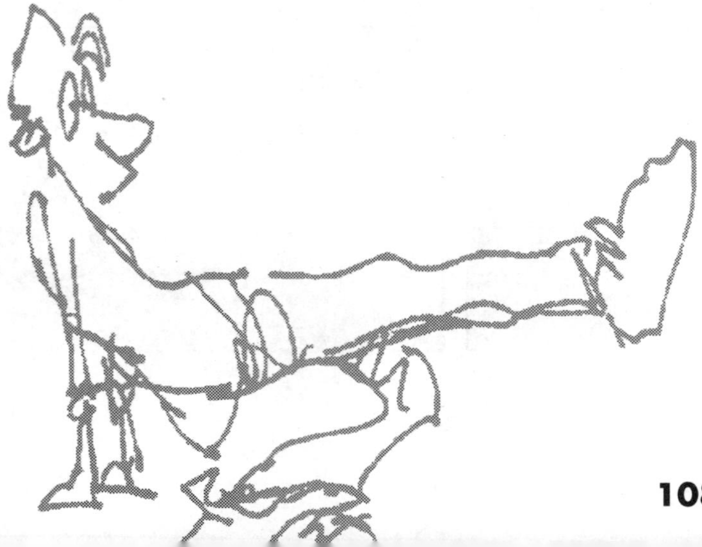

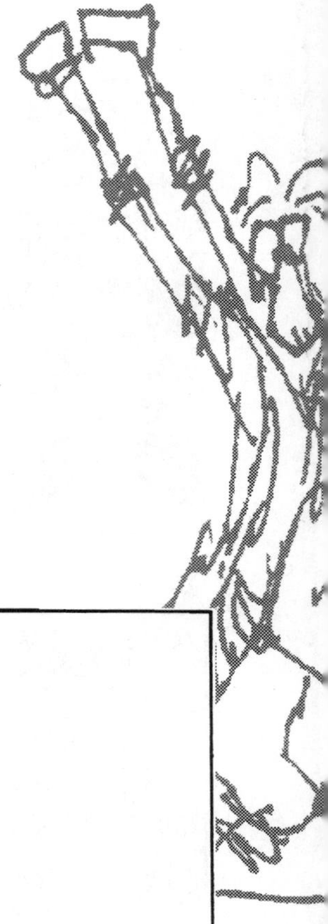

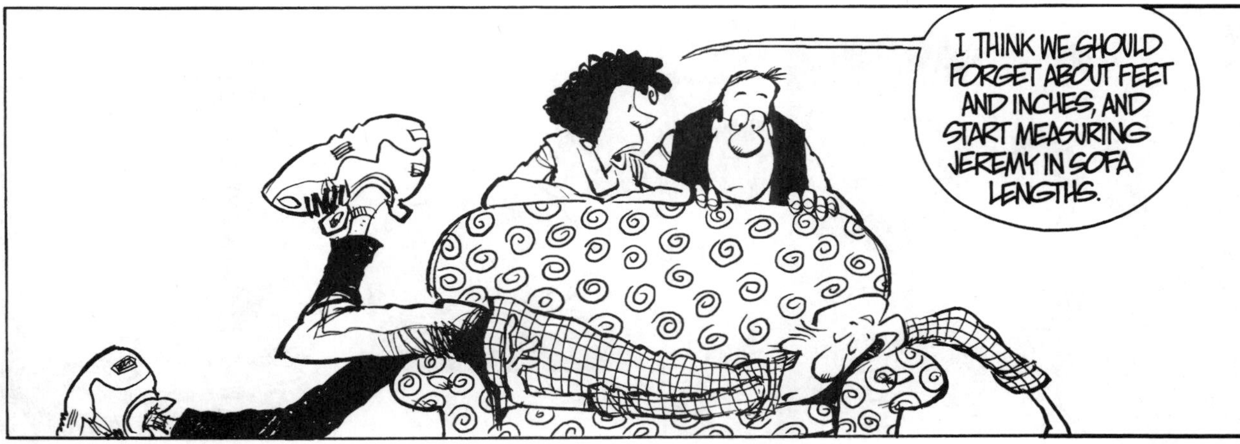
I THINK WE SHOULD FORGET ABOUT FEET AND INCHES, AND START MEASURING JEREMY IN SOFA LENGTHS.
SCOTT and BORGMAN

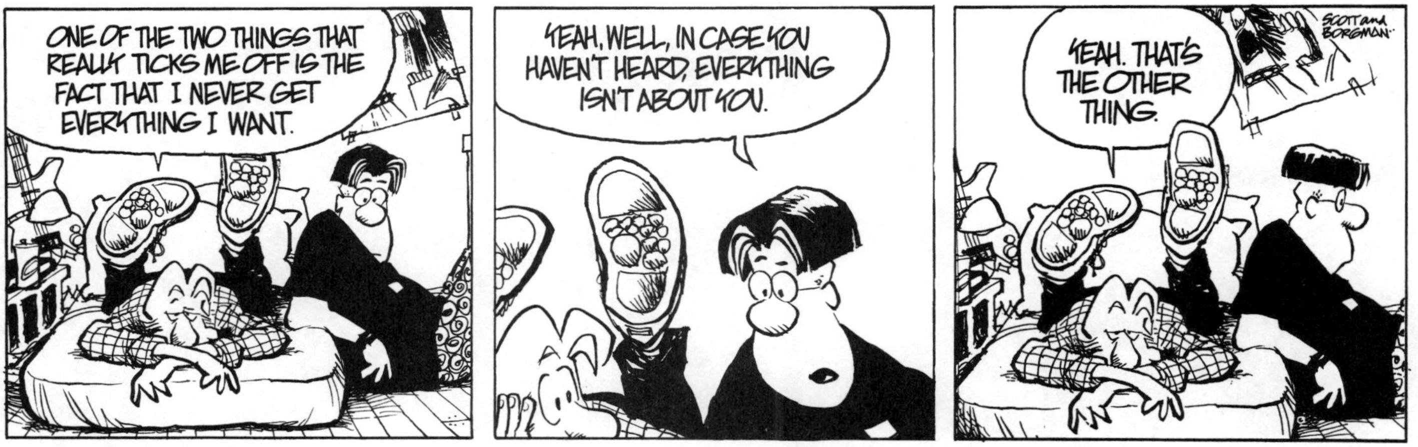
ONE OF THE TWO THINGS THAT REALLY TICKS ME OFF IS THE FACT THAT I NEVER GET EVERYTHING I WANT.
YEAH, WELL, IN CASE YOU HAVEN'T HEARD, EVERYTHING ISN'T ABOUT YOU.
YEAH. THAT'S THE OTHER THING.
SCOTT and BORGMAN

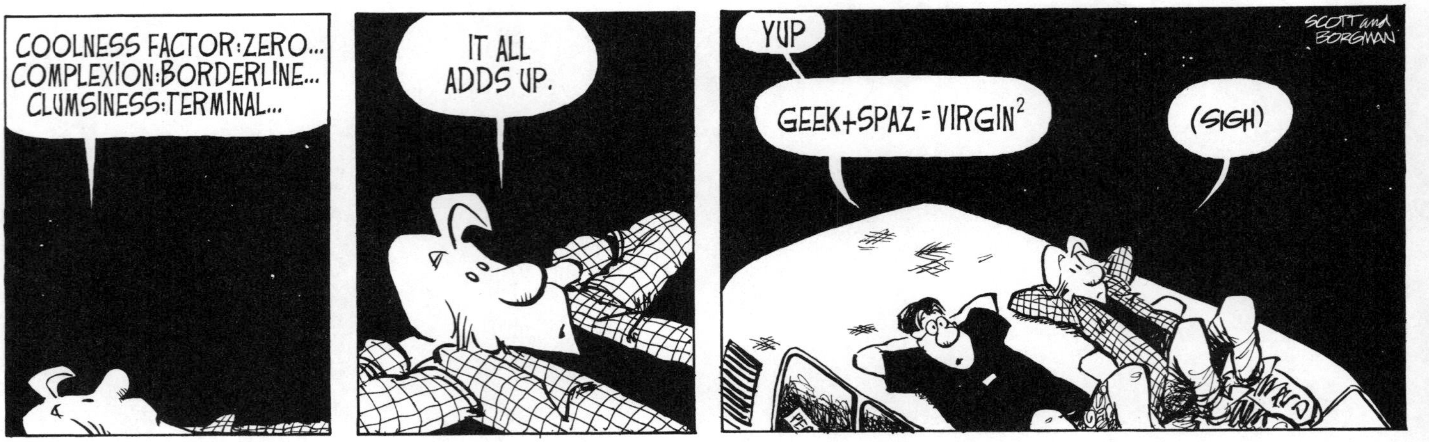
COOLNESS FACTOR: ZERO...
COMPLEXION: BORDERLINE...
CLUMSINESS: TERMINAL...
IT ALL ADDS UP.
YUP
GEEK + SPAZ = VIRGIN²
(SIGH)
SCOTT and BORGMAN

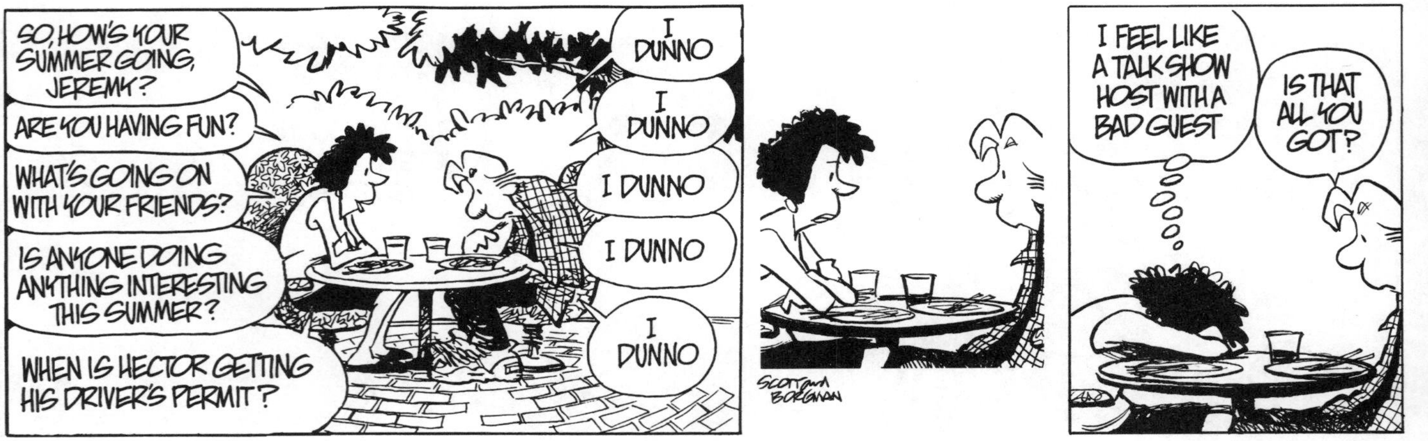
SO, HOW'S YOUR SUMMER GOING, JEREMY?
I DUNNO
ARE YOU HAVING FUN?
I DUNNO
WHAT'S GOING ON WITH YOUR FRIENDS?
I DUNNO
IS ANYONE DOING ANYTHING INTERESTING THIS SUMMER?
I DUNNO
WHEN IS HECTOR GETTING HIS DRIVER'S PERMIT?
I DUNNO
SCOTT and BORGMAN
I FEEL LIKE A TALK SHOW HOST WITH A BAD GUEST
IS THAT ALL YOU GOT?

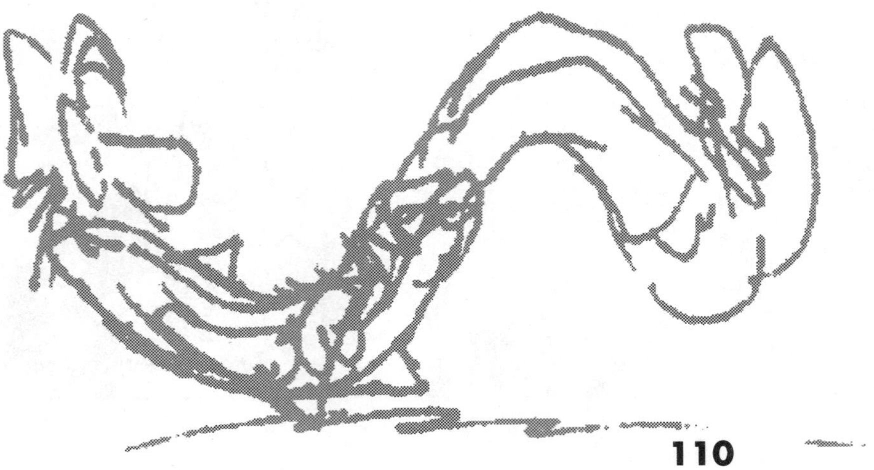

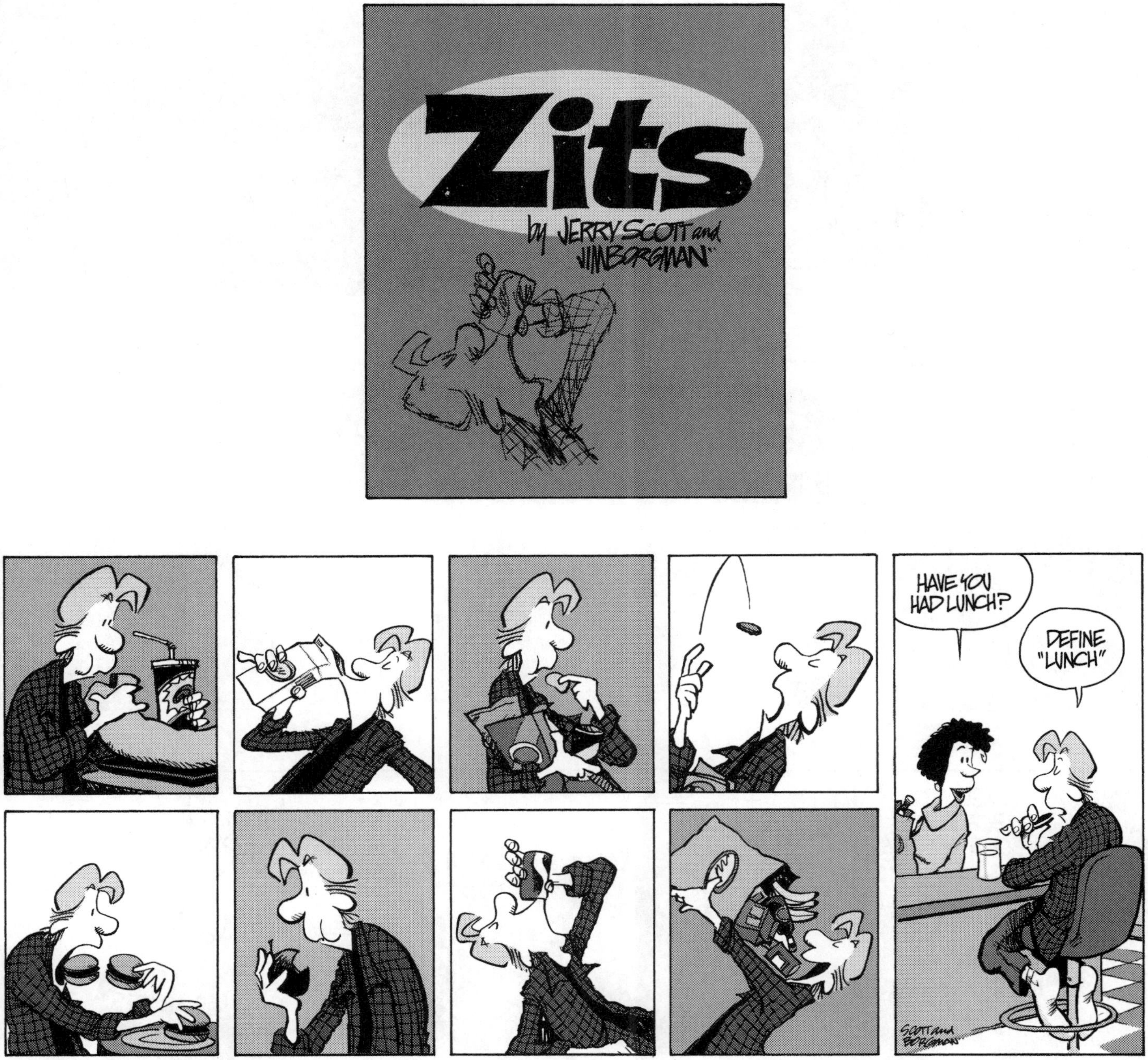
Zits
by JERRY SCOTT and JIM BORGMAN
HAVE YOU HAD LUNCH?
DEFINE "LUNCH"
SCOTT and BORGMAN

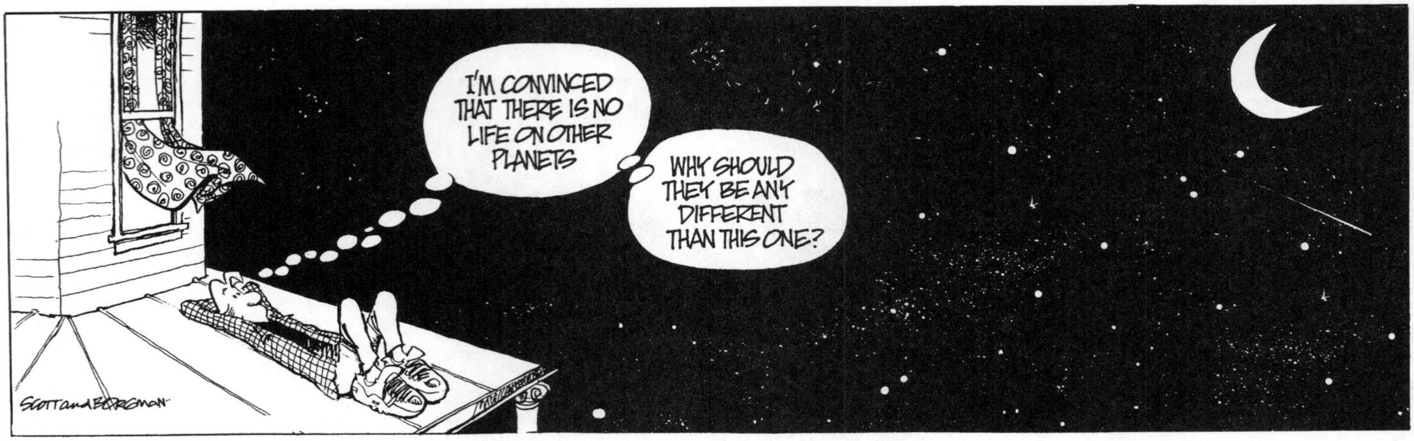
I'M CONVINCED THAT THERE IS NO LIFE ON OTHER PLANETS
WHY SHOULD THEY BE ANY DIFFERENT THAN THIS ONE?
SCOTT and BORGMAN

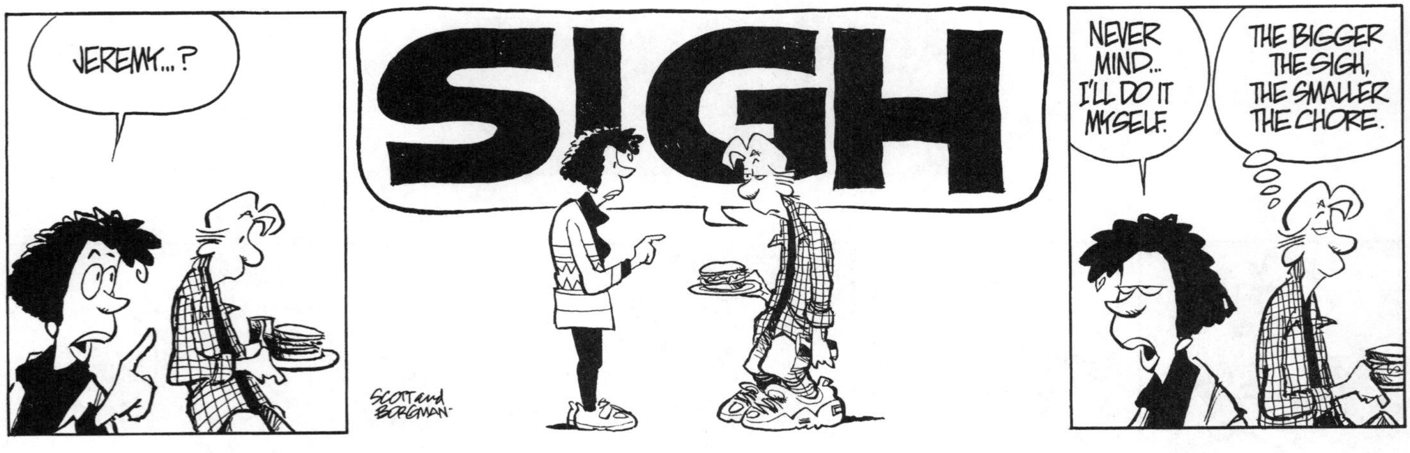
JEREMY...?
SIGH
SCOTT and BORGMAN
NEVER MIND... I'LL DO IT MYSELF.
THE BIGGER THE SIGH, THE SMALLER THE CHORE.

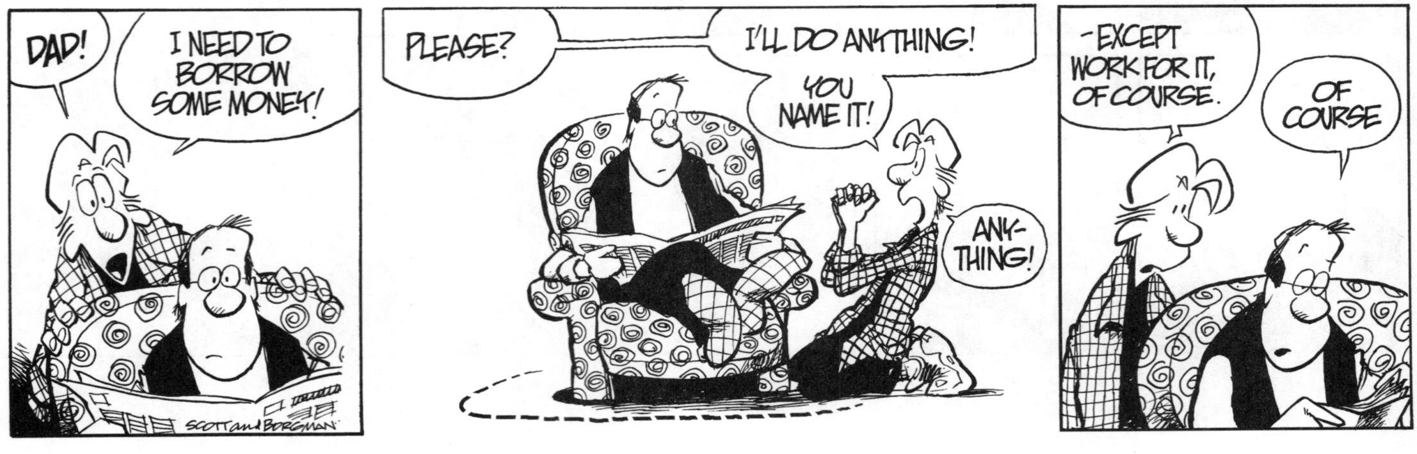
DAD!
I NEED TO BORROW SOME MONEY!
SCOTT and BORGMAN
PLEASE?
I'LL DO ANYTHING!
YOU NAME IT!
ANY-THING!
-EXCEPT WORK FOR IT, OF COURSE.
OF COURSE

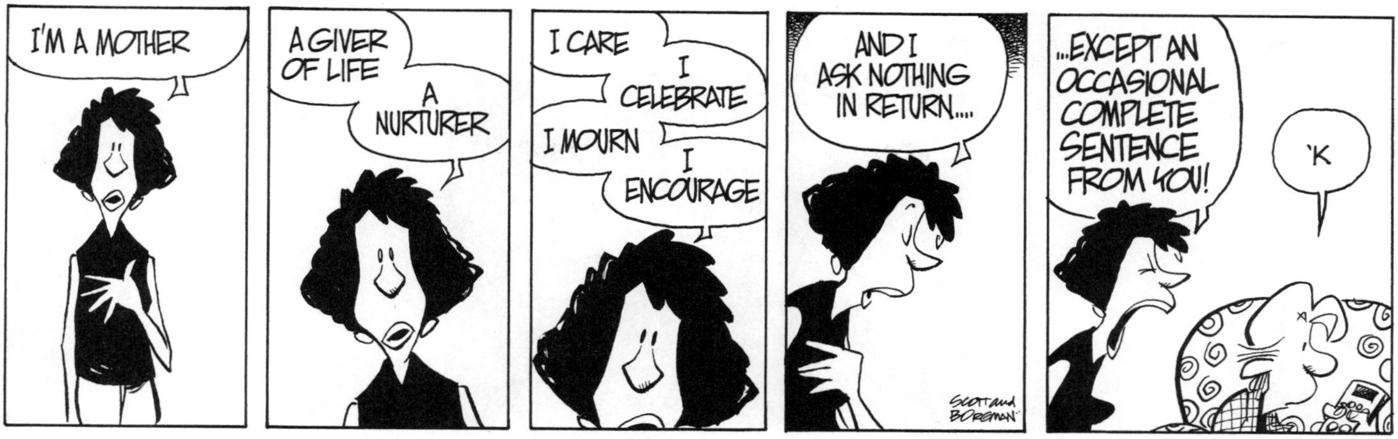
I'M A MOTHER
A GIVER OF LIFE
A NURTURER
I CARE
I CELEBRATE
I MOURN
I ENCOURAGE
AND I ASK NOTHING IN RETURN....
...EXCEPT AN OCCASIONAL COMPLETE SENTENCE FROM YOU!
'K
SCOTT and BORGMAN

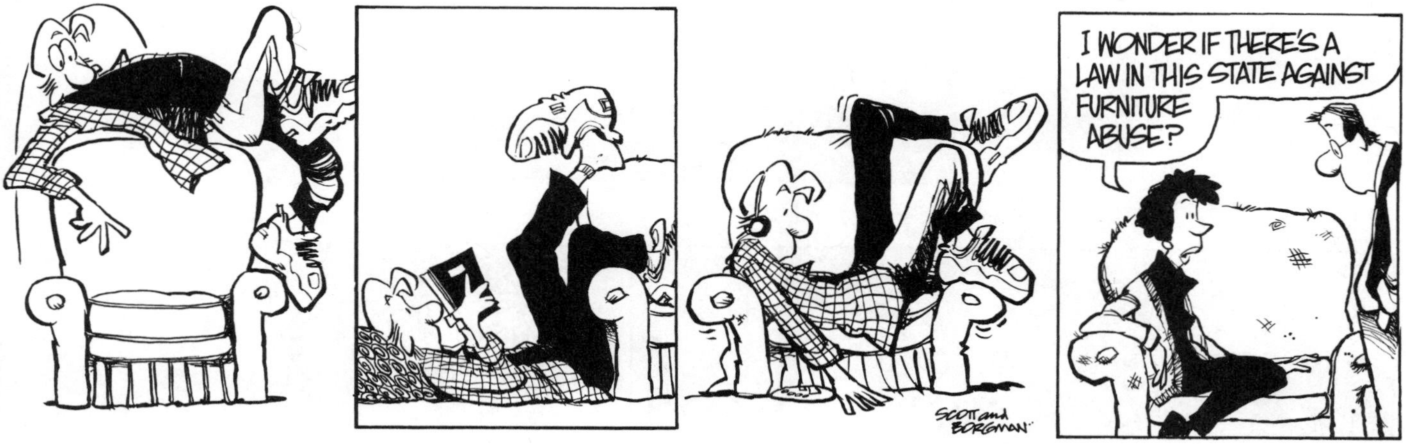
I WONDER IF THERE'S A LAW IN THIS STATE AGAINST FURNITURE ABUSE?
SCOTT and BORGMAN

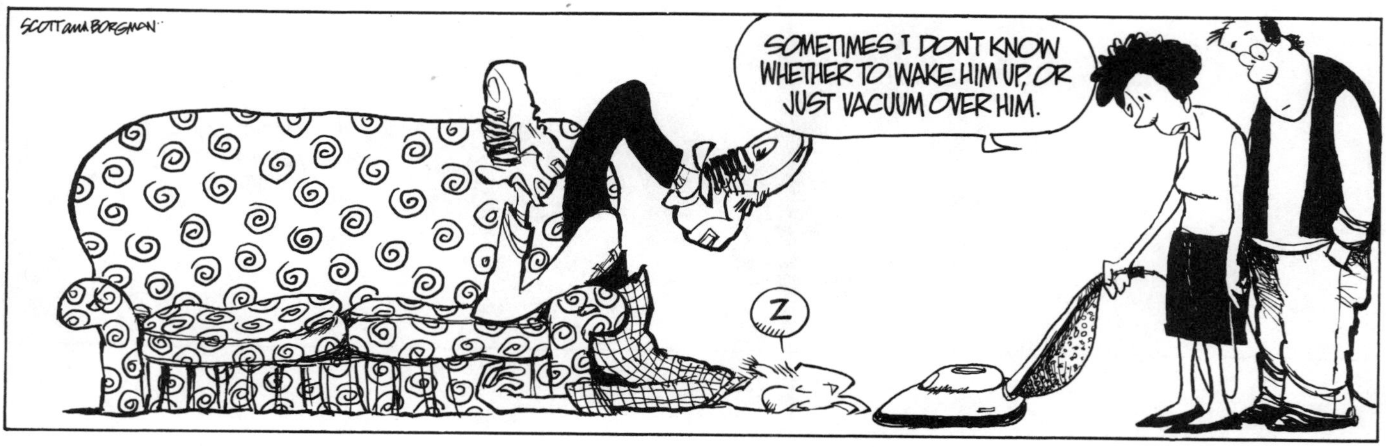
SCOTT and BORGMAN
SOMETIMES I DON'T KNOW WHETHER TO WAKE HIM UP, OR JUST VACUUM OVER HIM.
Z

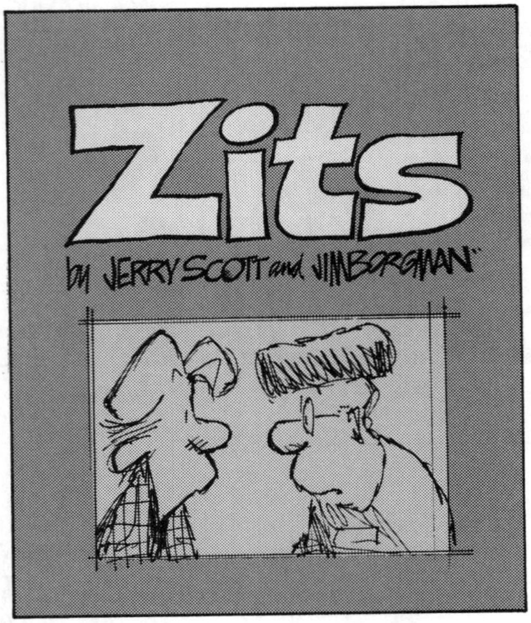
Zits
by JERRY SCOTT and JIM BORGMAN

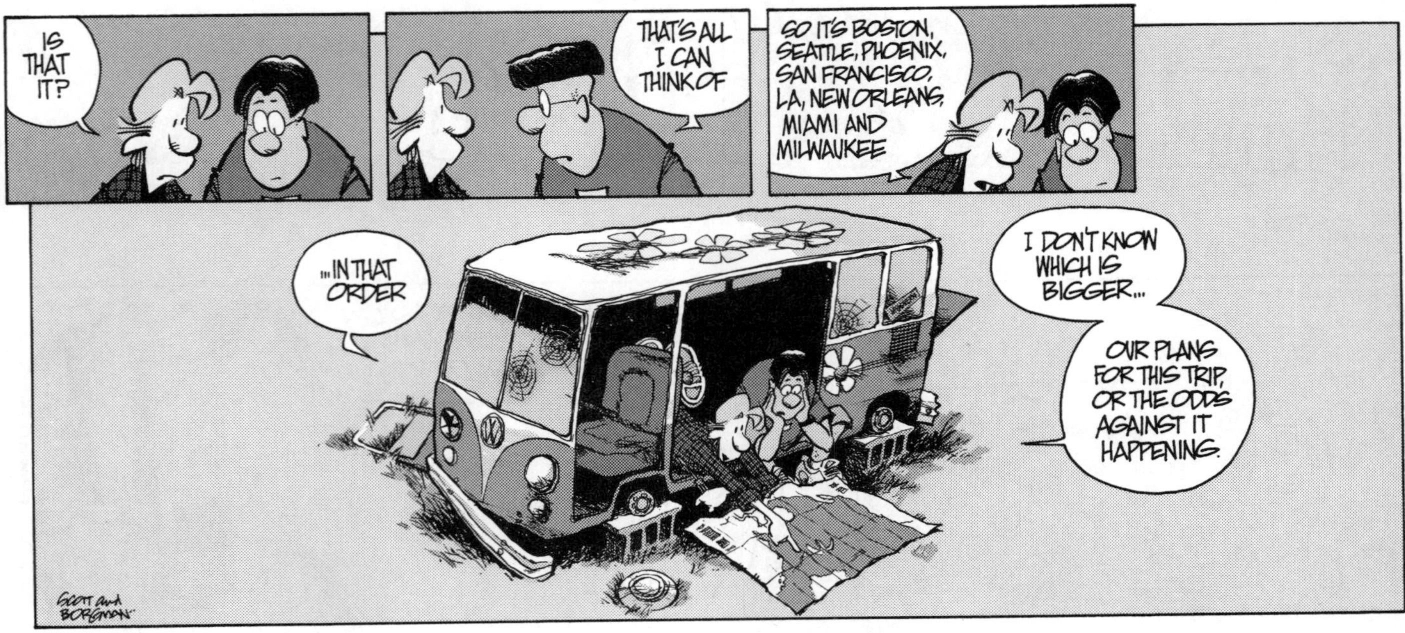
IS THAT IT?
THAT'S ALL I CAN THINK OF
SO IT'S BOSTON, SEATTLE, PHOENIX, SAN FRANCISCO, LA, NEW ORLEANS, MIAMI AND MILWAUKEE
...IN THAT ORDER
I DON'T KNOW WHICH IS BIGGER...
OUR PLANS FOR THIS TRIP, OR THE ODDS AGAINST IT HAPPENING.
SCOTT and BORGMAN

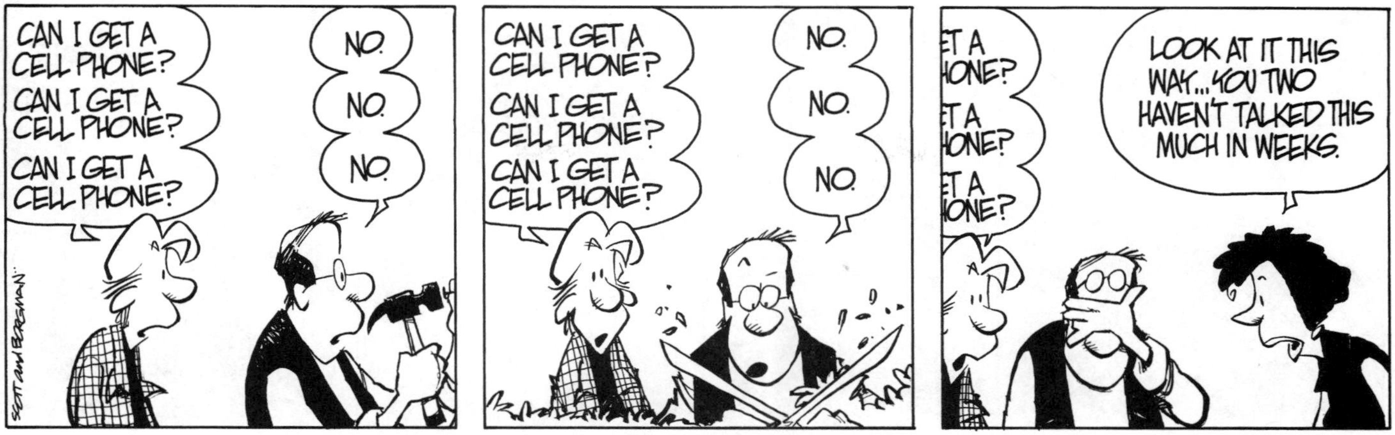
CAN I GET A CELL PHONE?
CAN I GET A CELL PHONE?
CAN I GET A CELL PHONE?
NO.
NO.
NO.
SCOTT AND BORGMAN
CAN I GET A CELL PHONE?
CAN I GET A CELL PHONE?
CAN I GET A CELL PHONE?
NO.
NO.
NO.
ET A HONE?
ET A HONE?
ET A HONE?
LOOK AT IT THIS WAY... YOU TWO HAVEN'T TALKED THIS MUCH IN WEEKS.

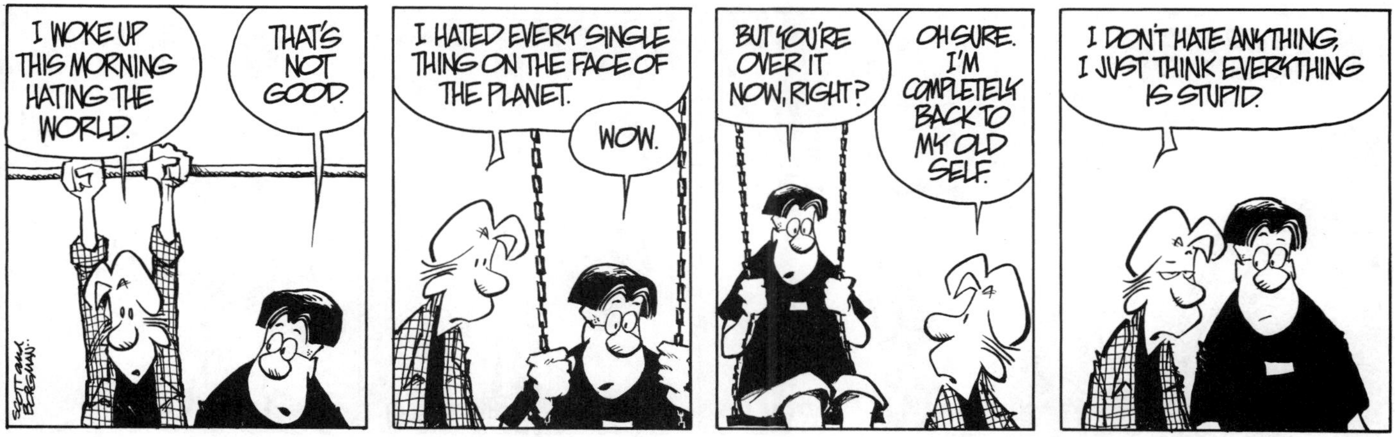
I WOKE UP THIS MORNING HATING THE WORLD.
THAT'S NOT GOOD.
SCOTT AND BORGMAN
I HATED EVERY SINGLE THING ON THE FACE OF THE PLANET.
WOW.
BUT YOU'RE OVER IT NOW, RIGHT?
OH SURE. I'M COMPLETELY BACK TO MY OLD SELF.
I DON'T HATE ANYTHING, I JUST THINK EVERYTHING IS STUPID.

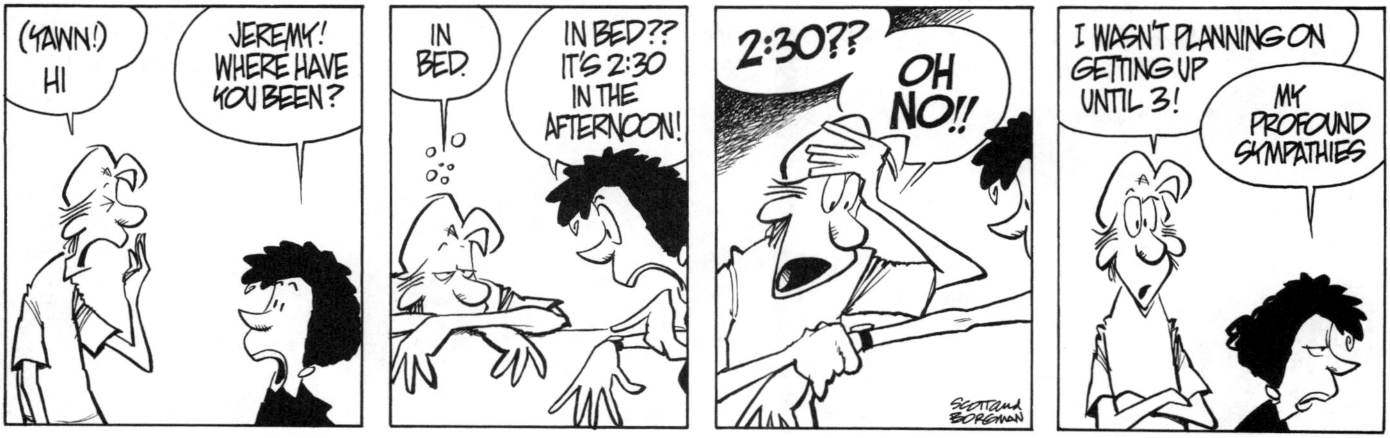
(YAWN!) HI
JEREMY! WHERE HAVE YOU BEEN?
IN BED.
IN BED?? IT'S 2:30 IN THE AFTERNOON!
2:30??
OH NO!!
SCOTT AND BORGMAN
I WASN'T PLANNING ON GETTING UP UNTIL 3!
MY PROFOUND SYMPATHIES

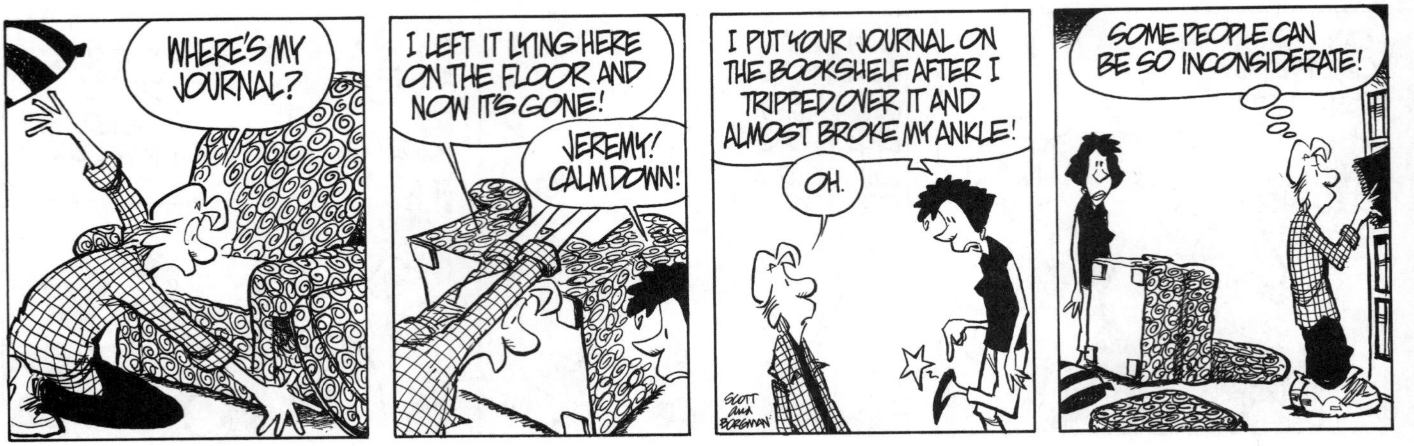
WHERE'S MY JOURNAL?
I LEFT IT LYING HERE ON THE FLOOR AND NOW IT'S GONE!
JEREMY! CALM DOWN!
I PUT YOUR JOURNAL ON THE BOOKSHELF AFTER I TRIPPED OVER IT AND ALMOST BROKE MY ANKLE!
OH.
SCOTT and BORGMAN
SOME PEOPLE CAN BE SO INCONSIDERATE!

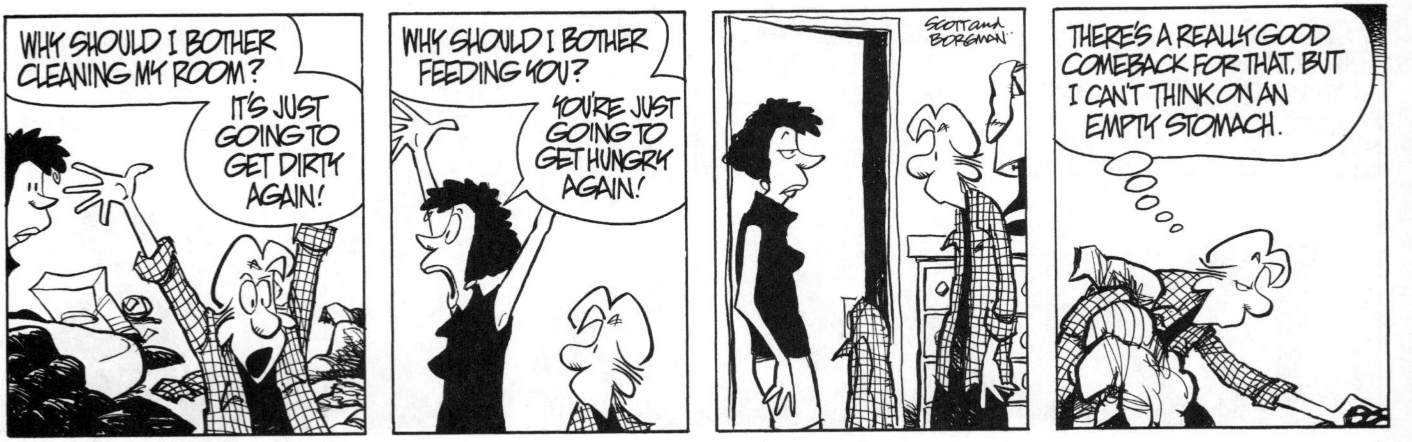
WHY SHOULD I BOTHER CLEANING MY ROOM?
IT'S JUST GOING TO GET DIRTY AGAIN!
WHY SHOULD I BOTHER FEEDING YOU?
YOU'RE JUST GOING TO GET HUNGRY AGAIN!
SCOTT and BORGMAN
THERE'S A REALLY GOOD COMEBACK FOR THAT, BUT I CAN'T THINK ON AN EMPTY STOMACH.

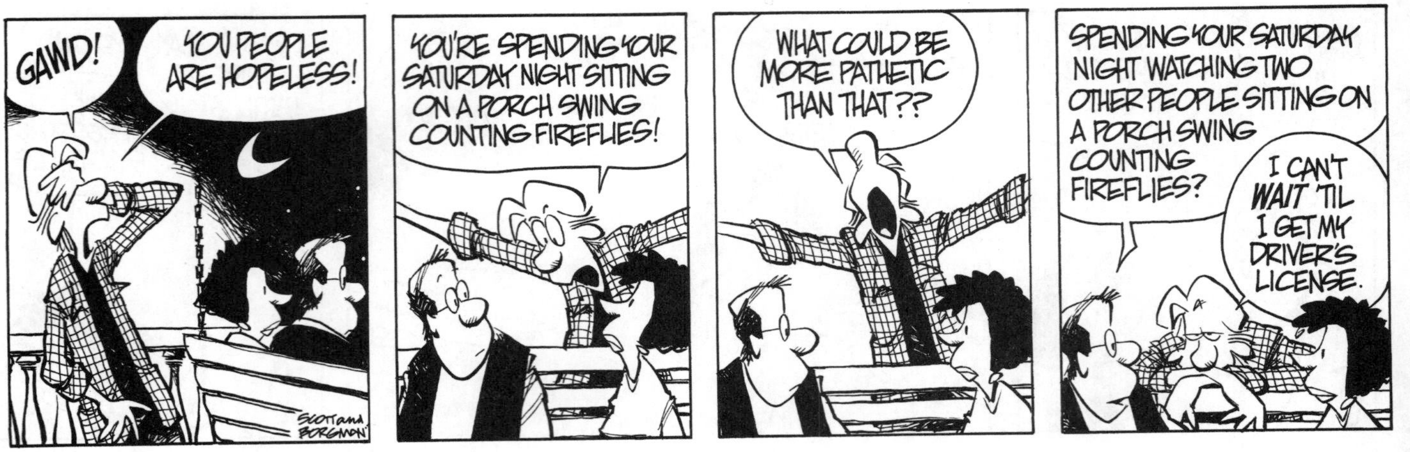
GAWD!
YOU PEOPLE ARE HOPELESS!
SCOTT and BORGMAN
YOU'RE SPENDING YOUR SATURDAY NIGHT SITTING ON A PORCH SWING COUNTING FIREFLIES!
WHAT COULD BE MORE PATHETIC THAN THAT??
SPENDING YOUR SATURDAY NIGHT WATCHING TWO OTHER PEOPLE SITTING ON A PORCH SWING COUNTING FIREFLIES?
I CAN'T WAIT 'TIL I GET MY DRIVER'S LICENSE.

Zits

by JERRY SCOTT and JIM BORGMAN

HEY DAD—

I'LL WASH YOUR CAR FOR TEN BUCKS

I CAN GET IT DONE AT THE CAR WASH FOR SEVEN

OH.

INCLUDING VACUUMING

UH-HUH.

THAT WAS GENEROUS OF YOU

GENEROSITY HAD NOTHING TO DO WITH IT.

PLUS, IT HAPPENS TO BE RAINING OUTSIDE!

GOOD POINT.

WELL, SINCE YOU'VE CRUSHED MY ENTREPRENEURIAL SPIRIT, I GUESS I'LL JUST HAVE TO GET USED TO THE IDEA OF LIVING AT HOME UNTIL I'M THIRTY.

SCOTT and BORGMAN

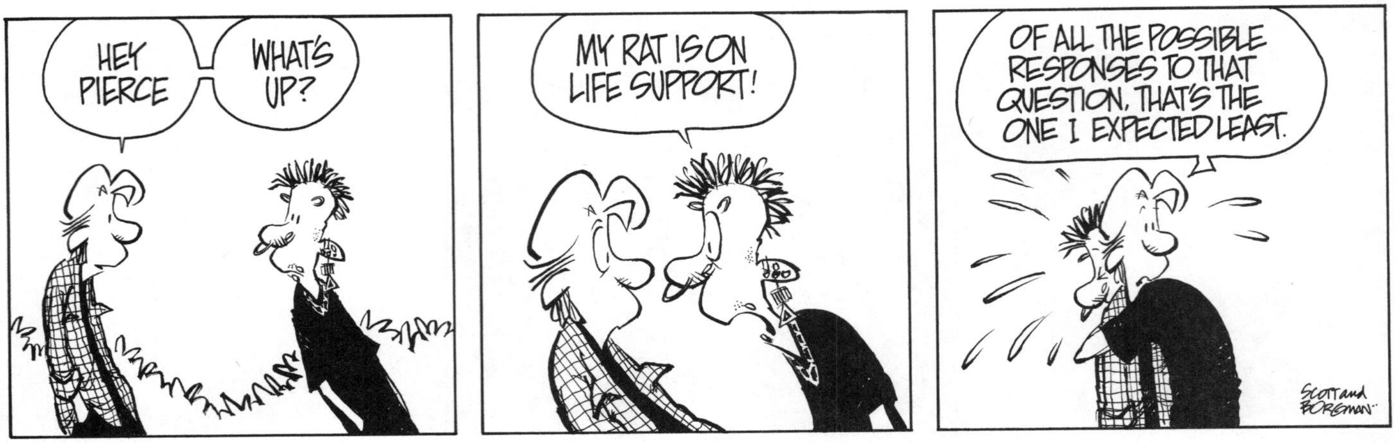
HEY PIERCE
WHAT'S UP?
MY RAT IS ON LIFE SUPPORT!
OF ALL THE POSSIBLE RESPONSES TO THAT QUESTION, THAT'S THE ONE I EXPECTED LEAST.
SCOTT and BORGMAN

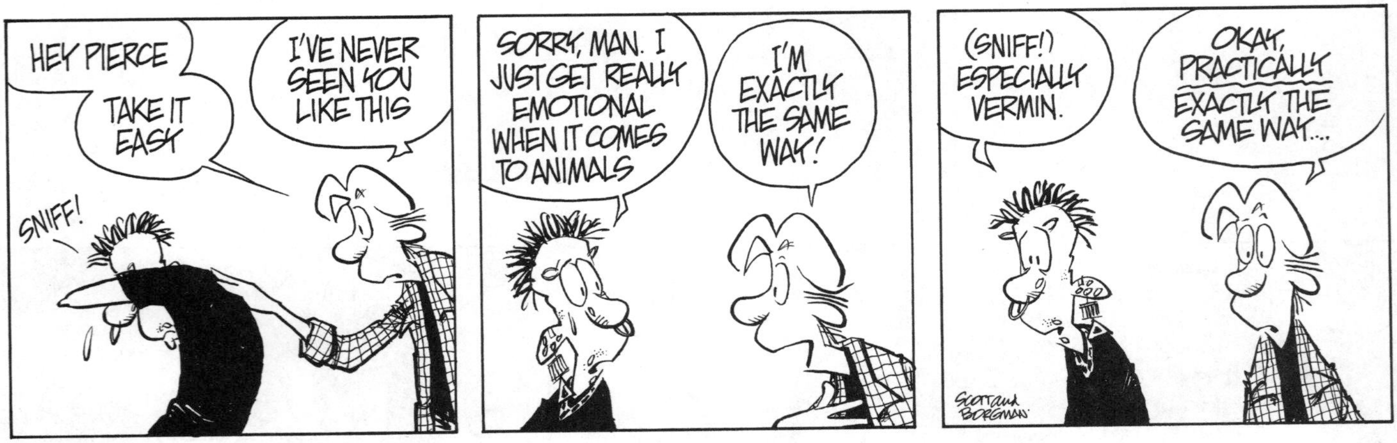
HEY PIERCE
TAKE IT EASY
I'VE NEVER SEEN YOU LIKE THIS
SNIFF!
SORRY, MAN. I JUST GET REALLY EMOTIONAL WHEN IT COMES TO ANIMALS
I'M EXACTLY THE SAME WAY!
(SNIFF!) ESPECIALLY VERMIN.
OKAY, PRACTICALLY EXACTLY THE SAME WAY....
SCOTT and BORGMAN

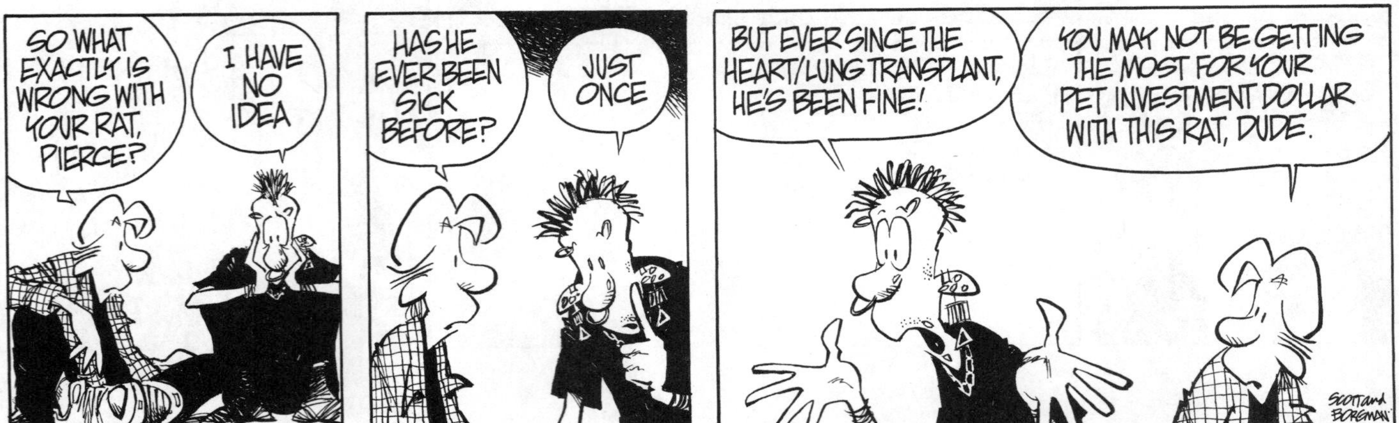
SO WHAT EXACTLY IS WRONG WITH YOUR RAT, PIERCE?
I HAVE NO IDEA
HAS HE EVER BEEN SICK BEFORE?
JUST ONCE
BUT EVER SINCE THE HEART/LUNG TRANSPLANT, HE'S BEEN FINE!
YOU MAY NOT BE GETTING THE MOST FOR YOUR PET INVESTMENT DOLLAR WITH THIS RAT, DUDE.
SCOTT and BORGMAN

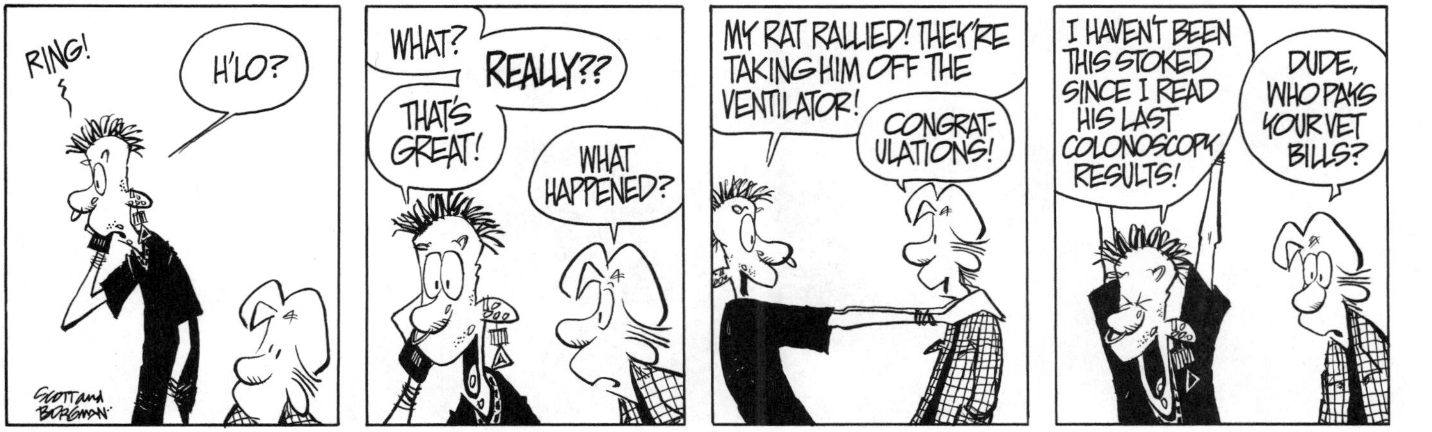
RING!
H'LO?
WHAT?
REALLY??
THAT'S GREAT!
WHAT HAPPENED?
MY RAT RALLIED! THEY'RE TAKING HIM OFF THE VENTILATOR!
CONGRATULATIONS!
I HAVEN'T BEEN THIS STOKED SINCE I READ HIS LAST COLONOSCOPY RESULTS!
DUDE, WHO PAYS YOUR VET BILLS?
SCOTT and BORGMAN

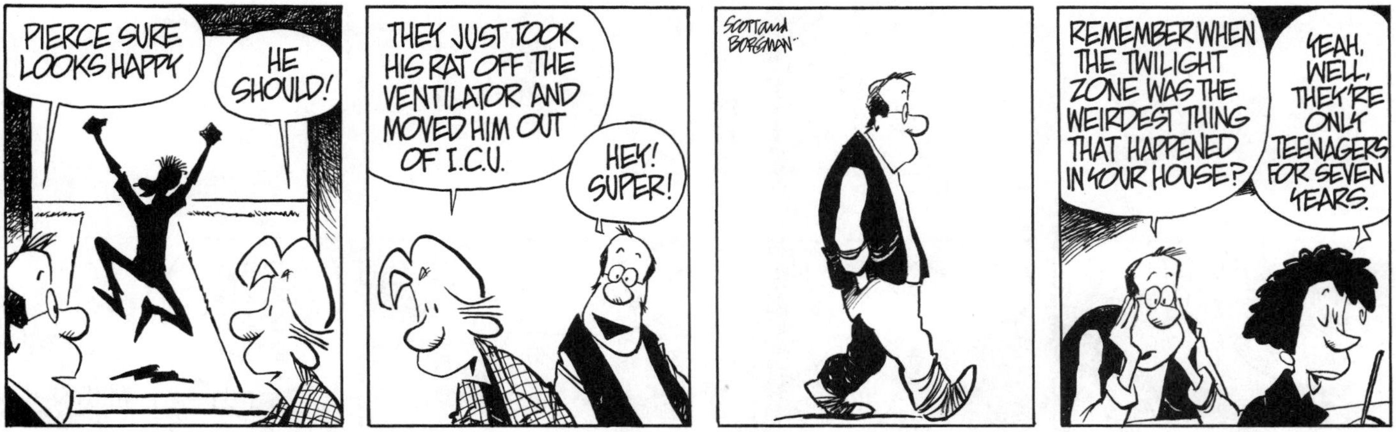
PIERCE SURE LOOKS HAPPY
HE SHOULD!
THEY JUST TOOK HIS RAT OFF THE VENTILATOR AND MOVED HIM OUT OF I.C.U.
HEY! SUPER!
SCOTT and BORGMAN
REMEMBER WHEN THE TWILIGHT ZONE WAS THE WEIRDEST THING THAT HAPPENED IN YOUR HOUSE?
YEAH, WELL, THEY'RE ONLY TEENAGERS FOR SEVEN YEARS.

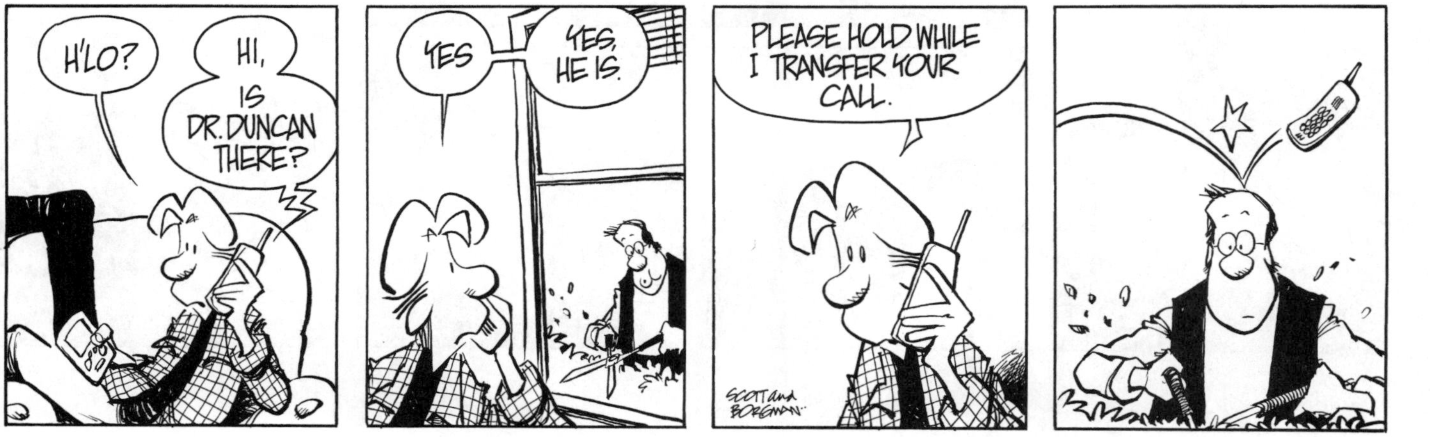
H'LO?
HI, IS DR. DUNCAN THERE?
YES
YES, HE IS.
PLEASE HOLD WHILE I TRANSFER YOUR CALL.
SCOTT and BORGMAN

Zits
by JERRY SCOTT and JIM BORGMAN
JEREMY, WILL YOU PUT THESE CLOTHES AWAY FOR ME?
YEAH. SURE.
AND I DON'T MEAN ON THE FLOOR!
--NEATLY!
PUT THEM IN YOUR DRESSER
CLOSE THE DRAWER...
AND STOP ROLLING YOUR EYES LIKE THAT!
YOU DON'T GET AWAY WITH MUCH AROUND HERE, DO YOU?
SCOTT and BORGMAN

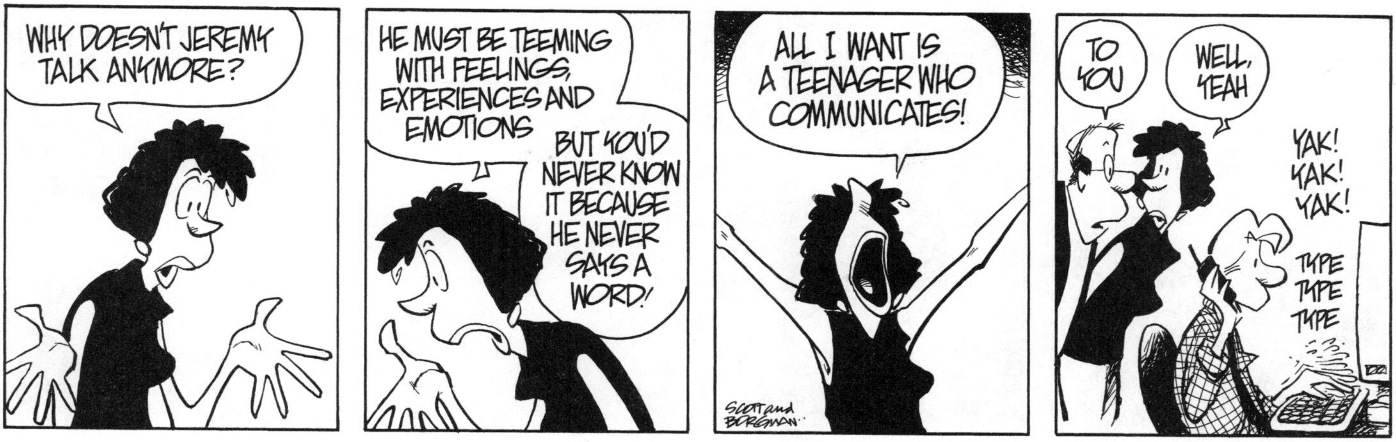
WHY DOESN'T JEREMY TALK ANYMORE?
HE MUST BE TEEMING WITH FEELINGS, EXPERIENCES AND EMOTIONS
BUT YOU'D NEVER KNOW IT BECAUSE HE NEVER SAYS A WORD!
ALL I WANT IS A TEENAGER WHO COMMUNICATES!
SCOTT and BORGMAN
TO YOU
WELL, YEAH
YAK! YAK! YAK!
TYPE TYPE TYPE

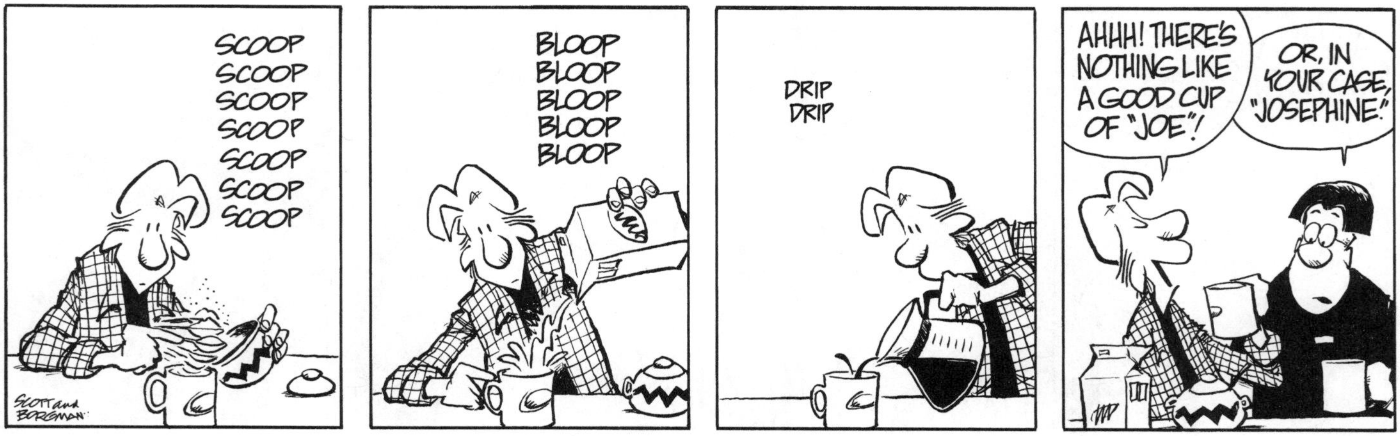
SCOOP SCOOP SCOOP SCOOP SCOOP SCOOP SCOOP
SCOTT and BORGMAN
BLOOP BLOOP BLOOP BLOOP BLOOP
DRIP DRIP
AHHH! THERE'S NOTHING LIKE A GOOD CUP OF "JOE"!
OR, IN YOUR CASE, "JOSEPHINE."

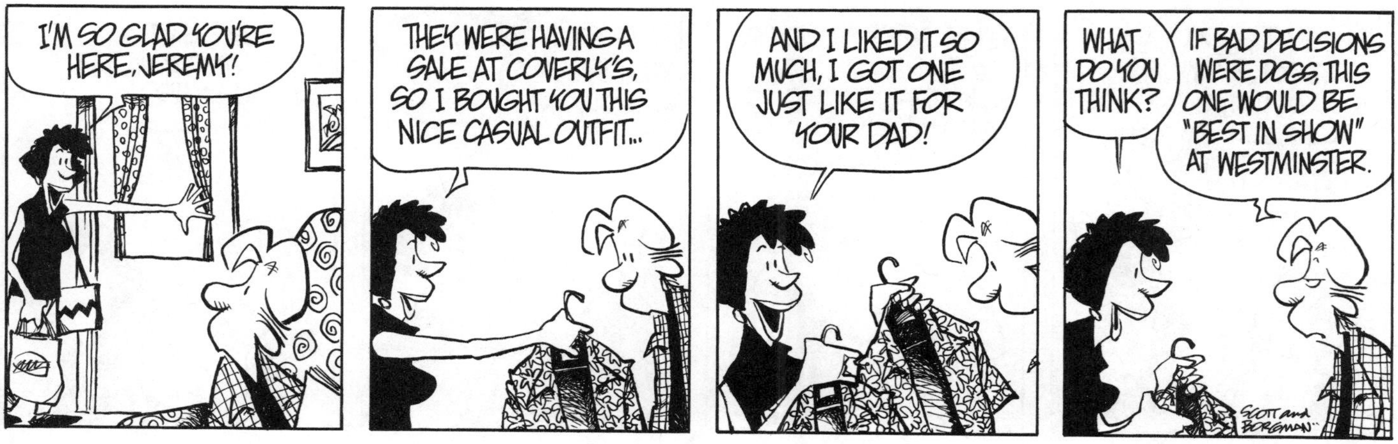
I'M SO GLAD YOU'RE HERE, JEREMY!
THEY WERE HAVING A SALE AT COVERLY'S, SO I BOUGHT YOU THIS NICE CASUAL OUTFIT...
AND I LIKED IT SO MUCH, I GOT ONE JUST LIKE IT FOR YOUR DAD!
WHAT DO YOU THINK?
IF BAD DECISIONS WERE DOGS, THIS ONE WOULD BE "BEST IN SHOW" AT WESTMINSTER.
SCOTT and BORGMAN

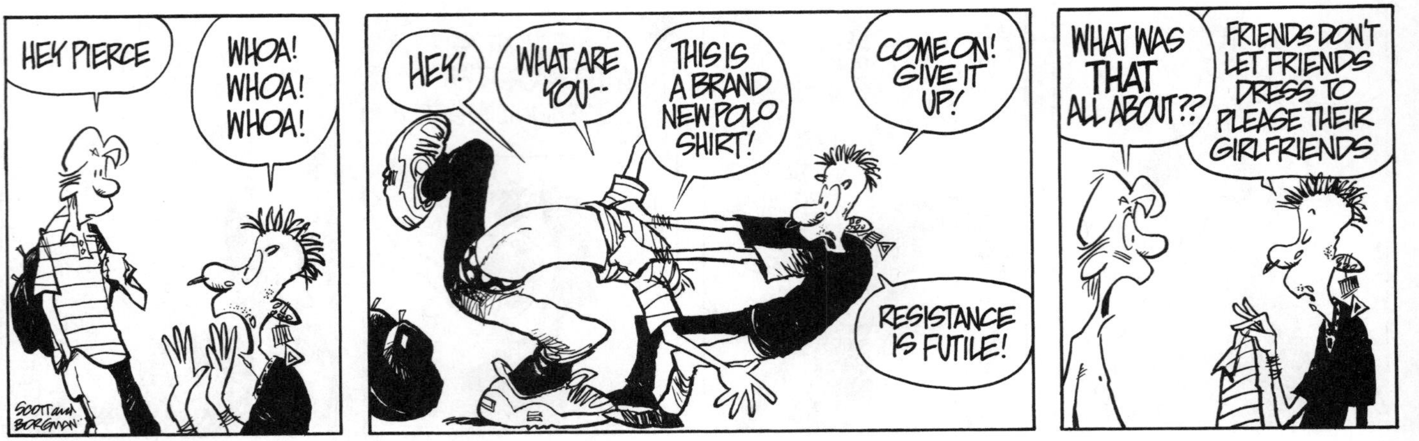
HEY PIERCE
WHOA! WHOA! WHOA!
HEY!
WHAT ARE YOU--
THIS IS A BRAND NEW POLO SHIRT!
COME ON! GIVE IT UP!
RESISTANCE IS FUTILE!
WHAT WAS THAT ALL ABOUT??
FRIENDS DON'T LET FRIENDS DRESS TO PLEASE THEIR GIRLFRIENDS
SCOTT and BORGMAN

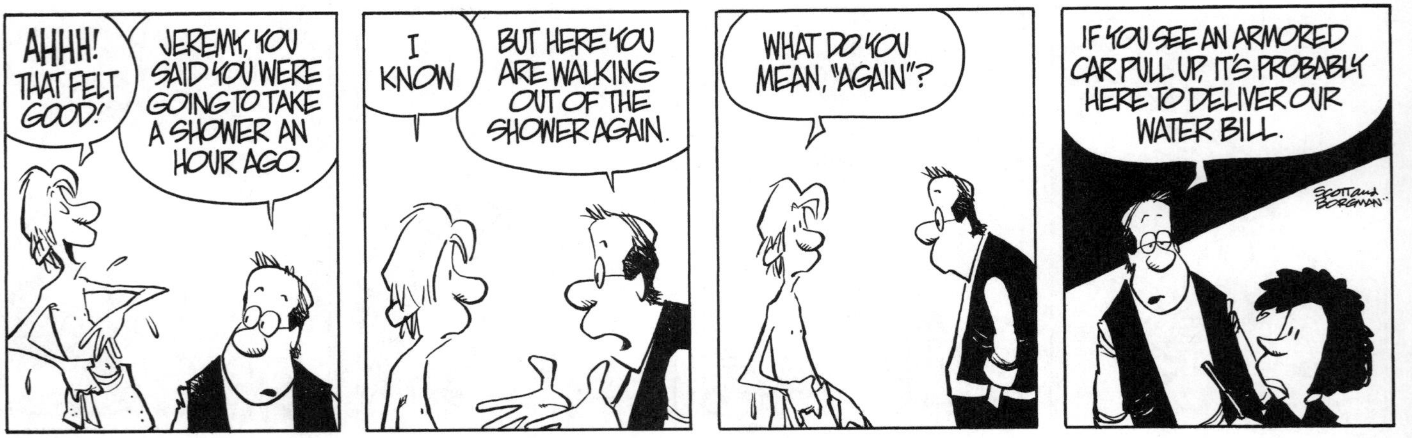
AHHH! THAT FELT GOOD!
JEREMY, YOU SAID YOU WERE GOING TO TAKE A SHOWER AN HOUR AGO.
I KNOW
BUT HERE YOU ARE WALKING OUT OF THE SHOWER AGAIN.
WHAT DO YOU MEAN, "AGAIN"?
IF YOU SEE AN ARMORED CAR PULL UP, IT'S PROBABLY HERE TO DELIVER OUR WATER BILL.
SCOTT and BORGMAN

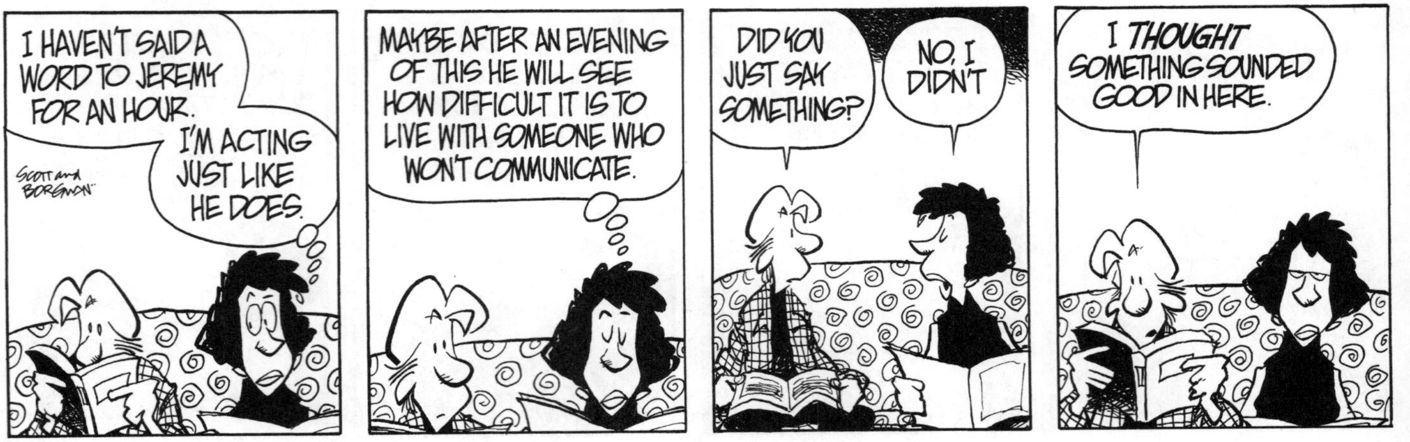
I HAVEN'T SAID A WORD TO JEREMY FOR AN HOUR.
I'M ACTING JUST LIKE HE DOES.
SCOTT and BORGMAN
MAYBE AFTER AN EVENING OF THIS HE WILL SEE HOW DIFFICULT IT IS TO LIVE WITH SOMEONE WHO WON'T COMMUNICATE.
DID YOU JUST SAY SOMETHING?
NO, I DIDN'T
I THOUGHT SOMETHING SOUNDED GOOD IN HERE.

Zits

by JERRY SCOTT and JIM BORGMAN

UH, HI PIERCE.

DUDE.

WHAT'S THE DEAL WITH THE CONE THING?

IT'S CALLED AN "ELIZABETHAN COLLAR"

WE PUT IT ON OUR DOG AFTER SHE HAD SURGERY SO SHE WOULDN'T PULL HER STITCHES OUT.

BUT MY PARENTS FOUND A NEW USE FOR IT

WHICH IS....?

FLIP!

BIP! BEEEP! BIP!

TOINK! TOINK!

CELL PHONE DETERRENT

HELLO? HELLO? IS ANYONE THERE?

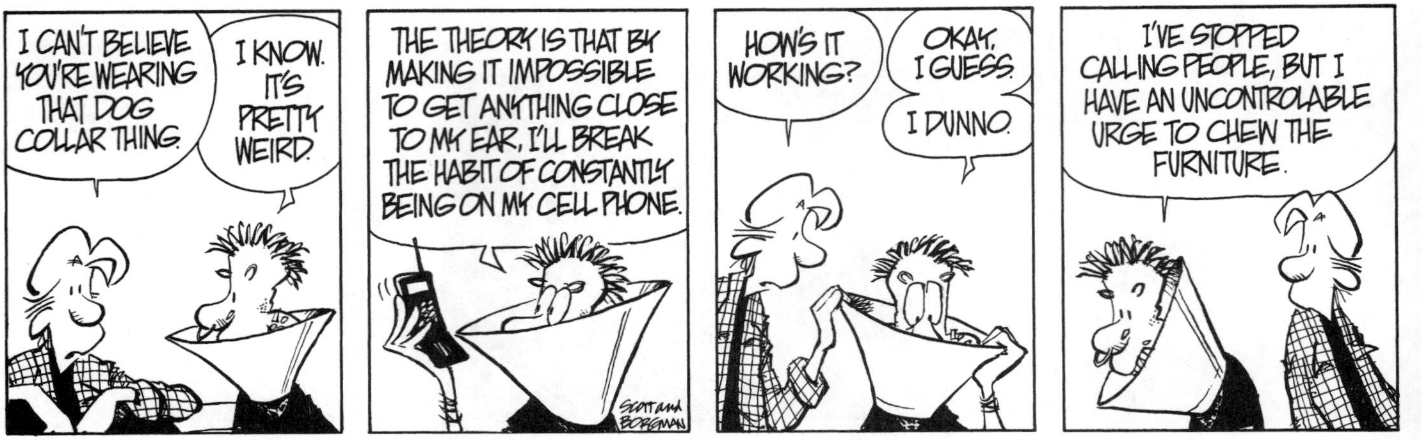
I CAN'T BELIEVE YOU'RE WEARING THAT DOG COLLAR THING.
I KNOW. IT'S PRETTY WEIRD.
THE THEORY IS THAT BY MAKING IT IMPOSSIBLE TO GET ANYTHING CLOSE TO MY EAR, I'LL BREAK THE HABIT OF CONSTANTLY BEING ON MY CELL PHONE.
SCOTT AND BORGMAN
HOW'S IT WORKING?
OKAY, I GUESS.
I DUNNO.
I'VE STOPPED CALLING PEOPLE, BUT I HAVE AN UNCONTROLABLE URGE TO CHEW THE FURNITURE.

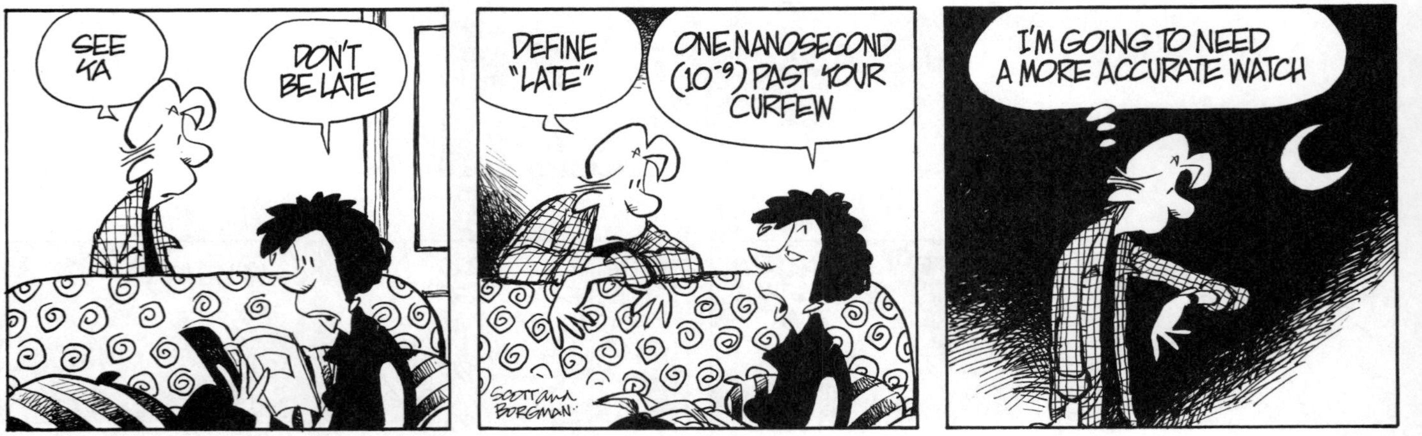
SEE YA
DON'T BE LATE
DEFINE "LATE"
ONE NANOSECOND (10^{-9}) PAST YOUR CURFEW
SCOTT AND BORGMAN
I'M GOING TO NEED A MORE ACCURATE WATCH

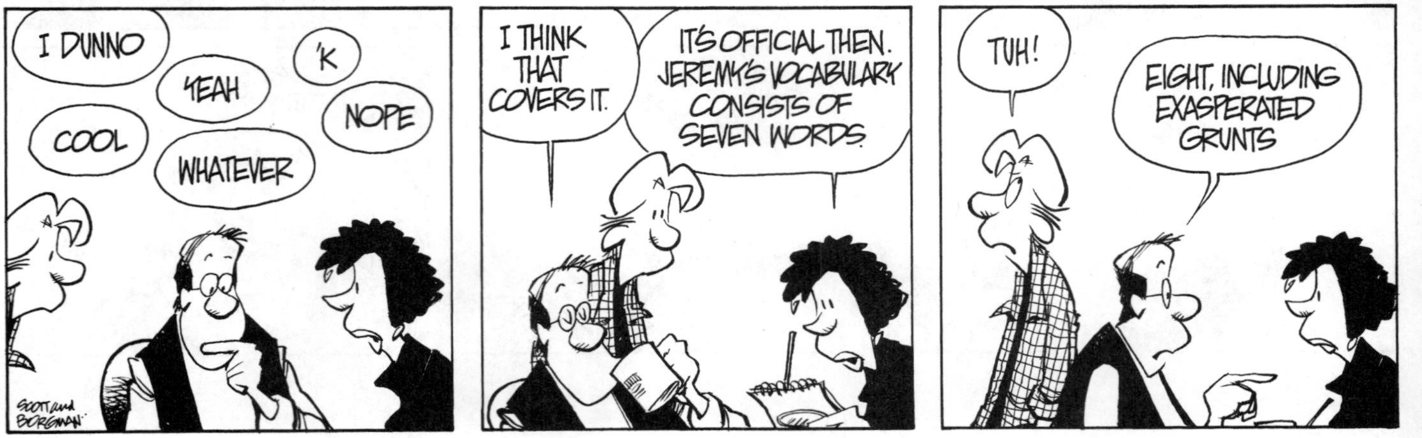
I DUNNO
YEAH
'K
COOL
NOPE
WHATEVER
SCOTT AND BORGMAN
I THINK THAT COVERS IT.
IT'S OFFICIAL THEN. JEREMY'S VOCABULARY CONSISTS OF SEVEN WORDS.
TUH!
EIGHT, INCLUDING EXASPERATED GRUNTS

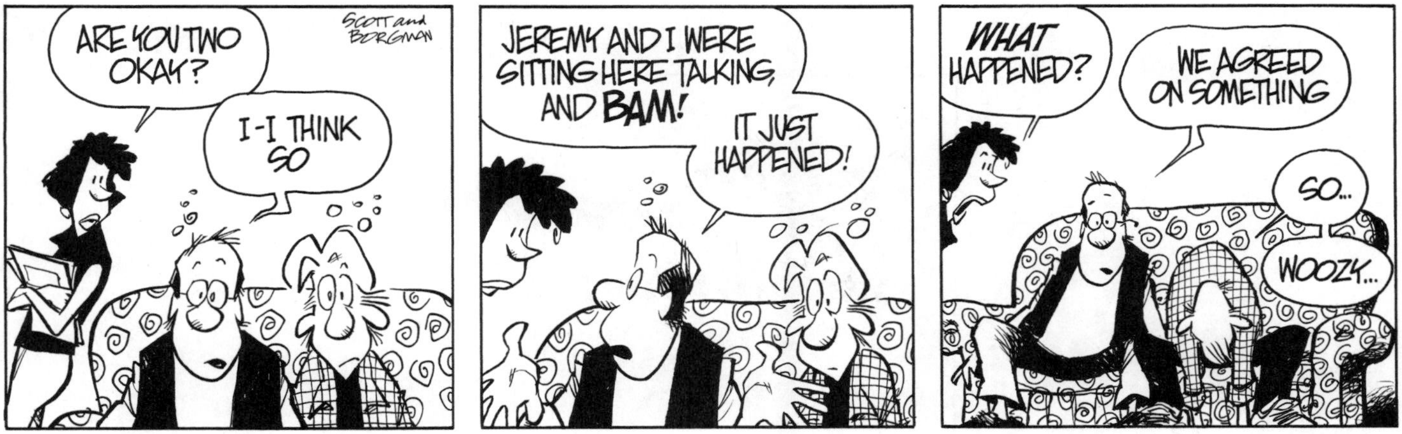
ARE YOU TWO OKAY?
SCOTT and BORGMAN
I-I THINK SO
JEREMY AND I WERE SITTING HERE TALKING, AND BAM!
IT JUST HAPPENED!
WHAT HAPPENED?
WE AGREED ON SOMETHING
SO...
WOOZY...

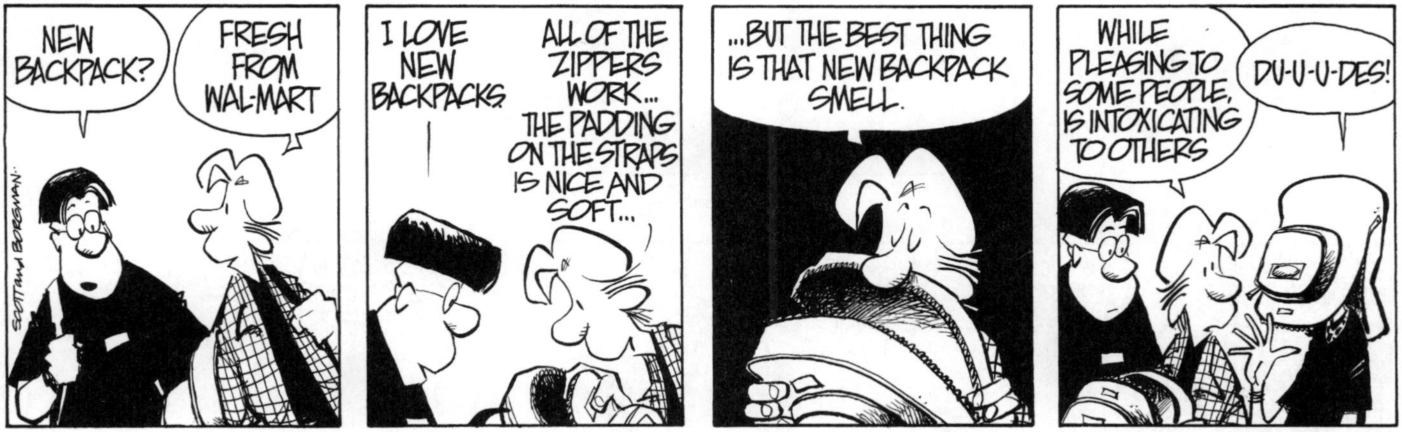
NEW BACKPACK?
FRESH FROM WAL-MART
SCOTT and BORGMAN
I LOVE NEW BACKPACKS.
ALL OF THE ZIPPERS WORK... THE PADDING ON THE STRAPS IS NICE AND SOFT...
...BUT THE BEST THING IS THAT NEW BACKPACK SMELL.
WHILE PLEASING TO SOME PEOPLE, IS INTOXICATING TO OTHERS
DU-U-U-DES!

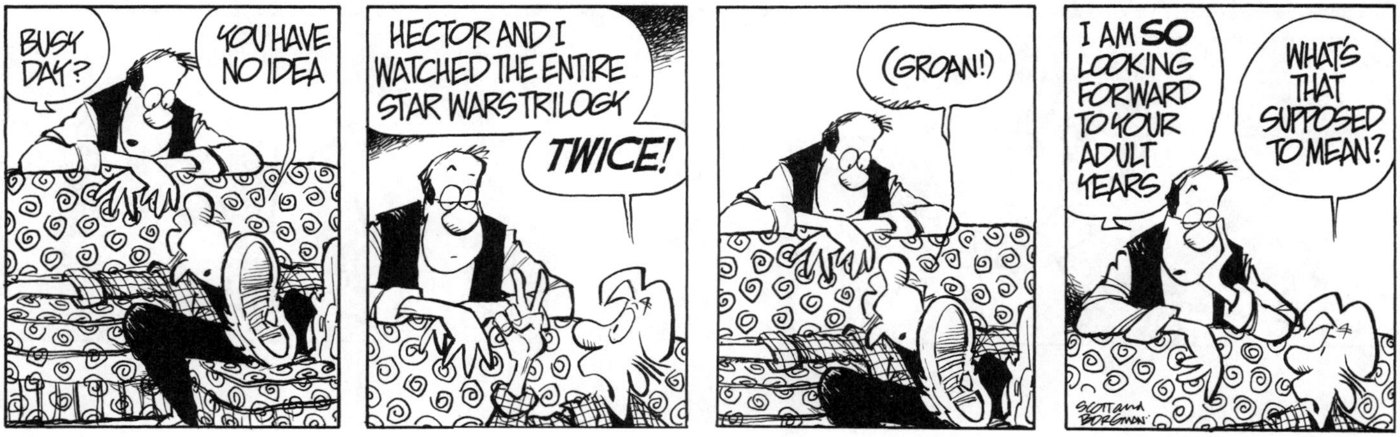
BUSY DAY?
YOU HAVE NO IDEA
HECTOR AND I WATCHED THE ENTIRE STAR WARS TRILOGY
TWICE!
(GROAN!)
I AM SO LOOKING FORWARD TO YOUR ADULT YEARS
WHAT'S THAT SUPPOSED TO MEAN?
SCOTT and BORGMAN

Zits
by JERRY SCOTT and JIM BORGMAN
HEY, MOM, WHERE ARE YOUR KEYS?
IN MY PURSE OVER THERE
HOW DO YOU TURN OFF A CAR'S PANIC ALARM?
SCOTT and BORGMAN
YOU MEAN AFTER THE PANIC BUTTON IS PUSHED?
YOU JUST PUSH IT AGAIN
THAT'S WHAT I THOUGHT
CLICK!
BEEP!
HONK!
BEEP!
WOOP! WOOP!
CLICK!
THANKS, MOM

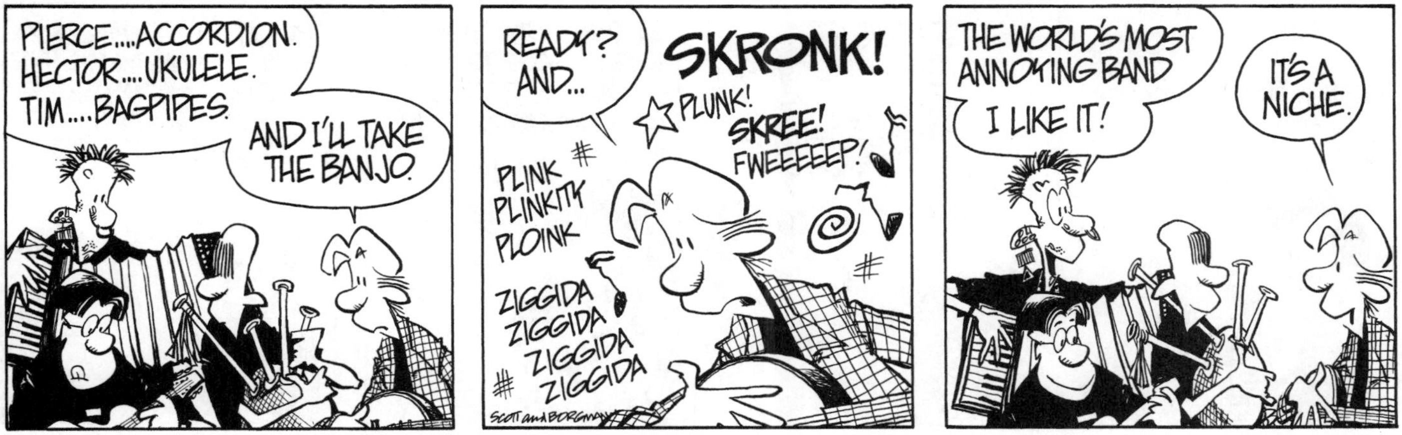
PIERCE....ACCORDION. HECTOR....UKULELE. TIM....BAGPIPES.
AND I'LL TAKE THE BANJO.
READY? AND...
SKRONK!
PLUNK!
SKREE!
FWEEEEEP!
PLINK PLINKITY PLOINK
ZIGGIDA ZIGGIDA ZIGGIDA ZIGGIDA
SCOTT and BORGMAN
THE WORLD'S MOST ANNOYING BAND
I LIKE IT!
IT'S A NICHE.

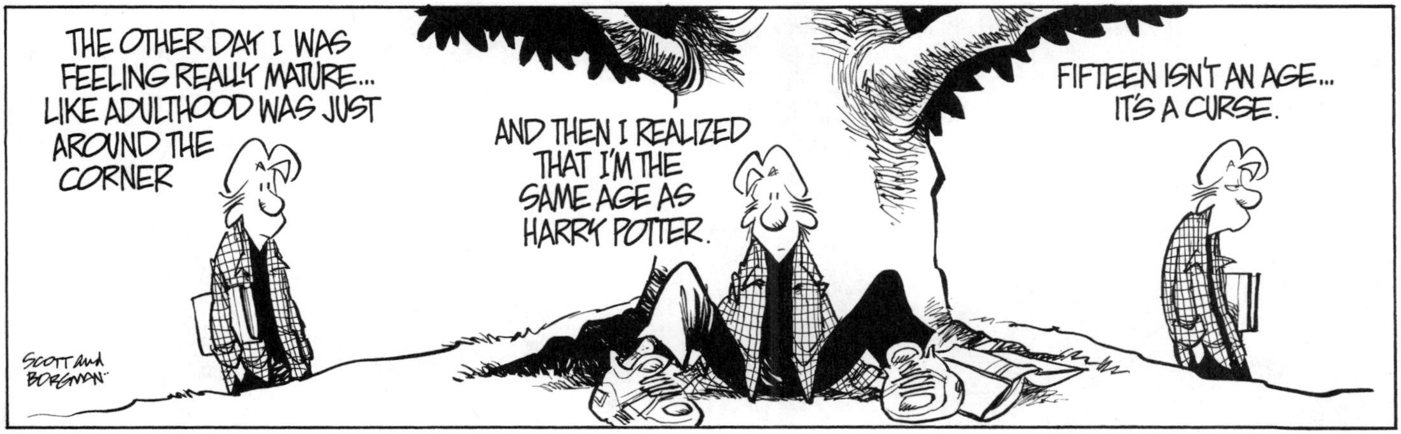
THE OTHER DAY I WAS FEELING REALLY MATURE... LIKE ADULTHOOD WAS JUST AROUND THE CORNER
AND THEN I REALIZED THAT I'M THE SAME AGE AS HARRY POTTER.
FIFTEEN ISN'T AN AGE... IT'S A CURSE.
SCOTT and BORGMAN

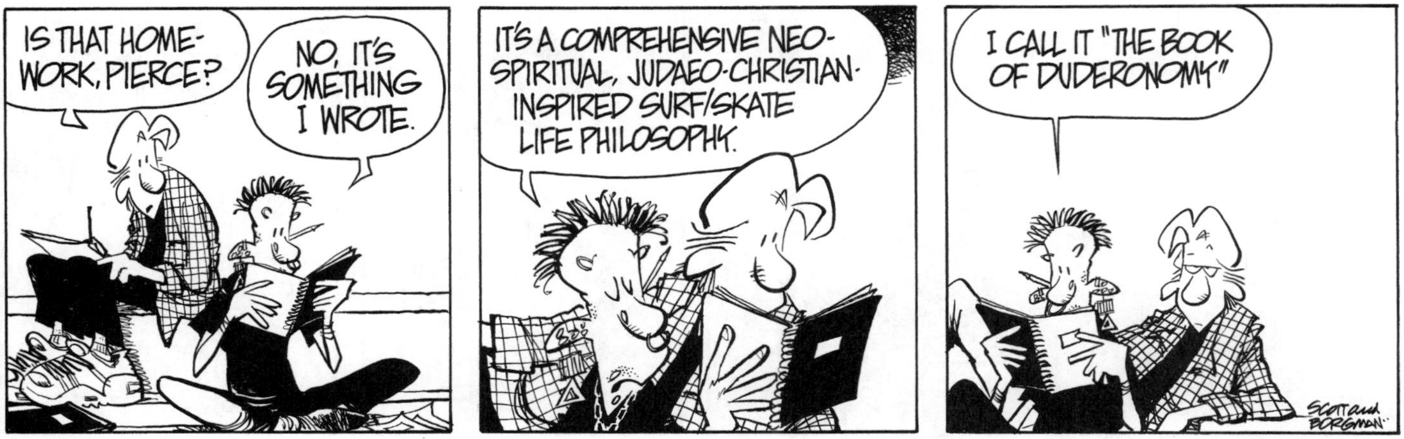
IS THAT HOME-WORK, PIERCE?
NO, IT'S SOMETHING I WROTE.
IT'S A COMPREHENSIVE NEO-SPIRITUAL, JUDAEO-CHRISTIAN-INSPIRED SURF/SKATE LIFE PHILOSOPHY.
I CALL IT "THE BOOK OF DUDERONOMY"
SCOTT and BORGMAN

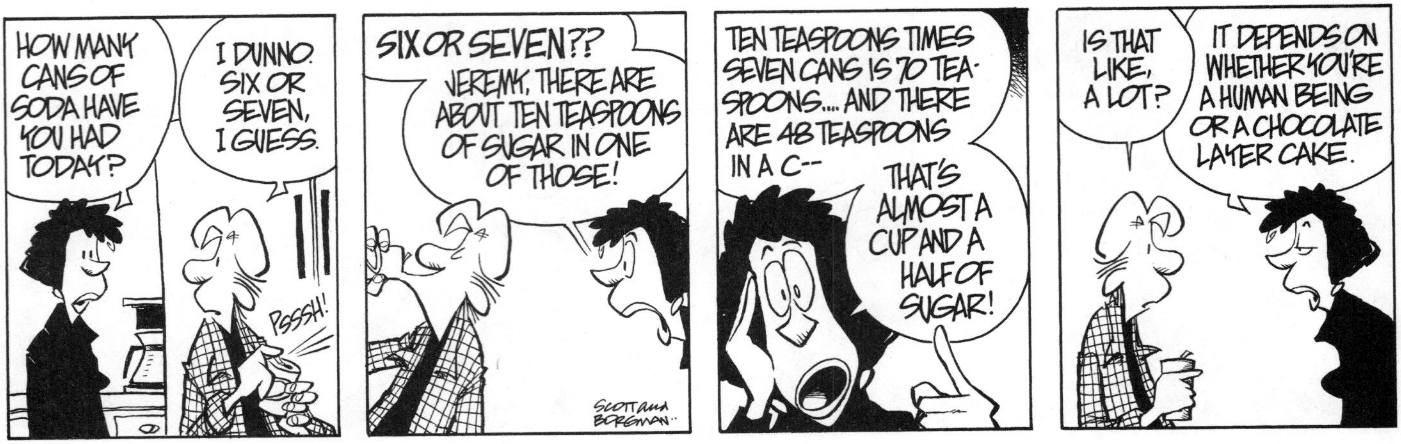
HOW MANY CANS OF SODA HAVE YOU HAD TODAY?
I DUNNO. SIX OR SEVEN, I GUESS.
PSSSH!
SIX OR SEVEN??
JEREMY, THERE ARE ABOUT TEN TEASPOONS OF SUGAR IN ONE OF THOSE!
SCOTT and BORGMAN
TEN TEASPOONS TIMES SEVEN CANS IS 70 TEASPOONS.... AND THERE ARE 48 TEASPOONS IN A C--
THAT'S ALMOST A CUP AND A HALF OF SUGAR!
IS THAT LIKE, A LOT?
IT DEPENDS ON WHETHER YOU'RE A HUMAN BEING OR A CHOCOLATE LAYER CAKE.

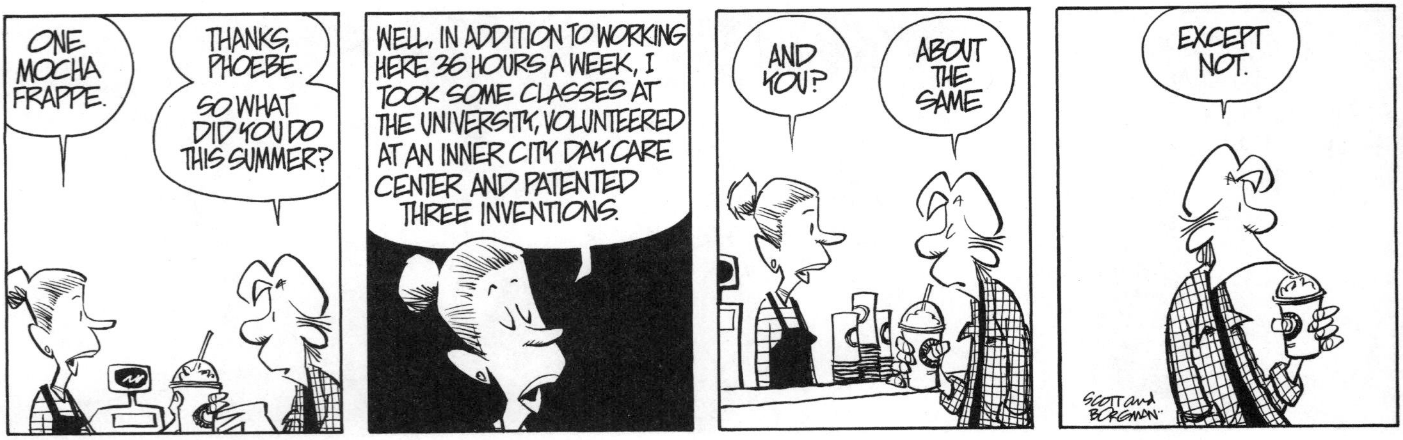
ONE MOCHA FRAPPE.
THANKS, PHOEBE.
SO WHAT DID YOU DO THIS SUMMER?
WELL, IN ADDITION TO WORKING HERE 36 HOURS A WEEK, I TOOK SOME CLASSES AT THE UNIVERSITY, VOLUNTEERED AT AN INNER CITY DAY CARE CENTER AND PATENTED THREE INVENTIONS.
AND YOU?
ABOUT THE SAME
EXCEPT NOT.
SCOTT and BORGMAN

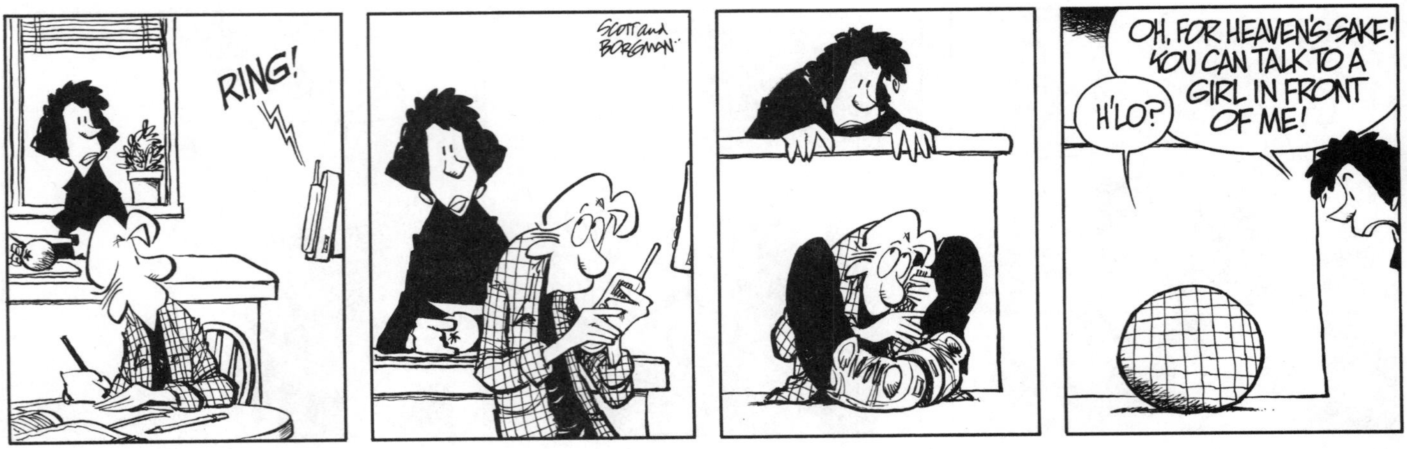
RING!
SCOTT and BORGMAN
H'LO?
OH, FOR HEAVEN'S SAKE! YOU CAN TALK TO A GIRL IN FRONT OF ME!